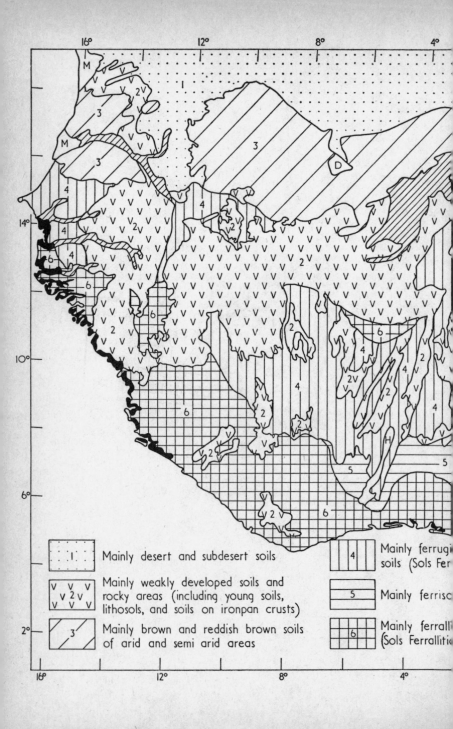

Mainly desert and subdesert soils

Mainly weakly developed soils and rocky areas (including young soils, lithosols, and soils on ironpan crusts)

Mainly brown and reddish brown soils of arid and semi arid areas

Mainly ferrugi soils (Sols Fer

Mainly ferriso

Mainly ferrall (Sols Ferrallit

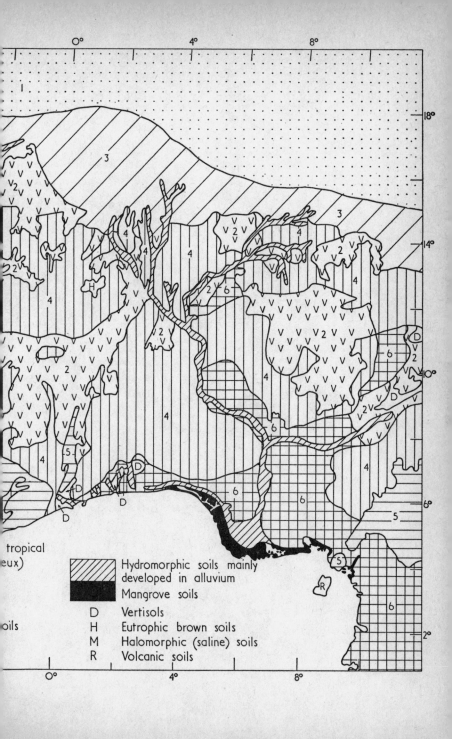

tropical
eux)

oils

Hydromorphic soils mainly
developed in alluvium
Mangrove soils
D   Vertisols
H   Eutrophic brown soils
M   Halomorphic (saline) soils
R   Volcanic soils

West African Soils

DEDICATED TO ELIZABETH (BORN 1965) AND
TO THE MANY MILLIONS OF HER GENERATION
WHO WILL, WE HOPE, INHERIT THE EARTH—
SUCH AS WE HAVE LEFT IT

West African Soils

PETER M. AHN

Professor of Soil Science, University of Nairobi
Kenya; formerly Department of Soil Science
University of Ghana, Legon, Accra

OXFORD UNIVERSITY PRESS

Oxford University Press, Walton Street, Oxford OX2 6DP

OXFORD LONDON GLASGOW
NEW YORK TORONTO MELBOURNE WELLINGTON
KUALA LUMPUR SINGAPORE JAKARTA HONG KONG TOKYO
DELHI BOMBAY CALCUTTA MADRAS KARACHI
NAIROBI DAR ES SALAAM CAPE TOWN

ISBN 0 19 859453 4

© OXFORD UNIVERSITY PRESS 1970

West African Soils and *West African Crops* by
F. R. Irvine (the third edition, in two volumes, of
West African Agriculture) were published in 1970.
Paperback edition 1974
Reprinted 1979

Printed in Great Britain
at the University Press, Oxford
by Eric Buckley
Printer to the University

CONTENTS

Soil classification
The soil series — Types of classification

General classifications of West African soils
The Ghana system of classification — The French classification system — The CCTA classification and soil map of Africa — The United States Seventh Approximation

Practical local classifications and land capability classifications
Land capability classifications — Soil classification for irrigated agriculture

Soil analysis
Soil sampling — Soil analyses and tests

Shifting cultivation
Shifting cultivation in the forest zone — Forest regrowth vegetation — Shifting cultivation in the savanna areas

Soil changes under shifting cultivation
The role of fallow — Soil changes during the fallow period — Clearing and burning — The effects of cultivation — Soil erosion — Advantages and disadvantages of shifting cultivation

The mechanization of agriculture

Fertilizers and manures
Animal manures — Green manures and mulches

Chemical fertilizers and their use
Methods of fertilizer application — The time of fertilizer application — Single and mixed fertilizers

Fertilizer responses in West Africa
Nitrogen responses — Potassium responses — Phosphorus responses — Sulphur and lime responses — Micronutrient deficiencies — The FAO fertilizer demonstrations

Nitrogen-containing fertilizers
Classes and specifications of nitrogenous fertilizers — Ammonia-containing nitrogenous fertilizers — Nitrate-containing nitrogenous fertilizers — Other nitrogen-containing fertilizers — Applying nitrogenous fertilizers

Phosphate-containing fertilizers
Classes and specifications of phosphate-containing fertilizers — Water-soluble phosphatic fertilizers — Water-insoluble phosphatic fertilizers — What happens when phosphate is applied to the soil — Applying phosphatic fertilizers

Potassium-containing fertilizers
Specifications of potassium-containing fertilizers — The principal potassium-containing fertilizers — Applying potassium fertilizers

Supplying calcium, magnesium, and sulphur to the soil

Correcting trace element deficiencies

LIST OF PLATES

x   WEST AFRICAN SOILS

Plate 28 is reproduced by courtesy of Ghana Information Services, and Plate 38 by courtesy of the Department of Agriculture, Eastern Nigeria. The remaining 46 photographs appearing in this volume were taken by the author.

PREFACE

In writing this introduction to West African soils and soil science the author has felt there was a need for a book which assumes little or no previous training, and which is written as simply as is consistent with accuracy. At the same time over-simplification of this wide subject was felt to be a disservice to the reader and it was felt desirable to indicate not only its breadth and complexity but also how much we still do not know or are not sure about. After 14 years spent studying West African soils the author is more than ever conscious of how little he at least knows about the subject and what conspicuous gaps in our knowledge remain to be filled.

It is felt that an understanding of soils and their characteristics is greatly helped by considering how soils are formed, and by trying to see them in relation to their natural environment. In this way we may begin to appreciate how soils can be expected to vary with differences in geology and in relief, in climate and in vegetation. To a point, therefore, the approach adopted is ecological. But man steps in, and is himself a 'soil forming factor' able to improve or destroy the soil he has inherited, and the longest section of this book is in fact the fourth section devoted to soil examination, management, and improvement. This is preceded by chapters on soil physics and soil chemistry.

There is a widely felt need for a soils textbook geared to the West African scene. Even this modest attempt to provide a short introduction to the subject has met with considerable difficulty, for what little is known about West African soils is not readily available. Research results are few, and often unpublished. Even the more fundamental data are hard to find: there are many misconceptions and unproved assumptions, and few reliable facts. It would be too much to hope that all these difficulties have been overcome, and it is perhaps inevitable that this book represents in some respects a personal point of view—even, perhaps, a personal set of values and prejudices.

This volume is intended mainly for use in West Africa and is concerned only with West African soils. It is hoped that it will be of use to a variety of readers—to sixth-form pupils, to school teachers, to university students, to agricultural assistants and agricultural officers, to soil surveyors, to farmers and agronomists, and to administrators and planners. This book is not intended primarily for fellow soil scientists in other parts of the world who want to learn something about West African soils—if it were, the approach would have been different, though if they find anything of interest, so much the better. They will certainly find much to comment on and criticize, and both criticisms and comments will be welcome.

P. M. A.

Legon, January 1968

PART 1

INTRODUCTION

1 LOOKING AT THE SOIL IN THE FIELD

Soil is only a thin layer at the surface of the earth which is sometimes easily lost but it is the home of the plant and the study of agriculture should logically begin with the study of the soil. The greater our understanding of it, the greater are our chances of using the soil wisely. This involves knowing sufficient about each particular type of soil—and there are countless different soils—so that each of them can be developed for agriculture, grazing, forestry, or other purposes in such a way as to make the best use of its particular characteristics. At the same time, wise use should keep the soil in good, productive condition for future generations.

To the geologist concerned with the rocks and minerals below it, the soil may be of little interest, something to be removed because it hides what is beneath. The farmer or the soil scientist, on the other hand, is not usually concerned with what is deep down except inasmuch as it helps him to understand the soil itself. He is interested in that part of the earth's covering which supports plants. Although soil is difficult to define exactly, we may consider it here as being that natural covering of the earth's surface in which plants grow. Similarly, although the soil can be studied in many ways—some of more practical value than others—we are interested here mainly in those aspects of the soil which influence plant growth.

Although the study of the soil as a science involves at least some knowledge of many other more basic sciences such as geology, chemistry, physics, and biology, soil science is not a theoretical subject but a practical one: it is an *applied* science.

The 1948 U.S. Department of Agriculture Yearbook contains the following statements by Henry L. Ahlgren:

The soil comes first. It is the basis, the foundation of farming. Without it, nothing; with poor soil, poor farming, poor living; with good soil, good farming and living. An understanding of good farming begins with an understanding of the soil.

An understanding of good farming begins with an understanding of, and respect for, the soil, but there is one thing that Ahlgren, in this short quotation, might well have added. Through understanding, poor soils can be made better, and good ones better still, just as careless and unwise use might soon lower the value of even a very good soil and perhaps reduce its productivity for a very long time. Further, soils differ in many ways, and what is a poor soil for one crop may be very suitable for another. Thus, understanding soils may involve getting to know the best use for many different types of soil, each used and managed according to its individual characteristics.

Soil formation

How is soil formed? What gives a soil the characteristics which differentiate it from other soils? When a farmer cuts down natural vegetation, as when he clears part of the forest and begins to cultivate, the soil undergoes certain changes. To some extent it continues to change as long as it is farmed. The soil is therefore changed and modified by man's interference and influence, but nevertheless soils are fundamentally natural objects which have formed slowly over long periods of time and the main factors affecting their formation and development are the natural ones of the environment.

Even a preliminary excursion to examine local soils should show the observer that soils are *natural bodies* related to their physical surroundings. Thus we find different soils over different types of rocks: e.g. soils developed over granites being distinct from soils developed over sandstones. We find that forest soils are not the same as savanna soils, so that clearly *vegetation* is another factor influencing soil development. We find that soils on the top of a hill may be quite different from those on the lower slopes and in the valley bottoms, so that *relief* also influences soil formation.

Because the environmental conditions of geology, climate, vegetation, slope of the ground, and so on, are never exactly the same in any two places, soils differ to a greater or lesser extent, and the soil in one place is never identical with that in another. But where the environmental conditions are similar, then the soils also are likely to be similar, and it is often of great practical use to consider together those soils which have certain characteristics in common. Thus, if we know that a particular crop or particular method of cultivation has proved successful on a soil, we might be well advised to try using a similar soil in the same way.

Sometimes the soil changes markedly over quite a short distance, particularly in hilly country. Anybody who has travelled in the forest areas of West Africa has probably noticed that the colour of the soil on the hill tops often differs in a striking way from that of the soils lower down the slope and in the valley bottoms. Other differences are also easy to see: some soils contain large quantities of gravel and stones, while others do not. Some soils are very sandy, loose, and easy to dig; others have a high content of clay and may be very sticky when wet and very hard when dry. The student of soils should as soon as possible get into the habit of examining soils whenever convenient and relating the soil examined to its environment.

The characteristics of a soil are conveniently considered as being the result of the influence of five main groups of soil-forming factors:

(1) The parent material from which the soil is developed.

(2) The climate, past and present, of the area.

(3) The vegetation supported by the soil (which is also influenced by climate) and the soil fauna (ranging from bacteria and other micro-organisms to worms and termites) which live in the soil.

(4) The type of relief associated with the soil.

(5) Time—i.e. the length of time during which the other factors have been influencing soil formation.

A sixth 'soil-forming factor' has already been mentioned: man himself who uses the soil and causes important changes in so doing. These factors are considered further in later chapters, particularly in Chapters 3 and 4.

The soil profile

To examine a soil in the field it is not sufficient to look only at the top 2 or 3 in of the soil, even though this is in some ways the part of the soil which most affects plant growth. The whole soil profile should be examined. A soil profile is a vertical cross section through the soil which shows the various horizons of which the soil is composed. These horizons are the different layers of soil material which together form the whole soil: each horizon differs in some respects from those above and below. Often the soil profile extends downwards from the surface horizon for many feet to hard rock below, although in West Africa rocks have in many areas been softened and decomposed to a very great depth so that fresh, hard, unweathered rock may not be found except at considerable depths, at several hundred feet, in some instances.

Soil profiles showing at least the upper horizons of the soil can be examined in road cuttings, in ditches if they are deep enough, in quarries and other holes dug in the ground, or in pits specially dug for the purpose, known as soil profile pits.

A typical local soil should be examined carefully and in as much detail as possible. The soil should, if possible, be one that has not been disturbed or cultivated for some time. The soil profile diagram shown in Fig. 1.1 represents a typical and widespread West African soil, and a discussion of some of its features will serve as an introduction to the study of soil profiles in the field.

The topsoil
The uppermost few inches of most soils which have not been disturbed by cultivation are darker than the soil below and form a fairly well defined horizon—the topsoil. The dark colour is due to the presence of humus and this varies considerably in amount with the vegetation and other factors. A good humous topsoil is typically a dark, greyish-brown in colour (although often loosely described as 'black'). Humus itself, when separated from the rest of the soil, is seen to be a sticky, black, amorphous and glue-like substance. It is derived from plant remains such as leaves, flowers, and branches which fall on to the surface of the soil, roots which die and decompose within it, and the bodies of soil microbes and other soil fauna. The humus coats and impregnates the soil particles, staining them the dark colour referred to above, and also helps to bind them together so that they are frequently more or less loosely aggregated to form soil crumbs.

Humus is derived from organic materials and has its own particular properties which are discussed in more detail below (particularly in Chapter 4), but it itself decomposes, or mineralizes, releasing plant nutrients as it does so. Humus has profound effects on the physical and chemical properties of the soil, and hence on soil fertility and productivity.

Leaves and other plant parts may be found on the surface of the soil, both fresh and partly decomposed. This thin layer on the surface is the *leaf litter layer*. In savanna areas this may be very thin and much of the ground may appear almost devoid of dead leaves. In the forest areas the leaf litter layer is better developed and there may be a thin, more or less continuous, covering of leaves. In a well developed West African forest, particularly one not yet disturbed by cultivation or not cultivated for a considerable period, the total weight and quantity of leaves, twigs, flowers, fruits, branches, and other plant parts falling on to the surface of the ground may be very great. Despite this great quantity of material falling down, the leaf litter layer is usually of surprising thinness. It remains thin because decomposition is so rapid that there is little time for it to accumulate. As soon as a leaf falls it begins to decompose, to be attacked by bacteria, fungi, and termites, or eaten and pulled into the soil by worms and other animals and insects.

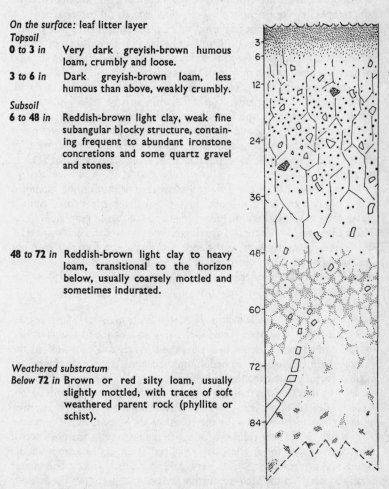

On the surface: leaf litter layer
Topsoil

0 to 3 in   Very dark greyish-brown humous loam, crumbly and loose.

3 to 6 in   Dark greyish-brown loam, less humous than above, weakly crumbly.

Subsoil

6 to 48 in   Reddish-brown light clay, weak fine subangular blocky structure, containing frequent to abundant ironstone concretions and some quartz gravel and stones.

48 to 72 in   Reddish-brown light clay to heavy loam, transitional to the horizon below, usually coarsely mottled and sometimes indurated.

Weathered substratum

Below 72 in   Brown or red silty loam, usually slightly mottled, with traces of soft weathered parent rock (phyllite or schist).

Fig. 1.1. Diagram of a typical well-drained upland sedentary soil developed over phyllite or schist. A short, simple description of the soil is given next to the profile. For more detailed work a fuller description would be necessary, subdividing the horizons shown further. Figures on the left refer to the depth in inches.

In cooler parts of the world forests often develop a much thicker leaf litter layer than is usually found in West African soils because the rate of decomposition there is slower. This suggests that the main reason for the rapid decay of leaf litter in West Africa is the climate, particularly the high temperature throughout the year which speeds up bacterial activity.

The topsoil itself is not uniform, but changes with depth, particularly if the topsoil has not been disturbed and mixed up by cultivation. In the natural soil the upper 2 to 3 in are usually darker and richer in organic matter than the lower 2 or 3 in of the topsoil.

A small handful of topsoil should be taken and examined in detail, preferably with a hand lens. The soil should also be felt by pressing it lightly between thumb and first finger. Soils should always be examined both by eye and by feel, and the experienced soil surveyor or agronomist can tell a considerable amount about the soil by rubbing it between his fingers in this way. The habit of feeling the soil should be learnt as early as possible.

Taking the soil apart carefully will allow the structure to be examined and the pores and natural spaces in the soil observed: it may contain gravel or stones, and there are probably a large number of very small roots. These fine roots in the topsoil are the feeding roots of the grasses, herbs, shrubs, and trees growing in the soil, and they often form a dense but shallow root mat, for this is the main root feeding zone. Further down the profile, in the subsoil, there may be far fewer roots.

The subsoil

Below the topsoil the soil colour may change quite markedly. It was noted above that the normal dark, greyish-brown colour of the topsoil is caused by the humus which stains and coats the mineral soil particles. In the subsoil there is usually very little humus to mask or modify the colour of the mineral particles so that subsoil colours are often more striking and varied than the relatively uniform colours of humus-stained topsoils. When a soil is described as being brown, brownish yellow, yellow, red, grey or any other colour it is usually the colour of the subsoil which is meant.

The red and brown colours of soils are mainly due to the presence of iron compounds, for if these are removed from a soil sample in the laboratory the resulting soil is very pale or almost white. The colour depends partly on the amount of iron present and partly on the form in which it occurs. In free-draining soils, i.e. in soils in which soil water moves downwards freely and oxygen circulates adequately, the iron is oxidized to reddish ferric oxide (as in the rusting of iron) and even small quantities of this dispersed in the soil and coating or absorbed on to the fine soil particles can give the soil a striking reddish colour. A red colour does not necessarily indicate a fertile soil but it does usually indicate a fairly well drained soil in which water drains downwards rapidly enough for the air to move freely in the larger soil pores. Red soils are therefore often found on upland sites, that is, on the summits and upper slopes of hills where free drainage is helped by the relief and position of the soil.

On lower-slope, less well drained sites the iron is often combined with water and occurs in a hydrated form which is generally more brown or yellow in colour. In very poorly drained soils the shortage of air oxygen brings about reducing conditions and the formation of compounds which give predominantly grey colours to soils.

After noting the colour of the subsoil sample examined, the *structure* and *porosity* of a handful of soil should be carefully examined. The soil may seem fairly dense and compact, but in fact it may contain up to 50 per cent by volume of air. It may seem unlikely at first glance that something so apparently solid should be half air, but a very careful examination, first with the naked eye and then with a magnifying glass, will disclose the presence of numerous pores between mineral grains, some of them very small, as well as larger cracks, channels, and irregular spaces. Some of the smaller pores and spaces are too small to be seen even with a powerful magnifying glass and a microscope is needed for their examination, but in many ways the spaces in the soil and their arrangement are at least as important and deserving of study as the solid particles between which they occur.

The pores and channels are essential for the circulation in the soil of both air and water, without either of which plants quickly die. If the fragment of subsoil examined really were solid, without pore spaces, it would feel much heavier. More important, it would be quite sterile, for no plant could grow in it. Soils which have been compacted or compressed have their pore space reduced. Footpaths are examples of this, and plants often find it difficult to grow even on old footpaths which have been abandoned for some time. The use of heavy agricultural machinery may also compact the soil. In these cases the soil becomes less favourable for plant growth because air and water cannot circulate as freely as before.

It is not only the total amount of pore space which is important, but the size and shape and arrangement of the pores. Some of the larger pores connect with each other, water drains out of them easily, and air circulates. The smaller pores attract water more strongly and water remains in them after it has drained out of the larger ones. The physical composition of the soil, the size and arrangement of its particles and of the spaces between them, and the circulation of air and water are all important aspects of soil physics which are dealt with in a little more detail in Chapters 2 and 5.

The subsoil should next be examined to see if it contains stones or gravel. Many West African soils have a well-marked subsoil horizon containing gravel, sometimes in very large quantities. Very gravelly material of this type is frequently dug out and applied to roads. It is often referred to as 'pea gravel' because much of it is about the size of a large pea and is also roughly spherical in shape. Strictly speaking, the gravel fraction of a soil consists of all the material between 2 mm and 20 mm in diameter, the larger pieces of rock or iron pan being referred to as stones or boulders.

To examine the pea gravel carefully, it may be necessary to wash it, and it may then be seen to contain a variety of different constituents. Ironstone concretions are often very common. These are more or less rounded, blackish or reddish, hard and sometimes smooth nodules of very impure iron oxides, or of soil material which has been impregnated by iron compounds and hardened. Contrasting with the concretions may be gravel-sized fragments of quartz, sometimes angular, sometimes more or less rounded. Gravelly horizons often also contain stones and boulders of quartz rock, and of ironstone or iron pan.

The gravel and stones together form the coarse material in the soil—all that material in the soil above 2 mm in diameter. This is often concentrated in a well marked band in the subsoil or in part of it, with less, or none, in the topsoil above or in the weathered substratum below. It is often desirable to separate the coarse material from the rest of the soil, the fine earth. To do this, it is necessary to sieve the soil using a 2 mm sieve. This should be done as follows.

(1) Sample a quantity of soil and, if it is not fairly dry already, allow it to dry out for a day or two.

(2) Break up the soil by crushing it gently, preferably in a small wooden mortar, to separate the coarse fraction from the fine.

(3) Pass a known weight of the soil through a 2 mm sieve. Weigh the fine earth which has passed through and calculate this as a percentage of the total soil.

A convenient sieve can be made from a piece of perforated zinc with holes 2 mm in diameter. For more accurate work, the coarse material has to be washed to remove the fine earth still adhering to it: this will also enable it to be examined and described more easily.

A very gravelly subsoil might be found to contain 50 to 70 per cent or even more of gravel and stones by weight, and only 30 to 50 per cent by weight of fine earth, while other soils may contain no stones or gravel at all, in which case the fine earth forms 100 per cent of the soil. Often the coarse material is of little or no value to the plant, and normally soil analyses are carried out only on the fine earth fraction, i.e. only on the soil material passing through a 2 mm sieve.

A large proportion of the upland soils in West Africa contain pea gravel in their subsoils, often in very large amounts, but there are also consider-able areas of upland soils which do not, while many of the soils of the lower slopes and valley bottoms are developed in material which is all or nearly all fine earth. These include the soils developed in alluvium deposited by streams and rivers, although these soils may contain rounded pebbles or rounded gravels whose shape indicates that they have been rolled and rounded in running water.

Whether or not a subsoil contains gravel, it also has other, more impor-tant, characteristics which distinguish it from the topsoil and the weathered substratum. It is normally the horizon with the highest clay content, and it usually has a different structure from the horizons above and below. Clay and soil structure are defined and described in the next chapter.

The weathered substratum

The boundary between the relatively thin topsoil and the subsoil below it is usually fairly easy to see because of the darker colour of the topsoil, caused by humus staining, and the fact that the topsoil is often more open, porous and easy to work whereas the subsoil may be relatively compact, with fewer roots, pores, and channels. In some soils, especially soils on steep slopes, the subsoil may be only a foot or two in depth, but frequently it is several feet thick. A normal subsoil thickness for many upland soils is 3 to 6 ft. If the soil profile pit or other soil exposure observed is deep enough, it may be possible to observe that the subsoil merges into a third horizon, the weathered substratum, below. However, in this case the tran-sition may be a gradual one and the boundary between the two horizons be more diffuse, irregular, and difficult to see. We may thus wish to speak of a transition zone between the two horizons. In some cases it takes considerable experience to separate the two horizons accurately, and the differences between the two vary somewhat according to the type of soil and the nature of the parent material below.

Generally speaking, the weathered substratum is the zone where the soil material has been less changed and modified by soil-forming processes than it has in the subsoil. If the soil is one derived from the rock below, then the weathered substratum contains the weathered products of that rock and perhaps also relatively unweathered fragments. This weathered rock material has already undergone some physical and chemical changes but bears a closer relationship to the freshly weathered material, or to the original deposit in which the soil was developed, than does the subsoil where soil-forming processes have resulted in more profound changes and greater reorganization and sorting of the soil material.

In the field, the weathered substratum may be distinguished by changes in soil texture, structure, and consistency (terms discussed further in Chapter 2) and may be lighter-coloured or more varied in colour because of mottles or the presence of traces or fragments of soft, weathered rock. The gravel and stones which often accumulate in West African subsoils may be rare or absent. The weathered substratum is often less compact and a given volume of soil weighs less than a similar volume of subsoil. It is, however, difficult to generalize about the nature of the weathered substratum because it varies very greatly according to the nature of the soil parent material.

The weathered substratum in turn may merge into hard, fresh rock below. This may or may not be similar to the rock from which the upper parts of the profile were ultimately derived and it may occur at such great depths—200 to 300 ft in some cases—that it cannot often be seen in a soil pit.

Comparisons between different soil profiles

Once a particular local profile has been examined in some detail, it should be compared and contrasted with other soil profiles, particularly with soils occurring on a range of topographic sites (i.e. soils on hill summits, middle slopes, valley bottoms, particularly steep slopes, flat hill tops, and so on) and with otherwise similar soils under a different vegetation cover or farmed in a different way.

A forest soil should, if possible, be compared with one developed under savanna vegetation. It will almost certainly be found that the forest topsoil is thicker, has more organic matter, and a darker colour than a corresponding soil under grass, especially if the grass is burnt every dry season. A soil which has remained under its natural vegetation for a long period will probably be found to have a better developed, more humous topsoil than one which has been recently cultivated or is still being farmed. The effects of vegetation on soils are discussed further in Chapter 4, and those of cultivation in Chapter 8.

The cultivation of the soil, particularly if the slope is steep, may have resulted in all or part of the topsoil having been washed away by rain and running water. This accelerated erosion endangers soils all over the world, especially those soils on steep slopes which are not protected by an adequate plant cover. The thickness and humus content of the topsoil greatly influences the agricultural productivity of soils, particularly in West Africa, and farming methods must therefore be such as to conserve and protect the topsoil as much as possible.

The soil catena

The subsoil of an upland soil may be red, brownish-red, reddish, or orange-brown in colour, and we may conclude that the soil is well drained but if soils lower down the slope are examined it is probable that they will have subsoils which are duller in colour—perhaps brown, brownish-yellow, or yellow. The colour of these soils and their lower position would suggest to us that they are less well drained than the red soils.

Further down the slope, and in flat or nearly flat valley bottoms, the subsoil colours may be greyish yellow, yellowish or brownish grey, pale grey, or even nearly white. Grey soils, sometimes with bluish or greenish shades or with mottles, are often found in poorly drained areas which are perhaps flooded during part of the wet season or seasons. These slow-draining, low-lying grey soils may be colonized by a particular group of plants adapted to damp soil conditions, plants which may differ markedly from the natural vegetation of the better drained, upland areas. Similarly, if these soils are cultivated, they may be planted to different crops from those on the higher soils, crops which prefer or at least tolerate marshy damp soils, such as rice and chewing cane.

There is thus frequently a sequence of somewhat different but related soils occurring from hill top to valley bottom. Such a sequence of soils is very common in West Africa and is often referred to as a *soil catena*. Catena is Latin for chain: the soils succeed each other like links in a chain. Typical soil catenas are described in a little more detail in Chapter 3.

2 SOME IMPORTANT PROPERTIES OF SOILS

In the preceding chapter the reader was urged to examine soils in their natural position in the field as frequently as possible, looking at as much of the soil profile as can be seen and relating it to its environment. In the U.S. Soil Survey Manual we read:

A soil is a natural thing out of doors. Like a river or a glacier or a volcano, it cannot be brought into a laboratory.

However, even if a whole soil cannot be brought into a laboratory, small samples of it can be. The examination, testing and analysis of soil samples in the laboratory can usefully supplement knowledge gained in the field, even if these samples once removed are never quite the same as the living soil in its natural position.

The composition of soils

The soil consists of the following:

(1) organic material in various stages of decomposition, including humus;
(2) mineral particles.

In the topsoil in particular, organic material and mineral particles are intimately associated, the first binding together the second to form soil crumbs. If the organic material is removed or destroyed, the mineral particles of the soil remain. These are conveniently divided up according to their size. The division of soil particles into clay, silt, and sand is a division into *size classes* based on the diameter of the particles (not on their nature or composition). These size classes are as follows:

Clay—less than 2μ (2 micron = 0·002 mm) diameter.
Silt—between 2μ and 60μ (0·002 mm and 0·060 mm) diameter.
Sand—between 60μ and 2000μ (0·060 mm and 2·000 mm) diameter.

It will be noted that the unit of measurement is a micron, i.e. one thousandth of a millimetre. This very small unit is used because of the very small size of the clay and silt-size soil particles. One millimetre is equivalent to 1000 μ, so that, since the fine earth fraction of the soil, as defined in Chapter 1, is that part of the soil passing through a 2 mm sieve, the upper size limit for sand is 2 mm or 2000 μ. Particles larger than this are referred to as gravel (2 mm to 20 mm), stones (20 mm to 200 mm) or boulders.

The fact that the fine earth fraction of the soil is composed of particles of different sizes can be conveniently demonstrated by the following experiment.

(1) Take a quantity of soil, preferably a subsoil sample with little humus.

(2) Dry and sieve through a 2 mm sieve to remove the coarse material. (If the soil contains no coarse material this can be omitted.)

(3) Put approximately 1 tablespoonful of fine earth into a 1 litre glass measuring cylinder or other suitable glass container. Almost fill with water. Covering the end with the hand, shake the soil and water vigorously.

(4) Stand the cylinder on a laboratory bench or table and carefully observe the way the soil suspended in the water falls to the bottom of the container.

As soon as shaking is stopped, the largest particles in the suspension, the sand, fall almost immediately, then the silt-size particles and, finally, after perhaps many hours or even days, the smallest soil particles, those of clay size, will also fall to the bottom. At the base of the cylinder or jar separate layers of decreasing particle sizes can be seen, with the coarser particles (the first to fall) forming the bottom layer, and the finest, which settled slowly, forming the top layer. The water has sorted out the soil particles according to size: they are now size-sorted. This simple but instructive experiment demonstrates a convenient way of separating soils into their constituent size particles. The fact that the settling velocity of particles is related to their diameter is used for the mechanical analysis of soils into particle size fractions in the laboratory.

The experiment has also shown us approximately the relative proportions of sand, silt, and clay in the soil sample taken. In addition, it has demonstrated what happens in nature when soil material is carried in suspension by a stream or river. As soon as the river water slows down or stands still, the larger particles are deposited, whereas the finer particles, including those of clay size, are deposited only if and when the water stands still for a sufficient period.

When a muddy river with soil in suspension overflows and floods its valley, as most West African rivers do frequently during the rains, the water slows down and may later stop moving altogether. The sand settles first, and sandy material is commonly found deposited on and near the

1   (*above*) A typical gravelly West African forest soil. There is a thin leaf litter layer overlying a gravel-free humous topsoil about 5 in thick containing frequent roots. The subsoil contains abundant gravel. In the example shown the gravel extends to about 36 in. The subsoil merges fairly gradually into the weathered substratum which is lighter textured and contains occasional traces of soft weathered parent rock (in this case phyllite). The pit shown is about 5 ft deep.

2   (*below*) A close-up of part of the gravelly subsoil shown in Plate 1. The gravel is mainly ironstone nodules and concretions with subordinate amounts of quartz gravel and quartz stones.

3   (*above*) Well-developed blocky structure seen in a sample of a heavy clay soil which has been dug out and allowed to dry. The blocks are angular and mostly 10 to 20 mm across, so that the **structure is** *medium angular blocky* (Table 2.2). The grade of structural development is strong.

4   (*inset*) Small, fairly angular soil aggregates brought up by ants. Soil fauna often contribute to topsoil structures.

5   (*below*) A well-structured soil. The dark topsoil has a strong fine to medium angular blocky structure. The paler subsoil has strong medium to coarse blocks with a tendency to form columns. The soil is a tropical black earth. Well-developed structures are found in West Africa mainly in soils with a high clay content, particularly in the relatively inextensive soils containing an expanding clay mineral such as montmorillonite. In many West African soils (including soils such as those shown in Plates 1, 2, 10, 11, 16, 18, and 22) structure in the subsoil is usually relatively weakly developed and may be difficult to see.

banks of the stream or river. Further away from the river the water, which has already dropped its sand, may stand long enough to deposit silt and clay, so giving a different type of deposit. Material transported, sorted, and then deposited by a stream or river is alluvium. Alluvium often shows marked water sorting of its particles. Soils near rivers are often developed in deposits of alluvium, and this material may have come originally, particularly in the case of large rivers, from areas a long distance away upstream.

The sand and silt fractions are commonly subdivided further as follows

Coarse sand	600 to 2000 μ (0·6 mm to 2·0 mm)
Medium sand	200 to 600 μ (0·2 mm to 0·6 mm)
Find sand	60 to 200 μ (0·06 mm to 0·2 mm)
Coarse silt	20 to 60 μ (0·02 mm to 0·06 mm)
Medium silt	6 to 20 μ (0·006 mm to 0·02 mm)
Fine silt	2 to 6 μ (0·002 mm to 0·006 mm).

With experience, it is possible to estimate the approximate content of sand, silt, and clay in a sample by feeling it between the thumb and first finger. Coarse sand is easily recognized in soils and is often angular, i.e. gritty. Most beach sand falls within the medium sand size class. Fine sand is common in many soils and is large enough to be felt distinctly between the fingers. Sand in a soil, particularly if it is fairly dry, can be heard if the sample is held to the ear and rubbed between the thumb and first finger. Silt, in contrast, is too fine to be felt as individual particles, and imparts a smooth and sometimes soapy feel to the soil. The amount of clay in particular greatly affects the feel and consistency of the soil, tending to make it heavier to work, sticky when wet, and hard when dry. For reasons discussed further below, the clay fraction is the most active size fraction in the soil and in many ways the most important.

Some of the size classes given above are arbitrary ones, chosen for convenience, though to some extent, particularly in the case of the clay fraction, these divisions separate classes with distinct natural properties. The sizes given are those of the international scale. The divisions used in various parts of the world do not always correspond exactly to those outlined: in some areas 50 μ is taken as the upper size limit for silt, and 50 to 100 μ particles may be described as very fine sand.

The finest particles, the clay, are so small that if they are well separated one from the other and not stuck together in larger aggregates they form an extremely fine suspension in water. In the soil test carried out above, the individual clay particles were probably adhering to each other to a considerable extent and settled much more quickly than they would have done if completely dispersed. To separate them completely, it is necessary first to destroy the humus in the soil which, because of its glue-like properties, tends to stick the individual clay particles together, and then to overcome the natural attraction that these small particles have for each other by shaking the soil-water suspension for several hours with a dispersing agent such as Calgon (sodium hexametaphosphate), or, if this is unavailable, with a little commercial detergent. If this has been done the finer clay particles may take weeks or even months to settle completely. A clay suspension passes through most laboratory filter papers, and a particularly fine paper is required if the clay is to be separated from the water by filtering. Such a fine suspension is somewhere between a normal suspension and a solution, and substances forming such fine suspensions are often described as colloids. Many colloids occur in nature: milk and glue are examples, as is the latex obtained from the rubber tree and the milky sap of other plants. Colloidal substances, on account of their fine particle size, have particular physical and chemical properties.

Soil texture

The normal soil does not consist of only sand, or only silt, or only clay, but is nearly always a mixture of particles of all three size classes. The characteristics of the soil, including its feel and physical handling properties, depend greatly on the relative proportions of the different size classes. The term 'soil texture' relates to the relative percentages of sand, silt, and clay in a soil. The feel of the soil gives some indication of these percentages. A soil with a high proportion of clay in it is described as a clay soil or, more concisely, as a clay. A very sandy soil is described as a sand. A soil intermediate between these without the characteristics of either is described as a loam. The term 'clay' and 'sand' here refer to the whole soil, implying the dominance of one size fraction, and must not be confused with the more specific use of the same words applied to a strictly defined particle size class.

The general terms which describe soil texture vary from area to area, but are usually defined exactly according to the range of sand, silt, and clay percentages which they include. In West Africa a relatively simple classification used in some areas is the following:

clay	light loam
light clay	loamy sand
heavy loam	sand
loam	

For greater precision, the adjectives 'silty' or 'sandy' (e.g. a sandy light clay) can be employed where necessary. The best way for the student to appreciate the soil properties implied by each of these terms is for him to carry out the following simple test on as wide a range of soil samples as is convenient.

(1) Sieve the soil and take approximately 1 tablespoonful of fine earth, enough to form a ball about 1 inch in diameter.
(2) Slowly add water, drop by drop, to the soil ball until the sticky point is reached: this occurs when the soil sticks to itself and can be shaped, but does not stick to the hand. (If it does, too much water has been added.)
(3) On a flat wooden board try to roll out the 1 in ball of soil into a cylinder about $6\frac{1}{4}$ in long. If it will bend without breaking, form it into a circle.

The extent to which the soil can be shaped is an indication of the texture. If the soil is a *sand*, it cannot be shaped or worked at all and the most that can be done is to heap it up into a pyramid or cone (Fig. 2.1), but if the sand contains sufficient finer material to enable it to be shaped into a ball it is a *loamy sand*. If the sample can be rolled into a cylinder, but breaks when bent further, it is a *loam* (a *light loam* forms a short, fat cylinder, an ordinary loam one which is full length). If the cylinder can be bent into a *U*-shape but no further, the sample is a *heavy loam*. If it makes a full circle without breaking, it is a light clay or clay: a *light clay* forms a circle with cracks in it; a *clay*, one without cracks.

This practical test is of considerable value since it gives an indication of how the soil handles when cultivated. A soil with a high clay content is relatively hard to work, and may be described as 'heavy', whereas sandy soils are usually much easier to dig, hoe, or plough and are referred to as being 'light'.

For a more accurate description of texture, it is necessary to disperse the soil and measure in the laboratory the percentages of the different size fractions defined above. In many parts of the world the textural terms used, such as clay, light clay, loam, etc., have been defined precisely in terms of the exact range of sand, silt, and clay which they contain. A diagram illustrating the latest classification in use in the U.S.A. is shown in Fig. 2.3. From this it will be seen that a soil there described as a 'clay' has over 40 per cent clay, less than 40 per cent silt, and less than 45 per cent sand, whereas a loamy sand must have between 70 and 90 per cent sand and less than 30 per cent silt and 15 per cent clay. The exact definition of the terms used varies in different countries, and is also liable to be modified from time to time.

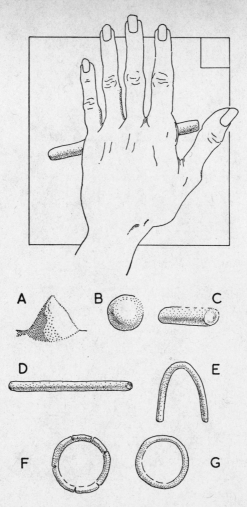

Fig. 2.1. A manipulative texture test which gives a practical indication of soil texture and consistency.

Enough fine earth is taken to make a ball of soil about 1 in across and water is dripped on to the soil until it reaches the sticky point, the point at which the soil adheres to itself but not to the hand. The extent to which the moist soil can be worked is an indication of texture. A sand can only be heaped into a pyramid A, but a loamy sand makes a ball B. If the soil can be rolled out to a short cylinder C it is a light loam. The remaining drawings indicate a loam D, a heavy loam E, a light clay, a circle with cracks F and a clay, a circle without cracks G.

The cylinder when fully rolled out, as in D, should be $6\frac{1}{4}$ in long. A board, shown below the hand, is marked with a 1 in square and a line $6\frac{1}{4}$ in long in order to standardize the test.

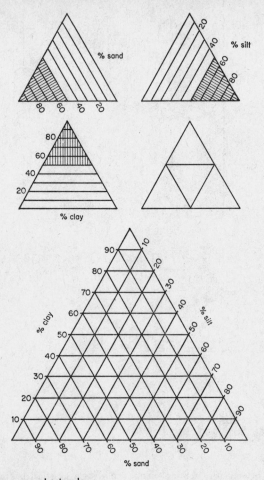

Fig. 2.2. The textural triangle.

The textural triangle really consists of three separate triangles (above) super-imposed on each other, one for sand (top left), one for silt (top right), and one for clay (centre left). In these triangles 100 per cent of sand, silt, or clay is at the left, right or upper apex respectively. The area shaded in each triangle represents over 50 per cent. In the fourth small triangle (centre right) areas with over 50 per cent sand, silt or clay form the outer triangles, while that in the centre represents soils with less than 50 per cent of each of these.

The full textural triangle (below) is so arranged that any point within it indicates three percentages, i.e. of sand, silt, and clay. Thus the texture of a soil or soil horizon can be indicated by a point in the triangle.

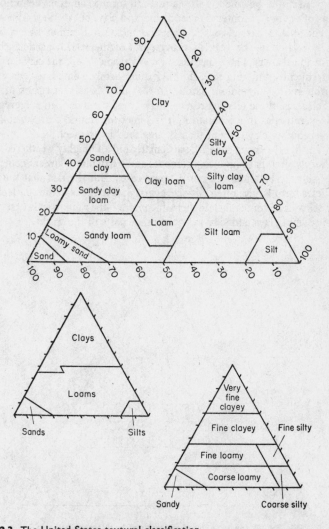

Fig. 2.3. The United States textural classification.
The larger, upper triangle represents the standard division into textural classes. The smaller triangle below it (centre left) is a much simplified version of the large triangle, indicating the broad divisions of clays, loams, sands, and silts. The third triangle (lower right) is a different type of simplification which is used in the U.S.A. for indicating broad textural classes used in the classification of soil families.

It is useful to be able to relate a textural term to an exact definition in terms of a range of contents of sand, silt, and clay, but in West Africa the content of these size classes and the feel of the soil cannot always be as closely related as they can in many parts of the world, particularly in non-tropical areas. This is because in many tropical soils the clay particles are frequently adhering to each other quite firmly, sometimes cemented by iron and/or aluminium oxides, so that they form aggregates of clay particles and these clay aggregates may be of silt size. If the aggregates are separated, as in a laboratory, it is sometimes found that the soil has a much higher clay content than is suggested by the feel.

Many West African soils are particularly old and highly weathered, and such soils often have high clay contents and particularly low silt contents: true silt may be almost absent in some cases. But the fact that the clay particles form larger, often silt-size aggregates may make the soil feel the same as soils having a much higher silt content—the same as soils described as silty light clays and silty loams in other parts of the world.

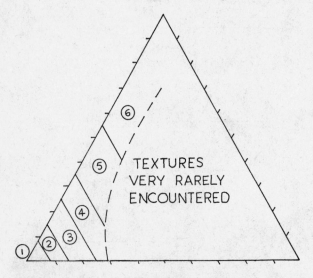

Fig. 2.4. A textural classification used in Western Nigeria. The classification shown above has been found practical for the generally sandy soils of Western Nigeria which usually contain little silt. The descriptive terms are (1) sand; (2) slightly clayey sand; (3) clayey sand; (4) very clayey sand; (5) sandy clay; (6) clay. (Adapted from Reference 25.)

The ring test described above is frequently used by soil surveyors in West Africa to describe the apparent texture of soils, and if carefully carried out gives a useful idea of how the soil behaves in the field and when cultivated. It is carried out on the sieved sample without prior destruction of the humus content and without any form of dispersion, so that it shows how the natural soil responds to manipulation: in fact, it is really a texture and consistency test.

Soil consistency

The term consistency refers to the resistance of a soil to the insertion of an instrument such as a cutlass, knife, or hoe, its resistance to deformation when handled, and its cohesion. These in turn depend very much on whether the soil is wet, moist, or dry, and for accurate work different sets of descriptive terms are used to describe the soil in each of these states, as shown in Table 2.1.

TABLE 2.1. Terms used to describe soil consistency at different moisture contents.

WET SOIL		MOIST SOIL	DRY SOIL
(a) *Stickiness*	(b) *Plasticity*		
non-sticky	non-plastic	loose	loose
slightly sticky	slightly plastic	very friable	soft
sticky	plastic	friable	slightly hard
very sticky	very plastic	firm	hard
		very firm	very hard
		extremely firm	extremely hard

Wet soil is described in terms of its stickiness, i.e. the extent to which it sticks to other objects, and its plasticity, the ability to be pressed into any shape without breaking, and to retain that shape. Both of these properties are related to the type and amount of clay present.

Moist soils, because of their lower moisture content, break into smaller aggregates more easily than do wet soils, even though these aggregates may cohere again when pressed against each other: the consistency is estimated by trying to crush a piece of soil in the hand and estimating its resistance. A very friable soil is easily crushed with gentle pressure, but a very firm soil is barely crushable between thumb and finger and an extremely firm one cannot be crushed in this way.

Dry soils are often relatively rigid, brittle, and hard, and may break into angular fragments which do not adhere to each other again when pressed together. A mass of soil should be held in the hand: if it is easily broken between thumb and forefinger it is no more than slightly hard, but a very hard soil when dry cannot be broken between thumb and forefinger and can be broken in the hands only with difficulty.

It will be observed that many of the above consistency properties are implied to some extent by the ring test. Unless otherwise stated, the colour and consistency described refer to the soil in its moist state. A more complete description may use such phrases as 'sticky and plastic when wet, very hard when dry', thus emphasizing the fact that some soils exhibit very different properties according to their moisture content.

Soil structure

Careful examination of the soil in the field shows that the soil is not uniform and homogeneous, but that it has a certain internal arrangement. The constituent sand, silt, and clay particles are not normally separate from each other, but adhere to each other and often form natural units or *aggregates* separated by pores, cracks, or planes of weakness. The term *structure* refers to this arrangement of the soil into natural aggregates.

When soil structure is described in the field attention is given to:

(1) the shape and arrangement of the structural units;
(2) their size;
(3) their degree of development, distinctness, and durability.

Structural units, often called 'peds', are fundamentally of four primary shapes: (1) those which are more or less flat or platy; (2) those which are prism-like with a predominantly vertical direction and bounded by fairly flat vertical surfaces; (3) those which are blocky or many-sided, arranged around a central point, and bounded by flat or rounded surfaces that fit into those of the blocky units surrounding the ped; and finally (4) those which are more or less round and spheroidal or many-sided which do not fit closely against adjoining peds but merely touch them at certain points so as to leave considerable space between them: these include crumbs (in which aggregates are bound by humus) and granules.

The size of the structural units is expressed by such terms as very fine, fine, medium, coarse, and very coarse: the actual sizes corresponding to these terms vary according to the type of structure, as shown in Table 2.2. The degree of development of the structure, if present, is indicated by the terms *weak* (barely observable in place), *moderate*, and *strong* (durable peds evident in undisplaced soil). A soil horizon without observable regular structure is described as *structureless*.

In the temperate regions of the world soil structure is often better developed than it is in many tropical soils, and textbooks written for those

TABLE 2.2. Sizes, in millimetres (mm), of structural units as conventionally described.

	VERY FINE	FINE	MEDIUM	COARSE	VERY COARSE
Granular and crumb structures (diameter)	Less than 1 mm	1 to 2 mm	2 to 5 mm	5 to 10 mm	Over 10 mm
Angular and subangular blocky structures (diameter)	Less than 5 mm	5 to 10 mm	10 to 20 mm	20 to 50 mm	—
Prismatic and columnar structures (diameter)	Less than 10 mm	10 to 20 mm	20 to 50 mm	50 to 100 mm	—
Platy structures (thickness)	Less than 1 mm	1 to 2 mm	2 to 5 mm	5 to 10 mm	Over 10 mm

regions usually describe structural types in detail. In West Africa, many soils have little or no structure in at least some horizons. Any soil when dropped will break into fragments, but these fragments are not structural units or peds unless they possess a certain regularity and are bounded by natural faces or planes of weakness and are not simply irregular pieces broken by force. Normally what structure there is, is best seen by digging a soil pit, and letting the exposed soil-face dry out for a few days. A structure that is obvious in the exposed surface is usually of moderate to strong grade; those structures that are not observed in the soil-face but can be seen by gently picking apart a soil sample in the hand are of weak to moderate grade.

In *topsoils* with a moderate to good humus content there is usually a fairly well developed *crumb structure* in which soil particles are loosely bound by the glue-like humus into very porous, more or less spheroidal aggregates. Worms, ants, and other soil fauna may produce rounded soil pellets and crumbs. Cultivation often has the effect of reducing the topsoil humus content and this brings about a loss of structure and of overall porosity of the topsoil, and with it a loss of soil productivity.

In *subsoils* the structure may be masked by the high gravel content of some soils. The better developed and more obvious structures are found in the heavier soils with relatively high clay contents, which may have blocky or angular blocky structures (an angular block is one with sharp corners fitting in neatly to the next block with little space between). Many old, highly weathered, iron-rich soils have little or no coarse structure but the soil, when examined carefully, is seen to consist of very small aggregates 1 mm or 2 mm across. If these are angular or nearly so, the soil may have a *very fine angular* or *subangular blocky* structure, if more or less rounded the structure may be *very fine granular* (less than 1 mm across) or *fine granular* (1 to 2 mm). Sometimes there is a compound structural pattern in which larger units, e.g. weak, very coarse blocks or prisms, break down into smaller component aggregates, such as weak, fine angular blocks. In some subsoils, however, the aggregation is so weak and irregular that the subsoil is best described as *structureless*, while in very sandy soils in which there is not sufficient humus, clay, or silt to bind the soil into aggregates, the soil may be *single-grained*, i.e. with separate sand grains.

In the *weathered substratum* there is commonly less structure, or a lower grade of structural development, than in the subsoil. Some structural patterns may reflect the nature of the weathered parent material.

In some soils, particularly some of the younger soils still containing material being weathered, clay may be moved downwards within a profile by percolating soil water. In these cases it may be deposited as distinct clay films or clay 'skins' on the surfaces of structural units. If such a unit is broken the clay film on the outside may be seen to be of a somewhat different colour or shade from the interior of the ped. Clay skins are not often found in the subsoils of the old, highly weathered, stable soils of much of West Africa, but may occur in younger soils and in some weathered substrata.

The structure or absence of structure of a soil greatly affects its agricultural productivity. A good crumb structure in the topsoil increases the amount of pore space and allows air and water to circulate. Spaces between structural units in the subsoil may assist water circulation there, particularly in the heavy soils where drainage might otherwise be slow. A well-structured soil may lose that structure through poor cultivation methods.

Soil porosity and density

If a sample of a given volume of topsoil is taken and compared with the same volume of subsoil (e.g. by filling containers of the same size without compacting the soil), it will almost always be found that the subsoil weighs more than the same volume of topsoil. This is because (1) the topsoil contains more humus, which is lighter in weight (has a lower specific gravity) than the mineral particles of the soil; and (2) the topsoil contains a greater number of air spaces, i.e. it has a greater total porosity.

The sand, silt, and clay of the soil, i.e. the mineral particles of the soil, probably have a specific gravity averaging about 2·6 (i.e. they weigh 2·6 times as much as the same volume of water). Let us assume that a small container when full holds water weighing exactly 1 lb: if the same container were filled with soil the contents would weigh 2·6 lb only if there were no air space at all between the particles, which is never the case. In actual practice the container might be found to hold only about 1¼ lb of soil if it were topsoil, and about 1 lb 8 oz or 1 lb 10 oz if it were subsoil, depending on the type of soil and its content of gravel and stones.

The *bulk density* of a soil (also called its apparent specific gravity) is the ratio of its weight to the weight of the same volume of water. Generally speaking, the higher the bulk density the less the pore space in the soil. A crumbly, porous topsoil in which air and water can circulate freely might have about 50 per cent of its total volume occupied by solid material and the other 50 per cent made up of pores of various sizes, cracks, channels, and other spaces; its bulk density would probably be about 1·2 (i.e. it would weigh 1·2 times the same volume of water). A typical bulk density for a non-gravelly subsoil would be somewhat higher, about 1·6, indicating less total pore space. In gravelly and stony subsoils, obviously, there may be still less air space, because the gravel and stones are themselves solid, without pores. In such cases the bulk density of the soil will be higher, perhaps as much as 2·0.

Our knowledge of the shape and distribution of small soil pores and of the microstructure of the soil has been greatly increased in recent years by the use of soil thin sections. Soil samples are impregnated and hardened with a colourless plastic resin, and then ground to form thin sections for examination in the microscope. Even without a microscope much can be learnt by using a hand lens and gently breaking open a fragment of soil with a needle and looking at the fresh surfaces, pores, and channels exposed.

The clay fraction

An optical microscope can magnify up to 1500 times, but this is not sufficient for the study of clay-size particles, which are too small to be seen with an ordinary microscope. The more recent invention of special techniques, such as the electron microscope and the X ray diffractometer, has allowed clays to be studied in much more detail. These techniques have revealed the fact that these minute particles are not merely very small, shapeless specks but are extremely small crystals, usually flat and flake-like, which possess a regular structure. Clay minerals can be divided into a number of distinct types with different structures and with different chemical and physical properties. As investigations continue, more different varieties of clay are being discovered.

The clay fraction in the soil was defined above as all those particles with a diameter less than 2 μ (0·002 mm), and this, it was emphasized, was merely a size class. Not every particle in the soil falling within this size class is necessarily true clay, for there are very small fragments of quartz (quartz flour) and amorphous iron oxides which, among other things, are small enough to be included but which are not true crystalline clays. The true clays, which nevertheless normally dominate the clay fraction, are often much smaller than 2 μ. Although some well developed individual clay crystals may reach 1 μ in diameter, most are even smaller than this.

Clay minerals are classified according to their chemical and micro-crystalline structure. The simplest type of clay and that which is by far the most common in most West African soils is *kaolin*. Kaolin, or kaolinite, has relatively large, flat crystal flakes, often more or less hexagonal, con-sisting of a number of adjacent sheets (Fig. 2.5). These sheets each consist of a double layer, one of a lattice of silica (SiO_2) molecules and the other of a lattice of alumina (Al_2O_3) molecules, the two being bonded together by shared oxygen atoms. Each double layer crystal unit is held to the next double layer by hydroxyl (OH^-) ions, and in kaolinite the distance between

---

Fig. 2.5. Clay minerals and their structure.

The drawing A indicates kaolin flakes as they appear in an electron microscope photograph. The flakes are less than 1 micron across so that the magnification is about 30 000$\times$.

B indicates the structure of a kaolin flake, composed of many double layers, each of silica and alumina sheets bonded by shared oxygen atoms (circles). Each double layer is bound to the double layer above and below by oxygen-hydroxyl bonds (double vertical lines) which allow very little expansion between the layers, so that ions and water molecules cannot penetrate easily. Because of the very limited amount of expansion possible kaolin is described as a non-expanding lattice clay.

C represents a montmorillonite flake in which each layer-unit consists of three layers, two layers of silica with a layer of alumina sandwiched between them. The bonds between the layer-units are relatively weak and the lattice can expand considerably, as represented in D. When wetted, water enters between the units of the lattice and the lattice expands.

Diagrams E and F represent clay flakes and their associated ions attracted to the negative charges on the clay. The flake E represents a soil which is saturated with metallic cations. All the negative exchange sites are occupied by calcium, magne-sium, and potassium ions, and the soil pH would be about 7·0 or slightly above. Diagram F represents what occurs when some of the cations are removed, as when soils are leached. The place of the cations is usually assumed to be taken by hydrogen ions and these give an acid reaction to the soil.

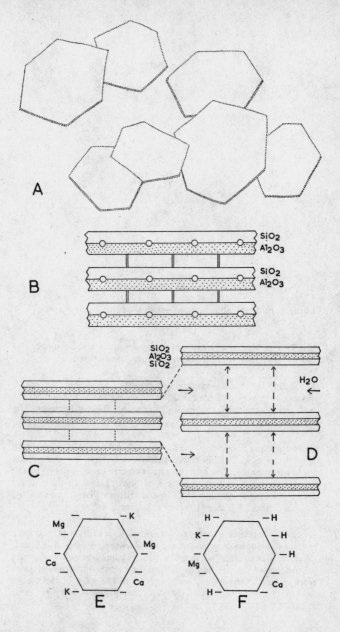

6 9   Photographs of soil thin sections seen through a microscope.

6   (*top*) Thin section of a forest topsoil showing very small crumbs. The area covered by the photograph is about 2 mm across.

7   (*top centre*) Thin section photograph of part of a sandy lower topsoil of a profile developed over granite, showing fairly angular quartz sand grains with small crumb-like humous aggregates between. The area shown is a little over 2 mm across.

8   (*bottom centre*) Soil channel. The channel is lined with clay which forms a clay skin. Dark lines and patches away from the channel are due to iron oxide. The distribution of this is partly related to the channel as is shown by the pattern of lines parallel to the channel walls. The magnification is the same as that for Plate 7, so that the channel is about 0·1 mm (100 micron) across.

9   (*bottom*) Thin section photograph of part of the weathered substratum of a soil developed over biotite granite showing decomposing biotite (left), opaque areas of ferric oxide (centre) and areas of reddish and yellowish clay (in the middle and to the right). An irregular small crack extends across the photograph from the edge of the biotite flake at the left to the right hand edge. The magnification is the same as that for Plate 6.

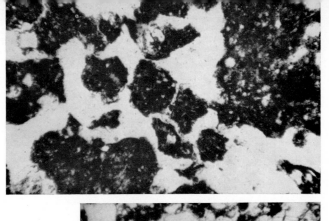

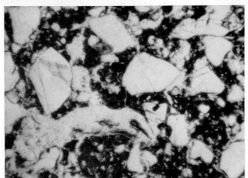

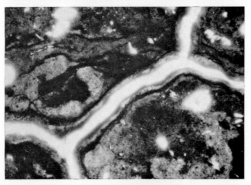

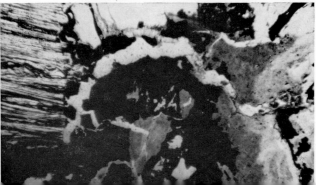

10   (*above right*) A stone line in a savanna soil. The stone line here consists of an irregular band of generally angular stones of quartz and quartzite which occurs at about 2 ft below the surface. The soil above the stone line contains abundant stones and gravel. Lesser quantities are found in the weathered substratum below the stone line.

11   (*below right*) A deeper soil developed under forest (under forest regrowth when the photograph was taken). The soil appears to be sedentary. A subsoil about 2 ft thick contains frequent pea gravel, mainly ironstone concretions 5 to 10 mm across. The weathered substratum is diffusely mottled and contains little or no stones or gravel apart from the broken quartz vein which passes through the weathered substratum from lower left to upper right, suggesting that this horizon is derived from a rock which has weathered *in situ*. (South-west Ivory Coast).

12   (*below left*) Profile comparable to that in Plate 11 showing the great depth of soil and soil weathering often found in the wetter forest areas of west Africa (a road cut in south-west Ghana).

13   (*centre left*) Coarsely mottled soil material similar to that found in the weathered substratum of the profile shown in Plate 11. The material is mottled but only slightly indurated. The dark areas are red to brown iron rich mottles; the pale areas are grey to white or pale yellow, and appear relatively iron free.

these double layers is small and fairly constant. Kaolinite therefore has what is called a 1:1 (one-to-one) layer lattice, i.e. one layer of silica to one of alumina, and the lattice itself is described as non-expanding because the distance between the sheets remains almost the same.

A second important group of clay minerals has a 2:1 (two-to-one) layer lattice. Each crystalline unit consists of three layers, two silica layers on the outside and an alumina layer between the two. Of this group of clay minerals the hydrous micas, such as *illite*, have a fixed distance between the sheets, as has kaolin. In a second type of 2:1 lattice clay, however, the individual three layer sheets can separate out a little to make more space between them, and thus form an expanding lattice: such a clay is *montmorillonite*. In montmorillonite the distance between corresponding points on adjacent sheets can vary to a considerable extent.

Clays with a fixed distance between the layers do not change much in volume when they become wet or when they dry out, but the expanding lattice clays allow water to penetrate between the sheets and cause them to expand. As a result, clays of this type such as montmorillonite, swell when wetted, but shrink and may form cracks when they dry again. Kaolin, in contrast, does not expand very much on wetting. Many other types of clay exist, some with properties intermediate between those discussed, and in a particular soil there is often more than one type of clay mineral.

Properties of clays

The colloidal properties of clays are related to their very small size. The smaller a particle of matter the greater is its surface area in relation to its volume, and the greater the proportion of its molecules which are at the surface. The important chemical properties of clays are due in part to their relatively enormous surface area as compared with silt-size and larger particles.

A molecule in the interior of a particle is connected to other molecules in a regular way, and is usually electrically satisfied, but a molecule at the edge may not be. At the edges of the clay flakes, and in some cases on the surfaces between the sheets which make up the flakes, are molecules with unsatisfied electrical charges. These unsatisfied charges are both positive and negative, but the negative charges are usually much more numerous than the positive. As a result of the fact that ions with opposite charges attract each other, these negative positions attract positively charged ions (or cations) in the soil, and these are loosely *adsorbed* on to the clay surface. When salts dissolve in water they become dissociated, i.e. they split up into a positively charged ion, the cation, and a negatively charged ion, the anion. Thus sodium chloride splits up in solution to provide a sodium cation and a chloride anion, and ammonium sulphate to provide two ammonium cations and a sulphate anion. The commonest cations in soils are usually those of calcium, magnesium, and potassium. It is these positively charged ions, the cations, which are attracted by the negative charges on the clay.

In addition, clays in soils are usually surrounded by water molecules, some of them attached to the cations to give hydrated cations, and some attracted to the clay, both to the outer surfaces and to the spaces between the sheets.

The negative charges on the clay give them their *cation exchange capacity*, their capacity to attract positively charged ions and to adsorb them in such a way that they can be relatively easily given up and are available to the plant. The cations do not enter into a chemical combination with the clay, but are merely attracted to positions on or close to its surface and are best visualized as being in continuous movement, changing positions with other cations in the water surrounding the clay. There is at any one time a fairly constant equilibrium between the cations attracted to the surface of the clay particles and those moving to the soil solution.

All clays are, chemically, aluminium silicates (the ideal simplified formula for kaolin, for example, is $2SiO_2 . Al_2O_3 . 2H_2O$) but in fact the crystalline structure is not quite regular and irregularities in structure and chemical composition may increase the number of exposed negative charges and therefore the cation exchange capacity.

In the case of kaolin, with its non-expanding lattice, the exchange capacity is due almost entirely to negative charges at the edges of the sheets only. In the case of montmorillonite there are additional negative positions between the sheets. Because of this and also because of the much smaller size of montmorillonite flakes, montmorillonite has a considerably higher cation exchange capacity than kaolinite.

The cation exchange capacity of a clay or a soil is conventionally expressed, for convenience, as the weight of cations which can be absorbed by 100 grammes (100 g) of the substance. As is often the case in chemical measurement it is more convenient to express this in terms of the equivalent weight rather than the actual weight. An equivalent weight of an element is the amount which, in chemical reactions, will replace or combine with 1 g of hydrogen. Since the quantities involved in clay exchanges are relatively small, the normal unit of measurement is 1/1000 part of the equivalent weight, the milliequivalent. Cation exchange capacity is thus expressed as *milliequivalents per* 100 *grammes* (m.e. per 100 g) of the clay, soil, or other substance referred to.

If a clay has a cation exchange capacity of 10 m.e. per 100 g it can absorb up to 10 m.e. of total cations. The actual weight of these cations will depend on which particular elements are involved, since they vary considerably in weight, and whether the cations are monovalent, divalent, or trivalent, i.e. whether they have one, two, or three positive charges each and therefore whether they each satisfy one, two, or three of the negative positions on the clay. These negative positions can be occupied by a range of different cations, but in many West African soils the commonest are calcium and magnesium, with smaller quantities of potassium and occasionally manganese and sodium cations. A negative position not occupied by one of the metallic cations is usually assumed to be occupied by a hydrogen ion.

Expressing the cation exchange capacity of clays as m.e. per 100 g, we find that kaolinite, the commonest clay mineral in West Africa, has an exchange capacity of about 10 m.e. per 100 g. This is only a very approximate figure, but comparison with approximate figures for other types of clay indicates that kaolin has a rather low exchange capacity. Montmorillonite has an exchange capacity which is about ten times as much, i.e. approximately 100 m.e. per 100 g.

The exchange capacity of soils is not, however, due only to their clay content, but also by their content of humus. Humus also has colloidal properties, and weight for weight, humus has a much higher exchange capacity than the clays discussed above—about 200 m.e. per 100 g. This is twenty times as much, approximately, as kaolin, and twice as much as montmorillonite. In topsoils with a good humus content most of the exchange capacity is usually due to the humus.

We may now summarize the nature and properties of the clay minerals discussed:

Kaolinite, the most abundant clay mineral in West African soils, has relatively large flakes up to 1 μ (0·001 mm) across and often more or less hexagonal in shape. Because its 1 : 1 layer lattice is non-expanding, kaolin does not swell appreciably on wetting; conversely, it does not shrink much or crack on drying. Its cation exchange capacity is relatively low, about 10 m.e. per 100 g, partly because its crystal flakes are not as minute as those of some other clays, partly because the negative charges are mainly confined to the edges of the lattice sheets.

Montmorillonite crystals are much smaller than those of kaolinite and may separate more easily into very thin flakes. Montmorillonite gives a heavier texture and more plastic consistency to soils than does kaolinite. The crystal lattice sheets expand away from each other on wetting, and the clay swells: on drying, the clay shrinks, and cracks may form in the soil. The cation exchange capacity is high, about 100 m.e. per 100 g, because of the small size of the flakes and the fact that negative charges on the interior surfaces of the sheets making up the flakes are also exposed.

Illite is intermediate between kaolinite and montmorillonite in its properties: it has a moderately high exchange capacity of about 30 m.e. per 100 g, but does not swell much on wetting because of the non-expanding lattice.

Many other types of clay also exist, but as stated above it is usually kaolinite which predominates in the normal, highly weathered soils of West Africa.

The origin of clays

Sand and silt particles in the soil are usually merely irregular particles of rock in the soil which have been broken down to a small size. Clays, in contrast, are built up or synthesized from materials liberated by the weathering of silicate rocks. The type of clay formed depends on the composition of the weathering rock and on the physical environment, particularly climate. (Climate and its influence on soils is discussed further in Chapter 4.)

The formation of soil horizons

The upper parts of a soil profile may or may not be related to the rock found at depth below. Soils which are related to the underlying rock and have been developed in weathered material derived from that rock are described as *sedentary*, suggesting that the soil material has not moved, or *residual*, a term suggesting the fact that the soil comprises residual material derived from the rock below.

In a sedentary soil (such as that shown diagrammatically in Fig. 1.1) the horizons are related to each other by genesis: the weathered substratum is composed of weathering products derived from material similar to that which forms the solid rock below it. Similarly, the subsoil is thought of as having developed from weathered material, such as that forming the substratum, while the topsoil is partly derived, largely through the influence and activity of plants and soil animals, from material similar to that in the horizons below. However, the soil is not a fixed, static, unchanging thing: it is alive in the sense that it contains innumerable living things (from viruses and bacteria to insects, animals, and plants) and that it is constantly subject to change and reorganization owing to physical and chemical changes and movements. Moreover, the landscape of which it forms part is also subject to change, with the higher parts being worn down slowly and the lower perhaps being filled up, and soils keep pace with these changes.

The nature of the soil parent rocks and their physical and chemical weathering is considered in the next chapter. The *weathered substratum* derived from these rocks is much lighter, i.e. has a lower bulk density than the parent rock because it is less compact and because of the removal during weathering of some of the rock constituents.

In the *subsoil*, soil-forming influences have been at work to a greater extent than in the weathered substratum, and all the soil material is more modified. More complete chemical and physical changes may have occurred, with a greater reorganization and perhaps concentration of constituents. The more soluble have now been removed and only the more resistant may remain. These resistant materials are mainly the clays, oxides of iron and aluminium, and quartz, though other resistant minerals may also survive considerable soil weathering and leaching. The subsoil is often referred to as the horizon of illuviation or 'washing in' since material is washed into it from the topsoil. Clay particles in particular may be carried downwards in suspension by percolating water from the topsoil to the subsoil, where clay is usually at a maximum. Most of the gravel so often associated with sedentary West African soils is usually in the subsoil.

The *topsoil* owes its very distinct properties to the fact that it is the soil horizon with the maximum biological activity, both of plants and of soil animals. Even in a fresh and unsorted deposit of soil material (deposited by a river perhaps) the topsoil would begin to develop almost immediately as worms brought up fine material, as worm casts, to the surface, and other soil animals and insects such as termites contributed to the formation of a surface layer. Plants begin to grow in the soil and their dead leaves and stems are added to the surface soil, decay and are incorporated within it. The plant roots also decay and most of these are in the surface few inches. Thus the topsoil may be formed relatively quickly in what was originally a uniform deposit without natural horizons. It has more organic material than the soil below and probably less coarse material, since the stones and gravel have not been brought up by soil animals and are thus left behind to accumulate in the subsoil. The humus helps the formation of a good crumb structure and thus the total air space is increased. Because of the supply of decaying plant material on which they feed, the activity of soil bacteria is greater here than in the subsoil.

The horizons of a soil profile are thus developed by natural forces, and the nature and properties of the profile will depend on the combined activities and influences of all the soil-forming factors. The nature of the rock or other parent material (such as alluvium) which forms the starting point will greatly influence the resulting soil, since some parent materials weather and alter more quickly than others, and provide different materials as they do so, thus influencing the chemical and physical properties of the soil derived from them. The forces acting on this material are largely the forces of climate and vegetation, helped by soil animals. The climate, particularly the temperature and the amount and distribution of rainfall, affects the rate of weathering of the parent material and the later modification of the weathered products, but temperature and rainfall also influence the type and amount of vegetation that will grow, so that climate has a double effect. Trees influence soil development in a different way from grasses, and every type of plant has a slightly different influence on the soil as well as being itself influenced by soil factors.

The relationships between soil, climate, and vegetation are therefore very close and complex, and it is difficult and sometimes misleading to consider one without reference to the others. The soil characteristics of practical importance to agriculture are the result of soil formation and of soil-forming processes acting over varying lengths of time. Chapters 3 and 4 consider some aspects of soil formation in more detail.

PART 2

SOIL FORMATION

3 THE INFLUENCE OF PARENT MATERIAL, RELIEF, AND SITE

SOIL PARENT MATERIALS

Parent rock and parent material

Some soils appear to be developed from material similar to the underlying rock. Soils of this type have been described (Chapter 2) as sedentary or residual. Not all soils are developed from an underlying parent rock: some are developed in more or less weathered and sorted material deposited by streams and rivers, i.e. in alluvium, while others are developed in colluvium, material which has moved down a slope largely under the influence of gravity. Soils may also be developed in materials as different as beach sands and organic matter deposits. Any material in which soil develops, and in which a soil profile begins to form, is parent material. The original parent material of a soil may therefore be a hard rock, or an unconsolidated deposit. The term *parent material* is therefore a wide one, whereas *parent rock* is a narrower term referring to those soil parent materials which are rocks.

The typical profile shown in Fig. 1.1 is a sedentary one and there are natural transitions from topsoil to underlying rock. Each horizon appears to be related to the one below. In other soil profiles there may be a sharp transition or discontinuity between the upper parts of the profile and the weathered substratum below. Such would be the case in a soil developed in shallow alluvium or colluvium: the upper horizons may be developed in the transported material (the alluvium or colluvium), but the lower may be derived from the underlying rock (Fig. 3.7). Profiles of this type are common in West Africa on the lower slopes of valleys and in valley bottoms. In the case of soils developed in alluvium it may be necessary to distinguish between soils developed in young, recent alluvium such as that which now forms the river banks and present floodplain, and the older river alluvium, often further away from the river and higher than the recent alluvium. The older alluvium will have been subjected to a longer period of weathering than the younger.

The study of soil formation therefore requires a knowledge both of the rocks which form the earth's crust and which become soil parent materials, and of landscape-forming processes which have carved out the present-day relief and resulted in the formation of secondary deposits which have subsequently also become soil parent materials.

The study of rocks is the province of geology, while landscape formation is the province of physical geology or geomorphology. The soil scientist needs to have some knowledge of both these subjects, particularly of those aspects which influence soil formation.

The main classes of rocks

The rocks which make up the earth's crust have been formed in three main ways. Molten rock material coming up from the interior of the earth cools and solidifies at or near the surface. These primary rocks, from which the other classes of rock are ultimately derived, are known as *igneous rocks*, 'ignis' (Latin for fire) suggesting the heat which kept them molten before they were cooled and hardened. When rocks are exposed at the surface they are liable to be weathered and worn down, and the weathered material to be transported and then deposited as a sediment. Rocks derived from these sediments are known as *sedimentary*. In some cases previously existing rocks, either igneous or sedimentary, are greatly changed by heat and pressure to form the third group of *metamorphic* rocks. These three groups are briefly considered in turn.

Igneous rocks

Igneous rocks are derived from an original molten material or magma pushed up from the lower regions of the earth's crust to positions nearer the surface, or even at the surface, where the magma cools and solidifies. As the magma cools, crystals of different minerals form, and most igneous rocks consist of a number of different mineral crystals which interlock to form the rock. The slower the cooling of the magma, the larger are these crystals likely to be, for slow cooling gives them time to grow before the rock sets hard. Sudden cooling, in contrast, is likely to give a rock with very small crystals of individual minerals, too small perhaps to be seen with the naked eye, so that the rock will appear to be uniform and without individual mineral crystals until it is looked at through a microscope.

Rocks vary very greatly in the type of mineral they contain and in the size, arrangement, and chemical composition of these constituent minerals. A mineral can be defined as a naturally occurring substance with a fairly uniform chemical composition and with a regular, well defined structure. Under favourable conditions this structure shows itself in the formation of a crystal, though a particular mineral can vary slightly in its exact chemical composition because of the substitution of one element for another in the crystal structure.

Silicate minerals

The majority of minerals are silicates, i.e. combinations of silicon and oxygen with other elements. The basic structural unit of these minerals is simple: it is a silica tetrahedron or pyramid, a four-sided unit in which one relatively small silicon atom at the centre is bonded to four much larger oxygen atoms which surround it and which form the four corners of the regular tetrahedron, as shown diagrammatically in Fig. 3.1.

Silicate minerals can be classified according to the way these fundamental tetrahedron building units have linked up to form the mineral. In the first group there are separate tetrahedra linked only by other elements; in the second group the tetrahedra are linked to each other, by sharing oxygen atoms, to form groups or rings. In another group they form chains of tetrahedra, in yet another important group they form flat sheets. Finally they may link in all directions with other tetrahedra to form a three-dimensional lattice of silica tetrahedra. Since the structure of the silicate mineral helps in the understanding of how it weathers to form soil material, these structures are discussed briefly in the following paragraphs.

Nesosilicates (nesos = island) are those in which the silica tetrahedra remain separate from each other with no shared oxygen atoms, but are linked by intermediate cations. The olivine group of minerals form the best example of nesosilicates: in these the silica tetrahedra are linked by divalent magnesium (Mg^{2+}) and iron (Fe^{2+}) ions. In the case of olivine this gives a mineral which is easily weathered, because the ferrous iron and magnesium cations are exposed at the edge of the crystal and are oxidized or hydrated, so that the mineral disintegrates. Some nesosilicates containing other cations are more resistant than the olivines, so that resistance to weathering depends partly on the nature of the cations and partly on the structure.

Olivine is an example of a group of minerals termed *ferro-magnesian*, i.e. rich in iron and magnesium. These minerals, which include minerals of other structural groups than the nesosilicates, are usually dark in colour, weather relatively easily, and release magnesium and iron when they do so.

In a second group the silica tetrahedra form groups or rings, while in an important third group, the *inosilicates* (inos = fibre) the silica tetrahedra join to form chains. In the pyroxene family of minerals they form a single chain, in the amphibole family they form double chains. In both

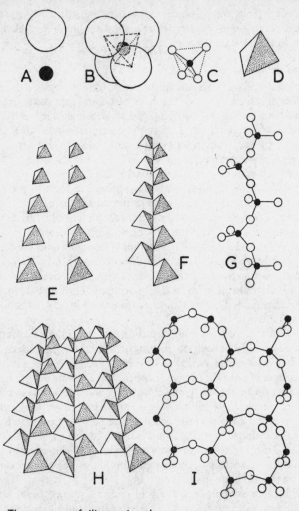

Fig. 3.1. The structure of silicate minerals.
At top left A an oxygen atom (circle) is shown in proportion to an atom of silicon
(black). B is a diagram representing a silica tetrahedron, showing the four relatively
large oxygen atoms almost hiding the smaller central silicon atom. The dashed lines
join the centres of the four oxygen atoms, indicating the four-sided pyramid-like
figure, the tetrahedron, which they form. C is a structural diagram of the tetrahedron indicating the relative positions of the atoms it contains. At D the silica
molecule is represented pictorially as a pyramid.

families the chains are linked to each other by Ca^{2+} and Mg^{2+} cations, the chains running the length of the crystal. Thus, pyroxenes and amphiboles (of which the most important is hornblende) are calcium magnesium silicates, but because of isomorphous substitution (see below) other cations such as Fe^{2+}, Mn^{2+}, or Na^+ can be introduced and give rise to different minerals within the family. The pyroxenes and amphiboles are often dark-coloured minerals which weather relatively easily and, as would be expected from their composition, release considerable quantities of calcium and magnesium to the soil.

Phyllosilicates (phyllon = leaf) are an extremely important group since they include not only the common rock-forming minerals, the micas, but also the silicate clay minerals (see Chapter 2). In these minerals the silica tetrahedra share three of their oxygen atoms to form flat sheets of tetrahedra. The sheets are tied to those above and below by linking cations. Micas are discussed further in a subsequent paragraph.

Tectosilicates form the extreme case of linking up of silica tetrahedra. Each tetrahedron shares all of its four oxygen atoms with other tetrahedra above, below, and on the sides of it. Since every oxygen atom is shared by two adjoining tetrahedra, there are half the oxygen atoms in relation to silicon that there are in the nesosilicates where the tetrahedra are all separate and none of the oxygen atoms are shared. The general composition for the tectosilicate is therefore SiO_2, as compared with SiO_4 for the nesosilicate. The best and purest example of a tectosilicate is quartz, a mineral consisting of silica tetrahedra and of nothing else. The simple, regular structure of quartz makes it extremely resistant to chemical weathering. A very important group of tectosilicates are formed by the felspars, tectosilicate minerals which have a more complex formula and less regular structure because of isomorphous substitution.

Isomorphous substitution is an important process in rock formation which modifies the basic structural patterns discussed above. Some knowledge of isomorphous substitution greatly helps an understanding of

---

In the central line the pictorial representation at the left, E, shows isolated silica tetrahedra as they occur in the nesosilicates. In this group of silicates the tetrahedra are linked by metallic cations (not shown). In the central drawing F the silica tetrahedra are linked to each other by sharing oxygen atoms: each tetrahedron shares two of its oxygen atoms with its two neighbours to form a chain. This structure is shown diagrammatically on the right: single and double chains of tetrahedra are characteristic of the inosilicates.

In the phyllosilicates the tetrahedra share three of their four oxygen atoms to link up to form sheets. This is shown pictorially at H and diagrammatically at I. Micas and clays are examples of phyllosilicates.

rock weathering and of the elements likely to be released when rocks weather, and is therefore very relevant to an understanding of soil formation. In many minerals the fundamental chain, sheet, or block structure is not as simple and regular as was suggested above because of the substitution, during the formation of the rock, of one ion in the crystal lattice by another of approximately the same size. 'Isomorphous' means 'same shape', thus suggesting that the ions introduced are approximately of the same size as those they replace. In practice they are either a little larger or a little smaller, and may also have a different valency. When an ion of a slightly different size is fitted into the crystal structure, that structure is no longer as perfectly regular as it was; the extra stresses and strains caused by this irregularity may weaken the lattice and help it to decompose or weather more rapidly than a more regular one. Secondly, when a cation replaces another it may have a different valency, as when aluminium (3 valencies) replaces silicon (4 valencies) or magnesium (2 valencies) replaces aluminium. In each case there will be one negative charge from the oxygen left unsatisfied. In order to restore electrical neutrality, an additional cation, such as sodium or potassium, or an alternate one has to be introduced, thus further modifying the structure.

The above can be illustrated by considering further two groups of common minerals, the micas and the felspars, in which isomorphous substitution occurs to a considerable degree, and contrasting them with quartz in which the simple, regular structure without isomorphous substitution gives the mineral a very high degree of resistance to chemical weathering.

Micas are sheet silicates (phyllosilicates) consisting of many layers, each layer in turn consisting of two sheets of silica tetrahedra held together, in the case of white mica, by a layer of aluminium and hydroxyl ions. The silica-aluminium layers are held to each other relatively weakly by potassium ions, and can be separated relatively easily, thus giving the micas their characteristic cleavage which allows them to be separated into very thin sheets. White mica, or muscovite, is therefore a potassium aluminium silicate. It has the formula $KAl_2(AlSi_3 O_{10})(OH)_2$: one quarter of the silica tetrahedra have had the silicon atom at the centre replaced by aluminium and in each case this has been balanced by bringing in one potassium ion.

White mica is not white so much as colourless and transparent. Another type of mica, black mica or *biotite*, is also common. Biotite is formed when the aluminium of white mica is replaced by iron or magnesium, so that $(Mg, Fe)_3$ replaces Al_2 in the formula for white mica given above. It will be noted that both types of mica contain potassium, but that biotite contains magnesium and iron in addition, so that it is the richer of the two as regards plant nutrients. As would be expected from the greater degree of isomorphous substitution, biotite is also considerably more easily weathered than the relatively resistant muscovite. Biotite, containing iron and magnesium, is one of the ferro-magnesian minerals referred to above and has the dark colour typical of these minerals.

Sericite is a form of white mica, usually but not necessarily of muscovite composition, occurring as small flakes. It is often a constituent of the metamorphic rocks discussed in a subsequent section.

Felspars are examples of tectosilicates, i.e. they have a three-dimensional block structure in which all the silica tetrahedra share oxygen atoms with all adjacent tetrahedra, and each oxygen atom is therefore shared between two tetrahedra, as in the case of quartz. However, a proportion of the central silicon ions have been replaced by aluminium ions. Since aluminium has a valency of three, as compared with the valency of four of the silicon it replaces, there is an excess negative charge which has to be satisfied by another cation. When that excess charge is satisfied by an introduced potassium ion, a potassium felspar is formed. Potassium felspars have the formula $KAlSi_3O_8$. They are of two main types, orthoclase and microcline, which have the same composition but slightly different crystalline forms because of different temperatures of formation.

Often the excess negative charge in the felspars is not satisfied by a single cation but by a combination of cations, particularly by a combination of potassium and sodium (the alkali felspars) or of sodium and calcium (the plagioclase felspars). The felspathoids are somewhat similar minerals containing less silica in proportion to alumina.

The felspars are thus not of fixed composition but can vary between potassium felspar ($KAlSi_3O_8$) and sodium felspar ($NaAlSi_3O_8$) and between calcium felspar ($CaAlSi_2O_8$) and sodium felspar. In physical appearance the various felspars are similar, being whitish, grey, or pink in colour, but calcium felspar is the most easily weathered of the group and potassium felspar the least easily.

Quartz has the same three-dimensional block structure as the felspars but in this case there is no isomorphous substitution and the mineral consists of silica tetrahedra and nothing else. It thus has the formula SiO_2. Because there are no basic cations to be attacked by the forces of weathering, and there has been no isomorphous substitution to weaken the simple regular structure of the mineral, quartz is extremely resistant to chemical weathering. In neutral and acid soils the chemical weathering of quartz is negligible and in practice it merely breaks down physically to smaller and smaller particles. Because of its resistant nature, it may survive in soils, and accumulate, after most of the other minerals have been broken down, and it is frequently the main or almost sole constituent of the sand fraction. Quartz is a hard, often transparent mineral occurring both as crystals in rocks, as in granite, and as veins of more massive quartz which may have been injected into previous rock formations.

A knowledge of the structure of minerals therefore helps in understanding two very important properties of a mineral from the soil point of view—how easily or otherwise it weathers, and what elements it is likely to release when it does weather. Quartz is the extreme example in each case, for it is very resistant to weathering and liberates nothing except silica on decomposition. The structural classification is obviously linked to some extent with the chemical composition of minerals. Chemical composition can be used by itself, without reference to structure, to classify rocks and minerals in a different way.

The chemical composition of igneous rocks

Chemically, rocks are frequently divided into the more basic rocks, those containing relatively high proportions of the basic metallic cations, and the more acid rocks in which an increasing proportion of the total composition is silica.

All silicate minerals contain some silica and all except quartz contain some basic cations. The usual division is as follows:

Acid rocks	Over 66% silica
Intermediate rocks	52% to 66% silica
Basic rocks	45% to 52% silica
Ultrabasic rocks	Under 45% silica

Rocks are frequently also subdivided into those in which the alkaline cations, potassium and sodium, predominate, and those more common rocks in which the calcic elements, calcium and magnesium, are the more important.

The more basic the rock, the greater the proportion of ferromagnesian minerals it is likely to contain. The more acid the rock, the greater the proportion of felspar and quartz it will have. Thus basic and ultrabasic rocks commonly consist mainly of olivine and pyroxene, with accessory hornblende or biotite. Intermediate rocks commonly contain hornblende, biotite, and plagioclase felspar while acid rocks contain quartz and felspars (often mainly orthoclase) and some biotite. Granite, an acid igneous group of rocks, consists essentially of quartz and felspar with some mica and/or hornblende.

Igneous rocks in practice are further divided into broad groups or families according to their grain size (reflecting the rate of cooling), as in Table 3.1. Thus basic rocks are collectively termed basalts when fine-grained, but dolerites when medium grained and gabbros when coarse grained. Similarly, rhyolites have the same broad chemical composition as granites, but rhyolites are very fine-grained whereas granites are medium- to coarse-grained rocks.

TABLE 3.1. The more important rock families classified according to chemical composition and grain size. Those in brackets are the alkaline (potassium- and sodium-rich) families, the remainder are calc-alkaline rocks (calcium and magnesium being the dominant bases).

	ULTRABASIC	BASIC	INTERMEDIATE	ACID
Fine-grained		Basalts	Andesites (Trachytes)	Rhyolites Felsites
Fine- or medium-grained		Dolerites	Porphyrites Micro-diorites	Micro-granites Granite-porphyries
Medium- or coarse-grained	Peridotites Serpentines	Gabbros	Diorites (Syenites)	Granites Granodiorites (Alkali-granites)

The weathering of igneous rocks

The soil scientist is interested in knowing how easily rocks weather and what they release when they decompose. It is helpful to distinguish between chemical and physical weathering. In *physical weathering* rocks are merely broken down by mechanical means to smaller and smaller particles without their chemical composition being altered, though this fragmentation may then make chemical attack easier. In *chemical weathering* the rock is decomposed chemically to liberate the constituents of which it is composed, and these are either removed or left to accumulate in the soil, in which case, as in the formation of clays, they may recombine to form new substances.

Mechanical weathering predominates in drier climates, as in deserts where changes in temperature cause shrinking and expansion and thus cracking and breaking up of rocks, and where physical forces such as winds and water break up rock particles by rolling, impact, and so on. In most of West Africa the rainfall is moderate to heavy, and the weathering is mainly chemical, of which the main agent is percolating soil water. Chemical weathering is now considered in more detail.

Dry air has little or no influence on rock weathering, and water is the main agent of chemical weathering. Rain falling through the atmosphere dissolves very small quantities of such constituents as nitrogen oxides, sulphur dioxide, oxygen, carbon dioxide, and perhaps traces of ammonia, sodium chloride, and other compounds. The first two give nitrous, nitric, and sulphurous acids, but of particular interest and importance are the oxygen and carbon dioxide which attack weathering rock by oxidation and the formation of carbonates. In addition, various organic acids derived from the decay of plant and animal material are added to the soil water as it seeps downward.

The percolating soil water is thus a weak but complex solution, and this attacks exposed rock fragments in the soil and penetrates into massive unweathered rocks along cracks and joints. The mechanisms of chemical weathering include solution, hydration (the combining of constituents with water), hydrolysis (the substitution of constituent ions by hydrogen ions), oxidation, reduction, formation of carbonates and bicarbonates, attack by acid and alkaline solutions, and the removal of the soluble products liberated. Thus chemical weathering is a complex process, the details of which vary according to the soils, rocks, and climate involved.

In igneous rocks one of the constituent minerals is often more easily attacked than the others, and its softening and breaking down will result in the disintegration of the rock and the separation of the remaining constituents which are then more exposed to further attack.

Granites form one of the commonest groups of crystalline rocks in West Africa and may be used as an example. They contain quartz, felspar, and a third mineral which may be either mica or hornblende. Micaceous granites are the most widespread in West Africa. The felspars (potassium, sodium, or calcium aluminium silicates) are the first to weather, the metallic bases they contain being removed, and the remaining silica and alumina often combining to form kaolin. The less easily weathered mica and the very resistant quartz may thus remain embedded in soft clay.

It is possible to put the common mineral constituents of igneous rocks in an order of weathering as follows:

> Olivine—most easily weathered
> Calcium felspar
> Pyroxenes and amphiboles (hornblende)
> Sodium felspar
> Black mica (biotite)
> Potassium felspar
> White mica (muscovite)
> Quartz—most resistant to weathering

Sedimentary rocks

When rocks weather, the sand, clay, and other residues may be deposited by wind or water to form sediments. These sediments are often size-sorted to some extent, since the load-carrying capacities of both wind and the water in streams and rivers vary according to the speed and other factors. As a result, sediments may consist mainly of clay size, silt size, or of sand size particles or of alternating beds of these. If weathering is rapid and the products accumulate near the place of origin, or if they are not much sorted in transit, then mixed sediments may be formed containing some rock particles not yet completely weathered, but often sediments consist mainly or entirely of materials which have already passed through a cycle of weathering. In highly weathered sediments, everything which can be easily broken down may already have been decomposed, leaving only the most resistant constituents, particularly kaolinitic clay and quartz sand.

These sediments accumulate on the lower parts of the landscape, in lakes, and in seas. Carbonates may also accumulate, as in the cases of chalk and limestone which are both calcium carbonate, in many cases derived from thick accumulations of the skeletons and shells of very small sea animals, and these form examples of the small group of minerals which are not silicates. Deposits of detrital sediments can be classified according to the size of their constituents, whether gravel and stones, sand, or clay. A careful examination of sediments tells much about their history: angular fragments, for example, have not been moved as far as those which have become rounded during transport.

The sediments derived from the weathering, transport, and deposition of rocks form the materials from which sedimentary rocks are derived. The sediments are subject to various processes which generally compact them and change them into rocks. They may be compressed by the weight of sediments above, and any water contained (particularly by the clays) squeezed out: pore space is reduced and the rock compacted and hardened. In addition to these physical changes, chemical changes occur, largely through the seeping of solutions, causing recrystallization, cementation, and other effects, including the formation within the beds of secondary minerals. Normally the hardening, cementation, and secondary mineral formation do not affect the overall structure of the sediment, or its characteristic arrangement in beds or natural depositional layers.

Coarse-textured sediments include conglomerates, in which gravels and pebbles are bound together by finer material, and breccias in which the stones are angular.

Medium-textured sediments consist mainly of the sandstones in which resistant, well-sorted quartz sand may be cemented together by quartz or other cements, e.g. iron oxides. Where the sand-size fragments are more angular, less sorted, and contain some unweathered material, a grey-wacke is formed. Sandstones containing both felspar and quartz grains are known as arkoses.

The fine-grained clay sediments form a range of clay sedimentary rocks depending on the type of clay, the content of other constituents, and the degree of alteration undergone by the original sediment. Compressed clay becomes a mudstone, but when secondary layers or lamina develop, the mudstone merges into shale.

Other classes of sediments include the limestones, siliceous deposits, rock salt, coal, and various iron carbonate and oxide minerals, in addition to the residual formations of laterite and bauxite considered in more detail in Chapter 4.

Metamorphic rocks

For a sediment to become a sedimentary rock, certain changes take place as a result of outside influences: when sediments and rocks are more fundamentally changed, or metamorphosed, a third class of rocks is formed. These metamorphic rocks may be derived from sediments and sedimentary rocks or they may be derived from the metamorphosis of pre-existing igneous rocks. The forces involved are those of heat, pressure, and chemical change, and the changes often take place at some depth within the earth's crust, as when folding and other earth movements subject rocks to great heat and to tremendous pressure, or when existing rocks come into contact with intrusions of molten magma.

The result of metamorphism is often the formation of a new structure and a reorientation of at least some of the components into secondary crystalline minerals, though the size of the crystals varies from very fine (discernible only with a microscope) to coarse.

Very characteristic of metamorphic rocks is an orientation of the constituents to give a banded effect. These bands or layers must not be confused with the depositional beds of sediments, but are secondary layers formed at right angles to the main source of pressure. They may be very fine, as in *phyllites*, or coarse, as in *schists*. Where plate-like silicates, such as micas, occur, the rock may split along cleavage planes. Coarser-grained rocks showing only a rough banding are grouped as *gneisses*.

Schists and gneisses are thus broad groups of metamorphic rocks defined according to their structure. They are usually further defined according to their most characteristic mineral. Thus a biotite schist or a sericite schist is a schist in which secondary biotite or sericite has formed, often mainly between the characteristic layers of the schist which may therefore show some cleavage. A quartz schist is a quartz-rich schist derived from an original deposit containing much quartz sand. Similarly, gneisses are named after a characteristic constituent, e.g. hornblende gneiss, a coarsely banded, crystalline rock of basic composition containing hornblende in addition to felspar and other constituents. The bands and layers formed during the original metamorphosis may later have been folded or contorted because of subsequent crustal movements and pressures.

The weathering of sedimentary and metamorphic rocks

Sedimentary rocks are derived from secondary materials which have already passed through at least one cycle of weathering, transport, and deposition. The more thorough the original weathering, the less likely is the material from which the sedimentary rock is derived to contain anything except resistant residues.

A sandstone consisting of little except quartz sand will break down on weathering to the original sand and perhaps little else, so giving rise to a very poor sandy soil. If the sandstone contains some felspar or sand other than quartz sand, then weathering may result in the formation of some clay and the soil will be less light-textured. Similarly, little-altered muds and clays will, on weathering, be likely to break down into the original clay constituents. Sedimentary rocks as a class are much less likely to contain crystalline silicates which can weather to give nutrients to the soil than are igneous and metamorphic rocks.

Considered as soil parent materials, metamorphic rocks show such a great range of characteristics that it is difficult to make general statements about them. Some, such as quartz schist derived from quartz sand, may be nearly sterile and break down only to more quartz sand. Others, in which secondary micas have formed, may be somewhat richer, while certain base-rich metamorphic rocks resemble the more basic igneous rocks and can give rise to very fertile soils. The rates at which these rocks weather show a similar broad range, with the more sterile, quartz-rich rocks often weathering rather slowly and those containing basic minerals often being subject to a much more rapid decomposition.

THE GEOLOGY OF WEST AFRICA

West Africa—like most of the African continent—consists mainly of a massif of very old rocks, the basement complex. There rocks, so old that they were formed before there was any life on the land capable of leaving fossils, belong to the oldest geological time period, the Pre-Cambrian. Here and there on the surface of this underlying block of older rocks occur later rock formations, including sediments deposited in lakes and shallow seas which once temporarily covered parts of West Africa. Today, about one-third of West Africa has the old Pre-Cambrian rocks exposed at the surface, while the remaining two-thirds are covered by more recent formations and sediments of various types. In that part of West Africa which is of the greatest agricultural importance, however, the proportions are reversed. South of 12° N in West Africa about two-thirds of the land surface consists of the ancient Pre-Cambrian formations and one-third of more recent rocks.

Pre–Cambrian formations

The ancient Pre-Cambrian massif of the African plateau consists partly of metamorphic rocks, formed from sediments derived from still earlier formations, and partly of later volcanic intrusions. Radio-active determinations have indicated ages up to about 2000 million years for some of these rocks. This so-called 'basement complex' consists largely of schists, phyllites, quartzites, granites, gneisses, and smaller areas of more basic intrusions. The general trend of the rocks is from north-east to south-west, a trend which is often reflected in the relief. Most of the West African minerals (diamonds, iron, chromium, manganese, and gold) are associated with the Pre-Cambrian rocks or with granite intrusions into them.

The Pre-Cambrian formations are subdivided by geologists into various formations which are more or less local, e.g. the Dahomeyan, the Birrimian, the Akwapim-Togo, and the Tarkwaian. Geologists are particularly concerned with the age of the various rock formations and with elucidating the geological history of the area, whereas the soil scientist and agriculturalist are interested more in which rocks occur at the surface and become soil parent materials. The rocks of the basement complex provide a wide variety of soil parent materials, and include many metamorphic and crystalline rocks ranging in composition from acid to basic. Generally speaking, because of their content of weatherable silicate minerals, Pre-Cambrian rock formations are richer soil-forming materials than the sediments of the later formations which rest upon the basement complex.

Later formations

The major areas where the Pre-Cambrian basement complex is covered by later deposits and rock formations are indicated in Fig. 3.2. Numerous shallow seas, often extensive, covered the basement complex at various times during the long period between its formation and the present day. This period can be divided geologically into four—the Primary (Palaeozoic), Secondary (Mesozoic), Tertiary, and Recent (or Quaternary) periods.

In the Primary period shallow seas resulted in the formation of beds of conglomerates, limestone, sandstones, and shales in the western Sahara, which reach south to the Senegal river, and east to the Niger bend. Subsequently sandstone deposits were formed in the Fouta Djallon area

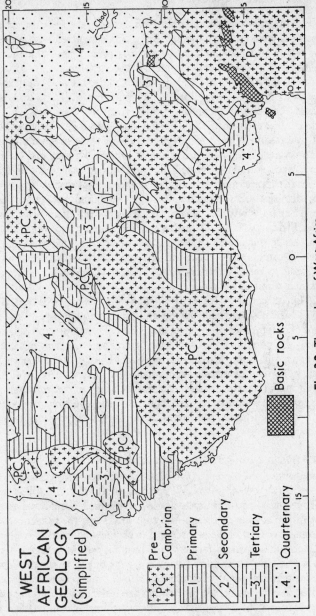

Fig. 3.2. The geology of West Africa.

WEST
AFRICAN
GEOLOGY
(Simplified)

Pre–
Cambrian PC

Primary 1

Secondary 2

Tertiary 3

Quaternary 4

Basic rocks

of the Republic of Guinea and elsewhere. Later in the Primary period the Silurian sea covered much of the Sahara, and associated with it are sediments which probably include the sandstones and related sediments of the Voltaian formations of central and northern Ghana.

Most of these early seas and depositions affected only western West Africa, so that to the east the area which now forms Nigeria was for long dry land, but in the Secondary and Tertiary periods arms of the sea invaded this area from the Gulf of Guinea, spreading along the Benue, Chad, and middle Niger basins. On the edge of these seas were deposited the sandstone, shale, and coal seams of eastern Nigeria, and later seas, lagoons, lakes, and mud flats are associated with other deposits of Tertiary age both in this area and in Senegal and other coastal areas of West Africa. These deposits include gravels, sands, shales, and limestones. In the western Sahara, stony rock wastes and areas of sand dunes were formed.

West African geology was further modified during Secondary and Tertiary times by intrusions and extrusions of volcanic material. Examples include volcanic extrusions round Jos and the island of Fernando Po, while later, in the Quaternary period, Mount Cameroon, a volcano not yet extinct was formed.

The Quaternary (or Recent) formations include areas of coastal alluvium in Sierra Leone and Nigeria and far more extensive areas in the interior of West Africa of sheets of loose sand. These were derived, during relatively dry periods of the Quaternary, from the weathering of sandstone formations, and were then spread by wind. The Quaternary period was marked by climatic changes with alternate wet and dry periods which have left their mark on the present relief and soils. Many of the ironstone sheets which mark the savanna areas are thought by some to have formed under a wetter climate whereas features of some present-day forest soils suggest drier conditions in the past.

West African geology in relation to soils

As stated above, the basement complex of worn down Pre-Cambrian rocks is exposed over two-thirds of West Africa south of 12° N. This gives a certain geological uniformity to these areas which is reflected to some extent in the soils even though the soils also show the influences of the climate and vegetation belts discussed in the next chapter. However, the Pre-Cambrian is a varied formation and the soils of the schists, phyllites, granites and occasional more basic intrusions of the basement complex vary considerably in both their physical and chemical characteristics. The soils over the basic rocks are the richest chemically and also often have the highest clay content. Those over granites vary in chemical fertility, since the granites and granitized rocks vary considerably in their content of dark minerals, but physically are usually sandy (sandy light clays, sandy loams, loamy sands, and sands) as contrasted with the soils (mainly light clays) of the phyllite and schist areas. The poorest basement complex soils are those over quartzite and other quartz-rich rocks.

In general, the soils of the basement complex tend to be more fertile than many of the soils associated with later sediments, particularly those associated with shales and mudstones and with the extensive areas of sandstone and other quartz-rich sediments. This is partly because the igneous and metamorphic rocks of the basement complex contain silicate minerals which break down to release plant nutrients, whereas since the sediments have already passed through one cycle of weathering they usually consist in the main of resistant residues, e.g. kaolinitic clay and quartz sand and gravel, without easily weatherable silicate minerals.

The contrast between the varied and often fairly rich soils of the basement complex and the more uniform and poorer soils of the later sediments may be illustrated by comparing the soils formed over Pre-Cambrian rocks in Ghana with those associated with the Voltaian sediments.

The Voltaian formations consist of massive sandstones overlying various beds of mudstones, limestones, conglomerates, and more sandstones. However, since the sandstones consist of little except quartz sand and lie at the surface over most of the considerable area covered by these formations, they give rise to fairly uniform areas of very poor sandy soils. Where the mudstones are exposed, poor clay soils are formed. These soils, which have developed in old sediments almost devoid of silicate minerals which can weather and release plant nutrients, generally have very low reserves of plant nutrients.

The Pre-Cambrian basement complex in Ghana is best represented by the extensive Birrimian formations, which extend into the Ivory Coast. These are subdivided into (1) the Lower Birrimian, which consist mainly of phyllites, schists, and related rocks, together with areas of granite and granitized rocks; and (2) the Upper Birrimian formations which resemble the Lower Birrimian, except that they are further diversified by intrusions and extrusions of igneous rocks, some of which were later metamorphosed.

As might be expected, the Birrimian soils are much more varied and chemically richer than the soils over the Voltaian sandstone which, in addition to having very low nutrient reserves, are low in clay and are therefore droughty. It is noteworthy that the forest-savanna boundary tends to follow the geological boundary, so that, in the forest fringe areas, forest is found on the Birrimian formations where the soils have moderately good water-storage capacities but savanna occurs on the drier, sandier soils associated with the Voltaian sandstones. The Birrimian soils under forest include the soils of the Ghana cocoa belt, some of which are particularly fertile. Both the granites and schists weather to give soils which are chemically moderately fertile except where developed under particularly high rainfalls, but the most fertile soils of the basement complex are those over the more basic rocks such as hornblende schist and gneiss and the basic igneous intrusions.

SOILS IN RELATION TO RELIEF AND GEOMORPHOLOGY

In West Africa soils frequently occur in a well defined and fairly regular sequence related to relief—the soil catena. Diagrams of typical soil catenas are shown in Figs. 3.3 and 3.4. Since a catena is related to relief, with a regular sequence of different soils encountered as one goes from hill top to valley bottom, it seems logical to assume that relief is the main soil-forming factor responsible for differentiating the soils. In fact, the influences of relief and geomorphology go together, and the sequence of soils in the catena is due to two main factors: differences in *parent material* on different positions in the catena, and differences in *site*. Differences in site include differences in slope, in drainage, and in position in relation to other soils. These two groups of factors will now be briefly considered in turn.

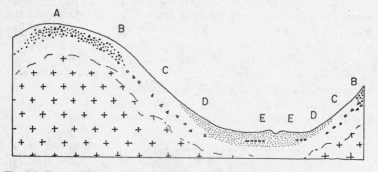

Fig. 3.3. Diagram of a simple forest catena over granite.
Gravelly red and brown upland sedentary soils are found at A and B on summits and upper slopes. These grade downslope into yellow-brown sandy light clay soils developed in middle slope colluvium at C and into yellow-brown sandy loam and loamy sand colluvium at D. The soils developed in local granite-derived alluvium at E are mostly grey to white sands with subordinate areas of gritty or sandy grey clays.

Parent material differences within the catena

Parent material differences in the catena occur even though the underlying geology is uniform. The whole area may be underlain by a single type of rock, e.g. by schists or phyllites, by granites, or by sandstones, but the underlying rock is usually the direct parent material of only some of the soils of the catena, generally the upland ones. Other soils in the catena may have developed in transported materials which, though they may have been ultimately derived from rocks similar to those underlying the area, now consist of weathered or partly weathered materials which have been transported and perhaps sorted during transport.

In a typical, simple West African catena the weathering products of the underlying rock are the parent material of the summit soils and of the upper and perhaps middle slope soils, but the lower slopes may be covered by colluvium and the valley bottoms by alluvium and these form the local soil parent materials there.

Colluvium

'Colluvium' is a broad term for material which has moved down a slope under the influence of gravity. In typical West African catenas the colluvium is not deep, often 2 to 4 ft. It varies considerably in extent. In phyllite areas of somewhat rolling relief it may form only a narrow band a few yards wide at the foot of slopes. An example of such limited colluvium is shown in Fig. 7.1 which gives detailed soil and relief maps of a forest area developed over phyllite. In other areas of different geology and relief the colluvium may be much more extensive. In rolling forest areas of granite, for example, the upland sedentary soils developed directly in the granite are sometimes relatively inextensive since most of the slopes are occupied by colluvial material. Not only is this granite colluvium relatively extensive, being found on middle and lower slopes (and sometimes even upper slopes) but the colluvium has itself been sorted, so that there is often an upper area of typically brown to yellow-brown sandy light clay which grades downslope into yellow-brown, sandy loam and loamy sand. It thus appears that the lower slope colluvium has, compared with the upper slope colluvium, lost some of its clay and is therefore sandier and lighter textured.

Colluvium in West African catenas is typically only a few feet thick—much of it probably has a depth of 30 in to 4 ft—and overlies a weathered substratum, comparable to the C horizon of the upland soils, in which traces of the underlying rock may be found (Fig. 3.7). The boundary between the overlying colluvial material and the underlying weathered substratum is sometimes diffuse but is often fairly sharp, and it may be marked by a thin layer of stones or gravel (often referred to as a 'stone line'), or by mottling, or by both mottling and hardening to form an indurated horizon.

The extent of colluvium also depends very much on the relief. In hilly, dissected areas of short slopes, as in much of the forest zones of West Africa, the catena itself is not extensive—perhaps a few hundred yards to half a mile from hill summit to valley bottom—but in areas of more gentle relief the whole catena is more spread out. In the savanna areas of West Africa relief is typically nearly flat or very gently undulating, with long, gentle slopes; the catena may be spread over several miles. Each soil in the catena is correspondingly more extensive and the boundaries between soils more diffuse. In such cases the colluvium may also be very extensive, occupying long middle and lower slopes, but under these circumstances the colluvial material is likely to develop some subsoil induration and thus to merge into the groundwater laterites discussed further below (see p. 104 and also Fig. 4.5).

Alluvium

In even the simplest catenas the soils of the valley bottoms differ from those of the summits and slopes, and usually this is related partly to the fact that the parent material of the valley bottom soils is alluvium.

Alluvium is material which has been transported by a stream or river and then deposited. Water transport and deposition involve some sorting action: the material carried (the 'load' of the stream or river) is size-sorted, for fine particles such as clays are carried more easily and carried further by slow-moving water than are sands and larger particles. Whereas colluvium has merely moved downslope, alluvium may have been carried considerable distances before being deposited. In the case of big rivers the alluvium they deposit on their banks may have come from hundreds of miles upstream and from areas of different climate and geology.

Alluvium is generally deposited over a considerable period of time, and at different periods the stream or river may have deposited materials of different textures and composition, so that deposits of clay, silt, fine or coarse sand may be found side by side or in layers one above the other. These depositional horizons within the soil parent material should not be confused with the soil horizons that later develop in parent material as a result of soil-forming factors. Typically a stream or river deposits its coarser load, including the sand it carries, as soon as it slows down, as when it floods: thus, sand or sandy deposits are most likely to be found next to or near the river itself, often forming a marked bank known as the river levee. The silts and clays may be carried further from the bank and finally settle down and be deposited where the water slows down or ceases moving, often in flattish areas of the river floodplain between the banks and the lower slopes. In areas of gentle relief the river may change its course with time, so giving more complex patterns of alluvium, while old alluvium may occur above the present floodplain, representing former deposits made at a higher level when the valley floor had not yet been eroded down to its present level. These older, higher alluvial deposits are known as river terraces, and the soils here can be expected to be older and have reached a more advanced stage of development than those developed in the younger alluvium associated with the present-day floodplain.

As in the case of soils developed in colluvium, the profiles of soils developed in alluvium consist of upper horizons of which the parent material is alluvium, and an underlying substratum formed from the material below the alluvium. The alluvium may, however, be considerably deeper than is normal for colluvium—so deep that the underlying material is of little interest—and the alluvium itself, as suggested above, may contain many contrasting horizons, sometimes including pebble beds.

Soils and geomorphology

In simple catenas, therefore, the immediate parent material may be the underlying rock and its decomposition products, as in the case of the sedentary soils generally occurring on upper slopes and summits, or it may be local colluvium, or it may be alluvium deposited by streams and rivers. This relatively simple sequence is typical of young, dissected areas. In older areas—and much of West Africa has a very long and complicated history—the more complicated geomorphology results in other types of parent materials and in more elaborate soil patterns.

The oldest part of the landscape, associated with the oldest soils, is often the flat or nearly flat summit areas which represent remains of old peneplains, as explained further below. These old, flattish summit areas are in turn associated with reworked, often very uniform soil materials (referred to by some as mantle deposits or as 'drift' material) and also with sheets of ironstone. These ironstone sheets or crusts are particularly extensive in the savanna and savanna-forest fringe areas and are thought by many to be geologically fairly old. They occur associated with some hill summits in the forest areas, but the more dissected relief of the forest areas probably means that if they were once more widespread there, they have been broken up and so are now less extensive. The abundant ironstone gravel of both forest and savanna soils often appears to contain

14 (*above*) A shallow savanna lithosol. The profile consists of an irregular but generally thin topsoil overlying hard rock, in this case green-stone. (Near the Black Volta, north-western Ghana).

15 (*below*) A forest lithosol over fissile shale. Flattish fragments of little weathered parent rock can be seen in the lower half of the photograph. These come to within 6 to 8 in of the surface.

16 (*above*) A profile developed in yellow-brown clay alluvium. There is a well marked pebble bed about 1 ft thick in the subsoil.

17 (*below*) Close-up of the pebble bed in Plate 16, showing the sub-angular and subrounded stream rolled quartz of which it is composed.

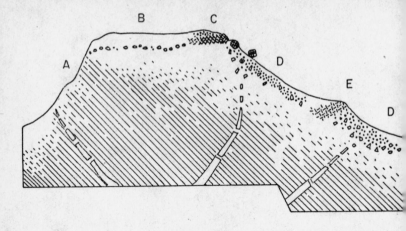

Fig. 3.4. A more complex forest catena over phyllite or schist.
For description, see text, and Figs 1.1, 3.6, and 3.7. A shallow, immature soils of
steep slopes; B upland 'drift' soils; C shallow gravelly soils over ironstone; D gravelly
upland sedentary soils; E 'shoulder' where indurated horizon comes to surface;
F soils developed in local light clay colluvium; G soils developed in clay alluvium
of valley bottoms; H soils developed in sandy alluvium of levees.

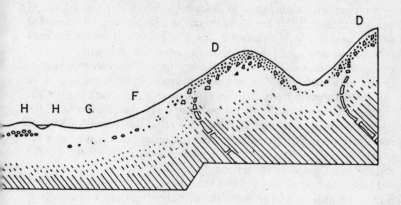

material derived from the breaking up and disintegration of these old crusts. Ironstone crusts are considered further in Chapter 4.

In order to understand the formation and distribution of West African soils it is therefore often helpful to take into account the history of the landscape, and its geomorphology. The ancient West African basement complex of Pre-Cambrian rocks has suffered a long erosional history. It has been lifted up and then worn down again by wind and rivers several times in succession over long periods of geological time. There is abundant evidence of it having been worn down to an almost flat surface or peneplain ('pene' = almost, i.e. almost a plain) at least twice. When these nearly flat plains are lifted up again relative to sea level, or when rainfall increases again after a dry period, then the rivers flowing on their gentle surfaces are 'rejuvenated' and begin to eat down into the old flat surface with renewed vigour, and carve it up afresh. Young valleys dissect the old surface, become more extensive, and finally most of the landscape may consist of valley slopes with the peneplain remnants remaining only as isolated, flattish hill summits separated by younger valleys, as shown diagrammatically in Fig. 3.5.

These old flat peneplain remnants, or 'surfaces', occur in West Africa on at least two levels, corresponding to two distinct peneplains of different ages. There is an upper and older peneplain thought to be of early- to mid-Tertiary age. The relatively inextensive and isolated remains of this upper peneplain often form flat hilltops on which there is a layer of bauxite (impure Al_2O_3), the ore of aluminium. Bauxite might be regarded as soil material so highly weathered that all or nearly all the silica has been removed, leaving behind the alumina. The lower peneplain surface is more extensive and is associated with ironstone crusts rather than with bauxite crusts. Both surfaces get lower nearer the coast and more dissected, so that the flat areas representing them are generally rare near the coast but more extensive inland. In Ghana and the Ivory Coast, for example, the upper surface is about 2000 ft above sea level at the latitude of Kumasi and the lower surface forms very extensive, broad, flattish summit areas at about 1000 ft above sea level. Such summit areas are represented in the soil and relief maps of Figs 7.1 and 7.2.

In addition to the ironstone and bauxite crusts which sometimes form such a conspicuous feature associated with these surfaces, particularly at their edges, there may also be areas of the 'drift' or mantle deposits referred to above. These are old soil materials, usually very highly weathered, and high in iron, which are characterized by a marked uniformity down the profile and lack of obvious horizons below the topsoil, suggesting a uniform deposit. This material varies in thickness from 1 to 2 ft to 20 to 30 ft. It is often characterized by the aggregation of the clay fraction to silt-size particles (by iron and aluminium oxides) so that although the clay content after dispersion in the laboratory may be high, the soil feels like a loam and there may be little or no water-dispersible clay. Such soil material is relatively inert and stable. It appears to be very old soil material from the surface of the old peneplain, perhaps deposited or at least reworked by wind or water action, and perhaps modified by termite activity. The profile of soils developed in this material is often very striking, with several feet of seemingly uniform material overlying the somewhat different material of the weathered substratum below (Fig. 3.6). As in the case of the soils developed in colluvium, the junction or unconformity between the overlying material and that below may be marked by a stone line, mottles, or an indurated zone.

The presence of peneplain remnants and of associated drift soil materials and crusts diversifies the local soil catenas. Even where peneplain remnants do not occur, the simple soil catena described earlier may be diversified by the presence of shallow, immature soils. These occur where slopes are steep, or where parent rocks are particularly resistant to weathering.

Immature soils are young soils—pedologically young in the sense that they have not developed a full, mature profile. Where slopes are very

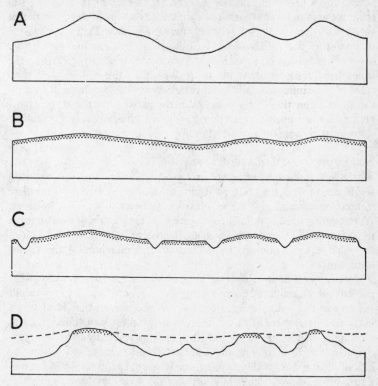

Fig. 3.5. Stages in the dissection of a landscape.

In diagram A a hilly landscape is undergoing erosion which, if sufficiently prolonged, will reduce it to a near flat, peneplain stage as shown in B. Old, highly weathered soils (shaded), often rich in iron, mantle the peneplain.

In the third diagram C the rivers on the peneplain have been rejuvenated, usually by a rise in the land relative to sea level, and new valleys are rapidly being cut into the old landscape.

Diagram D shows a later stage at which the original peneplain surface (broken line) is represented only by the flattish summit areas of occasional hills. The highly weathered peneplain soils (shaded) survive on these summits, though perhaps in modified form, and constitute the oldest soil materials in the area. The valley slopes and floors are associated with younger soils, though these younger soils may incorporate some of the older material, as when former ironstone crusts break up to give ironstone gravel in soils lower down the slope.

In West Africa the remains of at least two major peneplains are widespread. The upper peneplain is associated with bauxite crusts, the lower with extensive ironpan sheets.

steep, removal of soil material may be rapid enough to keep the soil shallow: such soils often consist of a topsoil directly overlying a weathered substratum containing rock relatively near the surface (Fig. 3.6). Shallow, rocky soils of this type are *lithosols* (lithos = stone). A similar profile may occur where the rock is extremely resistant to weathering. Where the lithosol is due primarily to the steep slope, then the relief may be considered the dominant soil-forming influence, but where it is due to the resistant nature of the rock, then the parent material is the dominant factor. In practice the two often go together, because particularly resistant rock formations often stand up as hills with steep slopes.

The influence of site and drainage

We have considered how relief and geomorphology provide, within a single catena over the same geological formation, a range of immediate soil parent materials. Differences between the soils of a catena, however, are not only related to differences in parent material but also to differences in position and in drainage, which are themselves related to relief. One of the most obvious outward signs of drainage differences is the colour of the subsoil.

Upland, well-drained soils in West Africa are frequently somewhat reddish—often reddish brown or brownish red, occasionally a very bright red or purplish red. These red colours denote a non-hydrated iron oxide in the soil, haematite (Fe_2O_3). The red colour indicates good drainage and a certain iron content in the soil (it does not necessarily indicate a particularly high iron content, nor does it of itself indicate soil fertility or lack of fertility). A good red colour can be given to the soil by as little as 1 to 2 per cent free iron or less: occasionally soils may have as much as 20 to 30 per cent free iron, but these are exceptional. The iron is dispersed in the soil, usually partly attached to the clay fraction, and thus the clay itself appears red unless the iron is removed, in which case the soil appears nearly white. Soil iron is dealt with further in the next chapter; here we are concerned mainly with the colour it gives the soil and the extent to which that colour reflects drainage conditions. The iron is red only so long as it is non-hydrated, i.e. not combined with a water molecule.

In the middle and lower slope soils drainage is a little slower than in the upper slope and summit soils, partly because they receive soil moisture seeping downslope from the upper soils. The fact that these soils remain moist longer and perhaps dry out less frequently and thoroughly is reflected in an increasing degree of hydration of the iron in the soil and in a brown or yellow colour rather than a red one. The hydrated iron oxides in these soils are mainly goethite ($Fe_2O_3 \cdot H_2O$) and limonite

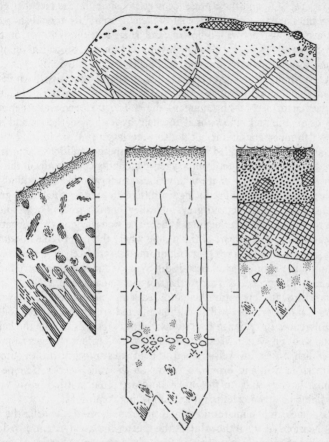

Fig. 3.6. Profile diagrams of an immature soil, a 'drift' soil and a shallow soil over ironstone pan.

At the left is a lithosol in which a topsoil directly overlies a weathered substratum containing weathering fragments of schist or phyllite.

In the centre is a soil profile developed in about 4 ft of fairly uniform red or brown clay 'drift' material. The overlying material is separated from the weathered substratum by a narrow transition zone, or discontinuity, which is slightly mottled and contains a stone line. Soils such as this, on old peneplain surfaces, are sometimes high in iron. In some cases they have a very high clay content but handle like loams because the clay is aggregated to larger particles.

The profile shown diagrammatically on the right is a shallow one with abundant ironstone gravel overlying solid ironstone pan at about 14 in. The depth and thickness of the ironpan varies considerably and it may outcrop at the surface.

($Fe_2O_3 \cdot 1\frac{1}{2}H_2O$), and their presence is responsible for the fact that going down the slope the colour of the subsoil changes first from reddish-brown to warm brown or orange-brown, and then to yellow-brown or even brownish yellow. Lower slope colluvium is typically brownish yellow in colour, as are the better drained soils developed in alluvium.

Where drainage is very poor, as in the valley bottom itself where the water table fluctuates and all or part of the soil profile is waterlogged, then another factor becomes prominent—the *reduction* of iron and other compounds in the soil, as opposed to their hydration in the upland soils subject to moist conditions but not to waterlogging. Waterlogging means that all soil pores are filled by water: under these conditions bacteria are forced to get their oxygen from oxygen-containing compounds in the soil, such as Fe_2O_3, and these are then reduced to form other compounds.

The colours typical of reducing conditions in soils are the bluish greys, greenish greys, and neutral greys of valley bottom soils. These colours suggest prolonged waterlogging. Where the waterlogging is intermittent or seasonal, as in that part of the profile where the water table fluctuates, then, instead of a uniform grey colour, mottles are likely to be produced. A mottle is a spot or small area of different colour from the surrounding material. The process giving to the soil a dominant blue, grey, or green colour through soil saturation and reducing conditions, is known as *gleying*, and poorly drained soils thus affected are known as gley soils.

Differences in drainage conditions are thus responsible for the colour catena so often seen in West Africa. The subsoil colour changes from red or reddish brown on well-drained upland sites to warm brown, brown, yellowish brown, and brownish yellow on the valley slopes. The poorly drained bottom soils on the other hand are often mottled or show the grey, blue or green colours typical of gleying conditions.

To some extent climate and rainfall are also involved: the drier the area and the more seasonal the rainfall, the greater the usual extent of reddish soils, but as rainfalls increase and dry seasons become shorter, so do the red soils become less extensive and the brown and yellow soils more so. In the very wet forest areas of West Africa, areas with over 70 in of rain and generally rather short dry seasons, really red soils tend to disappear or occur only occasionally, and most of the soils are brown or brownish yellow because of the hydration of the iron oxides they contain. This influence of climate on soils is considered further in Chapter 4.

Soil mottles are an important feature of West African soils, and are of two broad types. In the poorly drained bottom soils considered above, the mottles are generally faint, small, and diffuse. The soil matrix may be grey and the mottles yellowish, brown, or reddish, or the matrix may be yellowish brown and the mottles shades of grey, bluish grey or white. These small faint mottles are typical of poorly drained soils subject to occasional reducing conditions, i.e. to periodic gleying. As gleying gets more pronounced, so does the extent of greyish and pale mottles until the soil colour is generally grey, bluish grey, or greenish grey.

The mottles associated with gleying are rarely coarse, or very distinct and prominent, but this type of extremely coarse and pronounced mottling does frequently occur in the subsoils of upland soils. It has been called 'pseudogley' or false gley, particularly by French pedologists. The colours involved are often red or reddish-brown, with contrasting areas of pale grey or off-white. Coarse mottles like this may be present in horizons several feet thick in the profile, generally in the lower subsoil but sometimes extending into the weathered substratum, in which case the pattern of the mottles may be influenced by the structure of the softened rock. These mottles are caused by iron movements in the soil and by the concentration of iron in well defined mottles and patches whose reddish and brown colours often contrast with the pale, iron-depleted areas between them. These mottled, iron-rich horizons and the movement of iron in soils is part of the process of laterite formation and is related to the effects of climate on soils considered further in Chapter 4.

Valley bottom soils, both gleyed soils and the better drained alluvial soils, may receive valuable additions of material in solution and in suspension when the associated stream or river floods. In low-lying areas of prolonged waterlogging, the normally rapid decomposition of plant remains may be slowed down and a thicker, more humous topsoil than normal be formed. In extreme cases where water is at or above the surface for considerable periods, little altered plant remains may accumulate, but these accumulations of plant material are not common in West Africa.

The natural vegetation associated with poorly drained, lower slope and valley bottom sites may differ markedly from that of associated upland soils, so that vegetation, soils, and relief are closely connected. In forest areas the normal forest of well drained sites is usually replaced in the poorly drained areas by swamp forest, typically containing raphia palms. In savanna areas, fringing or gallery forest may occur along streams. Vegetation and its influence on soils is discussed further in Chapter 4.

Examples of typical catenas

The effects of differences in parent material, site, and drainage on the development of the soils of a catena can be illustrated by considering typical soil catenas developed over granites and over schists and phyllites, all of which are extensive soil parent rocks in West Africa.

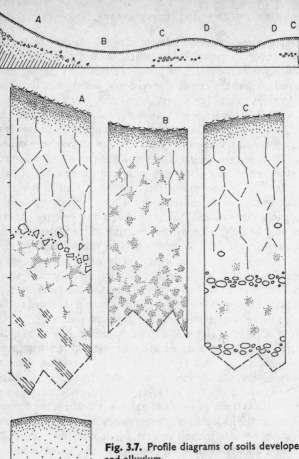

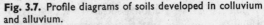

Fig. 3.7. Profile diagrams of soils developed in colluvium and alluvium.

The profile on the upper left is developed in about 3 ft of yellow-brown light clay colluvium which is separated by a discontinuity (often marked by a stone line, gravel, slight induration or mottling) from the weathered substratum below. The weathered substratum may contain traces or fragments of decomposing underlying rock.

The central profile is developed in clay alluvium of the valley bottom. Poor drainage is indicated by the grey colour and presence of mottles in the subsoil. The soil on the upper right is developed in somewhat deeper and better drained yellow-brown light clay alluvium containing pebble beds.

The profile at lower left is developed in yellow-brown alluvial sand of the levee.

Areas of *granite and granitized* rocks (the latter are often referred to by the French as migmatites) are often characterized by a distinctive rolling relief with rounded small hills and locally steep slopes (Fig. 3.3). All the soils of the catena are somewhat sandy, and they often also contain angular quartz grit and gravel, depending on the coarseness and quartz content of the parent material. Particularly coarse-grained granites high in quartz may have very large quartz gravel contents, but where the quartz content of upland sedimentary soils is high then the content of ironstone gravel may be lower than average. The content of free iron and of ironstone concretions in granite soils varies very considerably with the nature of the parent material: it is low in areas of pale granites poor in dark minerals, but can be high in granites rich in biotite.

The topsoils in granite areas are usually humous sandy loams to loamy sands: sand content is frequently highest in the lower topsoil (often 2 to 5 in) while clay content is at a maximum in the subsoil. Subsoil textures are often light clays (as assessed by the ring test) in the upland sedimentary soils and in the upper colluvium, but down the slope textures become lighter and the lower slope colluvium texture is typically a loamy sand to sandy loam. The local alluvium derived from granite consists generally of subordinate areas of sandy or gritty clays, grey where drainage is poor, and of more extensive areas of sands. The sands are often sharp medium sands and grey to white in colour.

The simple granite catena shown in Fig. 3.3 consists of summits and upper slopes of red, gravelly, sedimentary soils containing frequent ironstone concretions which grade downslope into brown but otherwise similar soils. These in turn merge into soils developed in brown to yellow-brown, sandy light clay colluvium of middle slopes which grades downhill into yellow-brown sandy loam or loamy sand colluvium. This in turn merges into the grey, sandy or gritty clay bottom soils and the areas of grey to white sands of the valley bottom sites.

This simple catena becomes more complex where it includes flattish summit areas representing old peneplain surfaces: these areas may be associated with red and brown sandy 'drift' soils and with ironstone crusts. On very steep slopes, shallow lithosols and granite outcrops may occur. On lower slopes old alluvium of river terraces might be found above the present floodplain. In some areas the lower subsoils of the upland sedimentary soils may be coarsely mottled and sometimes somewhat indurated.

In savanna areas the relief is typically more gentle and the catena more spread out than in the hilly forest areas: ironstone crusts may be fairly extensive in the higher areas and on the summits of flat-topped hills, but crusts and indurated horizons are also sometimes found on lower slopes

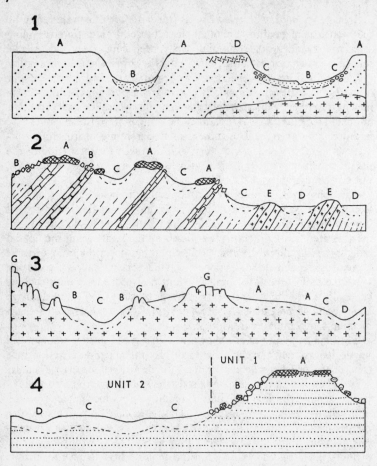

Fig. 3.8. Further examples of West African catenas.

1. A relatively simple catena developed in Tertiary sands. The catena consists of deep orange-brown sandy light clays A developed in the Tertiary sand formations, and associated grey sandy loams and loamy sands B developed in local alluvium. Additional soils which occur occasionally include those developed in river terrace deposits containing water-worn gravel and pebbles C, and upland soils with an indurated or partly indurated subsoil horizon D. (Adapted from Reference 78a.)

(continued opposite

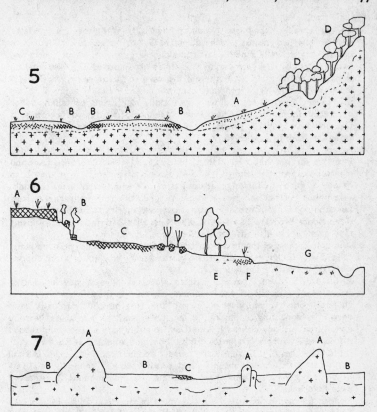

Fig. 3.8. (*continued*)

2. A soil sequence in the Duku area, near the River Niger, in Northern Nigeria. Alternating bands of softer rocks (schists) and harder, more resistant rocks (quartz schists, quartzites, gneisses, and pegmatites) form a series of ridges separated by depressions. At A a thick ironstone cap overlies quartzites and quartz schists of the highest part of the ridge area. The associated soils B contain quartz and ironstone fragments, and ironstone concretions, and some of these soils have indurated subsoil horizons. At C there are fairly shallow pale brown gravelly loams overlying weathered schist at 30 in, often with a stone line of quartz or ironstone gravel. The soils D are on gentle lower slopes and consist of brown to pale brown gravelly sandy loam over mottled weathered schist. The low pegmatite and gneiss ridges E have very shallow soils and rock outcrops. (Adapted from Reference 90.)

(P.T.O.

Fig. 3.8 *(continued)*

3. Another area near the Niger, Northern Nigeria. Here the soils are associated with porphyritic granites which outcrop at G. At A there are shallow red to brown very gravelly sandy loams containing large quantities of quartz and felspar crystals. The less shallow examples are mottled and also contain ironstone concretions. At B there are brown to yellow very gravelly clay loams containing many ironstone concretions and mottled below 2 ft. On the lower slopes C are yellow-brown sandy clay loams containing much quartz and felspar gravel. These soils grade into small areas of bottom soils D mainly pale brown to grey-brown non-gravelly loamy sands over clay loam (Adapted from Reference 90.)

4. An area over Nupe sandstones in Niger Province, Northern Nigeria, divided into two distinct soil-topographical units. Unit 1 consists of sandstone and ironstone capped flat-topped hills with steep scarps rising out of unit 2, an extensive, gently undulating sandstone peneplain with few drainage channels.

   In unit 1 the flat summits at A are capped with iron impregnated hard sandstone or with ironstone outcrops over weathering sandstone. The very steep slopes B consist of a very shallow (less than 1 ft thick) layer of loamy sand over rubble of sandstone and ironstone.

   In unit 2, most of the area is covered by orange-brown to red deep sandy clays C with duller, generally brown mottled sandy clay loams in the depressions D. (Adapted from Reference 94.)

5. An area in Sardauna Province, eastern Northern Nigeria, developed over acid crystalline rocks of the basement complex, mostly felspathic granite gneisses. Forest still survives on some of the steep hills but various types of derived savanna now occupy the lower, more gently sloping areas. In these lower areas a sandy clay with a mottled, concretionary and gravelly subsoil is found at A. Where the mottled subsoil becomes exposed at the surface, at the valley edges B, it hardens to a compact ironpan. In other cases C the soil has a partly indurated subsoil. Forest survives on the generally relatively deep sandy clays and loams of the steep hill sides and summits D. (Adapted from Reference 85.)

6. Ironpan formation associated with terraces of the river Milo, Republic of Guinea. The highest area shown A is 25 m above the river floodplain and is capped with an ironstone sheet 5 m (about 15 ft) thick which is breaking into blocks at the edge B. The terrace C, 7 m above the floodplain, also has an ironstone crust, partly covered by deposits from the neighbouring areas, and broken up at the edge D. The terrace below this, E, is 3 m above the present floodplain and induration is confined to its edge F, where it is due to lateral movement of iron and is only partial. The recent alluvium of the present floodplain G shows well developed mottling and the formation of ironstone concretions, but is not indurated. (Adapted from Reference 157.)

7. A diagram representing areas adjacent to the Red and White Volta rivers, Haute Volta, with granite domes and wall-like inselbergs A rising steeply from a very flat peneplain with 1 to 2 per cent slopes. The soils of the peneplain B are generally very shallow and poorly drained, with occasional indurated horizons outcropping, as at C. (Adapted from Reference 86.)

and in old alluvial terraces. The relatively extensive areas of gently sloping, lower slope colluvium of savanna areas may be underlain at 2 to 3 ft below the surface by a more compact horizon or a horizon which is mottled and more or less indurated. These soils form the so-called 'groundwater laterites' discussed further in Chapter 4 (Fig. 4.5).

Areas of phyllite and schist usually have a distinctive topography often characterized, in the more dissected forest areas, by relatively long steep slopes. Phyllites and schists weather to give soils containing more clay and silt, and less sand, than those associated with granites: the subsoil texture of the upland soils is typically a light clay. The silt content frequently increases markedly (often to 20 to 50 per cent) in the weathered substratum as the softened parent material is approached. Schists and phyllites usually weather deeply and are rarely seen in a fresh state in the wetter areas.

Catenas over phyllite and schist often differ from those associated with granites because of the relatively minor extent of colluvium: all or most of the summits, upper slopes, and middle to lower slopes are frequently occupied by sedentary soils containing moderate to large quantities of ironstone concretions and also some quartz gravel and stones. Quartz gravel and stones are derived from the veins of quartz which traverse the parent schist or phyllite and vary considerably in amount from place to place because of local variations in the parent rock.

The simpler catenas over phyllite and schist consist of red and brown upland light clay sedentary soils, similar in profile morphology to the soil shown in Fig. 1.1, which contains varying amounts of ironstone concretions, quartz stones and gravel. Most of the catena might consist of these soils, with only a narrow band of colluvium along the lower slopes immediately above the valley bottom soils. This colluvium typically consists of 2 to 4 ft of yellow-brown light clay. The valley bottom soils are also mainly yellow-brown to pale yellow light clays and loams where moderately well drained, and grey clays and loams where poorly drained. Areas of valley bottom sands are less extensive than in granite areas but a yellow-brown fine sand is often found on river bank (levee) sites.

A more complicated catena over phyllite is shown diagrammatically in Fig. 3.4. On the left is a flat hill summit area representing a peneplain remnant. Drift soils are found on the summit, and ironstone crusts occur at or near the surface of part of the summit area and outcrop at its edges, with some broken ironstone boulders detaching themselves from the crust and moving down the slope. The summit drift soils are frequently red, but they may be brown where drainage is slower, as on the flat central

18   (*above*) A soil with an indurated horizon. In this profile the upper 28 in of the profile consist of extremely gravelly light clay (the ruler at top right is 1 ft long). The gravel is mainly pea sized ironstone nodules and concretions. At 28 in there is a sharp transition to the mottled, indurated iron-rich material below. This material is sometimes referred to as plinthite.

19   (*below*) Close-up of indurated material which is similar to, but somewhat harder than, that shown in Plate 18. Small pale areas are present, though they are much less extensive than those shown in Plate 13, and numerous cavities (vesicles), pores and channels can be seen.

20 (*above*) A sheet of ironstone capping a hill. At the edge of the flattish summit the sheet has broken into boulders of ironstone, some of which have rolled down the slope. Sheets of ironstone and boulders derived from them are often very conspicuous in the forest-savanna fringe areas and in the savanna areas of West Africa, though they also occur in parts of the West African forest zone.

21 (*below*) A boulder of pisolitic ironstone, i.e. ironstone consisting of gravel sized material (mainly ironstone nodules and concretions) cemented together by iron oxides. In this case the boulders are resting on a fairly continuous sheet of ironstone or in gravelly material derived from its disintegration.

areas of the summit. The texture of drifts associated with phyllite and schist areas is frequently a clay according to the clay content when dispersed, but because of the stable aggregation of the clay fraction to silt-size aggregates, the texture often feels like a loam.

On the upper and middle slopes, red and brown more or less sedentary soils occur. In a typical profile the subsoil contains moderate to large quantities of ironstone nodules and concretions and varying amounts of quartz gravel and stones; some of the concretions may form *in situ* but in many cases most of them appear to be derived from the breaking up of ironstone crusts such as those found on the summit. In this case they are not true concretions but merely rounded gravel-size fragments of hardened, iron-rich material. The quartz gravel and stones are derived from veins in the phyllite and also accumulate in soils. The coarse material content of the subsoil is commonly 30 to 60 per cent by weight of the total soil, and may reach 70 to 80 per cent. Subsoil depth also varies considerably, with a gravelly zone which may be only about 1 to 3 ft thick in the less deep profiles but 4 to 6 ft or more in the case of profiles with particularly deep coarse material accumulations. The subsoil merges into the weathered substratum below: this is siltier than the subsoil and may contain traces and patches of softened schist or phyllite. A few mottles are normal, but occasionally, particularly in wet areas, there is a prominently and coarsely mottled zone in the lower subsoil and upper weathered substratum characterized by reddish brown, pale white, and grey reticulate mottling. This appears to be a zone subject to periodic reducing conditions, with local segregation of iron (see p. 100). Below the mottled zone, the deep weathered substratum has increasingly frequent traces and patches of softened parent rock, and softened rock material showing the original rock structure may be found.

Some of the upland sedentary soils have 10 to 15 in of gravel-free material above the gravelly subsoil. Downslope this upper gravel-free horizon thickens to 2 to 3 ft or more and becomes the colluvium which is the local parent material of the lower slope soils. The transition from the gravelly sedentary soils to the gravel-free soils developed in colluvium may therefore be quite gentle. The colluvium in turn grades into alluvium and the boundary may also be somewhat difficult to determine, especially where the alluvium is that associated with a small stream and consists of material similar to the colluvium.

On particularly steep sites, immature soils occur which consist of a topsoil directly overlying a weathered substratum containing weathered rock. Some of the upper slopes may have areas of non-gravelly material which was derived from the summit drift soils and has moved downslope.

'Shoulders' of soils with indurated subsoils sometimes occur, as shown diagrammatically in Fig. 3.4. These appear to be related to former levels of the valley floor or other flat areas, for subsoil induration is often best developed on flattish sites. Remains of old river terraces may also occur well above the present flood plain and further complicate the soil pattern.

Catenas of many other types occur over many diverse parent materials. Some relatively simple ones may consist of as little as two soils, as in some areas of Tertiary sandy clay deposits where an upland well drained sandy clay soil grades into a grey, more sandy soil developed in local alluvium, while others are very complex indeed. With all of them, however, an understanding of the nature and sequence of soils concerned is helped by considering the soils in relation to local parent material differences, and to differences in site and drainage associated with relief.

4 THE INFLUENCE OF CLIMATE AND VEGETATION

THE EFFECTS OF CLIMATE ON SOILS

Rain is the main agent of chemical weathering and it is also, in the tropics, the main climatic control of vegetation and agriculture. Climate therefore has a double effect on the soil. It has a direct influence on weathering, leaching, and soil development, and it has indirect effects on soils through its influence on the nature of the vegetation.

Since most chemical reactions are speeded up by higher temperatures and wetter conditions, both the chemical weathering of the original rock and the subsequent weathering and modification of soil material in the profile are more rapid in the wet tropics than in the drier and cooler areas of the world, and the processes involved may not be quite the same. This results, in each case, in the formation of soils broadly related to climate. It also means that statements which may be true of cool latitude soils do not necessarily apply equally well elsewhere. Since most soil textbooks have been written by, and for, workers in the temperate areas, such textbooks must be used with some caution by students of tropical soils. It is precisely in those characteristics of the soil which reflect the influence of climate and vegetation that West African soils are most likely to differ from those of other latitudes.

Weathering and translocation

Chapter 3 contains a discussion of the structure and resistance to weathering of rock-forming silicate minerals and of the mechanisms of chemical weathering. Once a mineral breaks down chemically the elements which are liberated may accumulate in the soil without further change, or they may combine to form new compounds in the soil, or they may be removed. In nature, the removal or translocation of weathering products goes on side by side with weathering but it is sometimes convenient to consider the two processes separately.

An analysis of stream and river waters indicates which elements and compounds are being removed in solution from the soils of an area. Such studies indicate that elements are removed in a fairly well defined order according to their different solubilities. Chlorides and sulphates are very soluble and quickly removed from weathering rock zones in the first stage of weathering, followed by calcium, sodium, magnesium, and potassium in what forms a second stage. Subsequently the combined silica in silicates is attacked and removed. This includes the silica in the clay minerals, which are also subject to slow decomposition, though it does not include the silica in quartz. The most resistant compounds to leaching are the sesquioxides of iron and aluminium, Fe_2O_3 and Al_2O_3. Sesquioxides are 'one-and-a-half' compounds in which one atom of iron, aluminium, manganese, or other metal combines with one and a half of oxygen or, more simply, two of the metal combine with three of the oxygen as in the formulae just given.

Slightly to moderately leached soils may thus have lost all the more mobile elements, those which are removed in stages one and two, but retain all or most of their combined silica and sesquioxides. In extreme weathering conditions, however, the silica is removed more than the sesquioxides. Further weathering, leaching, and translocation therefore have the effect of reducing the quantity of silica in the soil and thus of causing the proportion of iron and aluminium sesquioxides left in the remaining material to increase. For this reason a very broad, general characteristic of highly weathered soils developed under hot, wet climates is a relatively high content of iron and aluminium. Soils of this broad type have often been referred to as *latosols*, a term first suggested by the American soil scientist, Charles Kellogg.

Since one of the effects of the weathering and translocation associated with high rainfalls is the removal of combined silica from the soil and the relative accumulation in the remaining soil material of iron and aluminium sesquioxides, the ratio between silica and sesquioxides in the clay fraction of the soil can be used as an index of soil weathering. This ratio is often used as such, and as a basis for soil classification, particularly by the pedologists of French-speaking West Africa. In kaolinitic clay the ratio of silica to alumina is 2:1, but in the wetter areas of more intense leaching some of the silica is removed, leaving the alumina, and the silica/alumina ratio of the clay fraction falls below 2.

Many of the old and highly weathered soils of West Africa now contain little except the resistant compounds mentioned, since rock and mineral fragments in the soil capable of being easily broken down have long since decomposed. Long periods of weathering and leaching of weathering products have removed all except the most immobile constituents. Such soils consist largely of kaolinitic clay (some of which may have been broken down to leave alumina in the soil), of quartz silt, quartz sand and quartz gravel, and of hydrous oxides of aluminium and iron. Iron oxides may coat, impregnate, and sometimes bind together the clay and larger particles, and are often individualized as ironstone concretions or indurated iron-rich horizons and layers.

The type of clay mineral found in soils is also often related to climate. In soils of very wet areas without very marked dry seasons the normal clay mineral is mostly kaolin, and this is the dominant clay mineral in all West African forest soils except a few developed over particularly base-rich rocks. In areas of lower rainfall with more pronounced dry seasons, two-to-one lattice clays such as montmorillonite tend to become more common. The clay minerals in soils are in some cases inherited from clay sediments and deposits, but in the case of soils developed over crystalline rocks—and most West African soils developed over the extensive basement complex (see p. 55) fall into this category—the clay minerals form from the weathering of silicate minerals, particularly hornblende, micas, and felspars. The type of clay mineral formed depends on the materials liberated by the decomposing minerals, particularly on the ratio of silica to alumina and the presence of basic cations. When the more base-rich rocks weather, particularly under moderate to low rainfalls, montmorillonite is likely to be formed, but where the rainfall is very heavy and where the rocks are not so basic, then the dominant clay mineral formed is usually kaolin. Even if montmorillonite is formed initially under a heavy rainfall, weathering and silica removal may convert it to a kaolin type mineral. There is thus some relationship in West African soils between the type of clay mineral found and the climate and parent rock.

The tropical black earths form an example of distinctive soils which appear usually to be related to climate. Although a few exceptions occur, these soils are generally found under fairly dry savanna-type climates, and developed over base-rich rocks, i.e. either calcareous rocks or rocks high in ferro-magnesian minerals. In West Africa there are important areas of these soils in the Accra plains and south of Lake Chad, and there is a very minor area of them near Dakar. The tropical black earths, or Vertisols, are characterized by a very heavy texture owing to the fact that the clay fraction is dominantly montmorillonite; when wet the soils are very sticky, when dry they are extremely hard. They crack broadly on drying, and material from the upper horizons may fall down the cracks, so that in this way the soil horizons are mixed. The soils have a striking dark colour (hence the term 'tropical black earths') which is not due to a high organic matter content but probably to a calcium-humus compound which stains the soil. These soils are high in calcium, being generally neutral or slightly alkaline in reaction, and often have free calcium carbonate concretions in the profile (usually in the subsoil at the lower limit of cracking). These soils are too heavy to work with local hand tools, so have hitherto been neglected by the African farmer, but have been shown to be well suited to irrigated rice and sugar cane. They are mentioned here as an example of a West African soil which appears to be related primarily to a calcium-rich parent rock and a low rainfall. It seems that the tropical black earths do not normally form under high rainfalls and forest vegetation because the calcium would be leached out of the profile and the clay mineral would be converted, at least in part, to kaolin under those conditions, so giving a rather different soil over the same parent rock.

West African rainfall

Most of West Africa enjoys high temperatures which vary relatively little throughout the year, so that differences in climate are largely differences in the amount and in the distribution of rainfall. Climatically, West Africa can be divided into a number of distinct rainfall belts (Fig. 4.1) and these are related to broad soil and vegetation zones.

West African rains are caused by the seasonal movements of two main air masses: a dry, continental air mass to the north and a moist body of tropical or equatorial maritime air to the south. These masses move north and south with the apparent movement of the sun. As the sun moves northwards and approaches the Tropic of Cancer, so does the southern, moist body of air move northwards, bringing rain with it, and it is this seasonal north–south movement which is responsible for the wet seasons of West Africa.

South of about 8° to 9° N, that is in the southern and coastal areas of the Ivory Coast, Ghana, Togo, Dahomey, and Nigeria, there are two distinct wet seasons. The first and more important wet season occurs between April and July when the sun passes northwards. There is then a short break in the rains in August when the main wet areas are to the north. With the apparent movement of the sun south again there is a second rainy season in October and November as the moist southern maritime air mass again makes its influence felt. In December to March this moist body of air is too far south to have much effect on West African rainfall, and the dry body of air from the north is the dominant influence, so that this is the major dry season.

North of latitude 8° to 9° N the two distinct wet seasons so characteristic of the areas just discussed merge together into a single wet season, separated by a single long dry season.

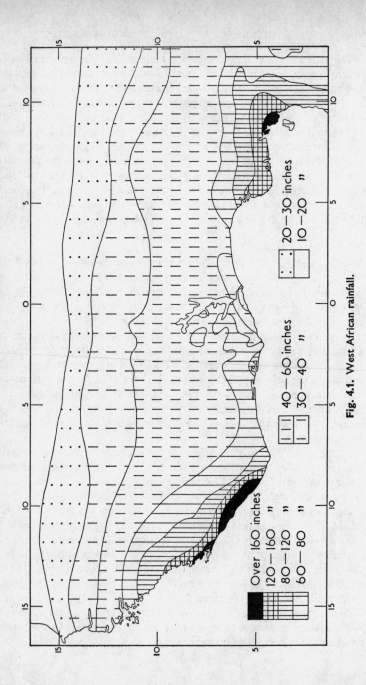

Fig. 4.1. West African rainfall.

The total annual rainfall varies very greatly and is influenced locally by the direction at which the winds cross the coast, the presence of ocean currents and the interior relief. With a few exceptions, the southern areas are generally the wettest and have fewer dry months; the total rainfall decreases to the north and the number of dry months increases. Except for the dry coastal areas of the Accra plains and southern Togo and Dahomey, the southern areas of West Africa have over 7 months of the year which are 'wet', i.e. which receive an average rainfall of over 4 in (Fig. 4.3). North of this southerly belt the number of wet months decreases until, in the general latitude of Dakar, it falls to under 3. We can therefore distinguish between a relatively heavy, two-peak rainfall in most of the southern areas of West Africa, and the generally lower total rainfalls falling in a single wet season to the north, these totals becoming progressively lower further northwards as the Sahara desert is approached.

Rainfall and leaching

It was stated above (see p. 84) that it is sometimes convenient to consider weathering and translocation separately: in some cases weathering products may form but there may be insufficient rainfall to remove them, so that they accumulate. The soil scientist is greatly interested in the ratio between liberation of weathering products and their removal. The latter depends on soil water, and we have next to consider further how rainfall influences soil development.

When rain falls on to the ground it may either be evaporated from the surface of the ground, or it may run off the surface and down the slope without penetrating the soil, or, thirdly, it may enter or infiltrate into the soil and thus be available to plants. The proportions of the rain which evaporate, run off, or infiltrate into the soil depend on a number of factors, such as the amount and intensity of rain falling, the amount and type of vegetation cover, the condition and nature of the soil itself (whether wet or dry, compact or porous, sandy or clay), the slope of the ground, the temperature of the soil, and other factors. Even the time of day may make a difference, for a light shower falling on hot ground in the middle of the afternoon would lose more by evaporation than if it fell in the cool hours of the early morning.

Of the rain entering the soil, some will later evaporate from the soil surface, some will be absorbed by plant roots and transpired through their leaves and some, if the rain is heavy enough, will move downwards through the soil profile. The subject of water retention and storage by soils is of great importance to practical agriculture and is dealt with in more detail in Chapter 5. Here, however, we are concerned with the effects of rain on

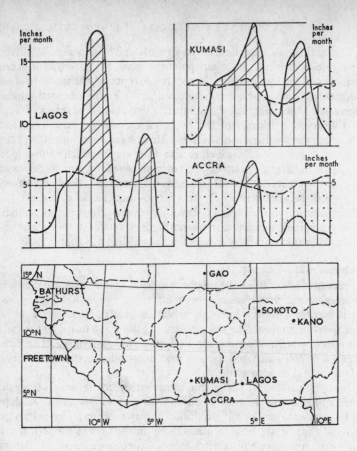

Fig. 4.2. (above and following page). Rainfall and potential evapotranspiration of eight representative West African climate stations.

In the southern areas of West Africa there is a two-peak rainfall regime, as shown in the three graphs for Lagos, Kumasi, and Accra on this page. Potential evapotranspiration—usually about 5 in per month—is shown by the broken line. The dotted areas represent the periods when rainfall is less than potential evapotranspiration and there is a water deficit. The shaded areas represent water received in excess of potential evapotranspiration.

The graph for Lagos, with very heavy rainfalls particularly in May and June, is representative of very wet areas in Nigeria, Ghana, the Ivory Coast, and parts of Liberia. In the wet seasons there is a marked excess of rainfall over evapotranspiration and through-leaching of the soil can be expected. The forest areas of more moderate two-peak rainfall are represented by the graph for Kumasi. Here the

(continued

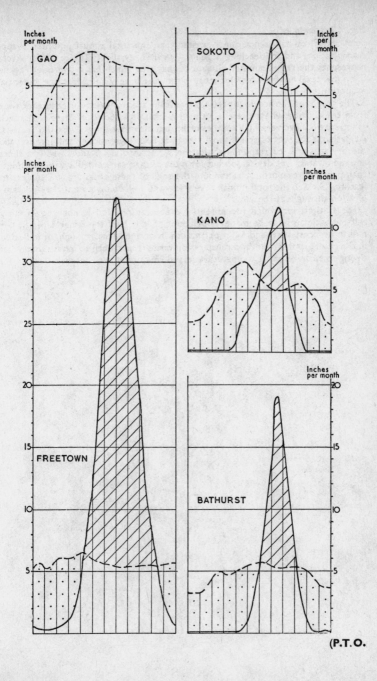

(P.T.O.

Fig. 4.2. (*continued*)

total annual rainfall is not much greater than the total annual potential evapotranspiration, and soil leaching is generally relatively slight. The graph for Accra represents the rather unusual climate of that area which has a two-peak regime but a low total rainfall which for most of the year is very much less than potential evapotranspiration.

The graphs on the previous page represent the areas of West Africa further away from the equator where there is a single rainfall peak. Some of these areas, such as Freetown, have very high total rainfalls, but also have long severe dry seasons. At Bathurst the wet season is shorter than at Freetown, though still intense, and the dry season is correspondingly longer. At Sokoto and Kano there is a short and moderately wet dry season but for most of the year rainfall is very much less than potential evapotranspiration and the soils of these areas are not subject to leaching. At Gao the total rainfall is very low and well below potential evapotranspiration throughout the year.

For stations for which the potential evapotranspiration is not known fairly reliable estimates can be made by assuming that it is of the order of $4\frac{1}{2}$ in per month in forest areas and $5\frac{1}{2}$ in per month in savanna areas though, as indicated in the graphs, potential evapotranspiration varies from month to month somewhat owing to such factors as temperature, cloud cover, and wind intensity.

soil development, and particularly with whether or not the soil is likely to receive more water than it can hold and thus be subject to water percolating through and out of the profile, i.e. to through-leaching.

Leaching means washing, and this washing or leaching caused by a temporary excess of water percolating down through the soil profile may occur relatively seldom, perhaps only after occasional, particularly heavy falls of rain or only in the wettest few weeks of the year. Through-leaching depends on whether there is at any time an excess of water which can remove weathering products in solution and suspension right out of the soil profile. Heavy concentrated rainfall in a short period is more likely to achieve this than the same amount of rain spread evenly over a longer period.

In the study of soil-rainfall relationships it is often helpful to compare the average total rainfall for a year, season, month, or even shorter period with the amount likely to be lost from the soil by direct evaporation and by transpiration by plants, the two processes together often being referred to as *evapotranspiration*. The potential evapotranspiration of an area, i.e. the total amount of water that would be lost by these processes if it were available, is sometimes assumed to be similar to the amount of water evaporated from an exposed water surface. The comparison between total rainfall received in a period and the estimated evapotranspiration losses gives some indication of the likelihood of there being a surplus for soil-leaching (Fig. 5.4), but the factors governing the behaviour of rainfall received and of soil water are immensely complex, and this is therefore only a very rough-and-ready type of calculation.

If the soils of West Africa are considered as a whole, they fall into belts related to climate and vegetation. Within these belts or zones there are considerable local differences between different soils of a single catena, and between catenas developed over different parent materials, but the soils of a zone tend to have common characteristics associated with rainfall. This is particularly true of the somewhat slower removal of soluble weathering products in the savanna areas and the progressively more intense weathering and subsequent removal, or translocation, of weathering products and of bases held in the exchange complex in the wetter areas. The differences between the soils of forest and savanna climates are now considered further.

Soils of the savanna zone

Most of the savanna areas of West Africa have annual rainfalls of less than 45 in, and totals of 20 to 40 in are widespread. Potential evapotranspiration losses are probably about $4\frac{1}{2}$ to 5 in per month, or 50 to 60 in per year, and it is only in the wet season that monthly rainfall is likely to exceed evapotranspiration. On balance there is a water deficit for all or most of the year and, as would be expected, soil leaching is not very pronounced, though there may be very temporary excesses of rainfall over evapotranspiration, and there is some percolation of groundwater downslope to feed the streams and rivers.

As a result of this general water deficit, the savanna areas are frequently characterized by soils which have neutral or even slightly alkaline reactions, particularly in the topsoil. In these soils the exchange complex (see Chapter 2) is relatively saturated, though many of these soils are sandy and low in humus so that the actual exchange capacity may be low. The neutral or alkaline reaction reflects the fact that soluble salts are not leached down and out of the profile. In dry areas they may even be concentrated in the upper few inches of the soil by evaporation. Thus, soluble substances liberated on weathering may be removed from the soil at a slower rate than they are formed, so that they accumulate. In dry areas, the soils may therefore be relatively rich chemically, with an alkaline reaction caused by the presence of calcium, magnesium, and other bases. In extreme cases salts of these elements or of sodium may be present in harmful quantities and impede or prevent plant growth, as in the case of alkaline soils (soils high in calcium and/or magnesium) or saline soils (soils high in sodium).

The main agricultural problems associated with savanna soils are shortage or poor distribution of water, with long severe dry seasons, the lack of organic matter in the soil owing to the sparse vegetation (aggravated by annual burning), and the frequent presence of ironstone or indurated layers at or near the surface so that many soils are shallow and cannot store much water. The low to moderate rainfall has, however, resulted in savanna soils in general not being subject to the leaching that some forest soils are.

Forest zone soils

The soils of the forest areas are in general subject to higher rainfalls than most of the savanna areas, and to two wet seasons rather than one.

In the less wet forest areas with a rainfall of 50 to 60 in a year, total rainfall does not exceed the estimated forest zone evapotranspiration, and only perhaps in 2 or 3 months, in the wet seasons, is there likely to be a surplus for through-leaching. As a result, these profiles are subjected to only sporadic leaching and, normally, the exchange complex is moderately saturated with exchangeable bases, and the topsoil has a near neutral or only slightly acid reaction. Since forest topsoils generally have a higher

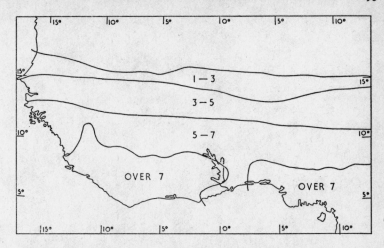

Fig. 4.3. Map showing number of months with an average rainfall of over 4 in. (Adapted from Reference 20.)

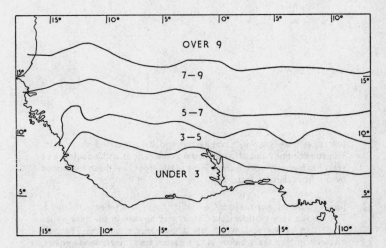

Fig. 4.4. Number of months with less than 1 in of rain. (Adapted from Reference 20.)

22 (*above*) A very gravelly savanna soil and its associated vegetation. The soil contains abundant ironstone concretions and nodules. The grass has recently been burnt. Some of the trees have been blackened by the fire (see also Plate 31).

23 (*below*) Savanna grass, almost without trees, north-western Ghana. The soil is a very shallow clay. Cracks may be seen in the dark upper 4 to 10 in of the soil, which has a columnar structure. The pale material immediately below is soft decomposed hornblende gneiss. The soil is unusually shallow. It is chemically very much richer than that shown in Plate 22 but subject to drying out in the dry season.

24   (*above left*) White sand areas in coastal Liberia (Maryland County) showing patchy distribution of white sands (supporting short tufted grass or almost bare of vegetation) and associated soils supporting thicket. White sand patches, generally small, are found along the West African coast in Ghana, the Ivory Coast, Liberia, and elsewhere where rainfalls are particularly heavy and the soils particularly sandy. In many cases these soils are groundwater podsols or giant groundwater podsols, with a dark organic horizon, sometimes indurated, in the subsoil. Their total area is very small and they are of little agricultural value.

25   (*centre right*) Somewhat podsolized soil, south-west Ghana. The soil is a very fine sand. A nearly white lower topsoil overlies a darker subsoil coloured by organic matter and iron oxides. The profile represents an early stage of podsolization. Often the white, eluviated horizon is thicker than that shown here and overlies a contrasting very dark brown somewhat indurated subsoil layer (an organic pan).

26   (*below left*) Derived savanna, western Sierra Leone. The area has a very heavy rainfall but the single dry season is long and severe: the present vegetation is a form of savanna resulting, it is thought, from cultivation and burning. The photograph shows a typical savanna tree, *Lophira alata*, invading farmed land. Numerous young Lophira seedlings about 1 ft high can be seen between the older Lophira trees.

organic matter content than those of savanna areas, and therefore a higher exchange capacity, the total quantity of bases held in the exchange complex may therefore be considerably higher than in the savanna areas, and also higher than in the very wet forest areas discussed next.

West African forest areas with a rainfall exceeding 70 in or more a year are much less extensive than forest areas of more moderate rainfall. Their higher rainfalls can be related to corresponding differences in soils, in natural vegetation, and in agricultural possibilities. These wetter areas are often characterized by a period of particularly heavy rain in May and June, when in 6 to 8 weeks up to 30 to 40 in or more of rain may be received. In such areas where there is a period of the year when rainfall greatly exceeds that which can be lost by evaporation and transpiration, very considerable soil leaching can be expected during the heavy rainfall period.

TABLE 4.1. Analytical data for 34 latosols from south-west Ghana. Above, average of 12 Ochrosols; below, average of 22 Oxysols.

The upper topsoils of the Ochrosols have an average pH of 6·1 and contain an average of 19·1 m.e. total bases, as compared with pH 4·4 and 3·74 m.e. for the Oxysols. The bases most affected by the greater leaching experienced by the Oxysols are calcium and, to a lesser extent, magnesium. (Adapted from Reference 79.)

LOWER HORIZON DEPTH (inches)	pH	FINE EARTH %	EXCHANGEABLE BASES, m.e. PER 100 g FINE EARTH, OVEN-DRY					% C	% N	C/N	% O.M.
			Ca	Mg	Mn	K	TOTAL				
2·7	6·1	73	14·42	3·81	0·32	0·55	19·10	4·35	0·383	11·36	7·23
7·9	5·8	63	2·87	1·26	0·08	0·17	9·38	1·24	0·130	9·54	2·09
20·8	5·2	63	0·73	0·60	0·02	0·09	1·44	0·83	0·080	10·38	1·38
44·4	5·2	58	0·45	0·49	0·01	0·09	1·04	0·51	0·060	8·5	0·98
2·2	4·4	85	2·26	1·02	0·14	0·32	3·74	3·49	0·275	12·69	5·98
6·5	4·5	69	0·65	0·42	0·05	0·14	1·26	1·44	0·129	11·16	2·48
17·2	4·8	50	0·41	0·30	0·02	0·09	0·82	0·85	0·087	9·77	1·45
33·2	4·9	55	0·34	0·29	0·01	0·07	0·71	0·58	0·071	8·17	0·10

High rainfalls are a widespread feature along the West African coast, being found in Liberia, the south-east and south-west Ivory Coast, south-west Ghana, and the wetter areas of Nigeria. The soils of these wet areas are normally thoroughly leached of their soluble weathering products and have an acid reaction, most marked in the topsoil, caused by the washing out of exchangeable bases from the exchange complex. Calcium appears to be the base most affected by this leaching, followed by magnesium. This is indicated by Table 4.1 which gives average figures for moderately leached and highly leached soils from the Ghana forest zone. Highly leached soils are characterized by a very acid reaction and a very low base saturation (the base saturation is the proportion of the cation exchange capacity of the soil actually occupied by basic metallic cations). The reaction is often in the range pH 4·0 to 5·0, but occasionally falls slightly below this. In acid soils of high rainfall areas the most acid horizon is often the topsoil, and the profile may become slightly less acid with depth. The reaction of the topsoil has been one of the soil characteristics emphasized in the Ghana method of soil classification (see Chapter 7, p. 206). An acid soil reaction has important effects on the availability of the soil nutrients to plants, as discussed further in Chapter 6 (see p. 180).

'LATERITE' FORMATION

Meaning of the term 'laterite'

The word laterite, originally applied by Buchanan in India in 1807 to iron-rich soil material which hardened on exposure, has been used subsequently to describe such a variety of materials that its present meaning is confused. It has been used to describe a range of hardened soil materials, including ironstone sheets and boulders, pea gravel, and also partly hardened, reddish, mottled soil horizons. In addition, laterite or the term 'lateritic soils' has also been applied loosely to almost any red soil. The word now lacks precision, therefore, and more accurate alternative words must be used instead, but all the aspects covered by the term are particularly related to soils of tropical climates and are conveniently considered in relation to climate.

Hard, rock-like sheets of indurated iron-rich material are best described as ironstone or iron pan; pan refers to a hardened soil horizon. Iron-rich concretions in the soil are similarly best described as ironstone concretions. Mottled, iron-rich soil horizons can be described as slightly or moderately indurated, according to the degree of hardening, or as soft or hard plinthite. Highly weathered tropical soils as a group are latosols.

Iron accumulation in soils

Weathering under tropical climates tends to result in the accumulation of oxides of iron and aluminium in the soil. In some cases this accumulation is purely relative, i.e. the sesquioxides form an increasing proportion of the residual soil material simply because of the removal of other constituents, particularly the combined silica referred to above. In other cases, sesquioxides which have been mobilized may actually come in from outside, as when they move downslope to lower soils, or from an upper horizon to a lower, thus giving an absolute accumulation since there are then more total sesquioxides than formerly. All sesquioxides appear to be capable of being moved under certain conditions, and this often results in local movement which in turn results in their concentration in certain areas or in well marked horizons in the soil. This formation of sesquioxide-rich soil horizons which may later become hardened (indurated) is particularly characteristic of many tropical soils and of certain tropical landscapes, particularly those of West Africa. These indurated horizons have had a great influence on subsequent soil development and the development of the associated relief, and thus on agriculture.

Soil iron may become mobile in two main ways, often associated. Iron in the ferric form (i.e. with a valency of 3, as in Fe_2O_3) is relatively immobile. If drainage is impeded, however, and soil water fills most or all of the soil pores, there will be a shortage of soil air, and micro-organisms requiring oxygen may be forced to obtain it from the iron compounds, thus reducing the iron from the ferric or trivalent form to the ferrous or divalent form (i.e. from Fe_2O_3 to FeO). Ferrous iron is mobile and may move in the soil solution until such time as it is immobilized by being oxidized back to the ferric form. When a soil is very wet or completely waterlogged, soil iron may thus migrate very locally within the same horizon to form the mottles characteristic of poorly drained soils subject to periodic reducing conditions (see p. 72) or it may move further to be concentrated in certain definite horizons within the same soil or in other soil profiles down the slope. In extreme cases, the iron may be removed into streams and rivers and so out to sea.

The second cause of soil iron becoming mobile and capable of migrating is mobilization by the action of organic compounds. These can include both secretions from living roots and some of the products of plant decomposition.

The concentration of iron within certain well defined horizons seems to be favoured by flattish topography in which lateral drainage down the slope is presumably unimportant and there is more likelihood of a fluctuating water table, or at least (since many upland soils may not have permanent water tables except at great depths) of the formation of a fairly saturated subsoil zone. Alternate wetting and drying within the zone appear to favour the local concentration of iron-rich mottles.

These mottled horizons are extremely widespread in West Africa, and are sometimes very thick, occasionally reaching a thickness of 20 ft or more: a mottled zone 2 to 3 ft thick is very common, particularly in soils of the wetter areas. The formation of soil mottles appears to involve the local concentration of soil iron in distinct reddish or brownish patches. At first these are separated by very pale, sandy or clay spots or patches from which the iron has been removed to such an extent that they are grey or nearly white in colour. Subsequently, as the horizon as a whole becomes more iron-rich, the dark mottles join to form a continuous network or matrix of soil material impregnated by reddish iron oxides. It is probably also impregnated by hydrous aluminium oxides, but as these are colourless their movement is not noticed so easily.

The hardening of iron–rich layers

If the sesquioxide-rich horizon remains covered by several feet of soil, it may remain relatively soft, or only slightly hardened, so that it can still be penetrated by plant roots. Such material can be dug out with a pick, and, though moderately firm or hard when undisturbed, may be brittle and break into angular fragments when dropped or struck. If the horizon is exposed at or near the surface, however, as by the removal of soil from above (or from the side, as in a road cutting), a hardening process may set in. This hardening or induration appears to be partly a further oxidation and partly simply a reorganization and crystallization of the constituent iron compounds under the influence of alternate wetting and drying. Microscope examinations of thin sections or hardened crusts have indicated that it is the formation of interlocking goethite crystals and of a more or less continuous crystalline phase of the iron oxides that causes induration. There may be little or no difference in total iron content between the soft and the very hard, rock-like forms.

From the point of view of practical agriculture, the important fact is that such mottled iron-rich horizons in the subsoil may, on exposure, harden irreversibly and thus reduce the productivity of the soil. Subsoil exposure is one of the dangerous results of accelerated erosion and topsoil removal discussed further in Chapter 8.

The mottled and partly hardened horizons are frequent in the forest zone, but extensive flat sheets of hard rock-like ironstone are more common in the savanna areas and in the forest fringe areas than they are in the forest zone itself. Many of these are considered very old (of Tertiary age) and therefore as 'fossil' formations inherited from a previous period. Their distribution has led some observers to suggest that the iron-rich, mottled horizons form under a forest or forest type climate but later harden irreversibly as the forest disappears during a subsequent dry period and erosion exposes the mottled, hardened layers at the surface. However, the relative absence of the harder crusts from the forest zone may also be attributed, at least in part, to the more dissected relief and the break up of former crusts. Large areas of both savanna and forest soil contain much pea gravel in their subsoils and this often appears to be derived partly from the breaking up of such older crusts at higher levels

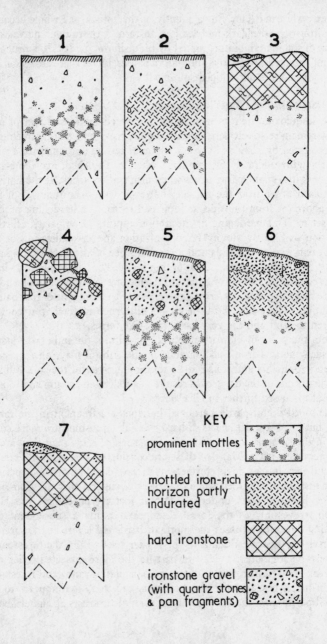

KEY

prominent mottles

mottled iron-rich
horizon partly
indurated

hard ironstone

ironstone gravel
(with quartz stones
& pan fragments)

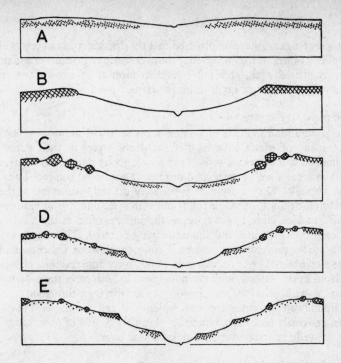

Fig. 4.5. (opposite page and above). Possible stages in the formation of ironstone crusts.

The profile diagrams 1–7 (opposite page) illustrate possible developments in the soil profile, beginning with (1) the formation of a mottled subsoil zone which becomes better developed and partly indurated (2). Later this indurated horizon is exposed at the surface and hardens to a rock-like ironstone crust (3). The crust subsequently breaks up (4) to provide the gravel in a later profile (5) in which a very gravelly layer containing ironstone fragments and nodules overlies a mottled, iron-rich layer. Later the overlying gravel layer is progressively removed and the mottled iron-rich layer becomes indurated (6), eventually being exposed and more completely hardened to form an ironstone crust at the surface (7).

The possible landscape changes associated with the profile developments shown opposite are indicated in diagrams A–E, above. These show the formation of a mottled, partly indurated subsoil horizon in A, which subsequently remains as a crust capping the hills of diagram B. In C the iron derived from the break-up of this crust moves downslope in solution and contributes to the formation of a new mottled and partly indurated horizon at a lower level. Further dissection of the landscape by streams and rivers has exposed part of this lower indurated horizon as a 'shoulder' in diagram D, while diagram E shows successive 'shoulders' resulting from a repetition of these processes, the older, higher shoulders having been further indurated to become ironpan.

Some investigators have emphasized that the disintegration of crusts also supplies a source of iron which may move downslope in solution and then be precipitated again at a lower level to form an iron-rich layer and eventually a new crust lower down the slope.

Groundwater laterites

The groundwater laterites of savanna areas form a widespread group of soils, many of which have mottled, hardened layers in their subsoils. Groundwater laterites are soils of the broad, gently sloping West African savanna areas which have a hard or at least somewhat compact layer in their subsoils. They are not very precisely defined, but many of them consist of shallow lower slope colluvium with some mottling or hardening of an iron-rich layer 1 or 2 ft below the surface, often at the transition between the colluvium and the underlying material. This seems to be related to the movement downslope of iron-rich soil water. Other examples have a compacted layer or 'clay pan' (a relatively impermeable, clay-rich horizon) in the subsoil, without induration. In both cases the movement of soil water appears to be an important factor in their formation.

Groundwater laterites are very widespread and extensive. They are often extremely poor soils, especially when they consist of poor, sandy or very gravelly material overlying an indurated layer.

Laterization and podsolization

The general process of laterization of hot wet climates has often been contrasted with the process of podsolization of cooler latitudes. Whereas laterization is essentially the removal of silica to leave behind the iron and alumina, podsolization is a process which tends to remove iron and the clays and leave behind a bleached, sandy, silica-rich soil horizon. The bleached horizon (the A2 horizon) is below the humous upper topsoil and it is the acid humus associated with these temperate podsols which contributes to the decomposition and mobilization of clay, iron, and humus in the bleached horizon; the mobilized materials move downward in the soil profile and accumulate in a dark horizon (the B horizon) below the A2. In some cases the dark B horizon in which organic matter and sesquioxides accumulate may become hardened. This type of podsolization is best developed in cool, wet, temperate areas under a pine forest vegetation, and since it is associated with both temperate climates and temperate vegetation it was for long thought that the process was the opposite of laterization and could not therefore occur in the tropics.

A more thorough examination of tropical soils has now revealed the existence of widespread soils which show some features typical of

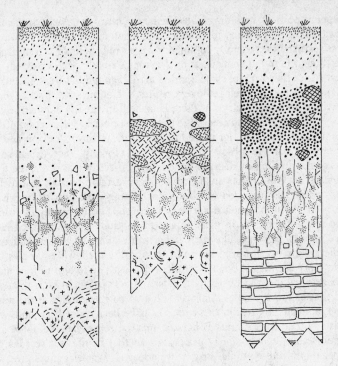

Fig. 4.6. Profile diagrams of groundwater laterites.

The term 'groundwater laterite' is a broad one applied to a range of soils, usually savanna soils of gentle relief, in which 1 or 2 ft of often light textured or gravelly material overlies a heavy and relatively impermeable layer, or a mottled indurated horizon. Drainage is often impeded by a clay layer or clayey weathered rock.

In the profile shown diagrammatically on the left about 30 in of loamy sand overlies a coarsely mottled clay horizon containing quartz stones and some iron-stone concretions. Below this the profile grades into a loam of weathering granite or gneiss.

The profile in the centre consists of about 20 in of loam overlying a partly indurated horizon containing irregular areas of discontinuous seepage pan. Below this is a mottled clay horizon grading into lighter textured material derived from weathered gneiss.

In the profile on the right the soil is gravel-free to about 1 ft but below this contains abundant ironstone gravel and some small ironpan boulders overlying mottled heavy relatively impermeable clay which in turn grades into clay shale at about 4 ft.

temperate podsols, including a bleached, grey, sand-rich A2 horizon and a dark B horizon of humus and iron accumulation in the subsoil. However, these features are generally confined to very sandy soils or soil horizons, and though found in many parts of the tropics are not of great extent. In West Africa the lower topsoil of sandy soils of high rainfall areas, including upland forest soils developed over granites, sometimes shows some slight bleaching and loss of clay but there is no well marked B horizon below: these soils therefore show no more than a more marked eluviation of the topsoil than is normal, for some loss of clay from the A horizon and its accumulation in the subsoil is entirely typical of many West African soils, as is shown in the clay distribution curves of Fig. 4.7. However, there do also exist in West Africa small areas of very striking podsols in which a deep, white sand horizon overlies a contrasting dark greyish brown or nearly black, humus-rich B horizon. These soils occur mainly in coastal sand areas, sometimes in what appear to be sandy deposits which have filled up old lagoons. The dark B horizon of organic matter and iron accumulation may be at about 30 to 40 in in the shallower examples but a few, very deep 'giant podsol' profiles occur with up to 8 to 10 ft or more of course, white sand overlying the dark humus layer. In both the deep and the shallow examples this layer seems to be precipitated at the water table, and for this reason these podsols have been named 'groundwater podsols'. The dark humus B horizon may be somewhat indurated and impermeable or only slowly permeable, so that in the wet seasons the upper part of these profiles may be waterlogged. Waterlogging in the wet seasons followed by drying out of the sandy upper part of the soil in the dry seasons favours the establishment of a grass and herb vegetation, so that these soils may be characterized by a savanna vegetation which forms distinctive savanna patches amid the surrounding forest or coastal thicket vegetation associated with other soils.

Podsols and white sand areas of the coasts are not extensive and though of interest pedologically have little agricultural value. They occur in south-west Ghana, the south-east and the south-west Ivory Coast, in the coastal areas of Liberia, and elsewhere. All these areas are very wet, and it appears that these soils form only in very sandy parent materials and under high rainfalls.

CLIMATE AND VEGETATION

The vegetation belts of West Africa (See front endpaper).
The most obvious division of the natural vegetation of West Africa is between the closed forest of the southern and generally wetter areas, and

the savanna woodland, savanna, and steppe areas of the generally less wet areas to the north of the forest belt. Both these formations can be subdivided further.

Forest vegetation cannot develop where there is a long severe dry season, so that closed forest is associated with the generally two peak rainfall regimes of the south: it is the distribution of the rain as well as the amount which is important. With a good rainfall distribution, and dry seasons no longer than 2 to 3 months, high forest can be found where the average annual rainfall is as little as 45 in a year. In contrast there are areas in coastal Guinea, for example, where the annual rainfall is over 100 in but the vegetation is now savanna grassland: this is because the rain falls in 6 months of the year and the remaining 6 months are extremely dry (less than 1 in per month).

Savanna vegetation consists of grasses and herbs which die back in the long, dry season and of trees (usually small and scattered) adapted to seasonal water shortages. Savanna of various types is therefore the vegetation associated with rainfall regimes which have a long severe dry season.

The forest zone

The forest is by no means uniform, but can be subdivided into forest associations according to the dominant species. These associations may differ in their structure, i.e. in the extent to which the trees form storeys at different heights, and the relative numbers of trees of different sizes, and these associations can to some extent be related to soils and rainfall.

The main division of the closed forest of West Africa is into the semi-deciduous forest of the moderately wet areas and the evergreen rain forest of the very wet areas.

The semi-deciduous forest contains species which shed their leaves at some time of the year and is characterized by such species as *Celtis soyauxii* and *Triplochiton scleroxylon* ('Wawa' or 'Samba'): it can be further divided into a number of associations corresponding more or less to differences in rainfall. Subdivisions of the semi-deciduous forest in Ghana are indicated in Fig. 4.8. The driest association is the *Antiaris-Chlorophora* association, characterized by frequent *Antiaris africana* and *Chlorophora excelsa*, while the rest of the semi-deciduous forest falls into the *Celtis-Triplochiton* association. Similar divisions can be made through most of the West African forest zone.

The evergreen rain forest of the very wet areas is characterized by a general absence of the indicator species mentioned for the semi-deciduous forest, and by the presence of trees such as *Cynometra ananta* and *Tarrietia utilis* which are characteristic of it.

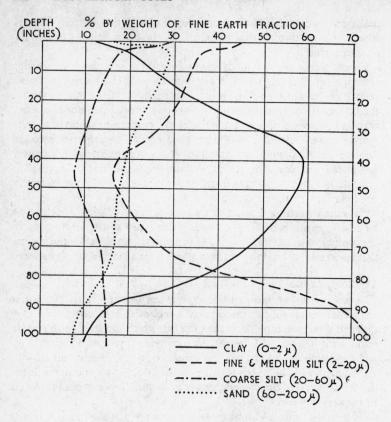

Fig. 4.7. Textural changes down two typical West African forest profiles.
Above: a moderately shallow soil developed over phyllite. The clay is at a maximum in the subsoil, at 40 to 50 in, and forms a distinct 'clay bulge'. Silt is about 40 per cent in the topsoil but falls in the subsoil, being least where clay is highest. It increases markedly in the weathered substratum where its presence reflects the influence of the silty phyllite parent material.

Opposite: a somewhat deeper sedentary soil developed over granite. This profile has more sand than the profile over phyllite, particularly in the first 5 ft and in the deep weathered substratum below 140 in. The sand accumulation is greatest in the lower topsoil, where it rises to about 80 per cent. Clay is at its highest in the deep subsoil, forming a relatively gentle clay bulge, but is low in the topsoil and falls off again in the weathered substratum.

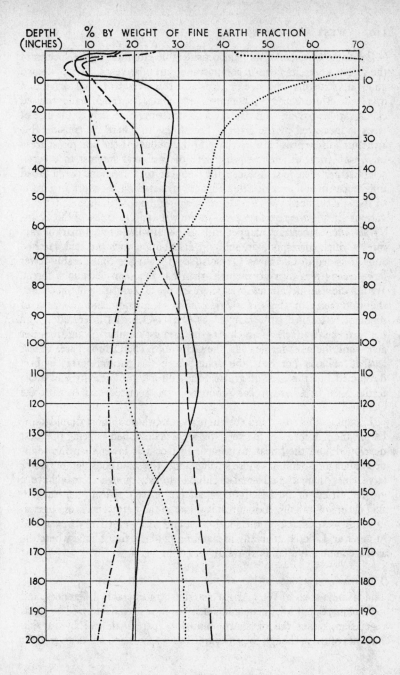

For some time botanists paid considerable attention to the species of the forest, i.e. to its floristic composition, but relatively little was known about its structure, the size of trees and the weight of total vegetation involved. More recently, botanists and foresters have made revised classifications paying more attention to structure, especially to the size of trees as measured by the girth at breast height. There are considerable structural differences between the semi-deciduous and the rain forest areas of West Africa, differences which are of particular interest to the soil scientist and ecologist because they appear to correspond with broad differences in soil and climate. Figure 4.9, based on the work in Ghana of the silviculturalist W. C. Mooney, shows the distribution of trees of various sizes in the rain forest and in the wet and dry facies of the *Celtis-Triplochiton* association mapped in Fig. 4.8. It will be noted that the rain forest, which corresponds roughly in distribution with the acid, leached soils classified in Ghana as Oxysols (see p. 206) has considerably fewer large trees (trees over 30 ft girth) than has the semi-deciduous forest. Within the semi-deciduous forest there is a broad correlation both between the wet facies of the *Celtis-Triplochiton* association and the area of moderately leached soils mapped as Oxysol-Ochrosol intergrades, and between the dry facies—which has the greatest number of big trees per acre—and the most fertile soils, the Ochrosols. The Ochrosol area of less leached soils is not only the zone where the natural forest is best developed but the area of greatest agricultural productivity and most fertile soils. In Ghana, cocoa production is associated mainly with the Ochrosol belt.

In popular literature, and even in textbooks whose authors should know better, the rain forest of the very wet areas is described as being the 'best developed' and the 'most luxurious'. In fact it is lower than the semi-deciduous forest and has more small spindly trees and considerably fewer large trees than a good semi-deciduous forest, though it may have a greater variety of species. Its comparative poverty reflects the leached, acid nature of its soils. Rain forest is found in the wettest parts of Nigeria, in south-west Ghana, in the south-west and south-east Ivory Coast, and in much of Liberia, generally in those parts of the forest zone where the average annual rainfall is above about 70 in.

The savanna areas

The savanna areas of West Africa also show considerable differences, and form belts related to climate and soils. Savanna is characterized by grass vegetation, either tall or short, annual or perennial, and by varying amounts of trees, though the trees are always sparse enough to allow light

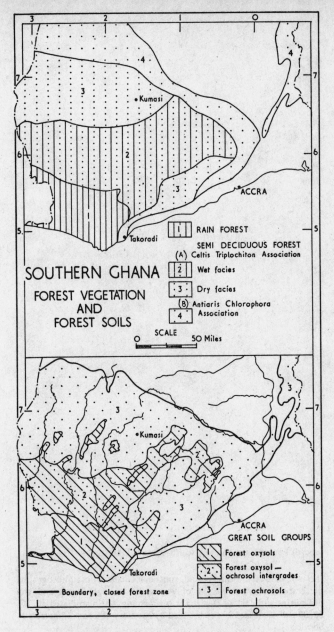

Fig. 4.8. Soils and vegetation of southern Ghana.

27   (*above*) Forest from the air, south-eastern Liberia.

28   (*below*) Forest from the ground, southern Ghana. These photographs illustrate the great weight of vegetation in high forest and the difficulties and cost of clearing it for farming. See also Plates 36, 37, 38, 39 and 41. (Plate 28 reproduced by courtesy of Ghana Information Services.)

29   (above) Typical savanna area showing gentle, almost flat relief and the dominantly grass vegetation with scattered trees. Some of the trees in the distance are economic species (including the shea butter tree, *Butyrospermum parkii*) encouraged by farmers.

30   (below) Medium grass savanna showing the appearance in the dry season before the dead grass has been burnt off (see also Plate 31).

to reach the ground and give a grass cover, and in some types of savanna are both small and very scattered.

Although the boundaries between closed forest and savanna are sharp the boundaries between the savanna belts are gradual: the zones merge into each other and a comparison of various maps of West African vegetation produced by different botanists indicates some disagreement about the definition of these zones and their extent. What is clear is that there is a general transition from wetter types of savanna in the south to dry types in the north which merge into steppe and semi-desert vegetation. Three broad zones may be distinguished. In the wetter southern areas of savanna there is a relatively wet type characterized by the presence of relatively frequent broad-leaved trees, and this type merges northwards into a less wet savanna in which there are fewer trees, and the trees are smaller and contain a smaller proportion of broad-leaved species. In the northern, driest type of savanna, trees are few, small, and often spiny and narrow-leaved. The terms Guinea, Sudan, and Sahel savanna are some-times applied to these three broad zones: they correspond broadly with zones of decreasing rainfall, but the effective rainfall is also affected by soil factors so that more local variations occur in relation to the depth and water holding capacity of the soil and the extent to which rain penetrates or runs off, as discussed further in Chapter 5 (see p. 127).

The effects of man

Despite the obvious relationship between West African vegetation belts and climate discussed above, it now appears that the present savanna vegetation is not as natural as was once supposed and that the climate could support (at least in the wetter savanna areas) a more woody type of vegetation than is at present the case. Present-day savanna reflects to a great extent the influence of man, and particularly of the annual fires which sweep across large areas of the savannas almost every dry season. Grass burning has probably been carried on for very long periods, both deliberately, in order to kill game and to clear away old, dead grass and to encourage a new growth from the underground parts for grazing animals, and accidentally, since a fire once started spreads rapidly through the dead grass and is difficult to control.

The effects of burning can be considered in relation both to the soil and to the vegetation. The effects on the vegetation differ somewhat according to the intensity of the burn and the heat produced: a burn at the end of the dry season when the dead grass material is thoroughly dry is hotter and does greater damage to trees and tree seedlings than a burn at the beginning of the dry season. Burning therefore eliminates seedlings of 'fire tender' tree species, and allows only fire-tolerant species to survive. These are often species protected from the effects of the burn by a relatively thick bark, but even these may be damaged and stunted by burning. The effects of burning are also shown by the grass. Burning encourages a change in grass species, and favours perennials at the expense of the annuals, for the perennials spring up again from their underground parts with the first rains after the burn.

It appears that burning has modified large areas of savanna both north and south of the Equator. In West Africa a number of experiments have shown that if a patch or plot of savanna is protected from burning for a period of years the vegetation changes. The species of grass present may alter, and the woody vegetation get thicker, until a low savanna woodland is formed. These experiments suggest that the natural climax vegetation which could be supported by the climate is somewhat different and more wooded, particularly in the Guinea and Sudan savanna zones, than the present vegetation which results from fires and from other activities of man. The vegetation is further modified by the effects of cultivation and by the fact that farmers protect and encourage certain species of trees for their food value, such as shea butter and *Parkia clappertonia*, or because they consider that they improve soil fertility, as in the case of *Acacia albida*.

The effects of burning on the soil include the fact that those parts of the grasses and herbs which are above the ground are not returned to the soil to form valuable humus, but merely provide ash. Although this ash settles and will later be washed into the soil, some of the nutrients are lost in the burning (particularly the sulphur). Furthermore, of those nutrients in the ash some are lost before they can be taken up by the plant. The most important effect of burning, however, is the loss of fresh organic matter which will decompose to provide humus and this contributes to the generally very low organic matter contents of savanna soils.

In the case of the forest zone, the influence of man is also important in modifying soils and vegetation, sometimes drastically. Man's penetration of the denser parts of the forest zone may in many cases have been more recent than his occupancy of the savanna and forest-savanna fringe areas where movement is easier, but moderately disturbed forest grows quickly again and may in time hide the temporary effects of man's activity. It is at the edges that the forest is most vulnerable and the balance between forest and savanna most easily upset in favour of the savanna. There is considerable evidence that the closed forest zone, particularly in the areas of denser population and heavier cultivation, has shrunk in size in recent years. Areas at the forest edges which at the beginning of this century were

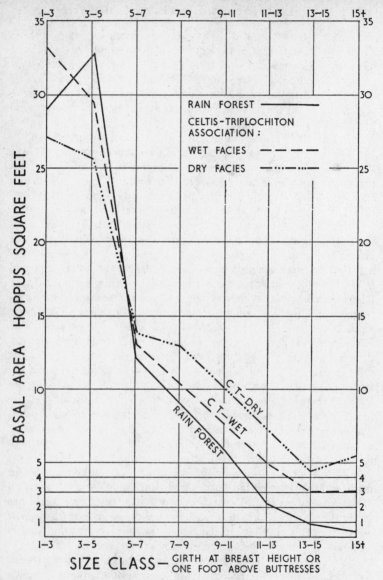

Fig. 4.9. All species girth size-classes for forest associations in southern Ghana. The graph indicates that there are considerably greater numbers of the bigger trees (over 15 ft girth) in the Celtis–Triplochiton association of the semi-deciduous forest than in the rain forest. (See Fig. 4.8.)

under high forest and full of game, are now relatively impoverished derived savanna areas with only scattered forest trees remaining. In some cases, as in many coastal areas, the forest has been replaced by a thicket growth, or invaded by savanna grasses which cannot be driven out again by forest species because tree seedlings are killed by the annual burning. In this way the derived savanna encroaches on the forest.

The encroachment of the savanna on the forest is easiest in the relatively dry areas and where the soils are shallow or sandy and cannot store much water. However, some observers believe that forest clearing can itself modify climate and result in a reduction in average rainfall, at least locally. When the ground is no longer protected by trees, run-off is likely to be increased and infiltration therefore reduced. Consequently there may be less water entering the soil even if there is no reduction in the rainfall. Water tables may fall, with the result that, in addition to the influence of annual burning, it may be more difficult for forest to re-establish itself through lack of water.

Microclimates

It is also important in ecology and in agriculture to consider not only the climate of a particular area but also of very small localized areas, e.g. the climate in a cocoa farm, or the climate in high forest as compared with the climate in an adjoining patch which has been cleared and left unshaded. Changes in local climates, or microclimates, may greatly influence agriculture. An example often quoted is the reduction in the water vapour content of the air (the relative humidity) which follows tree clearing, a factor thought to be harmful to cocoa in particular. The microbial activity of the topsoil depends very much on moisture and temperature, and may thus be very different in shaded and in exposed situations.

SOILS AND VEGETATION

A soil consisting of nothing except mineral particles of sand, silt, and clay develops as a true soil when colonized by plants and when receiving additions of organic matter from them. Often such colonization involves a succession of different plants or plant communities, each adapted to one particular set of conditions and replaced in their turn, as these conditions are modified through the plants themselves, by another community. The succession of vegetation types which succeed each other when a farm is abandoned and no longer weeded, forms a good example of a vegetation succession which can be observed in most parts of West Africa. This fallow vegetation, which grows up while the land is resting, is discussed in more detail in Chapter 8. It has an important role in restoring soil fertility which is still fundamental to the shifting agriculture generally practised in West Africa.

In general terms, any plant growing in a soil removes plant nutrients from the whole of the zone occupied by its roots, the root zone, and builds up its tissues, leaves, seeds, and so on. When plants decay the various elements which have been used to build up the plant are liberated again. The aerial parts of the plant (stems, leaves, branches, and seeds) fall to the surface of the ground and are decomposed with the aid of worms, bacteria, fungi, termites and a variety of soil animals. Most of these live, leave their droppings, and die within the top few inches of the soil. In effect, therefore, the plant is extracting nutrients from the whole of the root zone and returning them, with additions, mainly to the surface soil, and this is one of the principal actions of vegetation on soil development. This generally *upward* movement within the profile through plant action contrasts with, and is modified by, the generally *downward* movement caused by percolating soil water.

Vegetation and the humus content of West African soils

The most important differences between the two main classes of West African vegetation, the closed forest and the open savanna, as regards soil formation, are mainly those connected with the much greater weight of vegetation in the forest and with differences in the rooting systems between trees and grasses.

In the closed forest zone, the weight of the vegetation, that is, of the wood, leaves, roots, litter, and associated lianes of the forest, may well be of the order of 150 tons dry weight per acre, whereas in natural grassland the total weight of the grass vegetation might be only 1 to 5 tons dry weight per acre, to which must be added the weight of whatever fire-tolerant trees are also present. The chemical composition of the two types of vegetation is not quite the same, but it is clear from the difference in quantity of vegetative material that there is a far greater total amount of plant nutrients stored in the forest vegetation than in the savanna. These nutrients remain in the vegetation only as long as the plant part continues to live, after which they are liberated and return to circulation.

The much greater amounts of plant material which are returned to the surface soil in the forest areas account for the higher humus content of these topsoils as compared with those of the savanna.

Most of the above-ground parts of the savanna grasses may be eaten by grazing animals or be burnt off when the grasses die back, and do not decompose to humus. The humus in savanna soils is mainly that derived

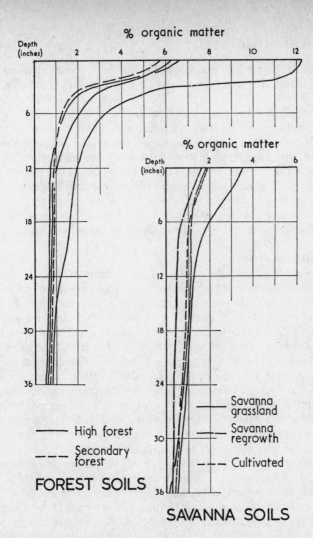

% organic matter

FOREST SOILS

— High forest

- - - Secondary forest

% organic matter

SAVANNA SOILS

—— Savanna grassland

– – Savanna regrowth

– · – Cultivated

Fig. 4.10. Organic matter distribution in typical West African forest and savanna profiles.

The graphs show the percentage of organic matter in the first three feet of four representative West African forest soils and four savanna soils. The forest profiles were sampled under high forest and under secondary forest vegetation. The savanna soils include profiles which were cultivated, under savanna regrowth and under savanna grassland at the time of sampling. (Based on analytical data contained in References 79 and 84.)

The graphs show the generally relatively high organic matter contents of the forest soils in the upper 4 to 6 in, but indicate that there is less difference between the organic matter contents of the subsoils of forest and savanna soils.

from the decay of grass roots. Grasses renew their roots more frequently than trees, and they may form a deep, close root network which contrasts with the generally surprisingly shallow rooting system of forest trees, as can be observed when a forest tree blows over.

The total amount of humus in a savanna soil in West Africa is usually much less than in a forest soil, and its distribution is also somewhat different, with a greater proportion of the total humus in the savanna soils being below the topsoil and spread down the first foot or two of the profile (Table 4.2). In a forest soil in contrast, there is typically a relatively high humus content in the upper 5 or 6 in. Below this, however, there is a rapid decline and a sudden transition to a subsoil in which the humus content may be as low, or even lower, than that of the subsoil of a savanna soil.

The nutrient cycle

Whenever plants colonize a soil and then return dead plant material to it, nutrients are moving in a circle, or cycle, from soil to plant and then back to soil. In some cases the cycle is such that there is little loss of nutrients and the same ones continue to circulate in a more or less closed cycle. This seems to be the case in a well developed high forest. As soon as a leaf, branch, flower, or seed decays at the surface of the soil the varied mineral nutrients released, of which the most important are nitrates, phosphorus, and potassium, are absorbed almost immediately by the very dense network of fine feeding roots which characterize the normal forest topsoil. Losses will occur through leaching and, perhaps, the removal of seeds and other plant parts, but in undisturbed conditions these losses may be very small indeed—so small that they are compensated by additions from the deeper parts of the soil and from the atmosphere. Soil fertility may actually be built up slowly in this way, but it must be remembered that the nutrients circulating in the closed cycle may be almost entirely in the vegetation itself and in only the top few inches of soil. On the other hand the subsoil and weathered substratum of the soil may, through prolonged and severe weathering and leaching, be extremely poor in nutrients. We thus have the apparent contrast between the seemingly luxuriant vegetation which is using the same nutrients again and again, circulating from plant to soil, and the poverty of the lower horizons of some, though not of all, forest soils.

When the forest is thinned or cleared for agriculture, the closed cycle is broken. If once the topsoil fertility is lost or used up, there may be little left except the relatively poor subsoil, and hence the so-called 'fragility' of this type of soil which can thus rapidly lose its initial productivity.

Soil organic matter

In the preceding paragraphs the amount and distribution of soil humus has been shown to be related to the type of the vegetation supported by the soil. It is now appropriate to consider the formation and functions of humus in a little more detail.

Organic soil colloids, collectively referred to as humus, result from the decomposition of plant and animal remains but they are only a temporary end-product as the soil colloids are themselves subject to decomposition. When separated, humus is seen to be a sticky, dark-brown, amorphous, glue-like substance (or, more accurately, mixture of substances), but in the natural soil humus is absorbed by soil particles or forms thin coatings on them. It is nearly insoluble in water, but soluble in dilute alkali solutions. Chemically it contains about 5 per cent of nitrogen and 60 per cent of carbon.

The formation of humus appears to be a very complex process, varying with the type of organic material from which it is derived. Plant and animal remains are attacked by fungi and bacteria (including actinomycetes), or eaten by worms and other soil animals, or by insects such as ants and termites, the latter in particular attacking the relatively resistant cellulose.

The easily decomposed substances soon break down to liberate carbon dioxide, water, oxygen, hydrogen, and a range of elements such as phosphorus, potassium, calcium, magnesium, and other constituents. The more resistant organic compounds, however, decompose less quickly and may persist in modified form. Another group of compounds is synthesized by bacteria, becomes part of their bodies and is added to the humus when they die.

Complex as it is, humus can be said to be quite distinct from the organic material from which it is derived, and also from the simpler products of its later mineralization. Thus, although fresh organic matter added to the soil decomposes quickly, it leaves behind complex colloidal organic residues—collectively termed humus—which remain in the soil considerably longer. While they remain, they greatly affect the chemical and physical properties of the soil, and when they are ultimately mineralized they release a range of major and minor plant nutrients.

The colloidal properties of humus resemble those of clays. Humus can absorb many times its own weight of water and therefore increases the water-storage capacity of the soil. Like clays, humus has a predominantly negative charge and humus particles in the soil are surrounded by a swarm of adsorbed positive ions attracted to the negative positions, particularly by calcium, magnesium, and potassium ions.

However, humus has an effect on soil structure which clays do not have. Because of its glue-like properties, humus binds together the surface soil into crumbs and so increases the total pore space and improves the circulation of air and water. It holds together the more sandy soils and gives them body, but it has the effect of lightening the heavier, clay soils. As a result, humous topsoils are often crumbly in structure and loamy in texture even if the subsoil below is particularly light or particularly heavy. Agriculturally, therefore, humus tends to even out extremes of texture and gives that loamy, well structured soil which is so valuable for crop production.

Humus itself mineralizes slowly and releases plant nutrients as it does so. As a result of this mineralization if new sources of humus are not added to the soil, the amount of humus in the soil decreases.

The effects of a reduction in the amount of humus in the soil, either by mineralization or by the physical removal of all or part of the topsoil by accelerated erosion, involve a deterioration in soil structure, a lowering of the cation exchange and water storage capacities of the soil and the loss of the potential nutrients contained in the humus itself. Reductions in the amount of humus may lead to a spectacular decline in the productivity of the soil. This is particularly important because humus levels can usually be built up again only rather slowly. Once the topsoil is lost or partly lost, the power of the soil to recover depends in part on the nutrients remaining in the subsoil and weathered substratum; but these horizons were described above as being often relatively sterile, as well as so deep that the rotting rock zone where fresh nutrients might be liberated may be out of reach of most plant roots.

Since soil humus is a complex carbon compound with an average carbon content of about 60 per cent., a simple way of estimating the humus content of a soil sample is to measure the total carbon it contains. This is the method normally adopted in soil laboratories. Carbon and organic matter are usually expressed as a percentage by weight of the oven-dry soil, i.e. of soil dried at 105 °C to drive off the uncombined water it contains.

A good forest topsoil may contain 3 to 4 per cent of organic carbon, equivalent to 5 to 7 per cent of organic matter, but once the forest is cleared and the soil cultivated this level falls. A forest soil which has been cultivated for a period may have 1 to 2 per cent carbon, equivalent to 2 to 3 per cent organic matter, while in savanna areas poorly humous topsoils may contain less than 1 per cent carbon. Table 4.2 gives some typical figures for West African soils and indicates that:

(1) Cultivated forest soils contain less organic matter than virgin ones.

(2) Savanna soils contain considerably less organic matter than forest soils.

(3) Fallow has the effect of raising the low amounts of humus that prevail after cropping.

(4) In both forest and savanna soils the content of organic matter falls off rapidly to very low levels in the subsoil, the contrast being greatest in the case of forest soils.

TABLE 4.2. Typical organic matter contents of West African forest and savanna soils. (Degraded soils may have considerably lower contents).

Horizon	FOREST SOILS				SAVANNA SOILS	
	Virgin %	Culti-vated %	3 years fallow %	10 years fallow %	Culti-vated %	Fallow %
Upper topsoil	5·0–12·0	2·0–4·0	3·0–5·0	3·0–7·0	1·0–1·5	1·0–3·0
Lower topsoil	1·0–3·0	1·0	1·0–1·5	1·0–2·0	1·0	1·0–2·0
Subsoil	0·5–1·5	0·5	0·5	0·5–1·0	0·5	0·5–1·0
Weathered substratum	0·1–0·2	0·1	0·1	0·1	0·1	0·1

PART 3

THE SOIL AND THE PLANT

5 SOIL WATER AND SOIL AIR

Plant roots require both air and water, and normally the soil has to be able to supply the plant with both of these. If all the soil pores are filled with water, then air cannot circulate in the soil and the roots of most plants are unable to live. On the other hand, if there is insufficient water in the soil, air circulation may be adequate but the plant will die for lack of moisture. Well drained soils normally have some of their pores, the larger ones, free of water, and in these pores oxygen and carbon dioxide can circulate, but the soil must also retain enough water in the smaller pores to supply the plant.

The study of soil texture, structure, and porosity, the circulation of air in the soil, and the movement and retention of soil water are often referred to by the collective term of soil physics. In many ways the physics of the soil are at least as important as its chemistry, partly because physical properties are often less easy to alter than chemical ones and partly because shortage of either air or water can cause rapid death of the plant. As G. W. Leeper put it:[1]

> The physics of soil is just as important as its chemistry. Most chemical shortcomings may be made good simply by adding the necessary fertilizer; but no amount of nutrient will make up for poor physical properties.

Before considering soil chemistry and the supply of plant nutrients (see Chapter 6) it is therefore appropriate to consider briefly those factors which govern the ability of a soil to supply air and water.

Individual species and even varieties of plants vary considerably in their water requirements. Some plants, such as the rubber tree and the oilpalm, require abundant water and are adapted to heavy rainfall areas. At the other extreme are plants which have adapted themselves to areas of very low and unreliable rainfall by a reduction in leaf area and by other measures which minimize their water losses through transpiration.

The *effective rainfall*, i.e. the amount of water actually available to the plant, depends, however, not only on the total rainfall received, but on the

[1] *Introduction to Soil Science* (Melbourne University Press, 1957).

nature of the soil and other factors. Even in an area of similar rainfall, differences in the nature of the soil result in differences in the effective rainfall, so that the plant species found on sandy soils with a low water-storage capacity may be different from the species established on other soils better able to store water for the use of the plant.

The entry of water into the soil

In the previous chapter, rain falling on to the soil was divided into that which evaporates immediately, that which percolates into the soil, and that which runs off the surface without penetrating the soil. Evaporation may be considerable if there is only a light shower of rain falling on to soil or plants heated by the sun. If the topsoil is porous, humous, well structured and absorbent, then perhaps much of the rain will enter the soil, particularly if the rainfall is not too intense. Run-off is increased when the rain falls in heavy downpours (as is frequently the case in West Africa), when the slopes are steep, and when the surface soil is compacted and lacks large pores and channels in which the water will enter.

In heavy clay soils, such as the black clays of the Accra plains and the Lake Chad area, shrinkage on drying often causes the formation of soil cracks, particularly during the dry season, which may penetrate the soil for several feet. A fall of rain, at the beginning of the wet season, for example, may at first enter the cracks and penetrate the soil easily, but as the clay becomes wetter the soil expands again and the cracks close up, thus making further entry of water slower. A wet, heavy clay may be relatively impermeable, so that water may penetrate only very slowly, and thus a relatively large proportion of the total rain received may be lost as run-off, or through evaporation.

Sandy soils, on the other hand, particularly if they contain a high proportion of medium or coarse sand, may have far more of the larger pores into which water can enter quickly, and even light falls of rain may therefore sink in deeply and quickly into these porous soils and, once within them, be protected from evaporation.

In general, infiltration is improved (a) when the topsoil has a good humus content and crumb structure; (b) when there is a good vegetation cover to break the fall of the rain and allow it to drop slowly on to the soil; and (c) when run-off is slow because the ground is relatively flat, or because there is a sufficient cover of litter or mulch to slow down water movement. If the water runs off slowly, it has more time to penetrate the soil and thus become available to plants.

The storage of water by the soil

Every soil and soil horizon can hold a certain amount of water beyond which additional water is lost by downward percolation. After a heavy fall of rain, the upper few inches or even feet of soil may be saturated with water, and all or most of the soil pores filled, but water quickly drains out of the larger cracks and pores owing to gravity, and thus moves to lower horizons. This excess water has usually drained downwards in about 24 hours, leaving the soil horizon holding as much as it can against the force of gravity. The excess water which has drained down is known as *gravitational water*, since this part of the water received is lost again from a saturated soil horizon by gravity. When the gravitational water has drained downwards, leaving the soil holding as much as it can against the force of gravity, the soil is said to be at *field capacity*.

The amount of water which soils hold at field capacity varies from soil to soil, depending on the content of soil colloids (both clay and humus) and the number and size of the soil pores. The smaller pores hold water by capillary attraction, i.e. the natural attraction between the water and the walls of the pore, and for small pores this attraction is enough to hold water against gravity. When the soil is at field capacity, these pores are full of water, and are known as *capillary pores*. The larger pores, in contrast, are quickly drained of their water, and when the soil is at field capacity these pores are empty, and thus available for the circulation of soil air. These larger pores, too big to remain filled with water when the soil is at field capacity, are termed *non-capillary pores*.

A productive soil should have a satisfactory balance between the capillary and non-capillary pores. If there are too few of the larger, non-capillary pores, circulation and diffusion of soil air are slowed down. This may reduce percolation and thus increase run-off. If there are too few of the smaller capillary pores, the amount of water held by the soil against gravity when it is at field capacity is reduced.

The total porosity, and the proportion of capillary to non-capillary pores, depends on the structure of the soil and on its texture. Good structure increases porosity by increasing space between structural units or 'peds'. A clay soil usually has a higher total porosity than a sandy soil, but most of the pores may be very small capillary ones, thus tending to give a high water content at field capacity but poor aeration, particularly if there is little soil structure. A coarse, sandy soil, in contrast, often has a much greater proportion of its total porosity as non-capillary pores: this gives rapid percolation of water and good aeration, but reduces the amount of water held at field capacity.

However, the water held at field capacity depends not only on the pore sizes, but on the content of colloids. At field capacity, water remains in the capillary pores, but water is also absorbed by the clay and humus colloids. This absorption contributes to the fact that soils high in clay hold more water at field capacity than very sandy soils, and that topsoils high in humus often store more water in proportion to their weight than the lower horizons of the soil. The greatest water-storage capacity in proportion to weight of soil is found in horizons very high in organic matter and in organic accumulations. Adding humus, compost, or animal manure to the soil thus increases its water-storage capacity and may greatly increase plant growth and improve crop yields for this reason alone, apart from the additional beneficial effects of structure improvement and the supply of plant nutrients provided as the humus mineralizes.

It is now necessary to consider how water held by the soil at field capacity may be lost again.

Water losses by plant removal

Since a soil or soil horizon at field capacity has already been drained of its gravitational water, it will not lose further water by downward seepage. Subsequent loss of water can take place in two ways: loss from the soil, mainly from the surface, through evaporation, and, secondly, if there are plants growing in the soil, loss through removal by plant roots.

Not all the water held by the soil when it is at field capacity can be removed by plants: the soil gives up part of this water more easily than the rest. Plants take in water through the very small root hairs, and soil water enters the root through the force of osmosis, the tendency for water from a weak solution to move across a semi-permeable barrier towards a stronger one. Thus the soil water moves from the soil solution to join the denser solution within the plant tissues, the cell sap. The water which is more loosely held by the soil is given up most easily and will move first, but as the soil water is reduced the root will have to extract water further away from the root hair and water which is relatively tightly held by the soil, and the extraction of the more tightly held water will require more force as the soil water gets less. Finally, a point comes when the suctional force exerted by the plant is not sufficient to extract enough water for the plant's needs. When this occurs the plant wilts and dies. At this point there is still some water left in the soil, but it is not available to plants because it is held with a greater force than the plant can exert to remove it (it could be driven off by heating the soil in an oven, for example). A soil from which all the water available to plants has been removed is said to be at *wilting point* (Fig. 5.1).

Water contained by the soil when it is at field capacity can therefore be divided into that which is available to plants, and that which is not. The *available water* stored by the soil is the difference between the water held

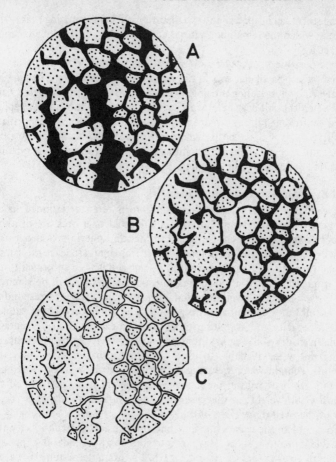

Fig. 5.1. Diagram representing the soil when saturated, when at field capacity and when at wilting-point.

The upper diagram A represents a small portion of the soil when saturated. Both the capillary and the non-capillary pores are filled with water.

The centre diagram B shows the same soil after the gravitational water has drained out of the non-capillary pores, leaving the soil at field capacity. Water is retained in the capillary pores.

In the lower diagram C all the water available to plants has been removed, and the plant wilts and dies. The soil is at wilting-point. The soil contains some water but this is held too tightly to be available to plants. Some of this tightly held water is held by the clay particles in the soil.

by the soil at field capacity and the quantity still held at wilting point—the point at which the remaining water is at such tension that the plant cannot extract it.

It is possible to measure how much water available to plants can be stored by any particular soil. If the water requirements of a growing crop are also known, it is then possible to estimate how long the available water held when the soil is at field capacity will last before it has to be replenished by further rain or by irrigation. Such calculations are particularly useful in the case of irrigation schemes, for such crops as rice, sugar cane, or bananas, for example, as they indicate how often and in what quantity irrigation water has to be supplied.

Soil moisture–storage capacities

The available water which a soil can store is often determined in the laboratory. If a wet sample of soil is subjected to a pressure of about 5 pounds per square inch, i.e. one third of atmospheric pressure, this is sufficient to remove the gravitational water from it and to leave the sample at field capacity. If a wet sample of the same soil is then subjected to the higher pressure of 15 atmospheres, the available water will be removed and the second sample will then contain an amount of water corresponding to the soil water content at wilting point. The water contents of the soil at field capacity and at wilting point are then calculated as percentages of the oven dry soil weight, the difference between the two percentages giving the water available to plants. At field capacity a soil may, for example, contain water weighing 25 per cent of the oven dry weight of the soil, while at wilting point the water content is 10 per cent of the oven dry soil weight: in this case the water available to plants is 15 per cent of the oven dry weight of the soil.

To complete the calculation and find out the actual quantity of water available to plants it is necessary to know the weight of the soil, expressed as its bulk density (see Chapter 2, p. 29). For example, assume that a soil horizon 1 ft thick has a bulk density of 1·5 and that its available moisture storage capacity is 20 per cent of its oven dry weight. Since the 1 ft of soil has a bulk density of 1·5 (i.e. it weighs 1·5 as much as the same volume of water), 1 ft of soil weighs as much as 1·5 ft of water: 20 per cent of 1·5 ft (or 18 in) of water is 3·6 in. The available moisture in the horizon, when it is at field capacity, is therefore 3·6 in.

The available water may vary considerably from horizon to horizon in the same profile, depending on the abundance of capillary pores and the content of clay and humus. In order to measure accurately the amount of water stored in a soil to a given depth, it is necessary to sample the soil horizon by horizon, to calculate the available water in each of them, and then to add this up to the depth required, i.e. to the depth exploited by the roots of the crop in question. An example of a calculation of this type is given in Fig. 5.2. This represents the results of the measurement of the available water which can be stored to a depth of 6 ft in a typical West African forest soil developed over phyllite. It will be noted that, for convenience, the available water is expressed as inches per foot of soil. In the case considered, the humous topsoil holds more available water per foot than the clay subsoil.

Clay horizons retain their water more tightly than lighter textured or humous horizons, so that the amount of water still left when they are at wilting point is higher. Thus, though clay horizons may hold much water at field capacity, relatively more of this is so tightly held as to be unavailable to plants and the amount which is available to plants may actually be less than that available in medium textured soils.

Sandy horizons hold the least available water, and may retain only $\frac{1}{2}$ in or even less per ft. Loams and light clays may hold 2 to $2\frac{1}{2}$ in/ft, but heavy clays may hold somewhat less because of the large amount of water still retained at wilting point.

The highest amounts of available water are held by horizons high in humus. The range to be expected in West African topsoils is fairly wide, depending on the humus content and other factors: in a very humous upper forest topsoil 3 to 4 in of water per ft of soil may be available, but in savanna soils, and in long cultivated soils relatively low in humus, much lower figures are the rule. Since a humous topsoil often holds more water in proportion to its depth than the lower horizons, it follows that the loss of this topsoil, by erosion for example, may reduce considerably the water storage capacity of the soil.

Water losses by evaporation

Even if there are no plants growing in the soil, water will still be lost by evaporation from the soil surface, and evaporation can remove more of the soil water than can plants and thus reduce the water content below wilting point. However, only the upper part of the soil profile is much affected by evaporation. It is common experience to find that although the upper layers of a soil in the field are dry, lower horizons may still be moist, even in the dry season after considerable periods without rain. Water may be lost from the surface soil by evaporation quite rapidly immediately after rain, this evaporation being in general faster when temperatures are high, when the ground is heated by the sun, when the air is dry, and when there is a wind blowing. When the first few inches of the soil have dried out,

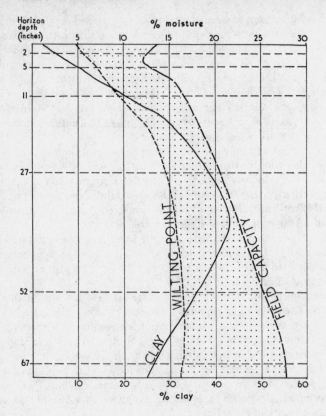

Fig. 5.2. The water storage capacity of two representative West African profiles. Diagrams A, B, and C (opposite page) show the available moisture which can be stored by a forest soil developed over phyllite.

Diagram A shows the moisture content of the soil (expressed as a percentage by weight of the oven dry soil) at field capacity. The soil was sampled to a depth of 72 in, with six sampling horizons as indicated. The percentage of water held at field capacity is shown by the broken line at the right hand side, while the percentage water still held when the soil is at wilting-point is shown by the central line composed of short dashes. The difference between the two is the water available to plants. The water available to plants in this case is about 25 per cent in the 0 to 2 in horizon but less than 10 per cent in the 40 to 50 in sampling horizon.

(continued

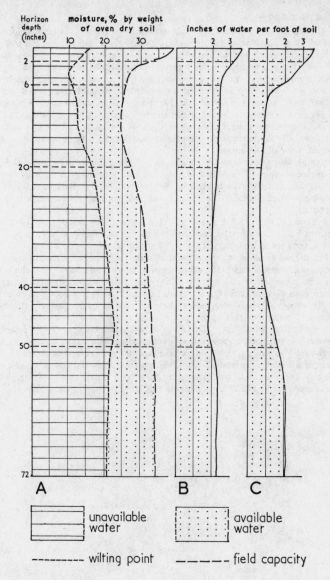

Fig. 5.2 *(continued)*

Diagram B shows the available water expressed in a more convenient form, as inches of water per foot of soil. However, these figures assume that the soil consists only of fine earth, for the percentage moisture figures shown in A refer to the fine earth fraction on which the laboratory determinations were made. In diagram C these figures have been corrected to take into account the fact that in the profile examined the coarse material (mainly ironstone concretions) reduces the fine earth to 40 per cent of the total soil in the 6 to 20 in and 20 to 40 in horizons, to 75 per cent in the 40 to 50 in horizon and to 90 per cent in the lowest sampling horizon. The coarse material therefore reduces the water storage capacity to 40 per cent, 75 per cent, and 90 per cent respectively of what it would have been if the soil were all fine earth.

The graph (page 134) shows the moisture held by a sandy forest soil developed in granite colluvium. The solid line indicates the percentage of clay in the soil (lower scale), and the two broken lines the water held at field capacity and at wilting-point (upper scale). The water available to plants is indicated by the shaded area.

The topsoil (0 to 5 in) has a very low clay content. The water retained at field capacity is held mainly by the humus in the topsoil. A relatively large proportion of the water held at field capacity in this horizon is available to plants.

In the subsoil (5 to 52 in) the amount of water held at field capacity increases, as does the content of clay in the soil. However, there is an almost parallel increase in the amount of water still held at wilting-point, so that the available moisture, the difference between the two, increases only slightly. This is because a relatively high percentage of the water held at field capacity is held relatively tightly by the clay and is not available to plants.

The weathered substratum (52 to 67 in) is of interest because the field capacity continues to rise in this horizon even though the clay content is lower than in the subsoil. The extra water held at field capacity is held by the relatively high content of silt in this horizon. The silt does not appear to hold the water as tightly as the clay, and hence a somewhat greater percentage is available to plants, so that there is more water available to plants in this horizon than in those above.

however, evaporation from the horizons below may be sharply reduced, and may then continue only at a very slow rate indeed. When the protecting, dry, upper layer is thick enough, further evaporation virtually stops.

A dry upper layer of soil reduces further evaporation losses by protecting the soil from the drying effect of sun and wind, so that the dry soil layer acts as a dry mulch. A similar protection is given when a farmer deliberately spreads mulch on the surface of the ground. This mulch may consist of plant remains (such as grass, leaves, or sawdust) or of compost, or of dry earth (dust mulch), or even of specially prepared rolls of paper or plastic spread over the ground to reduce evaporation (holes are left for the plants, and the cover also checks weeds). A suitable grass such as elephant grass (*Pennisetum purpureum*) may be grown on a separate plot and cut and applied as a mulch, particularly to such crops as coffee and bananas.

Both an applied mulch and the natural layer of dry soil formed when the first few inches dry out reduce further evaporation from the soil below. It used to be thought that if the surface soil dried out, water would continue to rise from deeper down the soil, by capillary attraction, to replace it, so that evaporation would slowly dry out the whole soil profile. This, however, is not the case. It is now known that upward movement of water from a water table or from a moist soil horizon is usually very slight and that the drying caused by evaporation from the surface alone is confined to a relatively shallow layer.

The fact that only the upper part of the profile can dry out through evaporation alone can be demonstrated in the following simple experiment. Soils of various textures are packed into glass cylinders, such as large 1 litre laboratory measuring cylinders. The soils are moistened so that they are more or less at field capacity, and then exposed to the sun and wind but protected from possible rain. The soils will lose moisture by evaporation from the surface, and the glass cylinder wall allows the extent of drying out to be observed, since the dry soil is usually paler than the moist. The lower limit of drying will probably fall fairly rapidly at first, especially in the sandy soils, but after some days or weeks it will move down only very slowly or not at all: in a sandy soil further losses may cease when the level is about 15 to 18 in below the surface. In loam and clay soils the level will fall more slowly, but it will probably fall further, eventually remaining steady at about 20 to 25 in from the surface in the case of the loam and slightly more for the clay.

Experiments of this kind and observations in the field suggest that evaporation alone can dry out only the top 15 to 25 in or so of soil, so that in the case of a bare soil or of a soil in which plant roots are confined to

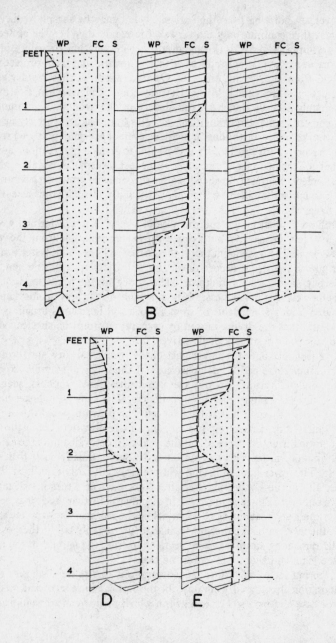

the upper 25 in, the lower horizons of the soil may remain moist almost indefinitely. Moisture in the lower horizons of the soil which are at field capacity or less can be removed only by plant roots in that zone, and not by capillary attraction (up, down, or sideways), or by evaporation, or by gravity.

Root depth

If moisture is in short supply, the deeper-rooted plants may be able to find enough to keep alive after the shallower-rooted ones have wilted and died. This is the case with the deep-rooted savanna trees which survive the dry season even though the associated grasses die back. The ability of an agricultural crop to survive a rainless period might depend on the depth to which it has been able to send its roots before the water shortage becomes severe, and in such cases it might be profitable to stimulate deep rooting (e.g. by supplying adequate soil phosphorus).

In some soils there is a natural lower limit to root penetration. This may consist of the rock below, or, as is much more frequently the case in West Africa, a layer of impermeable iron pan in the subsoil. A less obvious but equally effective barrier to downward root development is formed by the

---

Fig. 5.3. Diagrams illustrating water gains and losses in a soil profile.

In each diagram the vertical broken line WP represents the water held at wilting-point and the line FC the water held at field capacity. The line S, forming the right-hand side of the diagram, represents the water held when the soil is saturated. The gravitational water is the water held between the FC and S lines: this is that part of the water held when the soil is saturated which drains away in a day or so to leave the soil at field capacity. The water to the left of the WP line is held with a greater tension than 15 atmospheres and is therefore not available to plants.

In diagram A the whole profile has been depleted of the water available to plants and is at wilting-point. In addition, evaporation from the surface has brought the water content of the upper few inches to below wilting-point.

Diagram B shows the profile immediately after a heavy fall of rain. The upper foot or so is saturated and the next 2 ft are at field capacity.

Diagram C represents the profile about 24 hours later when the gravitational water has moved downwards in the profile. The whole profile is now holding as much as it can against gravity, i.e. it is at field capacity.

In D, water removal by plants has brought the upper 2 ft of the profile to wilting-point again. Only plants with roots extending below 2 ft from the surface could survive this stage. If no plant roots tap the water held in the lower part of the profile, below 2 ft, the water will be stored there almost indefinitely.

In E further rain has fallen. The top foot is at field capacity and the first few inches are saturated. That part of the profile between 1 and 2 ft is still at wilting-point.

water table or level below which the soil is saturated with water, leaving no air spaces. Except for a few specially adapted plants, such as rice and those found in swamps and mangrove belts, plant roots cannot penetrate the water table very far because of lack of oxygen, and are confined, therefore, to the soil above.

If plants grow in a soil with a water table near the surface and their roots are thus confined to a shallow soil zone, a subsequent sudden drop in the water table and drying out of the upper layers of the soil might result in their dying for lack of water, but if the water table falls slowly, the roots may be able to grow downwards to keep pace with it. In many ways the most difficult soils to develop agriculturally are those in which extreme water conditions succeed each other, as in the case of low-lying shallow sandy soils, for example, which are saturated at one season but rapidly dry out completely at another.

The drainage of wet soils helps deeper rooting, and there is now increasing use of irrigation to supply water when needed; these aspects of the subject are more the concern of the agricultural engineer. The movement and storage of soil water has in any case always to be considered in relation to the local climate, particularly to the length and severity of the dry season to be expected. A soil may prove very productive in the wetter parts of the forest zone, but a soil with very similar physical properties and water-storage capacity might, in the savanna areas, be droughty and of little agricultural value unless supplied with water artificially.

Making the best use of low or erratic rainfalls

West African rainfall is seasonal, and even those areas with a high total average rainfall have dry seasons during which water may be in short supply. It is true to say, therefore, that in almost all of West Africa water shortages may occur at some time of the year. Moreover, potential evaporation is high—probably about 5 in per month or 50 to 60 in per year, so that any month with less than about 4 to 5 in of rain will have a water deficit. The farmer's answer to this is to grow annual crops in the wet seasons, or to plant perennials with root systems deep enough to survive the dry periods.

By cultivation methods the farmer can, even without the use of irrigation, do much to lessen the harmful effects of low or erratic rainfalls and thus reduce the risk of crop failure. To do this he does, in effect, apply the principles of soil physics outlined above. He should try, first, to get as much of the total rainfall into the soil by reducing the proportions lost by evaporation or run-off. Secondly, he should reduce unnecessary losses of water from the soil, so that as much as possible of the water in the soil

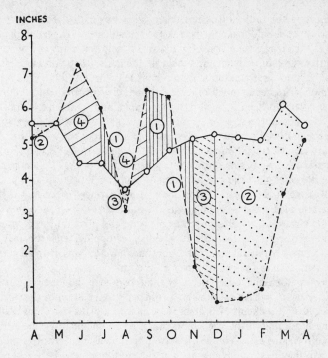

Fig. 5.4. Soil water relationships at Moor Plantation, Ibadan, Nigeria.

The broken line shows the average monthly rainfall, with two wet seasons (May to July and September to October). The continuous line shows average potential evapotranspiration, which is about 4 to 6 in a month. The rains of the first wet season cause soil water recharge (4) culminating in a water surplus (1). This is followed by soil water utilization (3) in the break in the rains, and water recharge again (4) at the beginning of the second wet season. There is a water surplus (1) during most of the second rains and into the beginning of the main dry season. After this about 1 month of soil water utilization (3) results in a deficit (2) for most of the major dry season. (Based on a diagram in Reference 25.)

is used by the crop and is not taken by weeds or lost by evaporation. Thirdly, he should make the best use of the wet season expected by planting at the right time crops which have suitable water requirements and length of growing season, and which are otherwise adapted to local conditions. These three aspects will now be briefly discussed in turn.

In order to get as much of the total rainfall as possible into the soil, it is necessary to keep it open and permeable, and to reduce evaporation and run-off. A well structured humus topsoil absorbs water like a sponge and the non-capillary pores, worm holes, and spaces between the crumbs ensure rapid percolation so that there may be no run-off except on particularly steep slopes or during very intense downpours. This is particularly the case when the soil has a good plant cover.

In parts of the West African forest zone, farmers practising shifting cultivation leave some of the original forest trees as shade, and these and a good cover of leafy crops such as cocoyam and plantain protect the soil from the direct force of the rain. Mixed cropping, and the fact that farmers may harvest their crops from time to time rather than all at once, together serve to keep some cover all the time.

In more densely settled parts of the forest zone, however, and in the much more extensive savanna areas of sparser vegetation to the north, it is much more difficult to protect the soil with a plant cover, particularly at the beginning of the rains, and this is also difficult when mechanized agriculture and complete clearing are introduced. The beating action of the rain may destroy the crumb structure of the topsoil, reduce the proportion of large pores and thus the permeability of the soil, and encourage run-off. Mulches and the maintenance of a plant cover, either dead or alive, are helpful when practicable, but other methods aimed at slowing down the run-off may be necessary.

If run-off can be slowed down, it has more time to enter the soil instead of being lost to the plant. This can be achieved by planting on the contour, or by making small retaining ridges along the contour. This latter method has proved effective in the drier parts of Nigeria. It is still more effective when small cross ridges are built at intervals, thus creating a series of small rectangular basins which retain water long enough to allow it to sink into the soil. However, one of the problems of low rainfall areas in West Africa is that when rain does come it may fall in very heavy downpours, so that although most of the year there is a marked water shortage, there are short periods of excess water and even flooding. At times such as this the basins may flood and plants die because of shortage of air, so to prevent this it has been found advisable to make the cross ridges across alternate pairs of furrows only, or to dig up the ridges towards the end of the rains so as to collect water at the end of the wet season only. Cultivation in large areas of the West African savanna zone is in mounds formed by scraping up the usually thin topsoil into heaps. Not only yams, but grain crops are planted in these mounds, and this is in part a measure designed to avoid flooding and to prevent crops dying from excess water during those relatively short periods of heavy rain. The farmer, therefore, has to cope with water shortages most of the year but at the same time be ready for occasional heavy storms and floods.

The second aspect of making the best use of low or erratic rainfalls concerns measures designed to reduce losses of water from the soil. Weeds compete for water but can be cut down, pulled out, or killed chemically with weedkillers. Cover crops, such as *Pueraria* or *Stylosanthes*, though desirable because they protect the soil, also compete for water with the crop. Evaporation losses are most effectively reduced with the grass mulch mentioned above. Mulches not only reduce evaporation and thus improve moisture relationships, they reduce run-off and add humus to the soil. Humus increases the water-holding capacity and improves structure, and adds nutrients when it mineralizes. In East Africa a growing practice is not to apply chemical fertilizers direct to a crop such as coffee, but to apply the fertilizers to a grass which is then cut and applied to the coffee as a mulch: in this way the uptake of the added fertilizer is improved.

The third approach is to find out exactly what the probability of rainfall is in the wet season, and choose or breed crops adapted to the local growing season. An examination of the meteorological data over a period will indicate, for example, that in three years out of four, or in seven out of eight, there will be a certain number of months with at least a certain number of inches of rain a month. A suitable crop variety must then be chosen or bred to suit these conditions. Thus, it might be better to plant a 4 month variety of maize, even though it has a lower yield, than a higher yielding $5\frac{1}{2}$ month variety which can be expected to fail because of inadequate rain about 1 year in 3. Varieties of some crops, such as sorghum, can be bred which are more resistant to dry spells than others (drought resistance being shown by the capacity to recover from a partial wilt, for example), or varieties with deeper rooting systems produced. If rainfall is likely to be inadequate, a simple method of increasing the water available to each plant is to increase the spacing, thus giving fewer plants per acre and allowing each to exploit more soil.

For many West African crops the correct date of planting is also very important. African farmers frequently plant some of their crops too late, and even a delay of 2 weeks after the optimum planting date may substantially reduce yields. This reduction in yield is mainly because of the lower

31   (*above right*) Savanna grass, similar to that shown in Plate 30, after the annual dry season burn. Plate 31 shows blackened tufts of grass with bare ground between and scattered trees with fire blackened trunks.

32   (*centre left*) Nodules on the roots of groundnuts (*Arachis hypogea*). The nodules contain symbiotic nitrogen fixing bacteria.

33   (*below right*) Banana plantation, Ivory Coast. The soils are grey sandy loam valley bottom soils. The banana plant requires a good water supply throughout the year and for commercial production (as here) the soils are both drained and irrigated. The ditch at the centre is for drainage and is designed to keep the water table at least 18 in below the surface in the wet season. In the dry seasons sprinkler irrigation is used. Heavy dressings of a complete fertilizer are given and the ground is mulched, often with elephant grass (*Pennisetum purpureum*) grown on a nearby plot, cut and spread round the banana plants. The bananas are of the dwarf *poyo* variety. The supports are to prevent wind damage.

34   (*above*) Digging a soil pit in the forest zone (south-west Ivory Coast). The vegetation seen behind the pit is regrowth thicket. A soil chisel can be seen in the foreground.

35   (*below*) A 'chisel hole' such as is often dug by soil surveyors in Ghana and Western Nigeria. The hole is dug to about 30 in. The chisel used is similar to that shown in Plate 34 and is manufactured locally from an old car spring. Similar chisels are widely used for cutting through the roots of the oil palm in order to fell it. Chisel holes are convenient for examining and sampling soils which are very stony or gravelly and therefore difficult to examine with a soil auger, though in the example shown the soil is a pale loamy sand developed in local alluvium in which an auger could have been used. A soil auger is frequently used for taking additional samples deeper than the 30 in of the chisel hole. Plate 35 shows a Dutch 'Edelmann' auger being lowered into the hole.

amount of water available to the crop and the shortening of the effective growing season, though with photosensitive plants (those plants sensitive to small changes in the length of day), including many varieties of rice, the length of day has an important influence on plant development and the time taken to reach maturity, and the optimum planting date may therefore be related more to day length than to rainfall.

The water available to a growing crop depends also partly on what was grown in the soil the previous season and on the extent to which the preceding crop or vegetation exhausted the soil of water and reduced the amount carried forward to the next season. Deep-rooted savanna trees can dry out a soil more thoroughly and more deeply than a shallow-rooted, short-season annual, and the effects of this may be felt by the succeeding crop. If there are no plants in the soil, or if they are confined to a shallow layer, water can be stored in the lower layers of the soil almost indefinitely. This is the principle practised in some areas of marginal rainfall where a crop is taken only every second year or second season, the rain received in the fallow season being stored in the soil until the following one.

In dry areas the choice and application of fertilizers may be particularly important. Too much nitrogen can stimulate abundant leafy growth and therefore increase water losses by transpiration, and be harmful for this reason, but an early application of phosphorus might be particularly helpful in dry areas if it stimulates a deep root system. Fertilizers and their use are dealt with in more detail in Chapter 9.

Soil air

There must always be a balance in the soil between the space occupied by the water and that occupied by air, and the air must be able to circulate. For this reason, and because the soil pores are the homes and workshops of many soil animals down to the most minute bacteria, it was stated in the first chapter that in many ways the soil spaces are at least as important and are at least as deserving of study as the soil particles.

Soil air is similar in composition to the air of the atmosphere except that, especially when confined in the smaller pores where the movement of gases and water vapour may be slowed down, it contains a little less oxygen and a little more water vapour and carbon dioxide than normal air, just as in the case of air breathed out by animals. This is due to the breathing action of the plant roots, whereby the plant is supplied with the oxygen needed for the breakdown of carbohydrates in its tissues and the liberation of energy. Soil air is also needed by soil animals and by a large class of soil bacteria, the aerobic bacteria, though a further group of anaerobic bacteria can work in airless conditions and these obtain their oxygen by breaking down oxygen-containing compounds.

Adequate circulation of soil air is essential to supply fresh oxygen to the plants and soil fauna needing it and also to remove the carbon dioxide which, if allowed to accumulate, would become toxic. The beneficial effects of a good soil structure, particularly of a crumb structure in the topsoil, are largely the result of the increase in non-capillary pore space and better circulation of air produced. The loosening and opening up of the soil by hoeing, digging, or ploughing has a similar effect. The increased oxygen supply benefits the soil bacteria as well as the plants.

6 SOIL CHEMISTRY AND THE SUPPLY OF PLANT NUTRIENTS

Elements needed by plants

Three of the major plant requirements have been discussed in the previous chapter: water, oxygen, and carbon dioxide. Using the energy of the sun in the process of photosynthesis, the plant combines carbon, oxygen, and hydrogen to form carbohydrates (sugars and starches), fats, and oils which it uses for its own energy or stores in seeds and other plant parts. Plant tissues are partly carbohydrates, including the cellulose of stems and woody parts. For the manufacture of protein, however, from which living plant cells are made, and which also occurs to a greater or lesser extent in seeds and all the young growing parts of a plant, a fourth major component is needed—nitrogen.

Other elements are also needed by plants; if analysed they are found to contain small amounts of up to ninety or more different elements. However, the functions of most of these, if any, are not known, and at the moment it is thought that only sixteen elements are essential to plant life in the sense that the plant cannot live without them.

These essential elements, in addition to the four already mentioned, are phosphorus, potassium, sulphur, calcium, magnesium, iron, boron, manganese, copper, zinc, molybdenum, and chlorine. The list of elements essential to animals is slightly different, and includes sodium, iodine, and cobalt; although these are not essential to the plant, clearly it is desirable that grasses and other plants eaten by grazing animals should contain sufficient quantities of them. The functions of a few of the essential elements are not known, and there is probably still a great deal to be learnt about the exact role of all of them.

Although the sixteen elements listed all appear to be equally essential in the sense that they must be available to the plant for life, they are not required in equal quantities: some are needed in relatively large amounts while others are required in such minute quantities that it was only very recently that they were shown to be essential.

It is convenient for practical purposes to divide the nutrients required into those needed in relatively large quantities and those needed only in traces—the trace elements. The major elements, apart from carbon, hydrogen, and oxygen (which are obtained from air and water), include the three so-called primary nutrients of nitrogen, phosphorus, and potassium. These are needed in relatively large quantities and are the elements frequently applied by farmers in various forms as fertilizers to stimulate growth (fertilizers are considered further in Chapter 9). The other major nutrients needed in fair quantities are calcium, magnesium, and sulphur. The remaining elements listed are required in very small quantities indeed, and some of them may be harmful or toxic if present in large quantities in the soil.

In studying plant nutrition it is necessary to know what nutrients the plant requires, how the plant takes in its nutrients, and how the soil stores and makes these available. While all three aspects are of importance in practical agriculture, the soil scientist is primarily concerned with the last—the forms in which plant nutrients are stored in the soil and the capacity of the soil to make these available to the plant as they are needed.

It is important to distinguish between the total quantity of an element in the soil and that quantity which is available to plants. Many soils have relatively large reserves of such nutrients as phosphorus, calcium, and potassium, but these reserves mostly occur tied up in forms which are not available to plants or available only very slowly. Thus it is often of little practical use to analyse a soil to find out the *total* quantities of any particular element it may contain. The plant depends on the *available* nutrients, not on the total nutrients, so that plant growth therefore depends on the rate at which a soil supplies essential elements in a form which it can absorb and not on the total quantities present in unavailable form.

A second important aspect in plant nutrition is the concept of balance between elements. One can imagine a soil which supplies all the essential nutrients in approximately the proportions needed: if one element needed by the plant is then added to the soil in excess, the plant may not be able to take up enough of some of the other elements it needs simply because the balance is now upset. Adding too much of one element has therefore caused an *induced* deficiency of another. Study of the balance between different nutrients in the soil often includes consideration of the ratios between different elements, or the ratios of one cation to other cations, or of one anion to other anions. Much has been discovered about plant needs by growing plants in sterile sand and giving them their nutrients in weak solutions of exactly known composition. However, valuable as these pot experiments are, they are no substitute for work on the natural soil or for experiments in the field.

A practical result of the need of a plant for a balanced supply of nutrients is summed up in the phrase sometimes heard—the 'law of the minimum'. This implies that in practice the growth of a particular plant is held up most by one particular requirement. This might be water, soil, air, sunshine, or any other factor, including a mineral nutrient. Clearly, if growth is held up by lack of water, it may be little use adding fertilizers to the soil, or if the plant is short of potassium, it is not going to be helped by adding phosphorus to the soil. This concept of the *limiting factor* is very useful since it shows what shortage must be remedied first and sometimes careful experimental work can indicate to what extent a particular limiting factor is reducing yields.

Nevertheless, the functions of plant nutrients are very complex and a plant may be unable to take up and use one element efficiently because it is short of another; in such a case increasing the supply of the first will not help without the second. The analysis of plant parts, such as leaves, can lead to the diagnosis of deficiencies, but even if leaf analysis shows that an element is present in less than average quantities it does not indicate why. A shortage might be due to lack of that particular element in the soil, to the imbalance of total nutrients, or to any of a wide range of other causes including plant disease.

In popular literature and some introductory books and articles it is often implied that one has merely to apply fertilizers to a soil in order to get better crops. It would be a distortion of the truth to suggest that the problem is always so simple. Plant nutrition is an extremely complex subject, and even those who have studied it in detail are quite capable of making practical mistakes, as when early trials on fertilizer applications to cocoa in the then Gold Coast resulted in the trees being killed. Knowledge is being built up slowly, mainly through careful practical work in the field. Sometimes a practice is found to be beneficial, but it is not known exactly why. There is still much to be learnt; some of the more elementary aspects of current knowledge are outlined in the following paragraphs.

Plant nutrient uptake

Although crop plants feed mainly by taking nutrients from the soil through their roots, essential elements can also be absorbed by the leaves and other plant parts, particularly through leaf stomata.

Nutrient uptake by plant roots is almost entirely through the root hairs, which are minute extensions of the outside cells of the plant root. The root hair obtains most of its needs from the soil solution, i.e. from soil water containing small quantities of nutrients in solution, not simply by absorbing the solution as such but by *exchanging* ions with it. Thus a positively charged ion, a cation, such as a hydrogen ion, is exchanged for another cation, such as potassium (K^+) or ammonium (NH_4^+), and in the same way in order to absorb an anion (such as the sulphate, nitrate, or phosphate anions) the root exchanges another anion for it.

In an earlier chapter, soil clays and humus were shown to have an excess negative charge, and to attract swarms of adsorbed cations to these negative positions. Cations such as ammonium (NH_4^+), potassium (K^+), magnesium (Mg^{2+}), calcium (Ca^{2+}), and others are held in a readily exchangeable way in this manner by the soil clays and by the negative positions on the organic colloids.

TABLE 6.1. Essential nutrients required by plants and the main forms in which they are absorbed.

	ELEMENT	FORMS IN WHICH ABSORBED BY PLANT
C	Carbon	Carbon dioxide (CO_2)—mostly through leaves, carbonate (CO_3^{2-}) and bicarbonate (HCO_3^-) anions
H	Hydrogen	Water (HOH), hydrogen ions (H^+)
O	Oxygen	Hydroxyl ion (OH^-), carbonate anion (CO_3^{2-}), sulphate anion (SO_4^{2-}), carbon dioxide (CO_2)—mainly through leaves
P	Phosphorus	Phosphate anion (mostly the dihydrogen orthophosphate ion, $H_2PO_4^-$, but also the monohydrogen orthophosphate ion, HPO_4^{2-})
K	Potassium	Potassium cation (K^+)
N	Nitrogen	Nitrate anion (NO_3^-) and ammonium cation (NH_4^+), also more complex forms such as urea (NH_2CONH_2) and soluble amino acids
S	Sulphur	Mainly as the sulphate anion (SO_4^{2-}); sulphur dioxide (SO_2) through leaves
Ca	Calcium	Calcium cation (Ca^{2+})
Mg	Magnesium	Magnesium cation (Mg^{2+})
Fe	Iron	Ferrous (Fe^{2+}) or ferric (Fe^{3+}) cations, also as complex organic salts (chelates)
Mn	Manganese	Manganous cation (Mn^{2+}), also as organic salts
Cu	Copper	Cupric cation (Cu^{2+}), also as organic salts
Zn	Zinc	Zinc cation (Zn^{2+}), also as organic salts
B	Boron	Borate anions ($B_4O_7^{2-}$, $H_2BO_3^-$, HBO_3^{2-} or BO_3^{3-})
Mo	Molybdenum	Molybdate anion (MoO_4^{2-})
Cl	Chlorine	Chloride anion (Cl^-)

The anions needed by the plant, the nitrates, sulphates, phosphates, borates, and molybdates, cannot be held by the clay and humus in the same way, and are in fact repelled by the negative positions since particles with the same charge repel each other. Some are held, however, by the positive positions which also exist on clays and humus, even though in smaller quantity than the negative. Other soil colloids, particularly the iron and aluminium oxides, also have positively charged positions giving them an anion exchange capacity.

In addition, plant roots are supplied with nutrient ions through their release into the soil solution from decomposing minerals and from the decomposition of organic matter. The supply from decomposing minerals is very slow, and in many deep, highly weathered tropical soils these are in any case often absent from the root zone. The main source of supply is then from the mineralizing organic matter.

Plants can also absorb elements through leaves and stems. The pineapple plant, for example, is able to absorb added fertilizer from the leaf bases. A range of major and minor elements is sometimes given to crop plants and to trees by spraying the leaves with nutrient solutions.

NITROGEN

It has been seen that the essential difference between a carbohydrate such as sugar or starch and a protein is that proteins contain nitrogen. Proteins are present in the growing parts of all plants, and in all parts of some plants such as the legumes. Nitrogen is one of the most important of plant needs, and has probably received more study than any of the others, while nitrogen fertilizers (both organic and inorganic) are used in greater quantities than other fertilizers. Nitrogen encourages vegetative growth of the plant and gives the leaves a good green colour; apart from its need by the plant as a constituent of protein it performs numerous regulating functions in the plant and influences the utilization of many other nutrients. Plants lacking nitrogen are stunted in growth with yellowish leaves and poorly developed root systems.

Although nitrogen comprises about four-fifths of the air and is thus abundant, it cannot be absorbed in this form by plants. Plants absorb nitrogen mainly when it is combined to form nitrates or ammonium, and their nitrogen nutrition therefore depends on the availability of one or both of these ions in the soil. The factors which lead to the combination of atmospheric nitrogen to give nitrates or ammonia have received a great deal of study and the various transformations involved together constitute the *nitrogen cycle*.

While the remaining plant nutrients are ultimately derived from igneous rocks, these contain very little or no nitrogen and almost all the nitrogen used by plants is thought to have come originally from the air.

Small but important amounts of nitrates are obtained from rainwater because lightning flashes during thunderstorms cause the combination of some atmospheric nitrogen with oxygen to give nitrates; under ordinary conditions, however, nitrogen is a very inert gas which does not combine freely with other elements. It can, however, be formed into compounds by bacteria of various types and these bacteria together form a major link in the nitrogen cycle.

The various bacteria which combine nitrogen from the air to form other compounds are described as nitrogen-fixing bacteria. Once combined, the nitrogen may form plant or animal tissues which in time will decompose and liberate nitrogenous compounds again for although nitrogen is inert as a gas, when combined it is mobile in the sense that it easily forms alternative compounds.

The processes of plant and animal decay and mineralization depend on further groups of bacteria, each of which is normally present in fertile soils in large numbers and which has one definite function or transformation in the cycle. Under normal natural conditions it is the decay of organic matter to give a succession of nitrogen-containing compounds which provides the plant with most of the nitrogen it needs.

The nitrification of organic material

Most of the soil nitrogen reserves are in the soil organic matter, mostly in the form of proteins and protein-clay complexes. Soil organic matter contains about 5 per cent of nitrogen, so that a determination of the organic matter content of the soil gives an approximate indication of total nitrogen reserves. To make the reserves available to plants, organic matter must be decomposed first to ammonia (NH_3) by fungi and bacteria. The ammonium cation (NH_4^+) can be held by the soil colloids and can be absorbed as such by plants, but under normal conditions most of the ammonium is rapidly oxidized to the nitrite (NO_2^-) form by one group of bacteria and then to nitrate (NO_3^-) by a second group, each obtaining energy in the process. The two groups are known collectively as *nitrobacteria* or *nitrifiers* and are to be distinguished from the nitrogen fixers which fix atmospheric nitrogen.

It is often stated that the oxidation of ammonia to nitrite and the subsequent oxidation of nitrite to nitrate takes place almost immediately, so that the intermediate products are hardly found in a soil. This is true, however, only where adequate numbers of each set of bacteria are available in the soil; sufficient research has not yet been carried out on West African soil bacteria for us to know if this is generally the case. One recent study in Ghana suggests that in savanna soils there is a low population, particularly in the dry season, of nitrite oxidizers: it was concluded that the deficiency of available nitrate nitrogen often observed in tropical grassland soils might be caused by an inadequate population of nitrite oxidizers.

The numbers of any particular strain of bacteria in the soil vary rapidly according to local soil conditions, including aeration and humidity, and the availability of a food supply: under favourable conditions bacteria multiply extremely rapidly. A comparison between the nitrogen bacteria of West African forest and savanna soils suggests that differences of vegetation, between forest and savanna, have a great effect on the amount and type of bacteria present.

Nitrate is very soluble and thus liable to be leached out of the soil, especially in the wetter areas. In practice it is formed at a fairly low, continuous rate, mainly in the topsoil, where it may be absorbed quickly by plant roots. Both the production of nitrate from the decomposition of organic matter and the loss of nitrate by plant absorption, leaching, and other causes (including denitrification) are affected by environmental factors, particularly climate, and thus vary from season to season.

There is frequently a slow build-up of soil nitrate during the dry season, for plant growth is slower then and leaching losses lower, and a flush at the start of the rains, so that nitrate levels are at their maximum a little after the beginning of the wet season. During the rest of the wet season they decline because of increased plant growth and absorption, and because of increased leaching and perhaps denitrification losses, and it is not until the next dry season that levels can be expected to rise again.

In the southern, mostly forest areas of West Africa with two wet seasons there is thus a double nitrate peak, one at the beginning of each rainy season. In savanna areas the single wet season may correspond with a slight single nitrate peak, though it appears that under grass or grass fallow nitrate levels remain low and fluctuate relatively little.

Soil organic matter contains both carbon (about 60 per cent by weight) and nitrogen (about 5 per cent by weight). The amounts present depend partly on the amounts of carbon and nitrogen present in the plant and animal matter from which the humus is derived, and partly on the different rates at which carbon and nitrogen in the humus are subsequently mineralized. The carbon/nitrogen ratio (C/N ratio) of West African forest topsoils usually stabilizes itself at about 10 to 12 : 1, but is much lower in the lower horizons. In savanna soils the topsoil C/N ratio may be somewhat higher, indicating more carbon in proportion to the nitrogen.

Raw organic material of plant residues has a C/N ratio of 20 to 30 : 1 for plant parts relatively high in nitrogen but as high as up to 90 : 1 for straw or cellulose-rich woody parts. Micro-organisms, on the other hand, have a much higher protein content and C/N ratios which may be as low as 4 to 9:1. Soil humus is derived from both plant and animal residues: lower C/N ratios therefore generally indicate higher microbial populations and more rapid mineralization, whereas the higher (or wider) C/N ratios suggest slower mineralization and a greater content of little-altered plant remains.

When large amounts of carbon-rich organic matter (such as rice straw or maize stalks) are added to a soil, the carbon stimulates bacterial growth, and bacteria (including actinomycetes) and other micro-organisms such as fungi increase rapidly and attack the carbon. These organisms need nitrate nitrogen to build up their tissues, however, and thus they might temporarily reduce the available nitrogen in the soil. The addition of organic matter to the soil will ultimately build up soil humus and supply nitrates, but the *immediate* effect may be an induced nitrate shortage, and it might be advisable to add nitrate fertilizers at the same time as organic residues to offset this temporary nitrate deficiency.

Nitrogen fixation

Nitrogen losses occur in a number of ways, including removal by leaching and by the harvesting of crops, through soil erosion, through denitrification and loss of nitrogen as gas, and other causes. These losses may be made good by additions from outside, from the nitrogen of the air.

Some nitrate (probably about 2 to 10 lb of nitrate per acre per year) is formed by lightning flashes during storms, though much of this may be washed out again by the rain. The more important source of nitrate is that obtained through the fixation of air nitrogen by bacteria, the nitrogen fixers. These fix nitrogen mainly when other sources of nitrogen are low, and use it to build up their tissues. Their life cycle is rapid, some dying after a life of only a few hours, and the protein of their bodies is decomposed to give ammonia and nitrates, as outlined above.

The nitrogen-fixing bacteria belong to two groups. One group is closely associated with plants, living in root nodules (Fig. 6.1) or other plant parts: they live in symbiosis with plants and are known as symbiotic bacteria. The second group live freely in the soil.

The symbiotic bacteria belong to the genus *Rhizobium*, a genus which includes many individual species of bacteria. Some of these are associated only with particular varieties or groups of plants. The plants generally associated with symbiotic bacteria are the legumes or *Leguminoseae*, but not all legumes have symbiotic bacteria, while nitrogen-fixing bacteria are also associated with a number of plants outside the legume family.

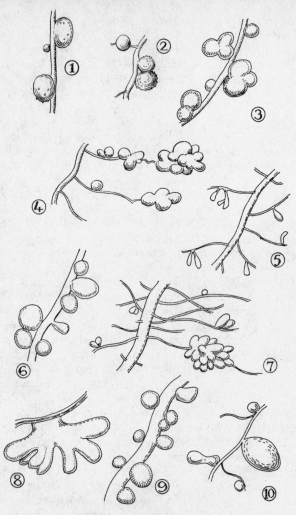

Fig. 6.1. Root nodules of some tropical legumes (not all to the same scale) showing the variety of shapes found.
1 *Arachis hypogaea*, 2 *Glycine soja*, 3 *Dolichos lab-lab*; second line: 4 *Lupinus termis*, 5 *Medicago sativa*; third line: 6 *Vigna unguiculata*, 7 *Crotolaria juncea*; bottom line: 8 *Pisum sativum*, 9 *Phaseolus mungo* and 10 *Cajanus indicus*. (Redrawn from Reference 17a.) (Reproduced by permission of Longmans, Green & Co.)

West African forests contain many leguminous trees and shrubs, including species of *Erythrophleum*, *Acacia*, *Albizia*, *Parkia*, and *Piptadenia*. West African savanna contains some leguminous trees and shrubs, but little is yet known about the extent to which they have root nodules containing nitrogen-fixing bacteria or the amount of nitrogen which is fixed in this way. Some leguminous shrubs, however, have been found to have a particularly high nitrogen and protein content in their leaves and to be valuable as a cattle browse for this reason.

In the temperate areas of the world, legumes (particularly annual and perennial herbs such as clover and lucerne) have been studied in detail and are widely used there as cover crops, green manures, fodder, and pasture. These temperate varieties do not normally grow in tropical areas, or, if they do, they may not form nodules. Apart from certain peas and beans, the tropical legumes most used so far are cover crops such as *Centrosema*, *Pueraria*, and *Stylosanthes*. Little is known as to how much nitrogen these add to the soil. Symbiosis depends on the mutual acceptability of the host plant and the particular strain of microbe: some plants accept only one strain, others several. If a suitable strain is not present in the soil, or not brought in artificially by inoculation, no nodulation takes place. Lack of suitable bacteria can therefore explain disappointing results with plants that might nodulate and add nitrogen to the soil if the right bacteria were present.

Nitrogen-fixing bacteria can also live in symbiosis with plants other than legumes, and these non-legumes might be relatively more important in the tropics than in other regions. Non-leguminous nodulators in the tropics and sub-tropics include the Casuarina family. Casuarinas have 'needles' (really slender green branches) resembling those of temperate pines, and often grow in poor soils or those which are seasonally swampy. Cycads—small, palm-like trees scattered in Africa and elsewhere—sometimes have nitrogen-fixing organisms in their roots, and other plants, including yams (*Dioscorea* spp.) may contain nitrogen-fixing bacteria in leaf glands.

Nodulation, even if suitable bacteria are present, can be restricted by shortages of molybdenum, calcium, or boron, though tropical legumes as compared with temperate ones generally have lower calcium requirements. Molybdenum or vanadium is required by the bacteria themselves in the fixation process.

The second major group of nitrogen-fixing micro-organisms are the non-symbiotic or free-living ones: they comprise aerobic and anaerobic bacteria and, particularly important in the tropics, blue-green algae.

Of the aerobic bacteria, i.e. those needing air oxygen, the most studied are the *Azotobacter*. These are the aerobic bacteria usually discussed at length in connection with temperate soils. They are very intolerant of acid soil conditions, however, and in the tropics another bacterium, *Beijerinckia*, is probably often more significant. It can fix nitrogen when the soil is as acid as pH 3, its range being pH 3 to 9, whereas *Azotobacter* ceases activity below pH 6.

The tolerance of *Beijerinckia* for acid conditions may be connected with the fact that it needs no calcium and little magnesium, which are lower in the more acid soils, but molybdenum is necessary for nitrogen fixation. In acid West African soils *Beijerinckia* is the dominant aerobic nitrogen fixer and it may also occur on the leaves of a number of forest trees and shrubs.

In neutral and alkaline soils, *Azotobacter* is dominant, and even in generally acid forest soils *Azotobacter* may appear in considerable numbers after the soil pH has been raised temporarily by the burning of the dead vegetation after clearing, thus illustrating the way in which bacteria respond rapidly to changing conditions.

The anaerobic nitrogen fixers belong to a genus known as *Clostridium*. They do not need air oxygen and can thus live in poorly aerated soils; they are also relatively insensitive to soil acidity.

In the tropics, blue-green algae, which also fix air nitrogen, are more important under some circumstances than the bacteria. They have been studied mainly in connection with nitrogen fixation in rice paddies, where they are sometimes found to fix more nitrogen than is removed by the growing crop, so that the soil has more nitrate after cropping than before. The blue-greens tolerate a wide range of moisture conditions and can live in moist and even dry soils, so that they may be found to have a wide application in tropical agriculture. Their main limitation seems to be that they do not like acid soils, but this might be merely a molybdenum shortage which could be corrected by applications of this element. The blue-greens are remarkably self-sufficient in that they can obtain all their needs from air, water, and mineral salts, and can thus colonize areas which other organisms needing organic residues cannot. This is a field in which research might bring important practical benefits.

The farmer adds nitrogen to the system when he brings in plant material as mulch or animal manure from elsewhere, or when he adds chemical fertilizers containing nitrogen. These aspects are dealt with in a later chapter.

One might summarize this section by saying that nitrogen, as an essential element of all living cells, is a major plant requirement, but that nitrogen is an inert gas which is absorbed by plants mainly in the form of the ammonium cation or the nitrate anion. Both are produced during the decay of organic matter by the action of micro-organisms, and the nitrogen reserves in a soil are closely related to its organic matter content. Apart from the release of nitrogen from plant and animal remains, nitrogen can be added to the cycle by bacteria and other micro-organisms living in the soil and by those which occur in symbiotic partnership with plants such as legumes.

PHOSPHORUS

Functions of phosphorus

Phosphorus, together with nitrogen and potassium, in one of the three major nutrients, although the amounts found in plants are smaller than the amounts of nitrogen and potassium they contain. Phosphorus is required as a small but vital ingredient in nucleo-protein. It is a constituent of cell nuclei and is essential for cell division and growth.

This nutrient is usually concentrated in the fast-growing parts of the plant, particularly in the root tips. Phosphorus affects the maturing period of crops, and is found in quantity in seeds and fruit. For a long time many agriculturalists have considered that adequate supplies of phosphorus have a stimulating effect on root growth in particular, and its application has been recommended in order to ensure a good root development.

The absorption of phosphorus by the plant

The plant is thought to absorb its phosphorus wholly or mainly in the form of the di- or mono-hydrogen orthophosphate ions, $H_2PO_4^-$ and HPO_4^{2-}. The $H_2PO_4^-$ ion is much the more important of the two, particularly in acid soils. It is further thought that the rate at which the plant absorbs phosphate anions is influenced by the concentration of phosphate ions in the soil solution. At any one time, the amount of phosphate ions in the soil solution is very minute—usually less than one part per million, i.e. less than one part phosphorus to a million parts soil solution. Expressed in another way, this is usually the equivalent of only an ounce or so of phosphorus in the soil solution in an acre of soil to a depth of 2 to 3 ft. Since a growing crop can easily absorb 10 lb/acre or more of phosphorus in a season (see Table 9.1) it is obvious that the amount in the soil solution at any one time is only a tiny fraction of the annual needs of the plant. The phosphate in the soil solution has therefore to be taken up by the plant and then replaced by fresh phosphate many times during the season if the plant's needs are to be met. Where other plant needs are not limiting growth, then the rate of plant growth may depend on the rate at which phosphate ions removed from the soil solution are replaced from

36–43   Shifting cultivation in the forest zone.

36   (*above*) A riverside village on the Liberian bank of the Cavally river (the far bank is in the Ivory Coast). The pale patch behind the village is being cultivated, behind it is a more extensive area of regrowth thicket. Nearer the village and in the foreground are some secondary forest trees. At the edge of the village itself coconut palms and plantains can be seen. The soils are mainly developed in river alluvium.

37   (*below*) A forest patch being cleared. Scattered tree trunks can be seen on the ground but a few trees in the clearing have been left standing. There is low secondary forest to the left and little disturbed high forest to the right and in the foreground.

38 (*above*) Clearing forest, south-east Liberia. The photograph shows a recently cleared steep hillside (1), bare of vegetation and vulnerable to accelerated erosion. A few tree trunks can be seen at lower right. Behind the clearing there is original forest to the right (2) and re-growth thicket and young secondary forest to the left (3). In the upper left-hand corner there is another patch of recent clearing (4). In the foreground there is low regrowth vegetation (5) with occasional patches of higher trees (6).

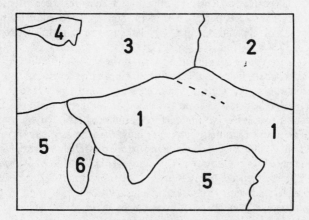

39 (*below*) General view of a more densely cultivated area than that shown in Plate 36 (central Liberia). There is a 'patchwork quilt' made up of recently cleared areas, patches of low regrowth vegetation and occasional areas of higher trees, illustrating successive stages in the process of land rotation cultivation.

the phosphate reserves in the soil. The nature of these phosphate reserves is considered in the next section.

Phosphate anions in normal well drained soils do not move very far in the soil—perhaps only a few millimetres from their place of origin. This is in strong contrast to some of the more mobile nutrients in the soil, particularly the nitrate ion. In practice, therefore, the phosphate anion has to be very near the plant root, if it is to be absorbed. Since the phosphate anion will not go far to the root, then the root has to go to the phosphate ion, and in fact adequate phosphate absorption usually depends very much on the plant being able to develop a good root system. The growing point of the root moves through the soil as the root system expands, exploring new soil areas. At any one time, the most active phosphorus absorption is usually from the root tips, with a slower rate of absorption from the older parts of the root system. The amount of phosphate absorbed thus depends partly on the extent of the root system and the total volume of soil which it explores.

Phosphate which is soluble and capable of entering the soil solution and of being absorbed by plants is known as *available phosphorus*. However, most of the total phosphorus in soils is usually *unavailable* to plants— unavailable because it occurs in compounds which are either insoluble or nearly so. Of the total phosphorus in the soil, by far the greater part is usually unavailable, and remains so as long as it remains in the insoluble or sparingly soluble form.

As the phosphate ions are removed from the soil solution by the plant, further phosphate ions are released from the soil reserves and take their place. They may come from anion exchange positions in the soil (see Chapter 2) or be released from inorganic or organic compounds in the soil. Plant growth may be limited by phosphate shortage if the replacement of removed phosphate ions is so slow that the amounts in the soil solution fall to very low levels. In that case the phosphate potential (which can be regarded as the degree of difficulty plants have in removing phosphate from the soil solution) is high, and the plant may be unable to absorb sufficient for its needs, so that its growth will be limited by phosphate shortage. If adequate quantities are, however, released from the soil reserves, or added by the farmer in the form of soluble phosphate fertilizers, then the potential is lowered, the concentration in the soil solution is increased, and uptake by the plant is also greater.

Forms of phosphorus in the soil

The unavailable phosphorus in the soil can in turn be divided into two types, that which forms *inorganic* compounds (such as iron or dicalcium phosphate, for example) and that which occurs in the form of *organic* compounds.

Phosphorus is not generally available when combined to form *organic compounds* but becomes so when these compounds are mineralized (see Chapter 4). Part or most of the soil organic phosphorus is in the soil humus, but certain additional phosphorus-containing organic compounds (such as nucleic acids or constituents thereof, and inositol phosphates) may occur in the soil independent of the humus fraction. The composition of soil humus is not fixed for, as was stated in Chapter 4, humus is a complex mixture of substances, and therefore the amount of phosphorus in soil organic matter and the ratio of that phosphorus to other constituents such as carbon and nitrogen is not constant. However, in very round figures the carbon-nitrogen-phosphorus ratios in organic matter are often found to be something like 100:10:1. The combined phosphate is made available as the organic matter mineralizes, and the free orthophosphate ions released in the soil solution are then either taken up by plants or combine with other soil constituents.

A high organic matter content and a good rate of organic matter mineralization should ensure an adequate rate of release of phosphate ions to the soil solution. Such conditions are likely to occur when a soil that has been left in fallow and built up a good humus content is first cultivated. Conversely, when a soil is left in fallow and when, particularly at the beginning of the fallow period, regrowth vegetation is actively increasing and adding to the soil organic matter content, then soil phosphorus is being locked up in unavailable organic forms in the new organic matter being added to the soil.

In soils low in humus there may be more of the total soil phosphorus in the inorganic form than in the organic, but in many West African soils, and particularly in the upper horizons of forest soils which are rich in organic matter, there may be more total phosphorus in organic than in inorganic combinations. For this and other reasons, most of the phosphorus absorption by the plant is usually from the topsoil where organic matter mineralization is greatest.

Inorganic phosphorus compounds in the soil fall into two classes. The first and most important in most cases consists of insoluble or nearly insoluble compounds of phosphorus with other elements, particularly with iron, aluminium, and calcium. The second class consists of insoluble phosphate-clay complexes.

In acid soils the phosphate is most likely to combine with either free iron or free aluminium to form ferric phosphate or aluminium phosphate or combinations of the two. These are relatively insoluble. In acid soils the supply of free ferric ions available to immobilize phosphate ions is usually high, and free aluminium is frequently also present so that these soils have a high phosphate fixing power.

In alkaline soils the free phosphate ions not taken up by the plant are most likely to combine with calcium ions to form calcium phosphate, which is also relatively insoluble, or they may react with particles of calcium carbonate in the soil.

The various compounds of calcium and phosphate found in the soil are of particular importance to the agriculturalist. This is not only because in the case of alkaline soils added phosphate is likely to be locked up and immobilized as one of these compounds but also because most of the commoner phosphate fertilizers applied to soils consist of, or contain, combinations of calcium and phosphate. The various compounds commonly found differ in

(1) the relative proportions of calcium and phosphate they contain, and
(2) their solubility in water.

It is helpful to be able to distinguish between the following calcium phosphates:

(a) *Monocalcium phosphate*. This has the formula $Ca(H_2PO_4)_2$, and it will be noted that for every calcium atom in the molecule there are two dihydrogen phosphate ions. The important fact about this compound is that it is water-soluble.

(b) *Dicalcium phosphate*. This has the formula $CaHPO_4$, so that for every Ca in the molecule there is only one monohydrogen phosphate ion. There is thus only half the phosphorus in proportion to the calcium that there is in the monocalcium phosphate. More important to the agriculturalist is the fact that dicalcium phosphate is relatively insoluble.

(c) *Tricalcium phosphate*. $Ca_3(PO_4)_2$, has even less phosphorus in proportion to calcium than dicalcium phosphate (it has three Ca to two PO_4 ions), and is even less soluble.

An alternative and better way of regarding the three compounds is to remember that the PO_4 radical has three negative valencies which are satisfied by calcium or by calcium and hydrogen in different proportions. In phosphoric acid, H_3PO_4, all three are satisfied by H^+ ions. In monocalcium phosphate only one of the charges, as suggested by the name, is satisfied by Ca^{2+}; in dicalcium phosphate two are satisfied by calcium and in tricalcium phosphate all three are satisfied by calcium and none by hydrogen. The important properties of these compounds to the agriculturalist are that:

(i) of the three only monocalcium phosphate is readily soluble; and

(ii) monocalcium phosphate in the soil can change (or revert) to one of the other forms and so become insoluble.

There are other calcium phosphate compounds present in soils. Of these the most important are the group of minerals known as 'apatites'. Mineral apatite is the original source of soil and plant phosphorus. Apatites have a structure rather like some silicates except that the tetrahedron is composed of phosphate instead of silicate. Apatites are compounds of calcium, phosphate, and a third component which might be hydroxyl (OH), fluorine (F), or chlorine (Cl). The first of these, hydroxyapatite, is the calcium phosphate compound found in bones and teeth, but the second, fluorapatite, is most important in soils and the main constituent of natural rock phosphate deposits (Chapter 9).

The fixation of phosphorus in the soil

'Fixation' is a broad term referring to the processes whereby available phosphorus forms combinations with other soil constituents and thus becomes unavailable to plants.

If a solution of soluble monocalcium phosphate is poured through a column of soil, the effluent collected at the outlet may contain little or no free phosphate. Some or all of the added phosphate anions have therefore been fixed by the soil in the column.

If we assume that the soil in the column is a sample of an acid West African latosol, then the fixation which occurs is probably caused by the reaction of the free phosphate anions (mainly $H_2PO_4^-$) with free iron or aluminium cations in the soil, or with their hydrous oxides, to form insoluble ferric or aluminium phosphates. These compounds when formed in the soil are either:

(a) precipitated as small particles or crystals; or

(b) absorbed on to the surfaces of iron or aluminium oxides or the surfaces of clay particles.

The extent of the fixation depends on a number of factors, as outlined below, the most important of which is the soil pH. The more acid the soil, the more is added phosphate likely to be fixed in this way and the greater the precautions necessary to ensure that some of it reaches the plant.

If, however, the soil in the column is an alkaline one then the fixation that occurs will be of a different nature. Most of the added phosphate will probably be precipitated as calcium phosphate. Magnesium phosphate might also be formed. If the soil contains free calcium carbonate (the tropical black clays of West Africa and other soils contain calcium carbonate concretions) then the phosphate may be precipitated as dicalcium phosphate or as apatite on the outer surface of the calcium carbonate particles, and this effect will be particularly important where the calcium carbonate is finely divided and thus has a large surface area.

The subject of phosphate fixation by soils is a complex one. For greater clarity, it is sometimes necessary to distinguish first between phosphate fixation and phosphate retention, and secondly, between these two and phosphate reversion.

Phosphate fixation, in the strict sense of the word, refers to the phosphorus which is locked up in compounds from which it cannot be extracted by dilute acids: this phosphate is considered unavailable to plants.

Phosphate retention refers to the phosphate which is held somewhat more loosely by the soil and which can be extracted by dilute acids (either weak acids such as citric or acetic or very dilute solutions of strong acids such as sulphuric). This dilute acid extractable phosphate is retained by the soil but is considered to be available to the plant.

Phosphate reversion is not a type of fixation, but is the process that occurs when soluble monocalcium phosphate changes or reverts to insoluble forms such as di- or tri-calcium phosphates. This is discussed further in Chapter 9 (see pp. 283–5) under the heading 'What happens when phosphate is applied to the soil'. This is, in effect, another way in which available phosphate becomes unavailable.

Factors affecting phosphorus fixation in West African soils

The extent to which phosphate ions are likely to be fixed depends on the intrinsic qualities of the soil itself and may vary considerably between different soils in the same area according to their chemical and physical properties. The following factors appear to influence phosphorus fixation:

(1) *The type of clay mineral and the total amount of clay in the soil.* One-to-one ($1:1$) lattice clays such as kaolin (see Chapter 2) retain or fix more phosphate than an equal amount of $2:1$ lattice clays such as montmorillonite. The amount of clay in the soil is also important. Clay-textured soils are likely to fix or retain more phosphate than loams and sands. This is simply because the total surface area of the soil increases as the clay content increases.

(2) *The presence of hydrous oxides of iron and aluminium* increases phosphate fixation. These are more commonly found in acid West African soils of high rainfall areas than in neutral or alkaline soils.

(3) *Soil reaction.* At pH values below 5·5 fixation through combination with iron and aluminium and with their hydrous oxides becomes increasingly important. At pH values of 7·0 and above, where the reaction is due to calcium and magnesium and not to sodium in the

soil, phosphate precipitation is caused by calcium, by magnesium, and by their carbonates. The intermediate pH range of 5·5 to 7·0 represents the soil reaction at which phosphate is most available to plants.

(4) *The presence of organic matter in the soil* may reduce fixation. It is thought that it does this by combining with some of the sesquioxides, or by coating them, so that they are less likely to combine with and immobilize free phosphate. Organic compounds, organic acids, and decomposition products may also dissolve fixed phosphate or displace it from compounds and thus release it into the soil 'pool' of available phosphorus.

Phosphate responses in West Africa

Much has been written and discussed about the capacity of tropical latosols in general to fix phosphate in insoluble compounds. Although some West African soils have a high phosphate-fixing capacity, this is not always the case. More research is showing that individual soils may differ considerably in this respect. Nevertheless it has been found that a wide variety of both forest and savanna soils do respond to phosphate applications and that phosphate shortages are frequently a limiting factor in West Africa. Apart from differences in soils, it must also be remembered that different plants not only have different phosphate requirements but that some are much better able to extract phosphate from the soil than others. In all cases a well developed rooting system assists phosphate uptake by increasing the volume of soil explored by the roots.

As a very general rule, it might be stated that savanna soils frequently respond to nitrogen and to phosphate, while forest soils are most likely to respond to potassium and to phosphate. Thus, phosphorus is the only one of the three major nutrients frequently deficient in both the forest and the savanna zones of Africa.

Responses to added phosphate depend on:

(1) The phosphate status of the soil before application, particularly the concentration of phosphate anions in the soil solution and the rate at which those removed are replaced from the soil reserves.

(2) The extent to which the added phosphate increases the ease of uptake by increasing the concentration in the soil solution and maintaining it at that higher level; this in turn depends on the type of phosphate fertilizer added, the way it is added, and the nature of the soil, particularly its phosphate-fixing capacity.

(3) The nature of the plant and the extent or otherwise to which it is held back by other factors.

If, as some agriculturalists have claimed, all the soluble phosphate fertilizer added to the soil is quickly fixed by the soil if not taken up by the plant, then it would be expected that the beneficial effect would be very short-lived and confined to the first season or year of production. This is sometimes the case. However, if the added phosphate has a residual effect, i.e. if it continues to produce yield increases in the second, third, or subsequent years, then it appears that not all of it was fixed or, if it was, then some of it became available again later to benefit subsequent crops.

Unfortunately, the number of carefully controlled experiments designed to test residual effects of phosphate applications in West African soils are very few. It should also be remembered that a result obtained on one soil will not necessarily be applicable to a different soil. However, one carefully conducted experiment in northern Nigeria, at Kano (quoted by E. W. Russell in *Soil Conditions and Plant Growth*, 9th edition, 1961) gave the following responses to a single application of about 15 lb of phosphorus per acre (applied as superphosphate) in 1937. Note that the increases obtained in 1938, 1939, 1940, and 1941 are residual responses obtained in the second, third, and fourth year after application, and that these residual responses suggest that not all the added phosphate could have been fixed in the first year:

TABLE 6.2. Residual responses to phosphate application in Nigeria.

YEAR AND CROP	YIELD WITH NO PHOSPHATE	YIELD WITH SUPERPHOSPHATE GIVEN IN 1937 ONLY	YIELD INCREASE
1937 millet	381 lb/acre	803 lb/acre	422 lb/acre
1938 guinea corn	617	781	164
1939 groundnuts	785	973	188
1940 millet	363	449	86
1941 guinea corn	356	459	103

In Ghana fertilizer trials on cocoa produced rather patchy results, but where responses were obtained this was usually considered to be caused by added phosphate. It is thought that, of the savanna zone crops, guinea corn is more sensitive to low phosphate levels, and therefore more likely to respond on low phosphate soils, than is maize, but responses have been obtained with most savanna zone crops, including groundnuts.

Since added phosphate in the soil is not very mobile and not likely, in well drained soils, to be leached out of the soil, it follows that regular applications of phosphate over a period of years must gradually and progressively increase the total phosphate in the soil, for only a fraction of that added is removed by plants. Even though most or all of the added phosphate is fixed in unavailable forms, it may nevertheless have some beneficial effect. This appears to be because added phosphate fixed in the soil must have neutralized to some extent the phosphorus fixation power of the soil, and partly because even the so-called fixed phosphorus becomes slightly available under some conditions: the greater the total phosphorus in the soil, the greater the effect of that very small part of it which becomes available each year is likely to be. In some areas of the world where the soils once responded well to phosphate applications, those soils which have a long history of cultivation and phosphate addition have sometimes ceased to respond to additional applications because of the progressively greater accumulations of added phosphate they contain.

In West Africa phosphate fertilizers, like other chemical fertilizers, have hardly been used as yet by the ordinary farmer, who, in effect, makes phosphorus available in his crop by resting the land at intervals in fallow, so that the fallow vegetation extracts phosphorus from its root zone which finally accumulates in the organic matter of the soil. As this organic matter mineralizes during the subsequent cropping period, phosphorus and other elements are made available to the growing crop. This is discussed further in Chapter 8.

One approach being tried experimentally is to add relatively large quantities of cheap rock phosphate to soils, particularly acid ones, in the hope that it will slowly satisfy the phosphate fixation power of the soil, and to rely on smaller quantities of more expensive soluble phosphate fertilizers to produce an immediate response. The most suitable kind of phosphatic fertilizer to apply depends, among other things, on the type of soil and the climate.

Phosphate-containing fertilizers and their practical use in West Africa are discussed further in Chapter 9, pp. 278–86.

POTASSIUM

Potassium, the third of the so-called primary or major nutrients is essential for the formation and transfer of carbohydrates in plants, and for photosynthesis and protein synthesis. Potassium occurs particularly in the growing points, fruits, and seeds of plants. Plants such as cassava which synthesize and store relatively large amounts of starch usually have particularly high potassium needs.

Potassium is absorbed by the plant as the potassium cation K^+, and is held by the soil colloids, together with the other exchangeable cations in the soil with which it may compete for exchange positions. The proportion of potassium cations to the other cations, particularly calcium and magnesium, held by the exchange positions and in the soil solution affects the ease with which potassium is taken up by the plant, so that these three cations are often considered in relation to each other. The root hair absorbs potassium cations from the soil solution or direct from the soil colloid.

Potassium is absorbed by plants in relatively large amounts—probably second in amount only to nitrogen in many cases. Potassium in the soil is also present in quantities which are relatively large when compared with the quantities in the soil of phosphorus, for example. In the rocks of the earth's crust, potassium is about twenty times as abundant as phosphorus, so it is not surprising that there should also be more potassium than phosphorus in soils.

The main original sources of potassium in soils are the potassium-containing minerals, principally potassium felspar, and both black mica (biotite) and white mica (muscovite). These minerals are discussed briefly in Chapter 3. The potassium in these minerals has to be released by the weathering of the mineral before it is taken up by the plant. On weathering, the potassium is liberated as the K^+ ion. When released, the potassium ions are either (a) lost in the water draining through the soil, or taken up by plants or other living organisms in the soil, (b) held by the cation exchange positions of the soil colloids; or (c) converted to less available forms.

Forms of potassium in soil

The fixing of potassium in soil in forms which are not available or only slowly available to the plant is not such an important phenomenon as the fixing of phosphorus in such forms. Nevertheless it is often convenient to distinguish in a general way between that potassium in the soil which is readily available to the plant, that which is slowly available, and that which is relatively unavailable or fixed.

The distinction between these three groups is not a rigid one, and in fact there is a tendency for the potassium in the three forms either to be in equilibrium or to move towards an equilibrium. What this means in practice is that if there is plant removal of the readily available potassium, then there will be a tendency for potassium in the slowly available form to become available, i.e. to move to the available pool of potassium to restore the equilibrium. Similarly, potassium appears to move from the unavailable, or fixed form, to the slowly available and the readily available forms, as these forms are depleted by plant uptake or other causes. Thus, in a soil where the uptake by plants is heavy and there is a steady drawing on the reserves of potassium in all forms, without additions in the form of fertilizers, the general trend might be as follows:

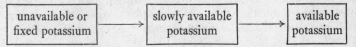

The general movement would therefore be to the right, i.e. from the less to the more available forms. If, however, large quantities of a potassium-containing fertilizer were added to the soil, in excess of that used by the crop and lost by leaching, the extra potassium in the available form would now tend to move to the left in order to maintain equilibrium between the three classes of soil potassium, i.e. some of the available potassium would be converted to slowly available forms and even perhaps to unavailable or fixed forms. The movement would therefore be the opposite of that shown above, and can be represented thus:

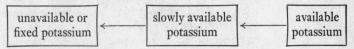

In practice, movement in soils can be in either direction depending on the extent of losses and uptake, potassium additions to the soil and other factors, and this two-way tendency for movement in a direction which will tend to restore equilibrium between the three forms is usually expressed diagrammatically by the combining of the two diagrams above to give the following:

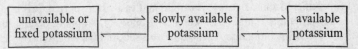

These general considerations are useful in understanding how potassium becomes available in a soil, but they do not of themselves tell us about the actual forms or combinations of potassium represented by the terms 'unavailable', 'slowly available', or 'available'.

The *available potassium* is that potassium which can be taken up immediately and easily by plants, and this is the potassium in the ionic K^+ form. The available potassium is therefore that potassium held as K^+ ions by the exchange positions of the soil, or that which is actually in the soil solution, or soluble and therefore capable of entering the soil solution. The readily available potassium is therefore the sum of the exchangeable and the soluble potassium. In practice it is very often measured or estimated by measuring the exchangeable potassium only.

If all the available potassium is removed from a soil, and the soil is left to incubate at a suitable temperature and moisture content for a period—a few weeks or months—then it is found that the available potassium is built up again. This available potassium must have come from the other forms in the soil discussed above—from the slowly available and the unavailable, thus illustrating the equilibrium movement illustrated in the first diagram. Obviously, the unavailable and slowly available forms of potassium constitute the *reserves* of potassium in the soil and even though not immediately available are of great practical importance to the farmer since, without added fertilizers, he must rely on release from the reserves to make good the available potassium taken up by his crop. What are these slowly available and unavailable forms in the soil, and how do they compare in quantity, in most West African soils, with the available potassium?

The unavailable potassium is that potassium held in the soil in the form of organic and inorganic compounds which are not soluble so that the potassium is not released until the compounds are weathered or mineralized. Normally the most important soil reserve of unavailable potassium is in the unweathered minerals—the felspars and micas. In young soils over rocks containing these minerals, rocks such as granites and mica schists, there may be a good supply of little weathered but gradually weathering felspars and micas in the root zone. In older, deeper, highly weathered soils the supply may be very much less in the upper part of the profile but may increase with depth as the weathering rock is approached. Biotite and the felspars weather relatively easily in hot, wet environments, but white mica is relatively resistant and may be found in much older and more weathered soils. Because it is light and easily transported, it is often found in alluvium. These little weathered but weatherable minerals constitute the main inorganic reserves in the soil and will obviously vary from soil to soil, depending on the nature of the parent material and the age of the soil and degree of weathering.

In addition to the inorganic potassium reserves, there are further reserves of potassium in the organic fraction of the soil which are released (together with a range of other nutrients) as the organic matter mineralizes. The amounts will again vary very much between soils, depending in this case on the vegetation, history of cultivation, and amount of organic matter, but unlike the inorganic reserves, those in the organic matter are mainly in the topsoil. In soils with very little potassium in the mineral fraction of the soil the organic potassium in the soil humus may constitute the main reserve of this element in the soil.

The slowly available potassium is that potassium which is intermediate in availability between the forms discussed above. Potassium in this form is thought to be mainly that potassium which is alternately fixed and then released, depending on conditions, by $2:1$ lattice clays in the soil, particularly illite (or hydrous mica). Clays are very similar in structure to micas, and a clay can change to a mica by absorption of K^+ ions just as micas weather to clays with the loss of these ions. In addition, illites appear to be able to fix K^+ ions, temporarily at least, in their silica sheets. This appears to be because the potassium ion is of the right size to fit in and be held in the silica sheets, a view supported by the fact that the NH_4^+ ion, which is about the same size, can also be held by illites but that calcium and magnesium ions, which are of different size, are not held or fixed in this way. Drying of the soil sometimes has the effect of releasing some of the slowly available potassium held in this manner, particularly in the case of soils low in potassium.

In West Africa this type of potassium fixation is probably generally of little importance. This is because potassium is not fixed by $1:1$ lattice clays in this way, nor is it fixed by the organic colloids in the soil. Most highly weathered West African soils are kaolinitic, and potassium fixation is thought to be negligible in these soils. A few younger soils contain a little or some illite, alluvial soils may contain a small proportion of illite, and some of the heavy black tropical clays containing montmorillonite might also fix small amounts of potassium, but in general potassium fixation is not important and for practical purposes can usually be ignored in West Africa. Temporary fixation is in any case not necessarily a disadvantage: it reduces the immediately available potassium but might hold added potassium that would otherwise be lost by leaching, and this may then be released slowly later.

Factors affecting potassium availability

In most soils the quantities of unavailable potassium are very much greater than those in the available form. Measuring the amount of *total* potassium in the soil gives an indication of reserves but does not necessarily give much idea of what is immediately available to the plant. Of the total potassium, about 90 to 98 per cent is generally in forms not available to the plant. About 1 to 10 per cent may be in the intermediate 'slowly available' forms. Only 1 to 10 per cent of the total, and often only 1 to 2 per cent, may be in the readily available forms, i.e. exchangeable or soluble.

These are general figures. In West Africa the ratios vary widely according to the nature of the parent material and the weathering stage. In young soils over potassium-rich rocks the total potassium can be 20 or even 100 or more times the exchangeable: in soils over rocks poor in potassium, e.g. many sediments, including sandstones, this ratio may drop to well below 10. In general the shallower, less weathered, savanna soils have higher total/exchangeable potassium ratios than the deeper, more weathered, and acid forest soils.

The ratio of total potassium to available potassium, while giving an indication of the reserves and perhaps of the rate at which the exchangeable might be expected to be made up from those reserves, does not of itself give an indication of the availability of potassium to the plant. The supply of potassium to the plant depends on the amount of readily available potassium and the ease with which it is taken up.

The ease with which plants actually absorb the readily available potassium in the soil is related, it appears, more to the *proportion of the soils cation exchange capacity* actually occupied by exchangeable K^+ ions than to the amount of exchangeable potassium. Thus, a stated quantity of exchangeable potassium will be relatively more available to the plant when held by a soil with a low cation exchange capacity than when held by a soil with a higher cation exchange capacity, because that quantity of exchangeable potassium occupies a greater proportion of the cation exchange capacity in the case of the first soil than it does in the second. Expressed differently, the same amount of exchangeable potassium causes a higher potassium saturation percentage in the first soil than it does in the second. If, for example, a soil has a cation exchange capacity of 10 millequivalents per 100 g, and the exchangeable potassium held is one tenth of a milliequivalent (0·1 m.e.) then the potassium saturation of that soil is 1 per cent. If the same 0·1 m.e. of exchangeable K is held by a soil with a total cation exchange capacity of only 5 m.e. per 100 g, then the potassium saturation percentage becomes 2 per cent. In the first case there would probably be a shortage of available potassium, but in the second case potassium uptake might well be satisfactory.

Some evidence suggests that a potassium saturation level of about 2 per cent or more is probably sufficient to ensure adequate potassium uptake by the plant in West Africa. With oil palm on Tertiary sands in south-eastern Nigeria it was found that potassium deficiency symptoms were shown when the potassium saturation percentage was less than 1·5 per cent, and that the percentage potassium saturation proved a better indication of the potassium nutrition of the palms than the actual amount of exchangeable potassium in the soil. On forest soils in Ghana, maize and cassava yields, after 7 years of continuous cropping, were severely reduced by potassium deficiencies when the potassium saturation percentage had fallen to 1·2 per cent. However, an elephant grass (*Pennisetum purpureum*) fallow included in the rotation, resulted in a potassium saturation percentage of 2·4 per cent and no drop in yields through potassium deficiency. This and other evidence appears to suggest that a potassium saturation level of about 2 per cent or above is normally satisfactory, but that saturation levels below this might result in potassium deficiencies.

Plants differ considerably both in their needs of potassium and in the efficiency with which they can extract it from soils low in this element. Responses to potassium are normally greater with cassava than with maize, probably because cassava, like all plants producing large quantities of starch, needs relatively large amounts of potassium, while grasses as a group appear to be relatively efficient extractors of potassium.

In West Africa in general it appears that responses to added potassium are more likely on forest soils than on savanna soils, and one of the striking facts about some of the trials made on savanna soils is that there is little or no response to potassium applications even during long periods of continuous cultivation. This might be partly because some of the savanna zone crops, such as guinea corn, maize, and millet, are grasses which are relatively good extractors of potassium and do not have particularly large potassium requirements, but it appears to be due mainly to the fact that savanna soils are generally of relatively low cation exchange capacity (this in turn being related in part to their generally low organic matter contents) so that relatively small amounts of exchangeable potassium released from the reserves are sufficient to ensure a satisfactory potassium saturation percentage and therefore a satisfactory level of potassium uptake by the plant.

Some savanna soils, being less deep and less weathered than many forest soils, have fairly high reserves of potassium-containing minerals and a high total to exchangeable potassium ratio, so that there is little difficulty in understanding why these soils can continue to release sufficient potassium during prolonged periods of cropping. Other savanna soils, however, with low or only very moderate potassium reserves—and these soils include those developed over dominantly quartz sand sediments—have low total potassium contents but still appear able to release sufficient to maintain a satisfactory potassium saturation level during long periods of cropping.

In forest soils the position is somewhat different, and here responses to potassium are generally larger and more frequent than in savanna soils. Since the cation exchange capacity of a forest soil rich in organic matter is relatively high, it requires correspondingly high amounts of exchangeable

40   (*above*) A forest farm, with cocoyam and plantain. A cocoa seedling,
      planted beneath the cocoyam and plantain for shade, can be seen in
      the left foreground. The picture shows the dense growth and irre-
      gular 'untidy' appearance of this type of land rotation cultivation.
      There are numerous weeds. However, the ground is shaded and
      protected from the force of the rain, and mixed cropping means that
      the soil is not likely to be much exposed after harvest. If the cocoa
      seedlings grow successfully there will be a smooth transition from
      the food farm to a cocoa farm. If they are not successful the farm will
      be abandoned to fallow regrowth vegetation for 6 to 10 years or more
      before being cleared and cultivated afresh.

41   (*below*) Recently cleared farm planted with hill rice (south-west
      Ivory Coast). Hill rice grows fairly well in the wetter parts of the
      West African forest zone and is frequently the first crop planted after
      clearing in the wet rain forest areas of the south-west Ivory Coast and
      Liberia. It may be followed by a crop of cassava. A few trees from the
      original forest have been left standing for shade. In the right middle
      distance are a few seedlings of the umbrella tree or parasolier
      (*Musanga cecropioides*) a common and widespread secondary forest
      species.

42   (*above*) Forb regrowth vegetation. Forbs are the soft-stemmed herbaceous weeds which spring up as soon as a cultivated forest patch is no longer weeded. This plate shows a typical tangle about 6 months old. The broad leaved herb to the left is *Solanum torvum*, in the centre is a young *Macaranga barteri* which will grow to a shrub or small tree. The broad leaved ribbed grass in the foreground is a species of *Setaria*. (See Reference 96).

43   (*below*) Forest thicket. At about 1½ to 2 years after the farm is abandoned the regrowth vegetation has usually become a thick tangled mass of shrubs, coppice shoots, climbers and small trees appropriately described as regrowth thicket. This persists for about 4 to 6 years, depending on local conditions, before becoming secondary forest. In the secondary forest stage, young, fast growing light-demanding trees are dominant, and these shade out most of the lower growth.

potassium to maintain a satisfactory potassium saturation percentage. There is not necessarily much difference in this respect between the generally more productive and less leached forest soils of the moderately wet forest areas, and the more leached and acid soils of the very wet forest areas of West Africa. This is because the cations most affected by leaching are calcium and magnesium (see Chapter 4) and the amounts of exchangeable potassium in the acid soils, though a little lower than the amounts in the less leached soils, are nevertheless not much lower. If the cation exchange capacity is also less in the acid soils (as it may well be, since organic matter levels are often slightly less and the cation exchange capacity is lower at lower pH values), then the potassium saturation percentage is not necessarily any lower in acid forest soils than it is in those which are only moderately acid or near neutral.

Responses to potassium and other added nutrients are discussed further in Chapter 9.

CALCIUM, MAGNESIUM, SOIL REACTION AND ITS EFFECTS

Calcium and magnesium

These two elements are both essential for plant growth and are absorbed as cations, but they also exert an important indirect effect on plant nutrition because the pH of the soil is determined by the extent to which the cation exchange positions on the soil colloids (see Chapter 2, pp. 34–7) are occupied by exchangeable metallic cations. The most important of these are usually calcium and magnesium, as is indicated by the average figures for Ghana Ochrosols and Oxysols given in Table 4.1. For this reason calcium, sometimes with magnesium, is often added to soils not so much to supply the calcium itself to the plant but in order to make a soil less acid and therefore improve the uptake by plants of other nutrients. This practice, known as liming, is much more common and widespread on temperate region soils than in tropical areas where relatively little is yet known about its effects. It is discussed further in relation to West African soils in a subsequent paragraph.

Calcium is an essential element for all higher plants and is found in relatively large quantities in plant leaves, but plants differ widely in the amounts of calcium they need. Deficiencies of calcium result in the terminal buds and root tips becoming stunted and failing to develop normally. Calcium is absorbed by the plant as the divalent cation Ca^{2+}. Exchangeable calcium is relatively low in the more acid soils such as are normally associated in West Africa with the particularly high rainfall forest areas. Plants such as rubber which tolerate or prefer heavy rainfalls and acid soils often have relatively low calcium requirements.

Magnesium is a constituent of every chlorophyll molecule, and therefore essential for photosynthesis; green plants cannot exist without it. Magnesium is also found in plant seeds. It appears to be connected with phosphorus metabolism in the plant, with the activation of enzymes affecting carbohydrate metabolism, and also (in association with sulphur) in the synthesis of plant oils. It is mobile in the plant, being transferred from old leaves to young ones if necessary, and deficiency symptoms, usually a chlorosis or whitening of the tissue between the veins, appear first on the older leaves. Leafy crops such as tobacco are particularly sensitive to magnesium deficiency, and deficiencies have been observed in West Africa in oil palms where they have been thought to be responsible for orange frond disease.

Both calcium and magnesium are taken up by the plant as the divalent cation, and to some extent the potassium, magnesium, calcium, and ammonium cations held by the soil colloids and present in the soil solution compete for entry into the root. The potassium and ammonium ions are taken up by the plant more readily than the calcium and magnesium. In West African soils the dominant cation is usually calcium, with magnesium second in quantity. The other cations present are usually present in relatively minor amounts. With increasing rainfall and leaching it appears that the calcium ion is the one washed out of the soil most, followed by the magnesium, so that the effects of leaching are to reduce the total amounts of both calcium and magnesium held in the exchangeable form, to alter the relative proportions of calcium and magnesium to each other, and to decrease these two relative to potassium and other cations.

Soil reaction

The acidity of soils is thought to have several sources, though soil acidity is a subject which is extremely complex and, despite much research, far from fully understood as yet. Soil acidity is thought to be connected mainly with the clay minerals and the nature of the ions attracted to them, but it is also affected by the soil humus, by hydrated oxides of aluminium and iron in the soil, by the presence of soluble salts and, in some cases, by the carbon dioxide in the soil atmosphere.

The reaction (acidity or alkalinity) of the soil broadly reflects the extent to which the cation exchange capacity of the soil colloids is occupied (or saturated) by exchangeable cations. In neutral or slightly alkaline soils most or all of the cation exchange positions are occupied by cations, usually mainly calcium and magnesium. When soils are leached, and the basic metallic cations such as calcium, magnesium, and potassium removed, then their places are taken by hydrogen ions and, in some cases, by aluminium ions (Al^{3+}). In acid soils the H^+ and the Al^{3+} ions are in equilibrium. At pH values below 5·0 much of the aluminium probably occurs as Al^{3+} ions which are attracted to the negative positions on the clays. At pH levels above 5·0 the aluminium ion combines with OH^- ions to form first $Al(OH)^{2+}$ and then $Al(OH)_2^+$ and $Al(OH_3)$, and H^+ ions are released which may or may not replace the aluminium and hydroxy-aluminium ions on the exchange complex. It is the concentration of H^+ ions in the soil solution which governs its reaction.

With increased leaching and cation removal, therefore, the soil becomes more acid and, as observed in Chapter 4, there is often a broad correlation between rainfall and soil reaction, particularly in the case of soils developed over similar parent materials.

Even in the more acid soils there may be sufficient exchangeable calcium and magnesium in the soil to satisfy the direct needs of the plant, but the indirect effects of the acid reaction may be important in reducing the availability of other nutrients.

For most nutrients, availability is at a maximum when the soil pH is between 6·0 and 7·0. In acid soils, phosphorus is likely to be locked up in relatively insoluble compounds, and phosphorus is considered most available in the pH range 6·5 to 7·5, with a marked decrease in availability below pH 6·0. Nitrogen, potassium, sulphur, calcium, and magnesium are all considered to be relatively less available below pH values of 5·5 to 6·0. Of the trace elements, molybdenum is relatively unavailable in acid soils, but an acid reaction increases the availability of iron, manganese, boron, copper, and zinc.

Liming

In temperate regions, the addition of rocks rich in calcium carbonate, such as limestone and chalk, is a widespread and long established practice which is designed to raise the pH of acid soils to less acid levels at which the availability of most nutrients is increased. Calcium may also have a beneficial physical effect on some clay soils by encouraging aggregation.

In the tropics in general, and certainly in West Africa, liming has been tried out only on a very limited scale and is not in general use. We do not yet know enough about its use, its beneficial effects, or the possible dangers of its application. Liming has sometimes increased the yields of certain crops when applied to soils with a pH below 5·0, but in other cases it has had little or no effect.

The danger in liming is always that the balance in the soil between nutrients might be upset, so giving rise to the induced deficiencies mentioned earlier. Liming may also seriously reduce the availability of trace elements with the exception of molybdenum. Many tropical plants, particularly those requiring high rainfalls, are in any case adapted to acid soils and some, including tea and pineapple, are thought to prefer them.

Much more information is required on the effects of liming in the tropics before it can be generally recommended, and it may never be as important as it is in cooler latitudes. The correction of magnesium deficiencies may be more important in some cases than the addition of calcium, and if limestone is used, the dolomitic variety—which contains magnesium carbonate as well as calcium carbonate—may be preferable for this reason. Liming materials and their use are discussed further in Chapter 9.

SULPHUR

Sulphur is an essential element particularly associated with protein synthesis, and is an ingredient of many plant proteins. It is needed for the synthesis of sulphur-containing amino acids, for the activation of certain enzymes, e.g. papain, and as a constituent of some vitamins. It is present in some plant oils, including that of the groundnut, and (together with magnesium) increases the oil content of others. Its role in the synthesis of proteins is suggested by the fact that if sulphur is a limiting factor, nitrates may accumulate in the plant tissue instead of being synthesized to proteins. Sulphur seems to be particularly needed by certain legumes, including the groundnut.

In the industrial areas of the world some sulphur is obtained from the air as the result of the burning of fuels containing sulphur, and many fertilizers also contain sulphates. For this reason sulphur needs in temperate regions did not for a long time receive the same attention and study as the needs of other nutrients. More recently, however, deficiencies of sulphur have shown an increase in these areas because of the use of both fuels and fertilizers containing less sulphur and because of generally higher yields resulting in heavier demands on the soil for essential plant nutrients.

In West Africa it appears that sulphur deficiencies are widespread in the savanna areas and are probably frequently a limiting factor for sulphur demanding crops such as groundnuts and cotton. This shortage is suggested by trials in northern Ghana, Northern Nigeria, and elsewhere which showed responses to additions of sulphur-containing fertilizers (usually single superphosphate). Low sulphur levels in the savanna areas are probably the result of very long periods of annual burning. During the burning the sulphur in the grass and other plants burnt goes up in smoke as sulphur dioxide. In the forest areas of West Africa burning is relatively infrequent and sulphur is released on the mineralization of the organic matter in the soil, which is normally present in considerably greater quantities than in savanna soils (see Table 4.2, page 123) so that forest soils with satisfactory organic matter levels are not likely to be short of this element.

Sulphur is absorbed almost entirely as the sulphate anion, SO_4^{2-}. Very small amounts of sulphur dioxide (SO_2) are absorbed by the plant through the leaves but sulphur dioxide at more than very low concentrations is toxic to plants. It has also been shown that elemental sulphur dusted on to fruit trees is absorbed by the plant. Sulphur-deficient plants are stunted and uniformly chlorotic, their general appearance often suggesting nitrogen deficiency.

TRACE ELEMENTS

All the remaining elements listed as essential—iron, manganese, zinc, copper, boron, chlorine, and molybdenum—are described as micronutrients or trace elements because they are needed by plants only in very small amounts. With the exception of iron and sometimes of manganese, they are present in soils in only very minor quantities, or traces: in some cases they may be toxic to plants if present in larger quantities.

Trace elements may limit plant growth either because (a) the amounts present in the soil are too low to satisfy even the very small requirements of the plant; (b) soil conditions (generally soil reaction) render unavailable to the plant those quantities present in the soil; or (c) they are present in sufficient quantity to be toxic.

All the micronutrients except molybdenum are more mobile and more readily available to plants in acid soils than in alkaline. The molybdate anion, which is needed by the bacteria responsible for nitrogen fixation, is more available in alkaline soils than in acid ones.

Iron is absorbed by plant roots in ionic form, either as the ferrous (Fe^{2+}) or the ferric (Fe^{3+}) ion, although the active form in plant metabolism appears to be the ferrous ion. Iron activates a number of plant enzymes and is connected with chlorophyll production. It can also be absorbed by roots as complex organic compounds known as chelates, and by plant leaves from foliar sprays. Even an iron nail driven into a tree trunk can supply iron to some species. Iron deficiency is most likely on calcareous and alkaline soils. Most West African soils contain very large quantities of iron and it is unlikely that iron deficiencies occur in acid West African soils.

Manganese is absorbed as the manganous ion Mn^{2+} and also in organic chelates. In either form it can be absorbed through the leaves as well as the roots, and foliar sprays are sometimes used to correct deficiencies. Manganese is associated with the activation of a range of plant enzymes. Manganese is toxic in large amounts, and toxicity is most likely to occur in very acid soils with a pH below 5·5. In many West African soils, particularly in some poorly drained soils, there are considerable quantities of impure manganese dioxide concretions which are bluish-black in colour and occasionally may become cemented into pan fragments or sheets. These concretions do not appear to be necessarily toxic to plants, possibly because MnO_2 is a relatively inert oxide; they sometimes occur in very productive soils.

Zinc is absorbed by plant roots as the zinc cation, Zn^{2+}, and, like iron, manganese, and copper, may also be absorbed as an organic chelate, and applied as leaf sprays. Zinc in plants is an activator of various plant enzymes. Zinc deficiencies are most likely in calcareous soils; zinc is toxic to plants if present in more than very small quantities. As in the case of the other metal trace elements, the quantities present in the plant in relation to the remaining trace element metals may be more important than the absolute amounts.

Copper is absorbed as the cupric cation, Cu^{2+}, and as organic chelates, and, as in the case of the other trace element metals considered above, may be conveniently applied as leaf sprays. Copper is concerned with the activation of plant enzymes and its proportion to the other trace element metals listed is of importance. Copper deficiency is most likely in organic soils such as peats.

Boron is absorbed by the plant root in a number of ionic forms including $B_4O_7^{2-}$, $H_2BO_3^-$, HBO_3^{2-}, or BO_3^{3-}. Its function in plants is not fully understood as yet; it is an essential element usually required in very small quantities.

Chlorine is now known to be another essential element, though bromine may partly substitute for it in the same way as sodium may partly substitute for potassium in some cases. The functions of chlorine in the plant require further investigation; it is required in small quantities and an excess has harmful effects on some crop plants, particularly tobacco and potatoes.

Molybdenum appears to be absorbed by the plant as the molybdate anion, MoO_4^{2-}, and is required by the plant in only very small quantities. Molybdenum is required by plants for nitrogen reduction and therefore for protein synthesis. A spectacular case of molybdenum deficiency in Australia was cured by adding a trace of molybdic oxide to the superphosphate fertilizer used, in the proportion of only 24 oz of molybdic oxide to 1 ton of superphosphate. Molybdenum, as stated above, is less available in acid than in alkaline soils, and since molybdenum is needed by *Rhizobium* bacteria for nitrogen fixation, molybdenum is sometimes given to legumes on acid soils.

There are a large number of other elements present in plant tissues which are thought not to be essential to the plant in the sense that the plant cannot live without them. Some of these elements nevertheless appear to fulfil useful functions or to be capable of acting as a substitute, in some cases and to some extent, for elements which are essential. *Cobalt* is not essential, as far as is known, to the plant itself but is needed by *Rhizobium* bacteria, and non-leguminous plants have sometimes responded to cobalt applications. Cobalt is an ingredient of vitamin B_{12} and is an essential element for animals. *Vanadium* has not yet been proved to be essential for higher plants, but is thought to be able to replace molybdenum to some extent in the nutrition of *Azotobacter*, and some crops have been reported as responding to vanadium applications, though its functions in the plant are not yet known. *Sodium* is an element taken up by plants (as the Na^+ cation) and a number of crops are thought to benefit from sodium applications, sometimes even when the potassium supply is adequate, but nevertheless sodium is not generally thought of as being an essential element. *Silicon* is a constituent of plants, particularly some plants such as sedges, and some investigators have shown that rice plants deprived of silicon grow less well than those supplied with this element, but silicon is not accepted as yet as an element which is essential to plant growth. *Aluminium*, *iodine*, *nickel*, and *tungsten* are other elements thought by certain investigators to fulfil some functions in plant nutrition.

Trace element deficiencies and their correction are discussed further in Chapter 9.

PART 4

SOIL EXAMINATION, MANAGEMENT, AND IMPROVEMENT

7 SURVEYING, CLASSIFYING, AND ANALYSING SOILS

SOIL SURVEYS

Aims of soil surveys

In many parts of West Africa, particularly in Ghana, the Ivory Coast, Senegal, and Nigeria, soil surveys were begun after the second world war and permanent survey teams and organizations are now engaged in soil mapping. Soil surveys are carried out in great detail in some of the more highly developed countries of the world, especially in the U.S.A. and are recognized as being of very great value to agriculture, as well as to other activities connected with the planned use of the soil such as forestry, town planning, and road building. Despite the increasing use of soil surveys, however, and the general realization of their necessity and value, there are many misconceptions about what they can and cannot do.

The fundamental aim of the soil surveyor is to examine, describe, and map the different soils which occur in the district or country surveyed. Once the characteristics, area, distribution, and agricultural value of the soils of a country are known it is possible to plan their best use. The wise use of the soil, as stated at the beginning of this book, implies using it so as to obtain a satisfactory yield or return now and, at the same time, preserving it in good condition for future generations.

The description and mapping of soils is only a beginning. It enables other work to be done on the soils and more information to be obtained by field experiments and laboratory determinations, and the knowledge obtained during a soil survey has to be interpreted in relation to our general level of knowledge of successful farming techniques in the area and on those soils. A soil survey is not an end in itself, but a valuable first step in compiling information about soils. It is thus a tool for agricultural development and improvement.

Although no two soil profiles may be exactly alike, they may be similar enough to be considered for practical purposes as the same soil. A single soil, often referred to as a *soil series*, includes similar soil profiles developed under similar soil-forming conditions, i.e. under a similar climate and vegetation, from similar parent material, under similar conditions of relief and drainage, and of similar age. The effect of these influences is reflected in the soil profile itself, so that an examination of the soil begins with an examination of the whole soil profile in the field.

For convenience, soils of a single series are usually given a name, often the name of the place, hill, or stream near to which the soil was first found and examined. Thus, a soil might be named Kumasi series, Nsukka series, or Rokupr series. This does not imply that the soil occurs only at the place after which it is named. On the contrary, the whole aim of a soil survey is to group together similar profiles wherever they occur, i.e. to correlate and compare one soil with another. Thus, if a soil from the Accra plains of Ghana, for example, is found to correlate with a similar soil from South Africa or from India, then it is likely that the agricultural crops and methods found suitable for that soil where it occurs elsewhere might also be found suitable for those areas of the soil occurring in West Africa. This is not a theoretical example, for the heavy black clays of the Accra plains are rather similar to the black so-called 'cotton soils' of South Africa, India, and elsewhere, and valuable information has been provided by careful comparison of actual soil samples from the three areas. Similarly, investigations by the Rice Research Station at Rokupr in Sierra Leone on the problems of reclaiming mangrove swamp soils for rice cultivation are likely to be of value wherever similar mangrove soils occur, both in other parts of West Africa and in the rest of the tropics.

Since the same climate and vegetation belts stretch across West Africa, often parallel to the coast, it is likely that in areas of similar geology and parent material very similar soil profiles may be found, and the experience and knowledge of a soil gained in one part of West Africa might profitably be applied to a similar soil in another part. Conversely, one should not expect a particular agricultural practice found successful on one soil to be equally suitable for quite a different soil.

A soil map, accompanied by detailed descriptions and analytical information on the chemical and physical characteristics of the soils mapped, can be of very great practical value to the agricultural research worker. It is of little value carrying out a fertilizer or other agronomic trial on a soil if nothing is known about that soil or where comparable soils occur elsewhere. When a soil survey of the whole area has already been made experiments can be deliberately sited on the more important soil series, and the information and recommendations obtained can be used where the series occurs elsewhere.

The soil survey report often contains broad recommendations for land use, recommending that some soils be used for tree crops, others for pasture, others for more intensive arable cultivation, and so on. However, methods of cultivation may change and new plants and plant varieties with differing requirements may be introduced. This means that the information which is of the most lasting value is on the chemical and physical properties of the soils themselves, information which can then be interpreted in the light of current knowledge of farming techniques and the requirements of different plants.

In some cases a soil survey is undertaken with the specific task of locating soils or a site for particular crops or a particular development scheme such as a rubber, oil palm, or coffee estate. Even in this case, a preliminary knowledge of the soils of the whole area will have to be obtained if the best site is to be chosen. More often, however, a soil surveyor is asked to map an area, not for its suitability for any one crop or scheme, but in order to assess the characteristics and map the distribution of all the soils in that area. It would be wrong to imagine that his sole aim is to find highly fertile soils on which agriculture will be easy and profitable from the start, or that he has failed if he does not find any such ideal soils; on the contrary, he is interested in all the soils, and in developing all of them in the best way according to their individual properties. An excellent soil for coconuts may be quite useless for cocoa, and one on which sugar cane gives good yields might be quite unsuited to, for example, groundnuts. Just as in nature certain plants and plant communities have adapted themselves to very different conditions of soil and climate, so in agriculture it is possible to make some sensible use of a very great range of soils.

Methods of soil survey

The methods best adopted for any particular soil survey depend in part on the nature of the area to be surveyed—whether forest or savanna, whether provided with roads or not, and so on—and in part on the aim of the survey and on the amount of time and money available.

In those forest areas of West Africa not yet much affected by clearing and cultivation, where the vegetation is still mostly little disturbed high forest and there are few roads, the soil surveyor will have to make use of footpaths, forest reserve boundaries and the like to walk along, and may have to cut traverse lines through the forest. His movement and progress will be relatively slow. Moreover, in thick forest areas he will receive relatively little help from aerial photographs.

In savanna areas conditions are different, for it is possible to see further and to gain an impression of the general relief at once, which is not easily obtained by walking in high forest. In open savanna areas movement is generally easier and it is often possible to walk and even to motor in any direction without having laboriously to cut lines through forest or forest thicket. Furthermore, air photographs of open savanna areas are of much more use to the soil surveyor than in areas where the vegetation is high and dense and where the photographs show little except the tree tops. Aerial photographs of open country can give detailed and accurate information on relief, vegetation distribution, land use, stream and river courses, and roads and footpaths. Even differences in soils can often be seen on the photographs so that, although observations on the ground are still essential, these may be needed less than in areas where air photographs are of less assistance. For all these reasons, soil surveys in savanna areas can often be made more cheaply, quickly, and accurately than in high forest.

The methods employed also depend very much on the detail required, the scale on which the soil map is to be published, and the time and personnel available. Soil surveys may range from sketchy reconnaissance surveys covering large areas in a short time to very detailed and careful surveys, generally of relatively small areas, published on a large scale. The reconnaissance survey may be published on a scale of perhaps 4 miles to the inch (1:250 000) or smaller and may show soil associations or broad groups of soils (a soil association is a naturally occurring group of associated soils, often a soil catena). A detailed soil survey, e.g. of an agricultural station or individual farm, may be made and published at a scale of several inches to the mile—perhaps 1:10 000 (about 6 in = 1 mile) or 8 in : 1 mile—and would show individual soils.

On a detailed survey, such as the survey of an agricultural station (Fig. 7.1), the soil would be examined at relatively frequent intervals, either with a soil auger, or by digging a considerable number of small inspection holes, perhaps at fixed intervals on a regular traverse grid. For gravelly soils, where the use of a soil auger is difficult, it is often convenient to dig holes with a soil chisel to a depth of 48 or 60 in, and then to take an additional sample from the bottom with a soil auger (soil chisels are similar to the flat chisels widely used in West Africa for cutting through oil palm roots: they can be made locally from pieces of car springs and fitted to a long, wooden handle). These inspection holes, often referred to as chisel holes, are widely used by the Ghana and Nigerian soil surveys in which labourers dig these holes at fixed intervals along roads, footpaths, or cut lines, and the holes are then later examined and sampled by trained soil surveyors or by field assistants. Where the soils are non-gravelly, a soil auger may be used, while many soil surveyors prefer to use a spade, particularly a long, narrow, ditching spade with which they can quickly dig a small deep inspection hole.

Once a preliminary idea of the soils is obtained, soil pits may be dug in order to examine the soils in more detail and to a greater depth, and to take samples. Soil pits can be about 3 ft×6 ft, and as deep as required: in areas of fairly shallow soils a depth of about 6 ft may be sufficient but in high rainfall areas of deep soils at least some of the pits may be dug considerably deeper to give information about the deep C horizons and the nature of the underlying rock material and how it weathers. On a detailed survey, particular attention will also be given to checking the soil boundaries, and if no detailed relief map is available, it is often useful to prepare a contour or form line map by levelling (usually with an abney level where great accuracy is not essential) and the relief map can be compared with the distribution of the soils, as in Figs 7.1 and 7.2.

On reconnaissance or preliminary surveys published at a relatively small scale, such as 1 in: 1 mile, it is possible to show only groups or associations of soils, and in this case it may be sufficient to make traverses along a network of roads, footpaths, or cut lines as available, sufficient to map the association boundaries and provide descriptions of the soils found within the associations. Such quick surveys give a preliminary idea of the soils and help in indicating the areas which may warrant more detailed investigation later. Considerable help in delineating association boundaries may be obtained from geological maps where they are available and from the relief, for often rocks or rock formations are associated with distinctive relief patterns.

In Ghana a method which has been found useful is the combination of a preliminary survey, mapping only soil associations, with some very detailed work, on a much larger scale, of small areas chosen as typical of each association. The small, detailed areas are often in the form of strips (frequently 1 mile long by ¼ mile wide) sited across the relief so as to give a sequence of soils from valley bottom to hill summit. These sample strips are mapped at the 8 in: 1 mile scale and in addition to a soil series map, there are also maps showing relief, vegetation, and current land-use. An example of such a sample strip is shown in Fig. 7.3. In other cases, detailed surveys of agricultural stations serve the same purpose of providing detailed soils information about a relatively small area selected as being typical of a larger area, the soil association, the extent of which is known though it has not been mapped in detail. This type of survey, which combines reconnaissance work with detailed studies of selected areas, is appropriately termed a 'detailed preliminary survey'. Recently the method has been used in the Ivory Coast and other territories and

44   (*above*) Farming in the savanna zone: looking west towards the Black Volta river, north-western Ghana. A typical compound house is in the centre. The fields near the settlement are cultivated relatively frequently and may benefit from the addition of household refuse and animal manure. Those further away are cultivated at longer intervals and then left to rest for several years: they do not receive additions of organic matter other than those left ocasionally by animals grazing them.

45   (*below*) Nearer view of crop mounds similar to those shown in Plate 44. The thin sandy soil, developed over pale granites, has been scraped up into cultivation mounds. These are used for maize, guinea corn and millet (often planted in that order) as well as for yams (*Dioscorea* species). Mounding gives a greater rooting depth and also minimizes the harmful effects of waterlogging and poor aeration after occasional heavy falls of rain.

UN-TREATED
to ACRE
YIELD of YAM 331 lbs
FARMER G·N·OKWOR
IDODO UDI DIV

TREATED
to ACRE
YIELD of YAM 554 lbs
INCREASE = 223
VALUE = 21/-

46   (*above left*) Giant crane digging out natural deposits of rock phosphate, north of Dakar, Senegal. High grade rock phosphates also occur, in West Africa, near Lome, in Togo. After preliminary treatment the rock phosphate is exported, mainly to Europe, to be manufactured into more concentrated and more soluble phosphatic fertilizers.

47   (*above right*) Laboratory technician subjecting a soil sample to a sieving test to assess the stability of the structural aggregates. The photograph was taken in the soil laboratories of O.R.S.T.O.M. at Adiopodoume, near Abidjan in the Ivory Coast. As yet, soil testing services in West Africa are on a very small and generally unimportant scale, and relatively little information or experience is available so far on the interpretation of soil tests for agriculture.

48   (*below*) Happy farmers in Eastern Nigeria posing for a photograph illustrating the increase of yield obtained by applying an 8–7–10 fertilizer to yams. Fertilizers are hardly used as yet by the West African peasant farmer and trials, demonstrations and extension activities (such as illustrated in this photograph) are necessary to encourage their wider use. Yams are a crop on which fertilizer applications are often relatively profitable, but with other crops yield responses have sometimes been uneconomic and discouraging. This is partly because of the relatively high cost of imported fertilizers in relation to local food prices and partly because yields are often limited by factors other than soil fertility. (Reproduced by Courtesy of Dept. of Agriculture, Eastern Nigeria.)

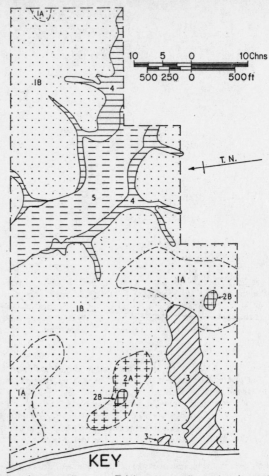

10   5   0   10 Chns
500 250 0   500 ft

T. N.

KEY

1. **Upland gravelly**
   sedentary soils

   [1A] Bekwai

   [1B] Nzima

2. **Indurated upland soils**

   [2A] Atonsu

   [2B] Nsuta

3. **Non gravelly upland soils**

   [3] Afrancho

4. **Soils developed**
   in colluvium   [4] Kokofu and Sang

Soils developed in local alluvium

   [5] Kakum and Oda

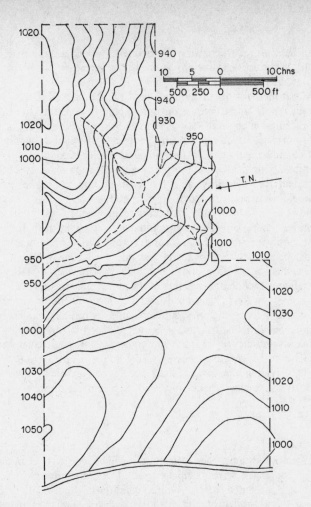

Fig. 7.1. An example of a detailed soil map showing soil series. The map is of Wamfie Cocoa Station, Ghana. The soils map (opposite) should be compared with the relief map (above).

The western end of the station (lower half of page) is a broad gentle summit area a little over 1000 ft above sea level. Most of the soils here are gravelly sedentary soils, but there are minor areas of soils over ironpan or with an indurated layer (2A and 2B) and an irregular patch of non-gravelly soils (3) developed in peneplain 'drift' material.

The eastern end of the station (upper half of figure) includes a small valley and here the distribution of soils developed in local colluvium (4) and in alluvium (5) is clearly related to relief. (From Reference 80.)

found to be a useful and relatively economical way of dealing with areas too large or too inaccessible to be worth surveying in detail in their entirety at the present time.

The exact methods of survey employed are often described within the soil survey report, and examples of these should be consulted in order to obtain information on methods as well as to form an appreciation of what kind of information such reports can be expected to contain. Some survey reports confine themselves to describing the soils encountered, others attempt in varying degrees to interpret the information obtained in terms of general advice to farmers and agronomists on how to use the soils. In more developed areas, a productivity rating might be given showing the probable crop yields to be expected on the major soils. Clearly, there is a considerable difference between a preliminary soil survey of thousands of miles of virgin forest, on the one hand, and a small agricultural station which has been cultivated for many years already on the other.

Reports may also differ considerably in the number of laboratory analyses, if any, included. A number of the more important reports which have appeared on West African soils include routine chemical determinations for the soils, sometimes supplemented by mechanical analyses. Determinations of moisture-storage capacity, structural stability, and the clay minerals present are given in a few cases. Soil analyses may not mean very much unless they are correlated with crop performances in the field, and these correlations are generally lacking. For this reason, interpretation of the analyses, particularly chemical analyses, remains difficult.

SOIL CLASSIFICATION

The soil series

Similar soil profiles form a soil series, and it will be recalled that, in theory at least, the soils of a series comprise profiles with a similar morphology which have developed under similar conditions—that is, they have developed from similar parent material, under a similar climate and vegetation, with similar relief and so on. Exactly what is meant by 'similar' may in practice, however, be partly a matter of opinion, so that different soil surveyors may rarely be in complete agreement. In practice, what is included under a single series also depends on the purpose of the survey, the amount of detail required, and the time and money available.

Soils of a single series are frequently subdivided into smaller units, such as subseries and phases. Conversely, it is also often desirable, particularly in soil classification, to group soil series together into larger units according to shared characteristics. Soil series may be grouped into families of series, and the families grouped into soil groups, and the soil groups into great soil groups, and the great soil groups into suborders and, at the highest level, into orders. Most world classifications divide soils into several orders which are subdivided in turn into suborders, great soil groups, and families.

At the other end of the scale, it is often of considerable practical importance to subdivide a single soil series into subseries and phases. A series may be divided into one or more *subseries* according to a characteristic not considered important enough to warrant separation at the series level, such as a slight variation in parent material giving a stonier subsoil than usual. A soil *phase* is another subdivision of the soil series. In English-speaking West Africa the term soil phase is very often applied to the *vegetation phase* of a soil as, for example, in the case of a high forest phase or a cultivated phase of a series. These distinctions, though at the lowest level in a system of classification, are very often of great practical importance, for the high forest phase of a soil can be expected to have more humus and be more fertile and productive than the cultivated phase. The term phase here applies to a characteristic of the series which is considered to be temporary. Given time, the cultivated phase of a soil, for example, may become the secondary forest phase. Similarly, we may talk about an eroded phase. This is also temporary if we take a long enough viewpoint for, given enough time, the soil might return to normal.

In the U.S.A. soil series are also normally subdivided into soil types according to the texture of the A horizon, so that a series might, for example, be divided into clay, clay loam, and loam types. Strictly speaking, these differences refer only to differences in texture in the topsoils, and the rest of the profile is the same in each type. In West Africa the type subdivision has been relatively little used so far, possibly because the textural range of the A horizon within a series is not great, or has not been studied in detail.

Soils which are not necessarily similar but which are associated in nature, as in a soil catena, may form a soil association, and it is frequently more practicable to map soil associations rather than the individual series they contain. A typical catena contains well drained soils on the upper slopes and summits which contrast with the genetically quite different, poorly drained soils developed in alluvium of the valley bottoms. The two types of soils may belong to different orders, and from the point of view of classification have little in common, but nevertheless they form members of a natural association which it may be convenient to map as such.

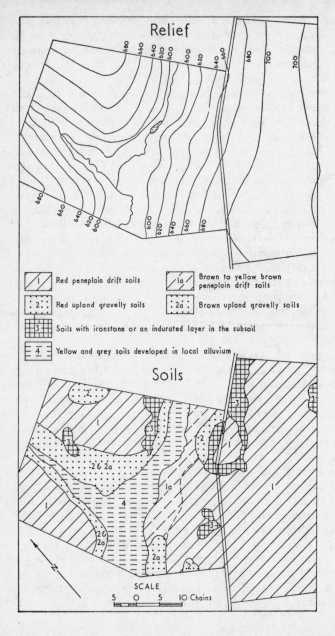

Types of classification

There are countless different ways of classifying soils. As in all classifications, the type used will depend on the *purpose* for which the soils are being classified.

A simple soil classification could be made on the basis of soil texture, separating the soils of a farm or area into clays, light clays, loams, sands, and so on. Alternatively, the same soils could be grouped and classified according to their drainage characteristics. This might divide them into well drained, moderately well drained, poorly and very poorly drained examples, and such a classification, though simple, might be of considerable practical use to a farmer or agriculturalist planning the use of the soils. Other possible classifications could be made taking into account other soil properties such as soil depth, the content of salt (sodium chloride), the fertility status as defined by the topsoil content of certain nutrients, the likelihood of the soil being subject to accelerated erosion if cultivated, or its suitability for mechanized agriculture or for any particular crop or group of crops. All these are more or less practical classifications which may prove of value, particularly on a local basis, provided that the information on which they are based is correct.

For a more fundamental, scientific type of classification into which all the world's soils can be fitted in a regular and logical way, something more is needed, and modern soil classification schemes usually place considerable emphasis on the mode of formation of the soil, i.e. on *soil genesis*, particularly on those properties of the soil profile itself which are held to reflect genesis.

If one examines soils in a relatively small area, then the most obvious differences between soils are likely to be differences due to position and relief, and to parent material. It might appear that the influence of these factors is locally dominant in soil formation, and a classification might be used based on parent material and site. In such a case, soils might be differentiated according to broad classes of parent material, to give soil associations, and within those associations the soils might be divided according to whether they were upland sedentary soils, lower-slope soils developed in colluvium, or valley-bottom soils developed in alluvium. This would provide the beginning of a classification based on genesis, and many further subdivisions could be made, but it should be noted

Fig. 7.2. Detailed soils map of Goaso Cocoa Station, Ghana. The south-eastern part of the station (right hand side of page) is covered with deep red peneplain 'drift' material. (From Reference 81.)

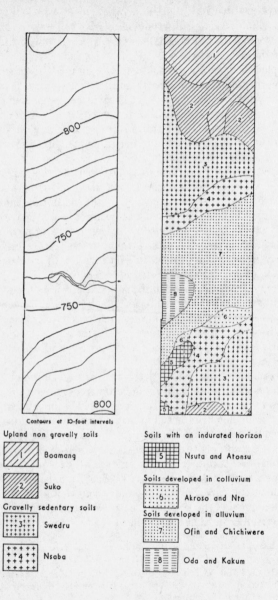

Contours at 10-foot intervals

Upland non gravelly soils

☐ 1 Boamang

☐ 2 Suko

Gravelly sedentary soils

☐ 3 Swedru

☐ 4 Nsaba

Soils with an indurated horizon

☐ 5 Nsuta and Atonsu

Soils developed in colluvium

☐ 6 Akroso and Nta

Soils developed in alluvium

☐ 7 Ofin and Chichiwere

☐ 8 Oda and Kakum

that the classification would be based on the detailed examination of soil profiles in the field and the grouping of those profiles according to characteristics thought to reflect differences in their origin.

Working in a single area in which climate and, perhaps, natural vegetation are similar throughout, it might be forgotten that many of the characteristics of the soils examined are the result of the influence of climate and vegetation. Work on a broader scale, however, will suggest that the soils of any single climate and vegetation belt tend to have certain characteristics in common, irrespective of more local differences due to differences in relief, parent rock, and soil age. These important *zonal* differences can be appreciated by comparing West African forest soils as a group with West African savanna soils. The forest soils are developed under a generally wetter climate, are more deeply weathered, and have the higher organic matter contents associated with the forest vegetation they support. Savanna soils, in contrast, are often shallower, less deeply weathered, and less leached of their soluble salts, and they have a much lower humus content because the associated vegetation is often sparse and smaller in total quantity than the forest vegetation.

If soils are being classified on a very large, broad scale, as when the soils of the whole of West Africa are being considered, it is often convenient to divide them up first into broad groups related to climate and vegetation, and then to subdivide according to more local differences.

A *zonal soil* is a soil whose characteristics reflect the environment of the zone to which it belongs. Such soils are the normal, typical, mature soils of the region. Certain soils will not fall into this general zonal grouping and can be classified as *azonal* or as *intrazonal* soils. Azonal soils are those which do not show characteristics typical of any particular zone, usually because they are too young or immature to have developed characteristics related to their environment. Such soils also include those whose parent material is so resistant that little or no development has taken place. Intrazonal soils, on the other hand, are those which, though more developed, are found in more than one zone; such soils include bog or

---

Fig. 7.3. Soils mapped on a sample strip.

The sample strip is 1 mile long and a $\frac{1}{4}$ mile wide, and is sited at right angles to the stream so as to give a representative cross section of relief and soils.

The left-hand diagram indicates relief, using form-lines at 10 ft intervals. The right-hand map shows individual soil series, as given in the key below. The strip shows forest soils developed over granite, and there is a fairly close relationship between the relief of the strip and the distribution of the soils. (From Reference 79.)

marsh soils in which profile development is dominated by the poor local drainage conditions rather than by other aspects of the environment.

GENERAL CLASSIFICATIONS OF WEST AFRICAN SOILS

The various political divisions of West Africa fall into two main groups, the French- and the English-speaking. The broad systems of soil classification in use in each group differ in their details, but both are based on soil genesis and both result in classifications which reflect to a considerable degree the influence of climate, particularly of rainfall. There is, however, often a fairly gradual transition between soils of the wettest and soils of the driest areas. Soil classification is often made more difficult by these transitions.

The Ghana system of classification

In Ghana and parts of Nigeria a system of classification originally worked out by H. Vine and C. F. Charter and outlined by the latter has proved useful. This classification begins by dividing soils into three main orders corresponding to the three broad groups of (1) normal, well developed, well drained upland soils whose characteristics reflect the local climate and vegetation; (2) low-lying and depression soils, including gley soils, affected for at least part of the year by high water tables; and (3) soils which are pedologically young—young in a few cases because they have been formed relatively recently but usually 'young' in the sense that they have not developed very much. This lack of development may be due to a resistant or inert parent material (such as quartz sand) or to the fact that the slope is so steep that the profile remains shallow and immature, as in a lithosol. Charter pointed out that in each of these groups one or two of the soil-forming factors could be considered dominant, and he named the three orders after the dominant soil-forming factors, as follows:

(1) *Climatophytic earths*, whose formation is dominated by climate and vegetation: these include most well drained, mature West African soils.

(2) *Topohydric earths*, whose formation is dominated by relief and water (drainage). These are the low-lying and depression soils affected by gleying and reducing conditions.

(3) *Lithochronic earths*, whose formation is dominated by parent material and time. These include the young soils referred to above—soils in very recent deposits, soils with resistant parent materials, and immature soils of steep slopes.

It will be observed that these three orders of Charter are little more than the zonal, intrazonal, and azonal soils of the early American classifications. The subdivisions of most interest in this system are the subdivisions of the first order, the Climatophytic earths. Most well drained, West African agricultural soils fall within this order, which is divided as follows:

Order	Great soil group family	Great soil groups
Climatophytic earths	Latosol	Savanna ochrosol
		Forest ochrosol
		Forest oxysol
	Basisol	Forest and savanna Rubrisols and Brunosols

The two main subdivisions of the climatophytic earths are the Latosols and Basisols. The underlying concept here is the relationship between the supply and the removal of bases from the soil, i.e. the relationship between the rate at which the parent rock supplies metallic cations such as calcium, magnesium, and potassium to the soil and the rate at which these are removed from the soil by leaching. The amount actually in the soil in exchangeable form is held to reflect this balance between supply from the parent rock and removal by percolating soil water.

With rocks and parent materials which are broadly similar, differences in this balance between supply and removal are largely due to differences in rainfall. There is thus a progressive transition from the highly leached and acid soils of the very wet areas, from which soluble nutrients and exchangeable bases may be removed relatively rapidly, first to the slightly leached soils of the areas of more moderate rainfall where through-leaching is less frequent and intense, and then to the non-leached soils of the drier, mostly savanna, areas where soluble salts may even be brought to the surface by rising soil moisture and form an accumulation there.

In practice, however, rocks and parent materials may not be the same and may not have the same base-supplying capacities over large areas, so that the broad transition described above, related to rainfall differences, is modified here and there by particularly poor or particularly rich rocks, especially by the latter. The soils over the particularly base-rich rocks usually differ considerably from those associated with the poorer and more acid rocks. These soils whose profile development is influenced by a base-rich parent rock are the Basisols of Charter's classification.

The *Basisols* usually have a near-neutral to slightly alkaline reaction in

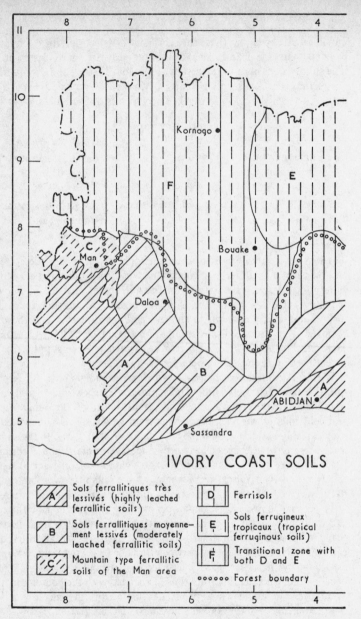

Fig. 7.4. Soil maps of the Ivory Coast and Ghana.

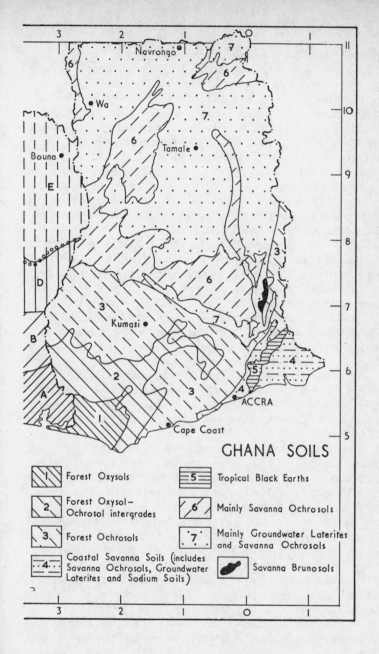

GHANA SOILS

1 Forest Oxysols	**5** Tropical Black Earths
2 Forest Oxysol–Ochrosol intergrades	**6** Mainly Savanna Ochrosols
3 Forest Ochrosols	**7** Mainly Groundwater Laterites and Savanna Ochrosols
4 Coastal Savanna Soils (includes Savanna Ochrosols, Groundwater Laterites and Sodium Soils)	Savanna Brunosols

both the topsoil and the subsoil because of the good supply of basic cations, particularly calcium and magnesium, from the parent rock, which is often a hornblende-rich rock such as hornblende gneiss. The clay fraction often includes some montmorillonite in addition to kaolin. The cation exchange capacity of the mineral soil is therefore higher than that of a typical Latosol. Soil structure may be better developed than in a Latosol, with blocky subsoils, and chemically these soils are relatively fertile. Unfortunately, in most of West Africa the rocks over which they are formed are scattered, and occur only in small patches amid less rich rocks. The Basisols are subdivided according to the vegetation (forest or savanna) and according to whether the dominant colour is red (the Rubrisols) or dull brown (Brunosols): the latter colour may be due to manganese staining, and does not necessarily reflect drainage.

The *Latosols* are far more extensive than the Basisols and are the typical, zonal soils of West Africa, developed over a range of parent rocks and parent materials of low to moderate base-supplying powers and under a range of rainfall conditions. In many cases, however, their development appears to have been influenced by the climates of the past as well as that of today. They are commonly more weathered than Basisols, and kaolin is the dominant clay mineral, usually associated with hydrous oxides of iron and aluminium and finely ground quartz, though some montmorillonite and illite may be present in the clay fraction and the less weathered Latosols contain some weatherable minerals in the silt and sand fractions. Structure in the subsoil is often poorly developed. In the wetter areas the profiles are often very deep. Both deep and shallow latosols may contain strongly mottled, iron-rich horizons, often partly indurated, or layers of hard ironstone.

It can be seen from the above that the Latosols are a very broad group of soils. Charter divided them according to the associated vegetation and the extent of leaching they had undergone. In practice, he found it convenient to make divisions reflecting the extent of leaching by measuring the reaction (pH) of the topsoil, as follows:

Ochrosols (ochre = reddish-yellow) are the generally bright-coloured latosols of the areas of more moderate rainfall, both forest and savanna. Leaching is slight to only moderate. This is reflected in the reaction of the upper topsoil, which is acid to neutral, i.e. pH 5·5 to 7·0 or above. The Savanna Ochrosols are distinguished from the Forest Ochrosols.

Oxysols (oxy = acid) are the more severely leached soils. They are generally associated with the higher rainfall areas. They are less red in colour than the Ochrosols, often being orange-brown, yellowish brown, or brownish yellow in the subsoil, and have very acid to extremely acid

TABLE 7.1. Analytical data for forest soils from Ghana and the Ivory Coast. The Ghana forest soils are classified as a *Forest Ochrosol* (above) and a *Forest Oxysol* (centre). The soil from the Ivory Coast is from the very wet south-west and is classified according to the French system as a *Sol Ferrallitique Fortement Désaturé* (strongly desaturated ferrallitic soil).

The Ochrosol is developed under 55 to 60 in of rain and has a topsoil pH of 6·4, in contrast to the very acid topsoils of the other two soils developed under heavier rainfalls. Total exchangeable bases in the subsoils of the Oxysol and of the Sol Ferrallitique are less than 1 m.e. per 100 g.

(a) SOIL / (b) LOCATION / (c) RAINFALL / (d) PARENT MATERIAL	1 LOWER DEPTH OF HORIZON (in)	2 pH	3 % FINE EARTH	4 % CLAY	5 % C	6 % N	7 C/N	8 % OM	9 EXCHANGEABLE BASES (m.e. PER 100 g) Ca	10 Mg	11 K	12 TOTAL	13 CATION EXCHANGE CAPACITY	14 % SATURATION
(a) Forest Ochrosol (Bekwai series)	2	6·4	100	36	6·11	0·454	13·5	10·51	23·74	7·87	0·30	32·93	43·13	76
(b) Kumasi, Ghana	11	5·1	94	40	1·28	0·137	9·3	2·20	1·63	1·24	0·10	3·17	16·00	20
(c) 55–60 in	21	5·0	42	46	0·71	0·085	8·3	1·22	0·50	0·30	0·07	1·08	13·20	8
(d) Phyllite	33	5·1	31	46	0·40	0·061	6·6	0·69	0·46	0·24	0·07	1·01	10·95	9
	46	4·9	79	44	0·31	0·069	4·5	0·53	0·32	0·33	0·03	0·85	9·99	9
(a) Forest Oxysol (Boi series)	3	4·7	95	22	2·47	0·189	13·1	4·25	1·70	0·79	0·22	2·46	12·60	20
(b) South-west Ghana	7	4·8	95	28	0·82	0·081	10·1	1·41	0·30	0·44	0·07	1·09	7·31	15
(c) 75 in	16	5·0	52	42	0·67	0·070	9·6	1·15	0·31	0·35	0·02	0·96	7·83	12
(d) Phyllite	27	4·9	93	53	0·52	0·059	8·8	0·89	0·26	0·31	0·04	0·78	8·42	9
	42	4·9	98	55	0·42	0·051	8·2	0·72	0·25	0·30	0·04	0·72	8·47	9
(a) Sol Ferrallitique Fortement Désaturé (Daobli series)	2	5·6	100	14	2·4	0·18	13	4·2	5·6	1·4	0·24	7·2	8·9	80
(b) South-west Ivory Coast	8	4·9	78	16	0·9	0·08	11	1·5	0·7	0·1	0·05	0·8	5·1	15
(c) 96 in	16	4·8	76	23	0·5	0·04	13	0·9	0·5	0·1	0·03	0·6	3·2	19
(d) Gneiss	26	5·0	70	42	0·6	..	..	1·0	0·8	0·1	0·03	0·9	5·6	16
	42	4·9	64	51	0·5	..	..	0·9	0·5	0·1	0·05	0·6	6·2	10
	53	5·1	88	51	0·2	..	..	0·4	0·3	0·1	0·03	0·4	6·4	6
	74	5·2	87	42	0·2	0·01	20	0·3	0·2	0·1	0·05	0·3	5·9	5
	96	5·2	84	51	0·2	..	..	0·3	0·1	0·1	0·03	0·2	4·6	4

upper topsoils (below pH 5·5, and often in the range 4·0 to 5·0). They are particularly associated with the very wet forest areas where annual rainfalls are above about 70 in and where the vegetation is usually evergreen forest, as opposed to the semideciduous forest normally associated with Ochrosols.

The system as briefly outlined above has proved of some practical value and there is a very broad correlation between these great soil groups and climate, natural vegetation, and agricultural possibilities. As it stands, however, the system requires further subdivisions. Its disadvantages include the fact that classification is based very much on the topsoil, which is easily lost or modified during cultivation: for this reason more emphasis on the subsoil characteristics might be desirable.

The French classification system

The French system is comparable to the Ghana system of soil classification inasmuch as soils are divided into broad groups based on the extent of weathering and of leaching of the soil, and these groups are broadly related to climate and vegetation belts. The actual criteria used are, however, somewhat different.

In addition to considering the removal of bases and the reaction of the soil, the French classification takes into account the extent to which soil weathering has removed the combined silica in the soil. It will be recalled (see p. 85) that under extreme weathering conditions the silica is removed more than the alumina, and that the ratio between silica and alumina in the clay fraction of the soil can be used as an index of weathering. The French have emphasized this ratio and the extent to which primary silicate minerals have been changed to kaolin and hydroxides of iron and aluminium. This process they refer to as 'ferrallitization' and the most weathered soils, normally found in the wettest areas, are referred to as ferrallitic soils for this reason. Account is also taken of 'ferruginization' (the liberation, movement, and accumulation of iron in soils), leaching, gleying, and mottling effects due to reducing conditions associated with waterlogging, the nature of the clay minerals and clay distribution in the profile, podsolization (bleaching of the lower topsoil because of decomposition and movement downwards of clay-humus complexes and the accumulation of these materials lower down in the profile), the silt/clay ratio and the C/N ratio of the humus fraction. Other classification criteria are indicated in the notes which follow.

The French classification system is associated with the work of G. Aubert and others and embraces all the world's soils, which are divided into ten classes. The class of most importance in West Africa is Class VIII,

TABLE 7.2. Analytical data for savanna soils from Northern Nigeria and northern Ghana.

The soils from Northern Nigeria are classified in the CCTA system as ferruginous tropical soils. They are developed over sandstone under rainfalls of 38 and 32 ins with a long and severe dry season (6 months or more with less than 1 in). The soil from north-east Ghana is classified according to C. F. Charter's system as a Savanna Ochrosol. It is developed over granite and has a higher clay content than the Nigerian soils developed over sandstone.

All three soils have topsoils which are slightly acid to near neutral, and organic matter levels which, though fairly low, do not fall off as rapidly below the topsoil as is normal in the case of forest soils (see Chapter 4, Table 4.2). The cation exchange capacity figures (column 13) should be compared with the clay contents (column 4).

(a) SOIL LOCATION / (b) RAINFALL / (c) / (d) PARENT MATERIAL	1 LOWER DEPTH OF HORIZON (in)	2 pH	3 % FINE EARTH	4 % CLAY	5 % C	6 % N	7 C/N	8 % OM	EXCHANGEABLE BASES (m.e. per 100 g) 9 Ca	10 Mg	11 K	12 TOTAL	13 CATION EXCHANGE CAPACITY	14 % SATURATION
(a) Ferruginous tropical soil (Busari series) (b) Northern Nigeria (c) 38 in (6 months less than 1 in) (d) Sandstone	4	6.9	94	4	0.63	0.041	15	1.08	3.7	1.9	0.24	5.9	5.6	100
	9	7.0	96	8	0.37	0.026	14	0.64	3.2	1.6	0.20	5.0	5.7	88
	16	6.6	98	6	0.27	0.021	13	0.46	2.4	1.0	0.16	3.6	3.7	97
	23	6.6	90	14	0.24	0.019	13	0.41	2.7	1.2	0.19	4.1	7.5	55
	33	6.7	89	26	0.22	0.022	10	0.38	4.0	1.7	0.28	6.0	10.0	60
	51	6.8	89	22	0.16	0.016	10	0.28	3.6	1.9	0.50	6.0	13.0	46
	74	6.8	86	22	0.16	0.012	13	0.28	2.8	3.0	0.62	6.5	7.7	84
	96	6.6	86	22	0.13	0.012	11	0.22	2.9	1.5	0.62	5.1	7.7	66
(a) Ferruginous tropical soil (Garintor series) (b) Northern Nigeria (c) 32 in (6–7 months less than 1 in) (d) Sandstone	2	6.4	96	0	0.57	0.057	10	0.98		2.91	0.14	3.5	5.3	66
	6	6.2	98	0	0.24	0.024	10	0.41	1.2	0.7	0.06	2.0	3.2	63
	9	6.2	96	0	0.06	0.008	7.5	0.10	0.54	0.38	0.04	0.96	1.6	60
	21	5.7	98	18	0.20	0.021	9.5	0.34	2.2	0.88	0.08	3.2	7.4	43
	44	5.5	68	26	0.14	0.020	7	0.24	2.5	1.4	0.04		13.0	31
	55	5.5	80	26	0.11	0.018	6	0.19	3.4	1.6	0.15	5.3	12.0	44
	55+	5.8	94	6	0.04	0.004	10	0.07	1.3	1.2	0.07	2.6	3.7	70
(a) Savanna Ochrosol (Mimi series) (b) North-east Ghana (c) 45 in (d) Granite	5	6.1	100	9	0.80	0.046	17.2	1.38	2.10	0.92	0.14	3.57	7.39	48
	11	5.4	99	19	0.68	0.043	15.8	1.17	0.92	0.39	0.05	1.65	8.15	20
	19	5.3	100	41	0.58	0.047	12.3	1.00	0.91	0.38	0.07	1.70	11.30	15
	30	5.9	100	39	0.34	0.036	9.4	0.58	0.79	0.40	0.07	1.70	9.96	17
	41	5.9	87	32	0.23	0.027	8.5	0.40	0.62	0.50	0.07	1.77	7.97	22
	50	4.9	99	12	0.10	0.012	8.3	0.17	0.21	0.25	0.03	0.75	3.33	23

comprising soils rich in sesquioxides and hydrated oxides, though soils belonging to some of the other classes are also represented in West Africa to a lesser extent, including soils of Class I—raw mineral soils, Class II—weakly developed soils, Class III—Vertisols, Class IX—halomorphic (saline) soils, and Class X—hydromorphic soils.

The soils rich in sesquioxides and hydrated oxides of Class VIII are divided into three sub-classes which are in turn divided into two to four groups each, and several sub-groups, as shown in Table 7.3.

The important sub-classes in West Africa are the Sols Ferrugineux Tropicaux (tropical ferruginous soils—also sometimes called fersiallitic soils) of the less wet areas, and the more completely weathered Sols Ferrallitiques of the high rainfall areas.

The *Sols Ferrugineux Tropicaux* are associated mainly with the savanna areas of West Africa. They are rich in iron (and sometimes manganese) oxides, but have no free aluminium. The clay fraction is mainly kaolin mixed with illite and hydrous oxides. The silt content can be quite high and the base saturation is at least 40 per cent. The tropical ferruginous soils are subdivided first into two groups: the non-leached and the leached. The non-leached tropical ferruginous soils are themselves divided into subgroups comprising young soils, soils with some migration of iron oxides and soils in which the iron oxide is stable. The leached tropical ferruginous soils are subdivided into four subgroups: soils without concretions, concretionary soils, indurated soils (with an ironstone crust or hardened horizon within the profile), and mottled hydromorphic soils with the pseudogley type of mottles—i.e. upland soils not fully gleyed but subject to periodic reducing conditions giving rise to characteristic mottling in part of the profile.

The *Sols Ferrallitiques*, or ferrallitic soils, are soils associated with heavier rainfalls than the Sols Ferrugineux, and usually with forest vegetation. The greater rainfall is reflected in deeper, more thorough weathering. These soils are often very deep and are characterized by a quicker and more complete transformation of the organic matter, a more marked decomposition of the mineral soil fraction and greater removal of decomposition products such as soluble salts, exchangeable bases, and silica. They are low in silt, and the cation exchange capacity is very unsaturated (less than 40 per cent, and often much less). The cation exchange capacity of the mineral soil is in general low, being defined as less than 20 m.e. per 100 g of clay, thus reflecting the fact that it is composed fundamentally of kaolin and sesquioxides. The Sols Ferrallitiques contain free aluminium, either amorphous or crystallized, and the silica/alumina ratio (SiO_2/Al_2O_3) is equal to, or less than 2. The free sesquioxides are

TABLE 7.3. The French soil classification system: major subdivisions of Class VIII, soils rich in sesquioxides and hydrated oxides.

CLASS	SUB-CLASSES	GROUPS	SUB-GROUPS
VIII Soils rich in sesquioxides and hydrated oxides	(1) Red and brown Mediterranean soils	A Sols Rouges Méditerranéens (Mediterranean red soils) B Sols Méditerranéens Lessivés (leached Mediterranean soils) C Sols Bruns Méditerranéens (Mediterranean brown soils)	(Not of importance in West Africa)
	(2) Sols Ferrugineux Tropicaux (Ferruginous tropical soils)	A Sols Ferrugineux Tropicaux non Lessivés (Non-leached ferruginous tropical soils) B Sols Ferrugineux Tropicaux Lessivés (Leached ferruginous tropical soils)	Divided into young (slightly ferruginous) soils and according to whether the iron oxides are stable or somewhat mobile. Divided into subgroups which are (i) without concretions; (ii) with concretions; (iii) indurated; and (iv) hydromorphic (mottled).
	(3) Sols ferrallitiques (Ferrallitic soils)	A Sols Faiblement Ferrallitiques (Weakly ferrallitic soils) B Sols Ferrallitiques Typiques (Ferrallitic soils) C Sols Ferrallitiques Lessivés (Leached ferrallitic soils) D Sols Ferrallitiques Humifères (Humous ferrallitic soils)	(i) Modal, (ii) ferrisolic (appreciable weatherable minerals); (iii) hydromorphic; (iv) indurated. (i) red; (ii) yellow or pale yellow-brown; (iii) yellow with red below; (iv) indurated. (i) leached of bases; (ii) leached of bases and clays; (iii) podsolized; (iv) indurated. (i) very acid and very low silica/alumina ratio; (ii) very humic; (iii) moderately leached; (iv) humous soils of high altitudes.

to a considerable degree closely linked to the surfaces of the clay minerals. The structural stability of these soils is often high due to aggregation of the clay fraction.

The Sols Ferrallitiques sub-class is subdivided into four groups, each further subdivided into a number of sub-groups, as indicated in Table 7.3. The Sols Faiblement Ferrallitiques (weakly ferrallitic soils) include an important subgroup described as 'ferrisolic'. The ferrisols are soils which only just fall in the Sols Ferrallitiques sub-class, since they are associated with both the savanna and the less wet forest areas (generally the forest savanna fringes) and are less deep and less weathered than the other Sols Ferrallitiques. They contain a proportion of weatherable minerals, though the nature of the clay fraction and the presence of gibbsite (crystalline Al_2O_3) puts them within the Sols Ferrallitiques sub-class.

The other important groups within the Sols Ferrallitiques sub-class are the Sols Ferrallitiques Typiques (typical, or modal, ferrallitic soils) and the Sols Ferrallitiques Lessivés, the leached ferrallitic soils. The latter are the most leached, weathered, and acid of West African soils and correspond more or less to the Oxysols of the British system. These show not only leaching of bases but translocation of clay, and some show podsolization of the lower A horizon. They are often indurated in the lower part of the profile. These characteristics serve to distinguish the sub-groups shown in Table 7.3. Very humous ferrallitic soils, with over 7 to 8 per cent organic matter in the top 20 cm (8 in) are associated with calcium-rich rocks and form the fourth group. The soils of this group are relatively very inextensive in West Africa.

More recently the typical and the highly leached ferrallitic soils have been renamed Sols Ferrallitiques Moyennement Désaturés (moderately desaturated ferrallitic soils) and Sols Ferrallitiques Fortement Désaturés (very desaturated ferrallitic soils). The former are characterized by a total exchangeable base content of between 1 and 3 m.e. per 100 g, a saturation in the subsoil of 20 to 40 per cent and a subsoil pH of 4·5 to 6·0. The Sols Ferrallitiques Fortement Désaturés are characterized by a total exchangeable base content of less than 1 m.e. per 100 g, a saturation of less than 20 per cent, subsoil pH values which are below 5·5, and topsoil pH values which are lower than those of the subsoil.

The relationships of these soils to climate can be appreciated from the soils map of the Ivory Coast shown in Fig. 7.4. This map was published in 1960 and is little earlier than the form of the French classification discussed immediately above, which represents a slightly modified classification concept published in 1965 in which the Ferrisols have been incorporated within the Sols Ferrallitiques. Nevertheless the main classification concepts show little change within the period and the map, which should be compared with the soils map of Ghana, indicates clearly the broad zonal distribution of soils in relation to climate and vegetation belts. The Sols Ferrugineux Tropicaux within the Ivory Coast are mostly the leached and concretionary tropical ferruginous soils and are found in the north-east of the Ivory Coast where the rainfall is less than 1100 mm (about 44 in). The remaining savanna areas of the Ivory Coast are mapped as being transitional areas where the Sols Ferrugineux are found mixed with Ferrisols. Ferrisols are dominant in the northern fringe areas of the forest zone where the annual rainfall averages 1300 to 1700 mm (about 52 to 68 in). The main part of the forest zone is mapped as Sols Ferrallitiques, both the moderately leached ferrallitic soils (rainfalls up to about 1700 mm or 68 in) and the highly leached ferrallitic soils found in the south-east and south-west corners of the country where average rainfalls range from 1700 to about 2400 mm (about 68 to 96 in).

The CCTA classification and soil map of Africa

The CCTA (Commission for Technical Co-operation in Africa) soil map of Africa was published on a scale of 1:5 000 000 in 1964. It represented about 10 years of work on the co-ordination of the results of regional soil surveys in Africa and attempted to bring together the various classifications used in Africa into a single classification adapted to African conditions. This classification, of very considerable interest to students of West African soils, is outlined in the following paragraphs. Figure 7.5 represents a small part of the CCTA soil map sheet of West Africa, slightly simplified and reduced to half the original scale. A much simplified soil map of West Africa mainly adapted from the CCTA soil map is printed on the rear endpaper.

The CCTA soil map has a mapping legend with 62 separate mapping units, but these are often combined into associations of two or more units. The 62 mapping units fall into the following twelve main groups:

1. Raw mineral soils   (*a*) Rock and rock debris
                               (*b*) Desert detritus
2. Weakly developed soils (*a*) Lithosols
                               (*b*) Sub-desert soils
                               (*c*) On loose sediments
                               (*d*) Young soils on recent deposits
3. Calcimorphic soils (*a*) Calcimorphic soils
                               (*b*) Vertisols
4. Podsolic soils
5. Brown and reddish-brown soils of arid and semi-arid regions
                                      (*a*) Of tropical regions
                                      (*b*) Of Mediterranean regions

6. Eutrophic brown soils of tropical regions
7. Red and brown mediterranean soils (*a*) Red
                                       (*b*) Brown
8. Ferruginous tropical soils
9. Ferrisols
10. Ferrallitic soils
11. Halomorphic (saline) soils
12. Hydromorphic soils

Of these, the most important groups in West Africa are groups 1, 2, 8, 9, 10, and 12. Much of the Saharan areas are mapped as group 1, desert detritus. These desert soils merge southwards into semi-arid area soils of group 5, but most of West Africa south of the latitude of Dakar is mapped as four main units, i.e. weakly developed soils (mainly ferruginous crusts and often mixed with ferruginous tropical soils), and broad belts, from north to south, of mainly ferruginous tropical soils, ferrisols, and, in the wettest areas, ferrallitic soils. These soils are associated with hydromorphic soils in the low-lying areas, and hydromorphic soils, usually developed in river alluvium, are mapped separately along the major rivers.

The following paragraphs give further information on the soils and mapping units of importance in West Africa.

The raw mineral soils are subdivided as follows:

Rock and rock debris
 Aa Rocks rich in ferromagnesian minerals
 Ab Ferruginous crusts (ironstone)
 Ac Non-differentiated rocks and rock debris
Desert detritus
 An Sands
 Ao Clay plains
 Ap Desert pavements (regs)
 Ar Non-differentiated desert detritus

These soils are hardly soils at all, for soil-forming processes in the desert climate have hardly begun, and the areas mapped consist of areas of little-altered rocks and rock debris, including ironstone crusts, sands, and clay sediments.

The weakly developed soils have little horizon differentiation. Their lack of development may be due to a number of different reasons. They may be little developed because of inert parent material, such as quartz sand, or because the very dry climate does not favour weathering. The profile might be immature because of very steep slopes and the rapid removal of soil material, in which case the soils are lithosols (see p. 70). Finally, they may be immature simply because they are developed in extremely recent deposits, but these cases are relatively uncommon. The CCTA map shows the following units:

Lithosols
  Ba   On lava
  Bb   On ferromagnesian rocks
  Bc   On ferruginous crusts (ironstone crusts)
  Bd   Non-differentiated lithosols
Sub-desert soils
  Bf   Non-differentiated sub-desert soils
Weakly developed soils
  Bh   On loose, non-recent sediments
Young soils developed in recent deposits
  Bo   River and lake alluvium
  Bp   Mangrove soils
  Bq   Wind-borne sands

Of the above, unit Bc, areas of soils on ferruginous crusts, is relatively widespread in West Africa, often associated with better developed soils such as the ferruginous tropical soils. Many of the crusts are considered to be old ones formed a long time ago, perhaps under different climatic conditions from the present, but some of them are contemporary ones forming now. Some of the crustal material is loose, some of it is in sheets; some crusts are forming now, others are being broken up. Another important and widespread mapping unit is Bo, the soils developed in alluvium, and these are often mapped as BoNa to indicate that they are associated with hydromorphic soils. The mangrove soils, Bp, form a fringe along some coastal areas.

The calcimorphic soils (soils whose characteristics are affected by the presence of calcium) include mapping unit D, the *vertisols*. The vertisols are the heavy, black, tropical clays associated with calcium-rich parent rocks and a relatively dry, savanna climate. They are found in West Africa in the Accra plains, near Lake Chad and near Dakar. They are characterized by a very heavy texture, and a dominantly montmorillonite clay fraction, and usually contain free calcium carbonate which forms concretions in the soil profile. They crack on drying, and are difficult to work because of their stickiness when wet and hardness when dry.

The brown and reddish-brown soils of arid and semi-arid regions are represented in West Africa mainly by a belt of mapping unit Ca, brown soils on loose sediments. These soils occur immediately to the south of the sub-desert soils where rainfall is generally less than about 20 in a year. These soils are sometimes formed from wind-borne deposits. They are little developed or weathered, being generally near neutral in reaction, and may contain weatherable minerals and have dominantly 2:1 lattice clays. Organic matter levels are very low because of the sparse vegetation. Unless irrigated, these soils are used mainly only for extensive grazing.

The eutrophic brown soils of the tropics—mapping unit Ha—are very inextensive in West Africa. These are formed in moderately dry to moderately wet areas (about 30 to 70 in per year) on parent materials which are relatively rich, including volcanic ash. They are young soils which often contain considerable reserves of weatherable minerals, and have dominantly 2:1 lattice clays. They are usually fertile and productive soils.

The ferruginous tropical soils correspond more or less to the Sols Ferrugineux Tropicaux of the French system discussed above, except that in the CCTA classification they have been separated not into leached and non-leached groups, but according to parent material. In West Africa the dominant parent rocks are the acid crystalline rocks (granites), schists, and phyllites of the basement complex (see Chapter 3). The mapping units are as follows:

> Ferruginous tropical soils
> Ja   On sandy parent materials
> Jb   On rocks rich in ferromagnesian minerals
> Jc   On crystalline acid rocks
> Jd   Non-differentiated, ferruginous tropical soils.

These soils are less weathered and less deep than the ferrisols and ferrallitic soils of the next mapping units, and often have appreciable reserves of weatherable minerals. The clay mineral is dominantly kaolin but often includes some 2:1 lattice clays: the cation exchange capacity and the silt content tend to be higher than those of comparable ferrallitic soils, and the base saturation percentage is also higher. These soils owe their name to the frequent marked separation and individualization of iron oxides, often present as reddish iron-rich mottles, or as concretions, or as partly indurated, iron-rich horizons. These are the dominant soils of the West African savanna areas.

The ferrisols of the CCTA classification are soils kept relatively young by surface erosion, so that the profile is less deep and the soil often somewhat richer than more mature and fully developed associated soils over comparable parent materials. Ferrisols have a better structure, higher content of exchangeable bases and greater fertility than associated ferrallitic soils. They correspond more or less to the Forest Ochrosols of the system of C. F. Charter (p. 206), soils which include many of the better West African cocoa soils. The CCTA mapping units are as follows:

Ferrisols
   Ka   Humic (at high altitudes)
   Kb   On rocks rich in ferromagnesian minerals
   Kc   Non-differentiated ferrisols

The ferrallitic soils of the CCTA classification appear to correspond to most of the Sols Ferrallitiques (except the ferrisolic ones) of the French system and to the Oxysols of the English (see pp. 206 and 210 above) and form one of the most extensive groups of African soils. These are the highly weathered soils of the wet areas of West Africa characterized by advanced leaching and weathering. The profile characteristics associated with this advanced leaching and weathering include a dominance of 1:1 lattice type clays (kaolin), low cation exchange capacities of the mineral soil, little or no reserves of weatherable minerals, a low percentage saturation and low pH values, and low silica/alumina ratios (generally below 2). The silt content tends to be lower than in less weathered soils over comparable parent materials, and the structure of the subsoil is generally rather weak, though the aggregation of the clay fraction, often to silt-size particles, generally gives these soils a good structural stability and makes them porous.

The CCTA classification of these widespread soils divides them mainly according to colour, as follows:

Ferrallitic soils
   (*a*) Dominantly yellowish-brown
      La On loose, sandy sediments
      Lb On more or less clayey sediments
      Lc Non-differentiated
   (*b*) Dominantly red
      Ll On loose, sandy sediments
      Lm On rocks rich in ferromagnesian minerals
      Ln Non-differentiated
   (*c*) Humic
      Ls Non-differentiated, humic ferrallitic soils
   (*d*) Yellow and red
      Lx Non-differentiated, on various parent materials.

Hydromorphic and halomorphic (saline) soils form only very small mapping units on the West African map, but hydromorphic soils are normally present to a minor extent along streams and rivers within the areas mapped according to the dominant upland soils; it is only occasionally that these soils are extensive enough to be shown as separate mapping units. Most of the major areas of river alluvium are mapped as BoNa, an association of alluvium (Bo) with hydromorphic soils (Na).

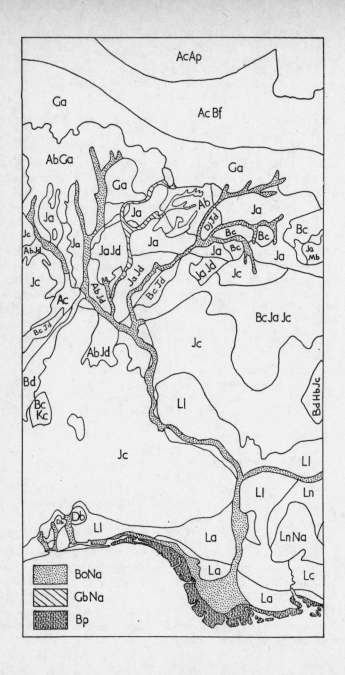

The CCTA system of soil classification has been adopted for use in Northern Nigeria.

The United States Seventh Approximation

The three main classification systems discussed above—C. F. Charter's system, the French system, and the CCTA classification—have all been based on a study of African soils and are therefore indigenous to the continent to a considerable extent. The French and English systems are based largely on West African experience, while the CCTA classification incorporates the experience of Belgian, Portuguese, South African, East African, and other soil workers. The U.S. Seventh Approximation, on the other hand, is an attempt to classify world soils which is based largely on U.S. experience, and as such is relatively strong and detailed on soils of the temperate zone but still relatively tentative as regards tropical soils— a fact which is stressed by those responsible for its production. Moreover, the U.S. experience of the tropics has been mainly in Hawaii and Puerto Rico, areas where the soils are not representative of many areas of Africa, and this further led to the fact that earlier versions of this classification were not found to be entirely applicable to West African soils. However, the classification is constantly being modified and the latest form of it incorporates more information on the African tropics.

The U.S. Seventh Approximation is a very challenging classification which summarizes an enormous amount of thought and work: it has been said that it is not only a new classification but a new vocabulary, for it includes large numbers of new and often odd-looking words which have been coined from Greek and Roman roots to name the various classification units set up. The new terminology has probably frightened some users, and the definitions of units are often very long and complex. Even in the U.S.A. the system has not yet been adopted for general use by the public, though it is much discussed and constantly modified by soil scientists.

The basis of the classification is that soils should be classified according to profile characteristics which can be measured, either in the field or the laboratory. This has led to the fact that sometimes a large number of

---

Fig. 7.5. Section of the CCTA map of Africa showing parts of Nigeria and of adjoining territories. For key, see text.
The original map was published on the 1:5 000 000 scale. The section reproduced here is reduced to about half the size of the original, and has been slightly simplified.

laboratory determinations and sometimes other information (such as the number of dry months) is necessary before a soil profile can be classified into its correct order, suborder, great group, subgroup, and family with accuracy. The system also makes considerable use of diagnostic horizons, i.e. soil horizons with specific characteristics, the definitions of which are also sometimes complex and introduce new concepts. Thus, the requirement of an Oxisol is that it possess an oxic horizon (an oxic horizon is defined below).

In the case of many tropical soils, the grouping is still relatively provisional and is not as detailed as for the temperate soils for which more information and analyses were available to the compilers.

The U.S. Seventh Approximation divides soils into ten orders of which those best represented in West Africa are probably, in order of increasing weathering and profile development, the Entisols, the Inceptisols, the Ultisols, and the Oxisols.

The Entisols are pedologically young soils in which soil-forming processes have not yet resulted in the formation of genetic horizons, or have resulted in the formation of only slightly developed horizons. This order includes soils which are young because of very recent formation, or young because of very inert and resistant parent material, and many of the soils belonging to the raw mineral and weakly developed soils of the CCTA classification, as well as some of Charter's Lithochronic earths, can be expected to belong to this order.

The Inceptisols are more developed than the Entisols but are nevertheless relatively young soils whose genetic horizons are thought to form rather quickly, and do not show much illuviation or eluviation or strong weathering. They include shallow, immature soils of steep slopes and also some poorly drained gley soils without well developed horizon formation.

The Ultisols are a varied group of soils found in many latitudes but normally confined to relatively wet areas. They are distinguished by an argillic horizon in the subsoil, i.e. by a horizon which has a considerably higher clay content than the horizons above and below. These include many of the upland West African soils previously included under latosols. Ultisols in West Africa are usually relatively highly weathered soils, with only low reserves of weatherable minerals, but they are not as extremely weathered as the next order, the Oxisols.

The Oxisols are the most highly weathered of West African soils and include some of the old and very highly weathered soils of old land surfaces such as the peneplain remnants discussed in Chapter 3. Oxisols must have an oxic horizon in the subsoil. The requirements of an oxic horizon are that it is at least 50 cm (20 in) thick, that it has a very low cation exchange capacity (defined as being less than 16 m.e. per 100 g of clay) that there are no more than traces of water-dispersible clay in at least part of the horizon and no more than traces of 2:1 lattice clays, and that the texture is no coarser than sandy loam. The boundaries of the oxic horizon are usually gradual and diffuse, and the horizon shows no rock structure or very little (less than 3 per cent by volume). The oxic horizon is thus not only highly weathered, but relatively inert and stable since there is almost no water-dispersible clay and no evidence of clay movement. This definition is rather narrow, and the Oxisol order probably includes only the oldest and most highly weathered of West African soils. Many of the West African soils formerly described as latosols probably do not fall within the Oxisol group but among the Inceptisols and Ultisols because they contain some weatherable minerals and some dispersible clay.

Numerous attempts have been made to fit West African soils into the Seventh Approximation: these have been limited in some cases by lack of analytical information. A recent survey of the south-west Ivory Coast conducted by U.S. soil surveyors is of particular interest since it classifies the soils according to both the French system and the U.S. Seventh Approximation. The area includes the very wet south-west corner of the Ivory Coast between the Sassandra and Cavally rivers where rainfalls are very heavy (up to about 100 in/year) and the geology is mainly granites, gneisses, and phyllites of the West African basement complex. According to the French classification, the soils are mostly Sols Ferrallitiques Fortement or Moyennement Désaturés (moderately or strongly leached ferrallitic soils), but according to the Seventh Approximation these ferrallitic soils fall into three different orders: most of them are either Inceptisols or Ultisols, with only relatively few series falling within the Oxisols. The Inceptisols include many Oxic Dystropepts, i.e. Tropepts (the Inceptisols of hot climates) with relatively low base saturation and low cation exchange capacity, while the soils included in the Ultisols are mainly classed as Paleudults, i.e. Udults (Ultisols that remain moist although they are not waterlogged) which contain no weatherable minerals.

Further consideration of the Seventh Approximation is outside the scope of this book, but readers are referred to the publications listed in the Appendix.

PRACTICAL LOCAL CLASSIFICATIONS AND LAND CAPABILITY CLASSIFICATION

The classifications outlined above, based partly on soil genesis, reflect to some extent the agricultural value of the soil and are particularly useful in obtaining a broad picture of the soils of West Africa and their relationship to each other. For more detailed work on a local scale, and for more precise recommendations for practical agriculture, it may be useful to employ additional or alternative classifications adapted to local needs.

The local, practical classifications are often based on a characteristic or group of characteristics considered particularly important in relation to the type of land use envisaged. In an earlier paragraph (page 199) it was pointed out that simple classifications could be made on the basis of soil texture, or according to drainage characteristics. A map of a farm showing these two soil properties would be of far more use to a farmer than a map showing whether the soils were Inceptisols or Ultisols.

When land is classified for irrigation (see next section) particular attention is directed to the relief, to the texture, and to the content of salts, particularly sodium chloride. When soils in the Sudan were classified for irrigation, the sodium chloride content was considered the most important single factor in assessing suitability. In the Yangambi area of the central Congo the generally deep, sandy soils differ somewhat in clay content, and in this case they were satisfactorily classified for cropping mainly according to one factor—their clay content. When growing tree crops (including forestry plantations) in the less wet areas of West Africa where the rainfall is very seasonal, the most important single soil factor is often perhaps the moisture-storage capacity of the soil. This in turn depends on the texture of the soil and its effective depth, which may be limited by an ironstone or indurated layer. A classification based on texture and on effective depth might be the most useful for this purpose, and would form a further example of the value of simple local classifications for selected purposes.

Land capability classifications

There have been many attempts to classify soils according to their agricultural 'capability' and to make the classification simple enough to be understood by the layman and by the ordinary farmer. Such classifications are widely used in the U.S.A. in particular. The capability assessed is one which normally refers particularly to the dominant local type of land use (the U.S. land capability classification, for example, was constructed for areas where annual crops and mechanized agriculture are the rule). However, the simplification necessary to produce a scheme easily understood by everybody sometimes leads to the classification saying very little which is not rather obvious and oversimplified. Capability maps can be useful for planning purposes and have often drawn attention to the need for erosion control measures, but they are no substitute for more detailed work on soils.

Because of the fact that the best known capability classifications were developed in areas of mechanized arable agriculture, they are not always easy to apply to rather different areas without the danger of being mis-leading. The usual method is to classify soils according to the severity of factors held to limit their use: the more severe the limiting factors, the narrower will be the range for which the soils are suited. Thus a Class I soil is a soil with very few or no limiting factors and is therefore the most versatile, but soils of Classes II to VIII suffer from progressively more severe limitations which narrow down their desirable and practicable range of use.

The land capability classification of the U.S. Soil Conservation Service, the best known and widest used of the U.S. capability classifications, places considerable emphasis on the liability of the land to suffer from accelerated erosion if cultivated. It therefore pays particular attention to slope gradients but it also considers natural soil productivity where this is a limiting factor, factors interfering with cultivation (such as stoniness), and climatic limitations. It should be emphasized that the normal practice is to adapt the general class definitions to local conditions prevailing in particular areas, and that this adaptation makes the classification of more value in those areas. The eight broad classes are the following:

Classes I to IV: soils suited to cultivation
    Class I—no special practices needed
    Class II—simple conservation methods necessary
    Class III—intensive conservation practices necessary
    Class IV—suited for occasional or limited cultivation with intensive con-
        servation practices
Classes V to VII: soils not suited to cultivation but suitable for permanent
        vegetation such as tree crops, forestry, and pasture.
    Class V—no special restrictions or practices
    Class VI—moderate restrictions in use
    Class VII—severe restrictions in use
Class VIII: not suitable for cultivation, grazing, or trees
        Class VIII land is usually extremely rough or steep land, or
        extremely sandy areas, or extremely wet or arid ones that may
        however have some value for wildlife or recreational purposes.

Land capability classifications have undoubtedly been of value in drawing attention to limitations of the land and the need for care to avoid accelerated erosion, but to be of maximum use in West Africa a very careful adaptation is needed to local conditions. In the forest areas of West Africa the most productive soils are often devoted to cocoa cultiva-tion; the most desirable soils for this purpose are chemically fertile ones, and the slope is relatively unimportant. Thus, this crop might be grown on all classes of soils up to Class VII, for the distinctions between classes based on gradient are of minor relevance to cocoa. Conversely, a soil which is flat, deep, loamy textured, not subject to erosion, and capable of supplying sufficient moisture would according to the classification be a Class I soil for arable mechanized agriculture, but might in fact be rather acid and infertile for cocoa.

These examples suggest that not only have land capability classifications to be adapted to local needs but that, although simple, they must also be well understood by the user. He should, for example, realize that the classification does not normally take into account soil fertility, except where it is so low that it is a limiting factor. Indeed this is not the aim and classification does not therefore indicate particularly fertile soils. He should also realize that with intelligent use he might in some cases be able to make more money from a Class IV soil than from a Class I soil and that the Class IV soil may even be the more chemically fertile of the two. The dangers of land capability classification thus also spring from the tendency to simplify still further on the part of the user, to think that Class I land is first class, and Class V or VI very inferior, whereas the more intelligent approach is not to think of good or bad soils but of soils with different properties each of which has certain advantages which the farmer should try to make use of.

Land capability classifications are in use in Ghana, in Northern Nigeria, and in other parts of West Africa. In practice many soils of an area often fall into a single class, as where, for example, moderately sloping upland gravelly soils cover most of the area, they might all be mapped as Class III (s). The suffix (s) indicates a soil limitation, in this case the high gravel content. The usual suffixes appended to the class numbers are (s) for a soil or rooting zone limitation, (e) for an erosion limitation, (w) for a wetness limitation, i.e. poor drainage or a liability to flooding and (c) a climatic limitation.

Soil classification for irrigated agriculture

Soils are often classified specifically for irrigation agriculture, usually according to a system somewhat comparable to the land capability classifications outlined above. A system widely used is that of the U.S. Bureau of Land classification, as outlined in their reclamation manual, or a modification of it to suit local conditions. This type of classification often divides land into six classes. Classes 1 to 4 are all suited to irrigated agriculture, with Class 1 land having the least limitations and Class 4 land the most. Class 5 land is that land which is not considered to be irrigable at present but which could become so under certain circumstances. It is therefore a 'holding' class in which land can be classified pending reclassification after the necessary engineering or other modifications have made it irrigable. Class 6 land is that land not considered to be irrigable.

For irrigation agriculture particular attention is given (a) to the gradient of the land, for only flat or gently sloping land is normally considered irrigable; (b) to the texture, which is preferably a loam, for very sandy and very clay soils are not particularly suited to irrigation, the first because they store so little water and have excessive permeability, the second because they are relatively impermeable and water moves very slowly through them, and (c) to the presence of high levels of salts, particularly sodium chloride, which might be increased to toxic levels during use.

It should be stressed that the definitions of the irrigation classes are normally suitably modified to suit local conditions. The following broad definitions of soils in Classes 1 to 4 may be found adaptable for general use in West Africa.

Class 1 soils are highly suitable for irrigated agriculture. They can produce sustained and relatively good yields at moderate cost. They are flat or nearly so and have little erosion hazard. The soils are (a) deep; (b) of medium to moderately fine texture; (c) have a structure and porosity allowing easy penetration of roots, air, and water; and (d) combine good drainage with an adequate moisture-storage capacity. No farm drainage works are normally necessary. The soils are free of salt or other toxic substances, or can easily be reclaimed.

Class 2 soils are well suited to irrigation agriculture but somewhat more limited than Class 1 soils. They may be more expensive to prepare for irrigation than Class 1 soils, and be more costly to farm and require more supervision. The limiting factors may include one or more of the following: shallow depth, texture which is either too coarse or too heavy, low moisture-storage capacity or slow permeability because of heavy texture or subsoil compaction. These soils may require some expenditure on drainage or reclamation works.

Class 3 soils are those with a somewhat restricted suitability for irrigation agriculture because of more serious limitations than are present in Class 2 soils. They may require heavier investment in land preparation, more care during use, heavier levels of fertilizers and amendments, or be restricted by heavy texture and slow drainage which can be corrected only partially and at high cost.

Class 4 soils are severely restricted in their irrigation possibilities: they may be suited only to special types of land use, such as pasture, or require heavy investment in engineering and drainage works before they can be used. Factors which could put a soil into this class include very poor drainage because of heavy texture and unfavourable low position which subjects the soil to periodic flooding or a very high water table.

It will be noted that, as in the land capability classification, soils are placed in groups of decreasing suitability for irrigation but that the particular factors or combinations of factors responsible for the soil being placed in that class are somewhat varied. Irrigation suitability maps are very useful for planning purposes and for deciding whether an irrigation scheme warrants the investment involved, but the individual user will often want to know exactly why a soil has been placed in a certain class and not merely what class it is in. He may, for example, have two soils both placed in Class 3, but for quite different reasons, and intelligent use of these soils will require knowing more about their limiting factors than the mere fact that they are classified as Class 3. As in the case of land capability maps, the irrigation suitability classification is therefore no substitute for more detailed work or for a knowledge of the properties of each soil series concerned. To some extent the type of limitation involved is indicated by the practice of adding suffixes to the irrigation class. The usual suffixes are (S) where soil characteristics are a limiting factor, (T) for areas limited by rough topography or too high gradients, (D) where the soils are limited by poor drainage, (R) where loose rocks occur within the plough layer, and (C) where a climatic factor (other than low rainfall) is considered to limit the use of the soil for irrigated agriculture.

There are enormous possibilities for irrigation agriculture in West Africa, particularly in savanna areas of gentle relief. Even in the forest areas, however, the dry seasons are often a limiting factor despite a high total annual rainfall, and it may be economical to irrigate. In the Ivory Coast forest zone, for example, intensive banana production always involves sprinkler irrigation in the dry seasons.

SOIL ANALYSIS

It is sometimes mistakenly assumed that one has merely to analyse a soil to know all about it, to be able to recommend how it should be used, and for what purpose. If this really were the case, the work of a soil scientist might be much easier, even if less challenging.

Analyses are very desirable, and may be very helpful but they are rarely enough by themselves, while in some cases not enough is yet known about their interpretation to make them of much practical value. Experience in interpretation comes by correlating laboratory analyses with actual crop performances, preferably in the field; without such correlations analyses enable soils to be compared one with another but do not necessarily indicate very much about their utilization for practical agriculture. This suggests that we need more analyses, and that the more we have the greater will be the value of each of them.

Soil sampling

Before a soil can be analysed it has to be sampled. An old saying states that 'the analysis is no better than the sample': accurate work in the laboratory is wasted and the results might even be misleading if the soil sample has not been taken correctly in the field. This is an aspect of the work which often fails to get the attention it deserves. Sampling methods need to be standardized just as much as laboratory methods, and, as with them, the best method depends on the purpose of the investigation.

Profile pits sampled primarily in order to characterize a soil series should be divided carefully into natural horizons and sampled horizon by horizon, beginning at the bottom and working upwards, sufficient being taken from each horizon for the sample to be representative. In shallow soil horizons this may mean taking soil material from the whole horizon and somewhat to the left and right of the starting point, so that a horizontal band of soil is sampled. In thicker soil horizons, a vertical band of soil may be sampled, care still being taken that the whole depth of horizon is sampled and sampled equally. If practicable, at least 3 to 4 lb of soil should be taken from each horizon, especially if very gravelly: a very small sample is less likely to be representative.

Samples should always be taken from a freshly dug soil face, not one that has been exposed for some time, nor should they be taken from an old road cutting or other exposure. Auger sampling is possible, but does not allow the detailed examination of the soil and the careful division into natural horizons that is possible when a profile pit is dug.

Profile pit sampling allows the soil series to be examined and analysed, and the analyses of successive natural horizons is of the greatest pedological interest, allowing much to be deduced about the genesis of the soil. Bulk density, permeability and other determinations can be made in the field at the same time as the sampling, and if thin sections of the soil for later microscope examination are required, undisturbed soil samples can also be taken.

However, examinations of a profile are, from the farmer's point of view, examinations of only a single spot in his field or farm, and invaluable as they are for the more fundamental knowledge of the soil, they do not necessarily say much about the soil either on the other side of the field or even as near as a yard away. If we wish to recommend a certain practice or fertilizer application to a farmer, then it is necessary to know the *average* condition and nutrient status of the field, plot, or farm in question. For this, a different type of sampling is necessary: in areas of apparently similar soils and land-use a number of bulk samples or 'cores' are taken to a standardized depth and then mixed to give a working average for the area. To give a sufficiently accurate average, on which management recommendations can be based, at least twenty core samples should be taken per acre, and only those samples from areas where soil and land use are similar should be bulked. The cores are sampled exactly to a given depth, often o to 6 in and 6 to 12 in, care being taken that a slice of soil of uniform thickness is obtained. The core samples are air-dried, bulked, and carefully sub-sampled to provide a final sample representative of the mixture of cores. The sampling is not carried out in this case according to the natural horizons of the soil, but to a fixed and carefully measured depth. In ploughed fields the natural horizons will in any case have been somewhat mixed by cultivation.

Soil analyses and tests

In areas of relatively advanced and standardized agricultural practices, such as the Netherlands or Great Britain, samples of known soils can be subject to routine analyses and appropriate fertilizer and other recommendations given to the farmer. Such advice is based on considerable experience of the soils in question, the crops and cultivation methods concerned, and the correlations of earlier analyses with growth. In West Africa, the relatively few and scattered analyses available serve to define and separate soils and give a broad indication of their characteristics in the field, but they have not yet (except in a few cases) been correlated with yields to the extent that precise fertilizer and management recommendations can safely be given on the basis of the analyses alone.

A soil can be analysed in many ways, and the type of analyses involved depends, of course, on what information is required. A soil can be subjected to chemical, physical, mineralogical, and other analyses by a variety of methods, and can in addition be subjected to certain treatments and tests other than analytical ones.

Chemical analyses of the soil can be used to determine the total chemical composition of the soil, or the total content of specific plant nutrients in it, but in the case of most elements a knowledge of the total amount present in the soil does not give much indication as to what is immediately available to the plant. Usually, analyses attempt to assess to what extent plant nutrients in the soil are available.

In the case of the metallic cations—particularly calcium, magnesium, potassium, sodium, and manganese—it is usual to determine the amounts present in exchangeable form. The exchangeable cations are leached out of the soil with a solution such as ammonium acetate: the ammonium cations replace all the exchangeable bases and the hydrogen originally present on the soil exchange positions, and these bases are collected in the leachate, in which they are then measured. At the same time the method allows the cation exchange capacity of the soil to be determined, for the amount of ammonium (or other cation used to leach the soil) which is held by the soil colloids gives the soil cation exchange capacity. Strictly speaking, this gives only its cation exchange capacity for that particular cation and at the pH (usually 7·0) of the leaching solution (the cation exchange capacity might be slightly different for other cations, and considerably different at other pH values) but since the method is standardized and widely used it allows the cation exchange capacities of different soils to be compared satisfactorily. The total cations in relation to the cation exchange capacity give the percentage saturation of the soil. With soils of dominantly the same clay mineral the percentage saturation correlates broadly with the pH, with very unsaturated soils having a pH of about 3·5 to 4·0 and saturated soils a pH of about 7·0.

The exchangeable potassium, calcium, and magnesium are assumed to be available to the plant, though this availability is influenced by other factors such as the nature and amount of competing cations and the cation exchange capacity. In the case of phosphorus, it is relatively difficult to assess what is 'available' by laboratory means, though a range of different methods are in common use. Usually a weak acid or alkaline solution is used to extract what is generally only a very small fraction of the total phosphorus in the soil, and this is assumed to be 'available' to the plant.

The various extractants commonly used are of different strengths and behave differently according to the nature of the soil and the forms of phosphorus in it. In all cases it is necessary to compare the amounts extracted with crop responses in the field: the better the method, the greater will be the correlation between amounts extracted and the response or otherwise of the soil to added phosphate. In practice, however, results are further complicated by differences between plants themselves in their extracting power and by the fact that much depends on the development of a good rooting system. In any case, results for so called 'available' phosphate should be compared only when they have been obtained with the same extractant. The measurement of the total phosphorus in the soil does not, in West Africa, give much indication of what is available to the plant.

In the case of soil carbon and nitrogen, on the other hand, it is usually the total quantity which is measured in the soil. The total organic carbon in the soil is usually measured by digesting the soil with an oxidizing agent (normally potassium dichromate), and the result expressed as a percentage of the soil by weight. Total nitrogen is measured by a thorough digestion of the soil with sulphuric acid which converts the nitrogen to ammonium sulphate: the ammonium is then measured in the digest and the nitrogen is also expressed as a percentage of the soil by weight. A comparison of the two percentages gives the C/N (carbon/nitrogen) ratio, a ratio widely used to characterize the soil organic matter (see p. 154). To convert organic carbon to organic matter in the soil, the percentage organic carbon is usually multiplied by 1·72.

The total nitrogen is, of course, not available to the plant until converted to ammonium or nitrate; the available nitrogen is the nitrate and ammonium nitrogen in the soil but these amounts are very small and fluctuate from day to day (they may be low immediately after rain, for example). They are therefore difficult to measure and are not normally determined for routine analyses.

The simplest, cheapest, and possibly the most useful single determination usually carried out is the measurement of the soil pH. This can be done with coloured indicators, but it is better done with an electric pH meter. A soil water suspension is made (often 1 part soil to 2 parts distilled water, but sometimes 1 part soil to 1 of water) and glass electrodes are inserted into the suspension after the soil and water have been well stirred and allowed to come into equilibrium. Portable battery-operated pH meters are now available for use in the field.

Examples of routine chemical determinations such as are frequently carried out on soils are given in Tables 7.1 and 7.2.

Physical determinations on soils often include a mechanical analysis which measures the percentages of sand, silt, and clay after destruction of the organic matter. The size classes into which the sand and silt are usually divided are indicated in Chapter 2 (see p. 18); for more detailed work more size classes may be determined. The sand and silt fractions may be examined to see what minerals they contain, and the nature of the clay minerals in the clay fraction may also be determined. Additional laboratory determinations on the soil might include the assessment of the soil moisture-storage capacity—particularly in the case of soils to be irrigated—and also of bulk density, porosity, permeability, and other physical characteristics, including practical tests to measure the strength or stability of the soil structure. Permeability and other characteristics may be measured on the natural soil in the field, and undisturbed soil samples may be taken in the field for subsequent impregnation with transparent plastic so that thin sections can be made and the soil examined under the microscope.

Practical soil tests, other than field trials, include the growing of carefully tended plants in pots. Test plants, such as tomatoes or rye grass, are grown in samples of different soils with or without various combinations of fertilizer, and growth rates compared by weighing the plants produced and sometimes by analysing them.

Soil analyses can sometimes be usefully supplemented by the analysis of leaves and other plant parts provided that they are carefully sampled and enough is known about what levels of the various nutrient elements can be considered to be normal or deficient. Analysis of oil palm and coffee leaves in the Ivory Coast and elsewhere is claimed to be useful in detecting low nutrient levels in the plant early enough for deficiencies to be corrected before they become harmful.

Recent advances in techniques now enable the soil scientist to analyse the soil in a bewildering and almost numberless variety of ways, some relatively simple and others very complex. It is important to define the aim of any particular investigation as precisely as possible, and then to select the techniques most likely to be able to provide useful answers. Analyses are in any case only one link in a chain which includes the correct sampling of the soil before it is analysed, and the interpretation of the results after they are obtained. The last is often the most difficult, and calls for the greatest all-round knowledge and experience.

8 SHIFTING CULTIVATION AND MECHANIZED AGRICULTURE

SHIFTING CULTIVATION

The details of current farming methods employed by the West African farmer vary considerably according to climate, soil, and vegetation, according to the group to which the farmer belongs and, among other factors, according to population densities and the pressure exerted on available agricultural land. Nevertheless, despite the variety of crops and agricultural practices involved, certain general statements can be made. Even though cash crops and permanent tree crops are becoming more important, most West African agriculture is still largely on a subsistence basis. Individual farmers aim at producing a range of crops mainly for their own consumption, as opposed to farmers who concentrate on one or two cash crops for sale which they then sell in order to buy their needs.

Most individual farmers cultivate only small or moderate-sized areas (Fig. 8.1), sometimes scattered in several separate patches. This is partly a consequence of the fact that cultivation is mainly carried out only with hand tools such as the hoe and cutlass, thus limiting the amount of land which can be cleared in any one year.

After clearing, the general practice is to cultivate a plot until it shows signs of exhaustion, as indicated by reduced yields, or has become infested by weeds. The farm is then abandoned and allowed to rest in fallow for a period in order to recover its fertility and productivity, after which it will again be cleared and cultivated for another cropping period of 1 or 2 years. This general system, involving the clearing of land for a short period of cropping followed by a generally somewhat longer period of fallow, is widespread in much of the tropics and sub-tropics, and has long been termed 'shifting cultivation'. More recently the alternative term 'land rotation cultivation' has been suggested as being preferable, since in the system described here the villages or settlements do not shift, though the land round them is cultivated in a rough and ready rotation.

Much has been written about this system and its alleged advantages and disadvantages. In the early days it was dismissed as primitive and untidy, and misguided, and usually unsuccessful efforts were made to substitute, with little modification, systems imported from Europe and elsewhere not yet proved satisfactory in the tropics. A greater understanding of the problems involved, of the advantages of shifting cultivation, and of the difficulties of introducing satisfactory alternative systems has now led to more cautious and balanced assessments both of its merits and of the dangers of trying to change too much too quickly.

Before attempting to assess the extent to which shifting cultivation, as practised in the various parts of West Africa, is adapted to soil and environmental conditions, it is necessary to describe the system in a little more detail. Both crops and methods change with rainfall and vegetation.

Shifting cultivation in the forest zone

In the forest zones the normal subsistence food crops are cocoyam or taro (usually *Xanthosoma*, rarely *Colocasia*), plantain (*Musa paradisiaca*), cassava or manioc (*Manihot utilissima*), usually of the so-called 'sweet' varieties with a relatively low prussic acid content, maize, and rice. These are supplemented by various vegetable crops, particularly garden eggs, okro, red peppers, shallot onions, and beans.

When high forest is cleared, either little-disturbed virgin forest or mature secondary forest, a few tall trees are usually left standing for shade (though some groups practise complete clearing) and the rest, together with the smaller trees and shrubs, are cut down in the dry season, allowed to dry out, and then burnt. The succeeding crop is then planted at the beginning of the rains and benefits from the ash left from the burning of the dead trash.

On good forest soils the first crops are often cocoyams mixed with plantain, the corms of the cocoyam and the suckers of the plantain being planted in small holes made with a cutlass (machete) at irregular intervals, the cocoyam somewhat closer than the plantain. These soon provide a leafy cover which shades and protects the ground. Other minor crops may be interplanted but in cocoa and coffee growing areas cocoa or coffee seeds or seedlings are frequently planted at this stage, especially if the farm has been cleared from virgin forest. In the wetter areas oil palm and rubber may replace coffee and cocoa. The cocoyams and plantain mature in about a year but continue to yield, from replanted corms and from new suckers growing at the base of the old, for a further 1, 2, or even 3 years, depending on the fertility of the soil. If the cocoa or other tree crop grows successfully,

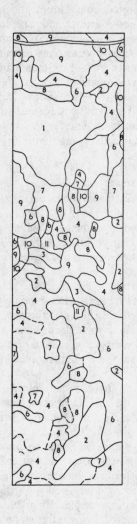

it is weeded regularly and takes over from the food crops before this; if it does not grow, the first food crops may be succeeded by crops of maize and/or cassava.

Where it is not desired to introduce a tree crop, particularly where the soils are cleared from a secondary growth of vegetation and are less fertile, the cropping might begin with a season or two of maize. Cassava, considered the least demanding of the food crops, comes last in many sequences, but in areas of poor soils might be planted immediately after clearing. Rice and, to a small extent, chewing cane, are often confined to the damper valley bottom and lower slope sites, though in very wet forest areas (as in Liberia) upland rice may be widespread and form the preferred first crop after clearing.

Forest regrowth vegetation

If the tree crop has been successfully introduced, then the farm becomes a more permanent one; if not, the farm is gradually abandoned, weeds, shrubs, coppice shoots, and small trees quickly take over, and the land is allowed to rest in natural fallow. This regrowth vegetation varies according to the soil and climate, according to the history of previous cultivation and possible soil degradation, and according to the presence of parent species nearby, but in many forest areas a distinct and fairly regular sequence of plant communities can be distinguished.

For the first $1\frac{1}{2}$ to 2 years after clearing the regrowth vegetation is dominated by forbs, i.e. by soft-stemmed, leafy, quick-growing herbs, and is known as *forb regrowth*. As shrubs and coppice shoots, together with

---

Fig. 8.1. The pattern of shifting cultivation: vegetation mosaics typical of moderately closely farmed forest areas. The vegetation and land-use were recorded on two sample strips, each 1 mile long and $\frac{1}{4}$ mile wide, in the western forest zone of Ghana.

1. Original forest.
2. Secondary forest.
3. Secondary swamp forest.
4. Thicket regrowth.
5. Swamp thicket.
6. Forb regrowth.
7. Newly cleared land.
8. Land under current food crop cultivation.
9. Cocoa.
10. Abandoned cocoa amid forb or thicket regrowth.
11. Abandoned cocoa or coffee amid secondary forest.
12. Built-over land (village site).

(From Reference 79.)

various climbers, become dominant a thicker and more impenetrable growth is produced, appropriately described as *thicket regrowth*. This is dense and difficult to clear.

At about 6 to 10 years after the farm has been abandoned, depending on local conditions, trees begin to dominate the vegetation formation, shading out the lower growth, so that the formation is now higher and less dense: it has become *secondary forest*. The trees which dominate at first are the fast-growing, usually soft-wooded and light-demanding species such as *Musanga cecropioides* (umbrella tree or parasolier), *Trema guineensis*, and *Ricinodendron africanum*, but with greater maturity the species composition of the secondary forest changes and slower-growing, shade-tolerant trees eventually drive out the earlier colonizers. The number of original shade trees spared during clearing and a host of other environmental factors influence the details of the succession but in most of the West African forest areas where cultivation has not been too intensive it follows a rather similar pattern.

In areas of long established cultivation and more degraded soils, the regrowth vegetation develops more slowly and is poorer in species, and in some areas, particularly coastal ones, the forest has now disappeared entirely, to be replaced by a dense coastal thicket, while on the drier northern forest fringes savanna encroachment, aided by annual fires, is widespread.

Shifting cultivation in the savanna areas

In the savanna areas the crops grown, the methods employed, and the regrowth vegetation are all different from those of the forest belt. There is usually only one wet season followed by a long dry season during which crop production on most sites is not possible unless irrigation water is available (as in the case of the dry season gardens below dams).

The savanna vegetation is relatively sparse, so that clearing is easier, but the soils are often thin and gravelly, and the long-established method of cultivation in many areas is to scrape up the soil into individual mounds on which the various crops are grown, particular grain crops and yams. These are often areas (such as the northern Ivory Coast, northern Ghana, and parts of Northern Nigeria) where population densities are relatively high and living standards lower than in many of the forest areas. In some areas settlements are in the form of scattered compounds rather than villages. Little of the natural vegetation may remain, except for such economically useful trees as shea butter. The regrowth vegetation which develops in savanna areas on farm land left for fallow consists mainly only of short grasses. These are in any case grazed by cattle and subject to annual fires, so that regeneration of the soil is relatively slow even if fallow periods are long, which they often are not, because of the density of population and the low yields from the areas which are under cultivation.

In general, savanna soils are particularly low in organic matter, and may have poor structures, poor nutrient reserves, and poor moisture-storage properties. In long-cultivated areas, sheet erosion (see p. 246) has further reduced their productivity. Very gravelly soils and those with indurated horizons fairly near the surface are often extensive. In some areas there is the contrast between very sandy upper slope soils which store little moisture, and areas of very heavy clay soils near rivers which may be too heavy to cultivate, or subject to floods.

Organic matter levels are of paramount importance in almost all West African soils: in the savanna areas in particular the main agricultural problems are possibly the raising of the organic matter content of the soils and water control. In many savanna areas some organic material is given to a more closely cultivated farm or garden near the house or compound which receives animal manure and other materials, and which is cultivated fairly permanently. These patches contrast with the more extensive fields, usually further away, which are cultivated for 2 or 3 years or even less and then left to recover; these receive little or no animal manure apart from that left by animals grazing them, and the normal short fallows are not sufficient to raise the fertility and productivity of these soils above a generally low level.

The normal subsistence food crops are yams (*Dioscorea* spp.), maize, millets and fonio (the last on some of the poorest and steepest soils), guinea corn, and groundnuts. Rice, vegetables (including tomatoes), and tobacco are widespread. The normal rotation employed for grain crops is maize–guinea corn–millet, the last being considered as best adapted to the most worn out soils, but grain crops are often preceded by yams.

In the derived savanna zone immediately to the north of the forest belt yams are particularly important, while in the western areas of West Africa, as in the coastal plains of Guinea, there is some tendency for the forest zone and savanna zone crops to be found side by side. Although the single long wet season is the rainfall régime associated with the interior savanna areas of most of West Africa, the annual totals here, 100 in or more, enable crops to be grown not normally associated with the savanna vegetation that now covers these areas.

The above summary of agricultural practices is brief but indicates the importance of fallow periods in the maintenance of fertility in a region where commercial fertilizers are as yet hardly used. It is now appropriate to consider further what effects fallow vegetation has on the soil.

SOIL CHANGES UNDER SHIFTING CULTIVATION

The role of fallow

The total nutrients in circulation clearly include both those in the soil and those in the associated vegetation, and together these constitute the 'nutrient capital' available for possible use by agricultural plants. The role of the fallow is to increase this total nutrient capital for the benefit of succeeding crops, and in particular to increase that part of it which is stored in the upper part of the soil profile in a form which will be available to those crops.

The land has been abandoned after a few seasons' cultivation and is clearly in a relatively exhausted state at this stage; the regrowth vegetation should ideally consist of those species best able to build up fertility again in the shortest possible time. One of the other important functions, however, of regrowth vegetation which is often overlooked, is that it drives out the weeds of cultivation which have established themselves during cropping and contributed to the reduction of yields. It is the difficulty of controlling weeds which often leads to a farmer seeking a new patch to clear. There are two aspects particularly deserving of consideration. The first aspect concerns the examination of the precise changes that take place in the soil as a result of being left in natural fallow, changes which together increase the fertility and productivity of the soil for the succeeding crop. The second aspect then involves the consideration of whether the regrowth vegetation is bringing about these changes as efficiently as possible alternative vegetation, or whether the functions of fallow could not be carried out by alternative methods, including green manures, mulches, fertilizers, manures, and improved crop rotations.

The improvements in fertility and productivity that result from natural fallows are connected with the increase in soil organic matter content during the fallow period. The soil humus improves the physical qualities of the soil, particularly structure and aeration, and also its cation exchange and water-holding capacity. In addition, the humus itself mineralizes to give a very wide range of nutrients, including phosphorus, sulphur, and nitrogen, and the improved topsoil thus contains greater quantities of total and available nutrients than it did before being left in fallow.

Soil changes during the fallow period

The factors which cause a reduction in the amounts of soil humus during the cropping period include a decrease in the quantities of fresh organic material received by the soil, and an increase in the rate of humus mineralization and loss because of the increased exposure of the soil to sun and rain.

When cropping ceases, the factors causing the humus decline under cropping are modified. The downward trend in humus contents may be halted and then succeeded by an upward trend, as the regrowth vegetation begins to provide a good protective cover for the soil and also to supply it with fresh organic material which provides a source of additional humus.

The amount and type of fresh organic material added to the soil will clearly depend on the type of regrowth vegetation concerned and how quickly it establishes itself.

In the forest areas a mass of stumps and tree roots left in the soil will quickly send up coppice shoots, while the growth of forbs is rapid too, particularly in the wet seasons. There is in any case a gradual transition from the later cropping stages, when the farm is no longer weeded but still being harvested, to the early stages of forb regrowth. The abandoned farm is therefore quickly covered by a usually dense leafy growth which shades and protects the soil and adds relatively large quantities of green material to it from an early stage, this being supplemented by dead roots.

It has been estimated that in a typical forest regrowth the weight of fresh organic material added annually to the soil may quickly reach the relatively high figure of 6 to 8 tons per acre, and a proportion of this is then converted to humus by the soil organisms.

In savanna areas the establishment of regrowth vegetation is much slower, and if the farm is abandoned, as it usually is, at the end of a wet season, the growth of a new grass cover may have to wait until the succeeding wet season. Even then, the establishment of a good cover is relatively slow, the shade it gives once established is less than in the case of the forest vegetation, and the weight of the vegetation supported by the soil and of the dead plant material added to it are both also much less than in the case of forest regrowth. The fallow vegetation therefore takes over from the farm more slowly in the savanna than it does in the forest, and is a less effective influence when it does so.

The amounts of plant material added to the soil annually under a grass fallow vary widely with climate and local conditions and are in any case usually severely reduced by annual burning, but they are unlikely in practice to exceed about 1 ton per acre—a small fraction of that provided by a typical forest regrowth—and in some cases may be much less than this.

Of the dead plant and animal material added to the soil under fallow, only a fraction will be converted to humus, the rest being oxidized or lost in other ways, and the humus which is formed is, of course, itself subject to a slower mineralization. The processes involved are complex, but it appears that about 10 per cent of the carbon in the added organic matter is retained as humus in the soil.

The rate of mineralization of the soil humus appears to vary with the amount present in the soil. When organic matter levels rise, so does the rate of humus mineralization also rise. This means that in a soil with a relatively low content of organic matter the rate of mineralization will also be relatively low and the addition of fresh organic material may result in comparatively rapid increases in the humus content. As the humus levels rise, however, so will rates of mineralization also tend to rise, and the net increase caused by further additions of fresh material will be less. Further increases in the amounts of humus therefore tend to become progressively smaller until an equilibrium is reached between the supply of fresh humus-producing material and losses through mineralization. The amount of humus then remains constant or nearly so.

In any one set of climate–soil–vegetation conditions there appears therefore to be a humus equilibrium level at which additions are balanced by losses. A soil well below its humus equilibrium level may gain humus rapidly at first if given an adequate supply of raw organic material from the fallow vegetation or other sources, but as levels rise and get closer to the equilibrium, further net additions will become progressively smaller, and the level rise progressively more slowly. As a result, the early stages of fallow regrowth vegetation tend to add humus to the soil at a faster rate than the later ones. This effect is reinforced by the fact that the early, leafy stages of forest regrowth in any case add more organic material to the soil than the later stages when new growth is more in the form of wood. Under a good secondary forest the humus content of the soil may have reached 75 per cent of what it once was under original high forest, but further increases may be relatively very slow. These considerations obviously influence the question of the most desirable length of fallow.

The concept of organic matter equilibrium has other important practical applications. Fresh organic material added to the soil, not only from a natural fallow but from a cover crop or mulch, will tend to result in a relatively large increase when the soil is well below equilibrium, but a small or negligible one if organic carbon levels are already near the equilibrium level.

Gains of organic carbon during the fallow period can be expected to be parallelled by gains in soil nitrogen reserves. If the C/N ratio is the same under the fallow vegetation as during the cropping periods, the nitrogen gain will be proportionate to the gain in carbon. Most or all of the added nitrogen is assumed to have come from the atmosphere and to have been fixed by bacteria, as discussed in Chapter 6, probably in the main by non-symbiotic ones.

The available phosphorus in West African soils is often largely the organic phosphorus, and this also is present in what appears to be a fairly fixed ratio to the soil carbon, so that increases in organic phosphorus under fallow can also be expected to be approximately proportional to the increase in organic carbon. The ratio between organic phosphorus and carbon has been estimated at very approximately 1:200, but varies considerably between soils. The phosphorus is subsequently made available to the plant as the humus mineralizes.

The increase in humus levels under fallow has other important chemical and physical effects on the soil, including a raising of the water-storage and cation exchange capacities of the soil. In most West African soils the cation exchange capacity of the topsoil is due mainly to the humus and this probably has an exchange capacity of 200 m.e. or more per 100 g. An increase in the organic matter content of the soil increases the cation exchange capacity, and the increase in the amount of bases which can be stored in the exchangeable form available to plants is also likely to be important to subsequent crop growth. If the amount of bases occupying the exchange positions on the humus does not also increase in proportion to the increase in exchange capacity which results from the higher humus levels, then the level of saturation will fall and the soil pH decrease. Since pH levels do not appear to decrease during fallows to an appreciable extent, it seems likely that the supply of exchangeable cations keeps pace with the increase in exchange capacity. This increased supply of exchangeable calcium, magnesium, and other cations might result from their being brought up from the lower horizons of the soil by the deeper plant roots but could also be due to cations formerly in the unexchangeable form in the upper soil horizons becoming exchangeable.

It must be remembered that of the net total increase of circulating nutrients which occurs during the fallow period—the nutrient capital referred to earlier—a considerable proportion, depending both on the amount and type of vegetation and the nature of the soil, is in the vegetation itself. By allowing the ground to rest in fallow, the farmer increases the total nutrient capital, but what happens to this capital and what proportion of it is subsequently used by growing crops depends on how the regrowth vegetation is cleared and the ground cultivated at the end of the fallow period. It is now necessary to consider what happens during clearing, burning, and subsequent cropping.

Clearing and burning

In the forest zone the forest or thicket vegetation cut down when a farm is cleared is allowed to dry and then collected in suitable heaps and set on fire. For the farmer armed only with axe and cutlass, burning is perhaps his most important tool, and in no other way could he clear away the dead plant material so easily and quickly. In the savanna areas the grass is also burnt before cultivation. Of the plant nutrients contained in the vegetation burnt, both nitrogen and sulphur are almost entirely lost during burning as gases, the first as ammonia, nitrogen, or nitrogen oxides, the second as sulphur dioxide. All the remaining nutrients, however, including the phosphorus and the potassium, are not immediately lost as a result of the burning itself but remain in the ash, largely as the phosphates, carbonates, and silicates of the cations calcium, magnesium, and potassium. The additions of often considerable quantities of ash to the soil have the effect, at least temporarily, of raising the soil pH, and may have a beneficial effect on succeeding crop growth for this reason.

Other effects of burning include the heating of the surface soil, though in the forest areas this is mainly in only a few spots where the burnt material has been heaped up or where large tree trunks have been burnt where they fall, while in the savanna areas the curtain of fire which sweeps through dead grass passes very quickly and may heat only a very thin layer of soil.

The burning has a 'partial sterilization' effect which is considered beneficial since it often increases the supply of nutrients in the soil solution and the rate of nitrogen mineralization, retards the growth of seeds which would compete with the new crop, and leads to an altered and generally increased microbial population. These effects are, however, probably rather minor compared with those of the addition of the ash itself.

Since the total weight of forest vegetation is so much greater than that of the savanna areas, the effects of ash addition to the soil after burning are correspondingly higher in the forest. The lowest topsoil pH values are normally found in the very wet forest areas and it is there that the beneficial effects of the additional exchangeable cations derived from the ash and of the raising of the soil pH to less acid levels is likely to be most important. Burning also destroys at least part of the pre-existing litter layer, but in normal forest clearing many groups of farmers leave numbers of shade trees standing and the burn is rarely complete, so that some plant material continues to be added to the soil to decompose and add humus.

Burning has been criticized partly because the organic material is ashed and might have a greater total beneficial effect, even if a much slower one, if allowed to decompose slowly, and partly because it appears that much of the ash produced on burning may be washed out of the soil before it can be taken up by plants. The proportion of the ash produced on burning which is lost through washing out of the soil obviously varies according to local conditions, including climate. In extreme cases some of the ash might be washed off the soil in the run-off, though most or all will normally first be washed into the soil.

The most critical period from the point of view of removal of soluble nutrients, and of general physical deterioration of the soil as a result of heating and the impact of rain, is that period between burning and the establishment of a plant cover some weeks after the onset of the rains. The humus in the topsoil is concentrated in the top 2 in or so and contributes to the crumb structure and hence to the high total pore space favourable to plant growth: both soil heating on exposure and the force of the generally short, heavy showers which mark the beginning of the rainy season in particular have the effect of reducing this crumb structure.

However, tropical soils high in ferric oxides are generally characterized by a well marked and stable aggregation of the clay fraction into larger, often silt-size, particles and by considerable stability for this reason. They may therefore retain much of their porosity under conditions which would adversely affect less stable soils, and the clay fraction, in particular, does not wash out easily from some of the mature soils high in iron. Soil water percolating through them might be almost clear, and profile pits dug in them appear freshly dug even months afterwards. This aggregation and structural stability is an undoubted advantage as regards the maintenance of soil porosity in the critical period after clearing and burning when the soil is exposed to heavy rains. However, some of the richest soils, the basisols developed over the relatively inextensive more basic rocks, are probably the least stable in this respect, being characterized by a high water-dispersible clay content and often by relatively slow internal drainage.

The effects of cultivation

The immediate effects of clearing and burning are succeeded by the longer-term effects of cultivation which may continue for 1 to 4 or more years, though perhaps 2 to 3 years would be an average figure. Yields decline during this period, but actual yield figures for small African-owned farms are difficult to obtain. In any case, mixed cropping is generally the rule and where different crops succeed each other in rotation, direct yield comparisons are not possible. Nevertheless, yields at the end of the cropping period of one half or even less than those at the beginning might be considered normal, and even more spectacular decreases can be expected on some soils.

The rate of yield decrease depends on management practices as well as on soil factors. The lowering of yields is caused by weeds, pests, and diseases, and other influences in addition to those due to a decline in the fertility of the soil itself. The soil factors contributing to this decline are themselves complex and include, in varying degrees, a loss of physical properties, a lowering of the nutrient status of the soil, changes in the soil microbial population, and physical erosion and removal of the topsoil.

The importance of weed growth in cropped patches and the increased labour needed to keep the farm under control is often forgotten in dis- cussions of declining yields during cropping. Diseases and insect pests are liable to be particularly important where the same crop is grown twice in succession and the normal practice of crop rotation is an advantage in this respect. The frequent use of mixed cropping, as when plantains are mixed with cocoyam, or maize with cassava or rice, spreads the risk of failure as well as providing in many cases a better protection for the soil, since harvesting is spread out over a period. Nevertheless, changes in the soil itself are usually the main factors reducing yields.

The decline in nutrient status is associated with declining soil organic matter levels, however caused. Since the supply of fresh organic material during the cropping period has almost always been severely reduced, while mineralization rates are either the same or, more probably, have gone up because of increased exposure, this decline in humus content is an inevitable consequence of clearing and burning which is usually reinforced by the effects of cultivation but which would occur even without it.

Decline in humus levels brings with it a reduction in the supply of a very wide range of major and minor nutrients, but particularly of nitrogen and phosphorus. Some observers have thought that in many cases the major limiting nutrient factor is the lowered supply of organic phosphorus. However, apparent humus loss on cultivation is partly due to mixing with the lower soil layers on cultivation and as humus levels fall so will the rate of further loss probably decline. The rate of loss and of mineralization becomes progressively less as the amounts of soil humus are lowered and approach the new equilibrium level associated with the changed and changing environmental conditions. Losses will in any case depend con- siderably on the type of crop grown and other factors.

To some extent the importance of decline in nutrient levels under cropping, as distinct from the contributory effects of physical soil changes, weeds, and other factors, should be reflected in the extent to which declines can be halted or prevented by the use of fertilizers. Not enough is known about the extent to which this is possible with chemical fertilizers alone. Fertilizer experience in West Africa is discussed further in Chapter 9 (see p. 266). In general, fertilizer responses are not common on soils newly cleared from an adequate fallow which have good organic matter levels, except in the case of nitrogen responses in savanna areas cleared from grass fallow. Responses become more common and more pronounced on long cultivated and exhausted soils where inadequate fallows have resulted in low humus contents. However, it is doubtful if chemical fertilizers alone can maintain productivity on many West African soils if their physical qualities decline.

Physical soil factors affect the availability of plant nutrients as well as the behaviour of soil air and moisture. It is often difficult to consider and assess the purely physical aspects alone since both the physical and chemical soil properties are greatly influenced by soil humus contents. Moreover, physical properties are less easily measured than humus or nutrient levels in the soil. In well aggregated soils the loss of structure due to humus decline alone may not greatly affect yields if nutrient levels remain adequate, but where rainfall is low or erratic the reduction in the moisture storage capacity of soils and in the available water supply might be important. Physical deterioration is in practice often accompanied to varying degrees by the actual removal of part of the surface soil by erosion.

Soil erosion

Soil erosion refers to the physical removal of all or part of the soil by wind, water, and other agents. It is better referred to as *accelerated soil erosion* since slight removal is normal even under the most stable natural conditions, as under virgin forest, and is in fact necessary if soils are not to become excessively deep or over-mature. It is when soil erosion is speeded up or accelerated that it reduces yields and endangers farmed land, and this is usually associated with a reduction in plant cover, however caused, and with the effects of cultivation itself.

The relief of the land is normally in equilibrium with the climate and vegetation. This implies that a balance has been reached between the protective effects of the vegetation cover and the destructive effects of climate. It follows that if the climate changes or, as is usually the case, if the vegetation is changed, as by clearing, this balance will also be altered. The net rate of removal might increase until erosion and deposition have produced shallower slopes and a new equilibrium is attained. The stable relief forms which result from the long interplay of these forces are, like soils themselves, related to climate and vegetation, as well as being influenced by the nature of the rock itself or the presence of ironstone and other crusts.

In the forest zone the protective effects of a high forest vegetation are much greater than those of a vegetation consisting of grasses and scattered small trees, so that despite the greater rainfall the stable slopes in the forest are relatively steep. In the savanna areas the rainfall, though perhaps lower in total, is a more effective agent of erosion because of the sparser vegetation, which is itself largely a result of the seasonal distribution of the rain, and the stable slopes are more gentle.

When a forest vegetation is removed, the protective influence of the vegetation is reduced or eliminated, but the potential destructive force of the rainfall is very high because of the steep slopes characteristic of forest topography. In savanna areas the relief is more subdued, so that even if the sparse vegetation is removed, the resulting increases in soil erosion and removal are not likely to be as great as in forest areas. It is in forest areas that soil erosion can be the most spectacular, particularly after clearing on steep hillsides, whereas in the savanna areas some soil erosion may be far more widespread but is less likely to be so immediately striking.

Vegetation protects the soil by sheltering it from the main force of the rain, much of which may then drip slowly and gently from the leaves, by shading the soil, by protecting it with a litter layer, and by holding it together and anchoring it with its roots. In a high forest there is usually a closed upper canopy and perhaps irregular strata of smaller trees below this, and the topsoil is bound by a dense mat of feeding roots.

In the savanna areas the frequently scattered and small fire-tolerant trees have a relatively small protective effect and often the grass itself is in clumps or tussocks with bare, exposed soil between. The annual grass burning keeps the tree densities low and clears away the dead grasses to expose the soil at the beginning of the rains. Under these conditions widespread sheet erosion is to be expected.

Sheet erosion occurs when water runs off most or all the ground surface taking with it some of the surface soil. It is likely to be most important when the soil surface does not absorb water readily, as when it has a poor structure through humus loss and when the soil is compacted or the pores blocked by silt particles washed into them. These factors result in a greater proportion of the total rainfall running off the surface and taking some of the surface soil with it.

Sheet erosion is very widespread in the savanna areas of West Africa, and has resulted in shallow soil profiles in some areas; it is particularly serious in the more densely populated and heavily cultivated areas, though its effects are generally gradual rather than sudden and spread out over the whole soil surface so that they may not be noticed as easily as those of gully erosion.

Gully erosion generally occurs on the steeper slopes and is a more local-ized and spectacular form of erosion which results from the run-off water being channelled into well-defined depressions which are rapidly deepened to form gullies. The two forms of erosion may be associated. Gully erosion is relatively difficult to control, and deep gullies may have the important effect of lowering the water table in their vicinity.

In general the traditional systems of land rotation cultivation in the forest areas minimize erosion by keeping at least some plant cover during clearing, by growing several crops together and by keeping soil cultivation and weeding down to a minimum. Erosion can be expected to be increased with complete clearing, with greater disturbance of the soil and with soil exposure that follows the harvesting of a single crop.

In savanna areas the ground is normally much more exposed than under forest and is often heaped into mounds or into ridges which may run down the slope and thus encourage gullying between them, but since the slopes of savanna areas are typically gentler than those of forest areas they are less liable to severe gullying.

Cultivation and engineering practices which reduce accelerated soil erosion are the province of soil conservation. They are generally designed to reduce run-off by maintaining an adequate plant cover, by keeping gradients moderate, and in general by adapting the types and methods of cultivation to the degree of erosion danger present on any particular farm. In dry periods *wind erosion* may also be important and can be reduced by planting wind breaks as well as by maintaining some plant cover for as much of the year as possible.

Erosion in West Africa has not been as serious or as alarming as it has in some other parts of the world. This is partly due to the nature of the traditional farming methods still employed and the lack, as yet, of wide-spread mechanical cultivation. The merits and disadvantages of present practices of land rotation are now considered further, together with the soils factors which appear to affect the prospects of modifying them successfully and of introducing greater agricultural mechanization.

Advantages and disadvantages of shifting cultivation

The disadvantages of shifting cultivation are perhaps more obvious than the advantages. The main disadvantages are (1) the great expenditure of labour needed when forest regrowth vegetation is cleared, labour which, unless permanent tree crops are planted, gives only a few seasons' returns before the land is again abandoned; (2) the generally low yields associated with the system; (3) the considerable proportion of the total land which is in fallow and therefore not productive at any one time; and (4) the fact that the system is stable only as long as fallow periods can be maintained for an adequate period. When fallows are reduced, yields can be expected to decline still further and thus lead to even shorter fallows, so that essentially the system works only where the ratio of land to people is high. To these general disadvantages can be added more specific considerations such as nutrient loss from the nutrient capital which might follow burning.

The advantages of the system can also be briefly summarized. The annual cycle of work imposed on the farmer is dictated by and adapted to the seasons: the dry season allows the cleared material to dry out and be burnt before the rains. The newly planted crop benefits from the ash derived from the burning, and nitrate levels have also been described (see p. 154) as being highest at the beginning of the rains when needed by the new crop. The fact that, in most forest areas, clearing is not complete and some shade trees may be left standing serves to give some protection to the soil, while existing roots are left undisturbed and only a relatively superficial cultivation with hoe or cutlass is practised to plant seeds, corns, or suckers. Mixed cropping helps to protect the soil. Although inadequate weeding, particularly towards the end of the cropping period, may reduce yields, it further serves to protect the soil against heating up and erosion, to supply it with some organic material and to ensure that, once abandoned to fallow, the regrowth vegetation quickly takes over.

The farmer himself needs little capital except a few hand tools and his own labour. Provided that fallow periods are long enough, soil regeneration is usually sufficient to suggest that the system can be regarded as a permanent one. Under these conditions, it can be said to be well adapted to low population densities living in the West African forest environment, though it will be noted that most of the advantages apply more to forest soils than to savanna ones where the general level of productivity is lower as a result of the generally less favourable environment.

Increasing population densities and the desire to improve on living standards have naturally posed with increasing urgency the question of raising agricultural productivity in West Africa, both in terms of yields per acre and in relation to the amount of labour invested. In theory two approaches are possible, one being to modify the existing system in an attempt to improve it by overcoming some of the disadvantages and at the same time retaining the undoubted advantages it has, the other is to introduce new systems based partly perhaps on experience in other parts of the world. The supporters of the first approach can point to the failures of many large and too hastily executed schemes based on inadequate previous trials and knowledge of the local soils and environment, and these failures certainly emphasize the need to 'hasten slowly' and to try out improvements thoroughly before adopting them on a large and costly scale.

A relatively obvious method of improving the general practice of shifting cultivation which has been considered from time to time consists in substituting the natural fallow by specially planted fallows, perhaps of quick-growing leguminous shrubs such as *Gliricidia*, which would have quicker and better effects than the natural fallow. Competition and natural selection have however probably resulted in natural fallows including the more aggressive and faster growing species and the fact that, in most of the West African forest zone at least, the species present vary relatively little with rainfall and other factors suggests that this natural selection is not greatly affected by local shortages of seed.

So far no alternative fallow vegetation has been shown to be much better than the natural. Even if it were it would require planting, and one of the virtues of natural fallow is its variety and the speed with which, under forest conditions at least, both new weeds and new growths from existing stumps and roots ensure a rapid upsurge of growth and immediate cover. Artificial fallows might, however, be easier to clear, and lend themselves to mechanized planting and clearing. Grass is known as an excellent improver of soil structure. Some grasses grow extremely well under forest conditions, producing very high tonnages of green matter with or without added nitrogen, so that the use of a grass fallow for regenerating old farms in the forest zone deserves further study. It might be combined with stock raising.

One disadvantage of land rotation cultivation, particularly in forest conditions, is the large amount of labour needed to cut down and clear forest vegetation. This can be reduced to minor proportions if tree killing, either with poisons or with hormones, is substituted. The dead material decomposes slowly and is humified, rather than being burnt and reduced to ash. For large-scale oil palm cultivation in the Ivory Coast and elsewhere the burning of the cut down vegetation is also avoided: clearing is complete but the trash is pushed by heavy machinery into parallel lines, so that alternate lanes between palms are clear and allow access and easy weeding, while the remainder are occupied by rotting trees.

The rationalization of the land rotation methods used by local cultivators has also been attempted, as in the 'corridor' system in the Congo. This method divided land into regular blocks large enough to allow a cycle of 4 years cropping followed by 16 years of fallow. The strips owned by different cultivators were parallel and adjacent so that at any one time a fairly large area, across the strips, was devoted to a particular crop in the succession, thus allowing large-scale disease and pest control and other operations.

Farmers substitute one type of vegetation—the plants grown—for another, the natural vegetation, and obviously the character of the natural climax vegetation can be expected to be some guide as to what plants and types of plant grow best. There are strong natural indications that in the forest zone tree crops are preferable to annuals while in the savanna areas annuals, including grasses such as the grain crops, are likely to be more successful.

There is a particularly strong case for emphasizing tree crops in the forest areas. Highly weathered tropical soils are often not as fertile as the high natural forest might suggest, since the nutrients are largely revolving in a closed cycle between trees and topsoil. On clearing, burning, and cultivation, there may be a considerable loss both from topsoil and from vegetation. The highly weathered subsoils are often relatively sterile compared with the topsoil, and so deep that roots may not reach the lower horizons where rock weathering might release new nutrients into the system. Once degraded or eroded, the power of recovery of these soils might be very low.

Tree crops, as compared with most annuals and biannuals, make relatively small demands on the soil nutrients and avoid the losses due to successive stages of clearing, burning, and cultivation. Once established, they protect the soil from the destructive effects of the climate and anchor it with their roots much as did the original forest vegetation; they also feed it with their litter and in a well-established rubber, oil palm, cocoa or coffee farm one can visualize a fairly closed cycle of nutrient circulation, even if the amounts circulating are lower than under the original forest. When tree crops become too old, or (as with oil palms) too tall to be economic, they can often be relatively easily replaced by the same or another tree crop which is introduced beneath the first in order to minimize soil exposure. Tree crops thus protect and benefit the soil, while the farmer in turn benefits from the fact that once tree crops are established, routine weeding and maintenance might be small compared with the labour of clearing new land every year. He also has a permanent capital asset for his labour, instead of just the season or two of cropping which he gets when he practises shifting cultivation.

The farmer has not been slow to see at least some of these advantages and hence the large acreages now planted of cocoa, coffee, oil palm, and rubber in many forest areas, and of coconuts along the littorals. From the soil point of view at least, there is much to be said for encouraging tree crops at the expense of annuals, and they may also help to check forest shrinking and savanna invasion, as well as to maintain the existing forest climate and micro-climates.

In savanna areas the problems are different and in many ways greater, although there is perhaps scope for more spectacular improvements than are possible in the forest zone. These improvements can be expected to result from the combinations of many factors, some of which apply to all the agricultural zones of West Africa. These factors include better seed supply, better crop varieties, better control of insects and diseases, the wider use of irrigation, the development of improved rotations, the greater use of organic and inorganic fertilizers and the building up, by more enlightened methods, of the general level of soil productivity. However, it is in the increased scope for mechanization that savanna development possibilities differ mainly from forest ones.

THE MECHANIZATION OF AGRICULTURE

Agricultural mechanization is a broad subject which includes the application of all forms of power to agricultural operations of all types, so that the farmer is less and less dependent on his own physical labour and that of those helping him.

Mechanization in this broad sense includes the mechanization of the processing of crop products (e.g. rice and coffee hulling), weed control by both mechanical and chemical means, crop planting, fertilizing, harvesting, handling and transport, and other minor applications, but the major use of mechanization and the one primarily thought of by most people in connection with the term concerns the mechanization of clearing, and the preparation of land by ploughing and other operations.

Mechanization could enable the existing farming population to cultivate more land, but unless regeneration by quicker means than natural regrowth is introduced, more cultivation may increase pressure on the land and reduce resting periods. Moreover, mechanization does not necessarily increase yields per acre, even if it increases yields per day's work, and in fact large-scale mechanization in temperate areas is generally associated with lower yields than are obtained by more intensive methods. The use of heavy machinery also requires that fields and farms be fairly large: the present small cultivation patches might have to be merged into bigger, perhaps communally-owned ones. The smaller types of tractor and cultivator found suitable for use in temperate regions are often too light for tropical use and not designed for the heavy work and rough conditions of the tropics.

Mechanization implies the expenditure of money on the purchase and running of machinery, whereas the subsistence farmer has little source of

cash income for such capitalization, and his family might supply a source
of cheap labour. Mechanization could also encourage quick farming of too
large areas at the expense of careful farming, and it may lead to an
undesirable emphasis on certain crops which lend themselves more easily
to mechanization than others. Furthermore, if adequate servicing and
repair facilities are not available, and machines are not carefully maintained
by trained engineers, they may deteriorate so rapidly that mechanized
cultivation actually becomes more expensive than hand methods.

Nevertheless, the main difficulties and dangers of mechanization are
more fundamental and are related to the nature of the soil and the associated climate. If land is completely cleared, it can be ploughed, harrowed,
sown, fertilized, weeded, and harvested mechanically. This results in a
saving of labour at every stage but also in the soil being more exposed to
the effects of sun and rain, particularly before the planted crop has established itself and after it has been harvested. In most of the forest zone the
relief is typically steep and dissected, and most of the ground sloping. The
gradients, together with the normal heavy and intense falls of rain associated particularly with the line squalls common at the beginning of the
rains, could be expected to result in heavy erosion, both sheet erosion and
gullying.

Even without accelerated erosion and topsoil removal, the factors of
clearing, cultivation, and lack of adequate cover are likely to bring about
a greater fall in humus levels and greater structural deterioration than are
associated with some of the traditional local methods. The behaviour of
a soil once it has lost its humus depends on its texture and structural
stability. Many West African soils which are high in clay and iron are
firmly aggregated into silt-size particles, and this gives them considerable
stability: they may remain permeable and porous even when low in humus,
and percolating water may remove little if any clay from them. This structural stability (structure here referring to the aggregation of the clay to
silt-size particles and not necessarily into much larger units) is one of the
favourable properties of some highly weathered latosols. On the other
hand there are some soils, often the lighter ones, which completely lose
their structure under intense cultivation. If the finer particles are washed
downwards, cultivation may result in a relatively sandy, sterile topsoil
overlying lower horizons in which soil pores are clogged by silt and clay,
or which may even contain a clay pan below plough depth.

There remains the question of how to reduce or prevent yields falling
with successive cropping, or how to restore productivity by means other
than fallow when they do fall. No continuous system of arable mechanized
cultivation has yet proved workable and economic in the conditions which

prevail in the forest zone of West Africa, where the most profitable and best understood type of large-scale operation is still often the planting of tree crops. Nevertheless, the use of heavy grass mulches as well as chemical fertilizers, together with animal manures where available, offer some possibilities for the development of new systems adapted to the forest areas.

It is in the savanna areas of West Africa that the possibilities offered by increased mechanization appear relatively more important. This is partly because savanna crops, especially grains such as guinea corn, maize, and millet, lend themselves to mechanized cultivation more readily than do forest tree crops and such subsistence crops as cocoyam and plantain, but also because the relief is in general much flatter in savanna areas, while the initial clearing of savanna vegetation is easier and cheaper than the laborious and expensive stumping involved in forest clearing.

In general, savanna yields are so low that at least some improvement, with or without mechanization, should be possible on the less difficult soils. Mechanization and the increasing of productivity are both much more difficult on the very gravelly, shallow soils, on soils capped with ironstone sheets or boulders and on the extensive groundwater laterites in which a partly hardened subsoil zone near the surface may be exposed when the topsoil is removed.

Mounding and ridging by the local farmers is designed partly to help surface drainage during the rains and to prevent young plants being washed away, so that although the great need is for more water, drainage operations may also need to be envisaged in order to carry away temporary surpluses. In some dry areas of West Africa small dams designed to supply water for irrigation and for livestock have been very successful. They often have productive, dry-season vegetable gardens immediately below them in which the farmer can work during the dry season when other cultivation work is slack.

Irrigation possibilities in the savanna areas are very great. Even in the wetter, forest areas, rainfall is often so seasonal that irrigation in the dry seasons might offer economic returns. The construction of irrigation and drainage systems falls within the scope of agricultural engineering, though successful irrigation and drainage depends to a considerable degree on soil factors, particularly on physical soil properties.

9 MANURES, FERTILIZERS, AND THEIR USE

FERTILIZERS AND MANURES

Manures, in the wide sense, refer to all substances added to the soil in order to increase the supply of plant nutrients, and include therefore such diverse materials as wood ash, the bones, dung, and urine of animals and birds, fresh or composted plant parts, and other more or less naturally occurring substances such as rocks and sea shells. The use of at least some of these goes back a long way and information on manuring can be found, for example, in the works of Roman authors written 2000 and more years ago.

With the development of chemical manufacturing techniques in the last 100 years or so, combined with relatively recent advances in agricultural chemistry, has come an increasing use of chemical compounds of known composition. These were regarded at first with suspicion by some and considered as inferior to 'natural' manures. Organic manures, as considered further below, have beneficial effects on physical soil properties which chemical ones do not, but the plant absorbs its needs mainly or entirely in the forms described in Chapter 6 and the effect of these nutrient anions or cations on growth itself is the same whether they are derived from complex organic manures or relatively simple chemical ones. For clarity, the former are referred to here as manures, the second as fertilizers.

The complexity of the soil and other factors governing plant nutrition has been described in Chapter 6. Attention was drawn to the importance of soil reaction and of a balanced supply of nutrients, as well as to the distinction between total nutrients in the soil and those available to the plant at any one time. The beneficial effects of fertilizers and manures depend on a range of environmental and management factors as well as on the soil. For maximum increases in yield, attention has also to be given to such subjects as seed quality and the breeding and use of improved crop varieties, to disease and pest control, to times of harvesting and optimum planting densities, to irrigation and to drainage where necessary, and to other factors which affect growth and yields.

The final yield obtained depends on so many factors that it might be difficult in practice to assess the importance of nutrition in general or of the lack of any one nutrient in particular. If fertilizers are to be used wisely, however, some idea of their effects and hence of the optimum quantities to be used must be obtained.

The application of fertilizers and manures has the aim of increasing soil fertility and thus productivity, but the effects of these additions depend partly on the existing fertility of the soil and may in fact be greater when applied to an already productive soil than when applied to a very poor one. These effects will also vary according to the inherent physical and chemical properties of the soil, particularly on the nature and content of the clay and humus colloids. Broadly speaking, clay soils are more difficult to work than sandy ones, store greater quantities of water and nutrients, but may give up their nutrients more slowly than lighter-textured soils. Light, sandy soils low in both clay and humus are relatively easy to work, and may give up to the plant their stored water and nutrients more easily than heavier soils, though their reserves of both are usually much lower and therefore sooner exhausted. In this chapter, however, the emphasis is on the nature and composition of the manures and fertilizers themselves rather than on the soil factors governing uptake by the plant, some of which are discussed in Chapter 6.

Animal manures

Animal manures include animal dung and urine, and animal by-products such as bonemeal and dried blood. Dung contains the undigested portions of the animal's food, whereas urine contains only the soluble products resulting from the break-down in the animal of the digested part of the food. Dung, in particular, varies greatly in composition and hence in usefulness according to the nature and even age and health of the animal, and the quality and composition of its food supply. Urine has a higher nitrogen and potassium content than dung, and since these are in solution they are quickly available to plants. Dung has a much more varied composition, decomposes more slowly, and, because of its organic matter content, has beneficial physical effects on the soil which urine and chemical fertilizers do not.

The value of animal manures depends to a considerable extent on how they are handled and stored before being added to the soil and hence the extent to which they might have decomposed and lost some of their more soluble or volatile constituents before being applied, as when nitrogen is lost as ammonia gas. It is often better to mix together the manures obtained from different types of animal, if available, rather than apply only one type.

In West Africa the largest volume of available manure is cow manure, and this, together with horse manure, is relatively bulky and low in plant nutrients in comparison with that of other animals. If the cow feeds only on poor grasses with a low protein and a high silica content, such as those generally available in the dry season, its manure will be correspondingly high in undigestible residues of low nutrient value. Nevertheless, the application of cow and horse manures is highly beneficial and relatively long-lasting, and in the northern areas of Ghana, for example, the standard recommendation is 8 tons of manure per acre for all crops except yam, which is liable to be infested by yam beetle if animal manures are used. The manure is applied at the beginning of the maize—guinea corn—millet rotation.

Pig manure in particular depends in quality on the animal's diet, but is generally richer than cow manure. Sheep and goat manure are more concentrated than the other forms considered and are rich in plant nutrients: both animals, but particularly goats, feed on a great variety of plants.

The richest and most concentrated manure on the farm is that of poultry—the fact that the urine and solid excreta are mixed contributes to the higher nitrogen and phosphorus content—but because of its concentrated nature care is needed in the application of poultry manure. It ferments quickly, releasing ammonia, and is frequently recommended for vegetable production in particular. It has been estimated that a single, well-fed hen produces 33 lb of manure per year, containing approximately 8 oz of nitrogen, 6 oz of phosphate, 3 oz of potassium oxide and appreciable quantities of calcium, magnesium, and boron.

Bonemeal is derived from animal bones and is a source of calcium and phosphorus in the form of calcium phosphate. For quicker effects it is ground fine, though it is not a cheap form of phosphorus. Dried blood contains about 10 per cent of nitrogen but is also not a cheap source of supply compared with chemical nitrogenous fertilizers. Chemical phosphates are sometimes added to animal manures in order to reinforce their generally low phosphorus content and to reduce nitrogen losses as ammonia, and it is thought that phosphates are in some cases less likely to be combined in sparingly soluble compounds when added together with organic colloidal material.

A great part of the virtue of animal manures lies in their slow mineralization and the addition of organic matter to the soil which they produce, so that on a cost basis it is not correct merely to calculate the percentage of N, P, or K they contain and to compare this with the cost of an equivalent amount of that element in the form of chemical fertilizers. In any case, animal manures are simple to apply, are available locally and, if not wisely used, will be wasted: chemical fertilizers have usually to be imported and paid for and may require greater technical knowledge in their application. In addition, many of the advocates of animal and plant manures have drawn attention to their content both of a very wide range of elements and possibly of complex organic compounds such as vitamins and hormones which may also stimulate growth.

Much better use could be made of existing supplies of animal manures in West Africa, while the increased adoption of mixed farming practices in which crop production and stock raising are carried on side by side so that each benefits the other, undoubtedly holds out considerable prospects for greater productivity. Although cattle raising is thought of primarily in connection with the tsetse-free savanna areas, it has been successfully accomplished in the forest zone and the usual textbook generalizations about its absence from this area must be critically re-examined. In any case, sheep, goats, pigs, and poultry flourish in the forest as well as the savanna areas and, in conjunction with tree crops such as coconuts and oil palm, could provide the basis of a workable mixed farming system even where cattle are not kept.

Although animal husbandry is beyond the scope of this book, a brief digression on some of the factors likely to affect its success is relevant to the subject of animal manures. In essence, the maximum development of meat or milk production depends both on the genetic qualities of the animal and the extent to which its genetic potential is either realized or limited by the environment—and similar considerations apply to plants. Genetic potential is increased both by the informed, rigorous selection of local stock and by the introduction of new stock from outside, often crossed with the local. Selection implies the castration or separation of bulls and other male animals not up to breeding standard, a simple practice which by itself could raise West African stock quality, but the realization of the improved genetic potential is mainly a question of disease control, management practices and, above all, of food and sometimes water supply. In the case of pasture for cattle, in particular, the main problems are concerned with the dry-season shortage of pasture and the poor quality of what little grass is then available. Cattle may have to walk long distances in search of food and water and frequently lose in weight what they have added in the wet season, so that there is little or no net gain. Improved pastures through careful selection, the prevention of overgrazing, and, perhaps, the use of irrigation and fertilizers could themselves lead, among other things, to the manure being more abundant and of better quality, while if fodder crops were grown to supplement dry-season food shortages, a system of mixed farming could be envisaged which would lift the general productivity levels of both arable agriculture and stock raising.

Green manures and mulches

Animal manure consists largely of grass and other plants which have undergone some change during digestion, but green plants in the fresh state can also be added to the soil directly, and this also is a practice which goes back to Roman times and earlier, when beans and other leguminous crops in particular were recommended. The practice of adding to the soil fresh, undecomposed green plant material is known as green manuring. In some cases the plant is grown and dug or ploughed in where grown; in others it is cut and put on to other areas as a mulch.

The green manure crop while it is growing protects the soil and functions as a cover crop, so that green manuring and the use of cover crops and mulches are often considered together.

When green manures are added to the soil they supply organic carbon, nitrogen and a range of other plant nutrients to the soil, the composition of the green manure depending on the type of plant and on soil and other environmental factors. Green manure is particularly noted for the stimulating effect it has on soil bacterial activity, and in this respect it may differ in its effects from those produced by the addition of dead and decomposed plant material. If the green manure does not contain leguminous plants, it is assumed merely to be returning to the soil those nitrates which it has previously removed from it, but if a legume obtains nitrogen from the air fixed by the symbiotic nodule bacteria, then additional nitrogen is being added to the system. It is this additional nitrogen which is often thought of as being one of the main benefits of the use of leguminous cover crops and green manures in temperate regions, in which legumes and non-legumes are frequently grown mixed together, particularly in crop rotations.

In some respects the growing and then turning in of a cover crop is best considered as a short-term artificial fallow, for, like natural fallows, it might obtain nutrients from the whole rooting zone and then concentrate them in the topsoil in a more available form. Its efficiency should thus be judged by similar criteria to those used in the examination of the role of natural fallows in the previous chapter, the main difference being that, whereas the natural fallow is usually burnt when cleared, green manuring adds fresh plant material.

Although the theoretical possibilities and benefits of green manuring in the tropics are great, little is yet known as to its best use in practice or to what extent the tropical leguminous cover crops and green manures now used really add extra nitrogen to the system. It is thought by some that they often merely rest the land and may halt the decline caused by continuous cropping without bringing about any real improvement, in which case natural fallows might be cheaper and more effective.

Little careful experimental work has as yet been carried out in West Africa on which generalizations might be based as to the extent to which additional nitrogen can be added to the soil by this means, or the extent to which green manures and mulches raise organic matter levels in the soil more than very temporarily. The very rapid rates of organic matter mineralization in most of West Africa probably result in the fact that it needs very heavy applications of green manure to raise organic matter levels appreciably in the soil, and that any increase so obtained is quickly lost again. However, grasses such as elephant grass and Bermuda grass can produce very high tonnages of green material to the acre, particularly under a forest zone climate or when irrigated; and if they are added at frequent intervals to fields under cultivation they might greatly help in keeping up productivity.

Perennial plants have been found to be better capable of improving soil structure and organic matter levels than annuals, but in Africa so far grasses have been more effective than legumes. Grasses are widely recognized as being good structure-improvers because of their dense fibrous root systems, and grasses, of course, include such crops as sugar cane. The benefits of green manures and cover crops which are not also used for fodder and other purposes must be considered in relation to the loss of a year's cropping.

The wider and more effective uses of mulches is a separate but related question, the primary benefit of a mulch sometimes being its effect on reducing soil water losses and keeping down soil temperatures and erosion rather than the addition of nutrients which it also brings, so that mulches are particularly valuable when and where water supplies are marginal. The use of plant mulches in West Africa has sometimes been unpopular with local farmers because they may encourage termites which subsequently attack the growing crop when other food material is in short supply. In East Africa, however, grass mulches are widely used on tree crops such as coffee, and it has been found that if fertilizers are added to high-yielding grasses such as elephant grass (*Pennisetum purpureum*), and the grass is then cut and applied as a mulch to tree crops such as coffee, then the trees benefit from the added fertilizer as the grass is mineralized, and in fact a greater percentage of the added fertilizer is taken up by the tree in this way than if the fertilizer were applied direct.

CHEMICAL FERTILIZERS AND THEIR USE

Chemical fertilizers differ from organic manures in that they usually consist of relatively simple chemical compounds of known composition and that they contain, weight for weight, much higher percentages of fertilizing elements. They are therefore more concentrated and usually easier to transport and apply, and to store. Some chemical fertilizers are dug out or mined from naturally occurring deposits. Others, particularly the nitrogen-containing fertilizers, are manufactured in increasing quantities.

In the industrialized temperate countries where gigantic total quantities of chemical fertilizers are used each year, present levels of agricultural production would be impossible without them. In these countries a vast amount of experience has been gained in their use under local conditions, and advice is normally available to farmers from agricultural advisers and local agricultural stations and colleges, as well as from the manufacturers and sellers of fertilizers themselves who naturally have an interest in showing farmers how to use their products and in publicizing the results of successful fertilizer use.

In West Africa, as well as in many other areas of the world where agriculture is not highly commercialized, fertilizers are used to only a small and sometimes negligible extent. This is indicated by the fertilizer import statistics for the West African countries. The small quantities of fertilizers that are imported are used mainly by research stations and a few large plantations. Fertilizer use by the small West African subsistence farmer has hardly begun.

If fertilizers are to be used on a much wider scale in West Africa, it is necessary first to find out more about their use—when, and where, and in what combination they give the best results. Secondly, it is necessary to demonstrate their use to the farmer and persuade him that it is in his interest to apply them. Since fertilizers have normally to be paid for in cash, their increasing use is often associated with a more commercial approach to agriculture than the present general subsistence agriculture of much of West Africa. The small subsistence farmer may not be able to invest money in fertilizers even if he wishes, and may have to be helped by loans or subsidies, particularly in the earlier stages of their introduction.

The first need is to find out more about the kind of conditions under which applications of commercial fertilizers can give economic returns, this in turn depending on the cost of the fertilizer, the yield increase obtained, and the local selling price of the crop. Commercial agriculture is the art—or science—of growing crops for a profit and not just of growing crops. Yields can very often be increased given sufficient expenditure of time and money, but these increases might be totally uneconomic, while the unwise use of fertilizers can even reduce yields. A brief summary of our present knowledge of fertilizer responses in West Africa, and brief notes on the recent FAO fertilizer demonstrations and trials, is contained in a subsequent section (see p. 269).

TABLE 9.1. Very approximate amounts of N, P_2O_5, and K_2O, in lb/acre, removed by some important West African crops.

The amounts removed refer to the yield figures given in the second column, which themselves vary widely in West Africa. It should not be assumed that nutrients added in fertilizer should be in the same proportion as they are thought to be removed by the plant, for the type and amount of fertilizer required will vary with local soil conditions and will be affected by what is in the soil already and other factors. The table does indicate, however, that different crops require nutrients in different proportions and amounts, as can be seen by comparing, for example, coconuts with cassava (Table adapted from *Fertilizers and their use*, FAO, Rome, 1965).

CROP	YIELD (lb/acre)	N	P_2O_5	K_2O
Maize	3000	72	36	54
Cassava	25 000	161	39	136
Sugar cane	25 000	30	20	60
Groundnuts	1500	105	15	42
Tobacco	1700	90	22	129
Coffee (fresh berries)	5000	35	7	40
Oil palm (bunches)	15 000	90	20	135
Cocoa (dry pods)	1000	20	10	12
Coconuts	1500	13	4	12
Rice—grain	1600	35	9	7
straw	2750	11	3	29

Methods of fertilizer application

Chemical fertilizers, either single or mixed, can be applied to the soil and in some cases the plant itself in a variety of ways, the best method depending on the type of fertilizer used, on the crop involved, and on the local soil and climate. The influence of some of these factors is discussed in Chapter 6, and later in this chapter under the individual fertilizer nutrients. In general, fertilizers are applied to the soil by one or more of the following common methods:

1. *Broadcasting*. In broadcasting, fertilizers are applied fairly uniformly to the surface of the field or farm patch before the crop is planted. The fertilizer may be left on the surface or worked into the ground: the less soluble the fertilizer, the greater the need to mix it with the soil so that it occurs within the plant root zone.

2. *Row or sideband placement*. Row placement, or sidebanding, is mainly used where specially designed equipment for the purpose is available. It consists in placing the fertilizer in the soil a little away from the seed or seedling, often 2 to 3 in to one side, and 1 or 2 in below the seed or plant. In this way the fertilizer is near enough to be used by the plant but not close enough to injure it. In West African practice the equivalent, where

no special machinery is available, would be to put the fertilizer in the planting hole at similar distances from the seed or from the roots of the transplanted seedling. Some fertilizers can injure seeds and plants when placed too close to them or in too large amounts.

3. *Top-dressing.* Top-dressing consists of broadcasting fertilizer on to a field containing a growing crop. It is sometimes used for grain crops, cotton, and sugar cane, and is of value mainly for the relatively soluble fertilizers, such as nitrate, which are easily washed into the soil and quickly available to the plant. These are the fertilizers often applied as split applications (see below) during the growing season to give an extra shot of nutrient when needed.

4. *Side-dressing.* Side-dressing differs from top-dressing inasmuch as the added fertilizer is placed along rows of plants, or between rows, or next to or around individual plants or trees. It is thus more localized than top-dressing, but is also merely applied to the surface of the soil and therefore best used for very soluble fertilizers easily washed into the soil and the root zone. Less soluble fertilizers and nutrients which move relatively slowly in the soil are best placed in the soil where roots will reach them, and not merely top-dressed or side-dressed.

The time of fertilizer application

Correct timing of fertilizer applications is of great practical importance, and is connected with the method chosen. Row or sideband placement and broadcasting are done before the seeds or plants are put into the ground, or at the same time. With fertilizers such as the phosphorus-containing fertilizers which do not move far in the soil, and with the less soluble fertilizers which become available over a period, placement in the soil at or before planting is normally best. In the case of the very soluble, quick-acting fertilizers, particularly the nitrates, fertilizer can be added during the growing season as top or side dressings, or dissolved in irrigation waters. Trace elements are often applied as leaf sprays, and in the case of pineapples solid fertilizer may be placed in the leaf axils.

The application of the same fertilizer more than once to a crop is known as a split application. Split applications are useful in the case of very soluble fertilizers in high rainfall areas because they tend to increase the proportion of added nutrient taken up by the plant and reduce wastage through leaching out of the soil. Split applications are also widely used with nitrate applications to maize and other crops which have been shown to benefit from extra nitrogen at a particular stage in their development. In southern Nigeria, for example, a 4 year study from 1958 to 1962 showed that split applications of nitrate at 1 month and at 2 months after planting were more effective than single applications either at planting or at 2 months after planting.

Single and mixed fertilizers

In the following sections on fertilizer materials the commoner commercial fertilizers are discussed. Many of these contain only one major nutrient and are referred to, somewhat loosely, as single fertilizers, though in many cases the accompanying elements may also have beneficial effects. In addition to these generally single fertilizers, a wide range of ready mixed fertilizers are available containing stated proportions of all three major nutrients, or of the major nutrients with additions of other nutrient elements. The conventional method of designating the nutrient content of these mixtures is to give the percentage by weight they contain of nitrogen, phosphorus pentoxide (P_2O_5) and potassium oxide (K_2O). Thus a mixture labelled 10–10–10 would contain, in every 100 lb, 10 lb of nitrogen, 10 lb of P_2O_5, and 10 lb of K_2O. If the amounts of elemental phosphorus or potassium rather than P_2O_5 and K_2O are required, then these figures have to be multiplied by the conversion figures given on pp. 278 and 286.

The grade of the fertilizer, such as the 10–10–10 given as an example above, tells the user both the ratio of nitrogen to phosphorus to potassium in his fertilizer and also how concentrated the fertilizer is. A 15–15–15 mixture obviously contains more of the three nutrients per 100 lb than the 10–10–10 mixture, and is therefore more concentrated, though the ratio of the nutrients to each other remains the same. More concentrated fertilizers may save transport and handling costs, but in some cases the additional materials in the low-analysis fertilizers may also be of value.

Although a fairly large number of fertilizer materials are discussed in the following sections—and this list is by no means complete—there are only three fertilizer materials imported in any quantity in West Africa, and these three, ammonium sulphate, muriate of potash, and single super-phosphate, are frequently mixed on the spot to make various combinations and grades of mixed fertilizers. Mixing is easily done if the N, P_2O_5 and K_2O percentages of the single fertilizers are known. Table 9.2 gives the quantities of fertilizer ingredient needed. For example, if a farmer desires to apply 20 lb of N, 20 lb of P_2O_5 and 10 lb of K_2O, he will have to take 98 lb of sulphate of ammonia containing 20·5 per cent N, 111 lb of single superphosphate containing 18 per cent P_2O_5 and 16 lb of potassium chloride (muriate of potash) containing 60 per cent K_2O. He will therefore apply a total of 225 lb of his mixture per acre to give the application rates desired. A large part of this total weight is made up of the sulphate and the calcium in the ammonium sulphate and the single superphosphate. The more concentrated commercial mixed fertilizers are made possible only by using ingredients containing higher percentages of the nutrient elements desired, such as ammonium nitrate and ammonium phosphate.

TABLE 9.2. Quantities of a fertilizer ingredient of known nutrient content required to give a specific weight of nutrient (Adapted from tables prepared by FAO).

PERCENTAGE OF NUTRIENT IN THE FERTILIZER INGREDIENT	WEIGHT OF NUTRIENT REQUIRED (lb)							
	10	20	30	40	60	80	100	120
3	333	667	1000	1333	2000			
4	250	500	750	1000	1500	2000		
5·5	182	364	545	727	1091	1455	1818	
6	166	333	501	667	1000	1333	1667	2000
7	143	286	428	571	857	1142	1429	1714
8	125	250	375	500	750	1000	1250	1500
9	111	222	333	444	667	889	1111	1333
10	100	200	300	400	600	800	1000	1200
11	91	182	273	364	545	727	909	1091
12	84	166	254	333	500	666	833	1000
13	77	154	231	308	426	615	769	923
15	66	133	201	267	400	533	667	800
15·5	65	129	193	258	387	516	645	774
16	62	125	188	250	375	500	625	750
18	55	111	167	222	333	444	555	666
20	50	100	150	200	300	400	500	600
20·5	49	98	146	195	293	390	488	585
21	47	95	144	190	286	381	476	571
25	40	80	120	160	240	320	400	480
30	33	67	100	133	200	267	333	400
33	30	61	91	121	182	242	303	364
34	28	59	90	118	177	235	294	253
42	24	48	71	95	143	190	238	286
44	22	45	69	91	136	182	227	273
45	22	44	67	89	133	178	222	267
46	21	43	66	87	130	174	217	261
48	21	42	62	83	125	167	208	250
50	20	40	60	80	120	160	200	240
51	20	39	58	78	118	167	196	235
60	16	33	51	67	100	133	167	200
62	16	32	49	65	87	129	161	195

Not all the fertilizers listed in the following pages can be safely mixed. Ammonium-containing fertilizers may lose ammonia gas if mixed with some basic fertilizers such as rock phosphate and basic slag. Fertilizers containing free calcium cannot be mixed with soluble, phosphate-containing fertilizers. Hygroscopic or very soluble fertilizers cake or form lumps if kept in mixtures. Complete fertilizers obtained by chemical reaction and the formation of new, more concentrated compounds are often preferable to mechanical mixtures of single fertilizers because of their increased concentration and greater uniformity.

The use of mixed fertilizers has several advantages over the use of single fertilizers, particularly in unskilled hands. Mixed fertilizers in general are less likely to cause an unbalanced supply of nutrients in the soil than the uninformed use of single fertilizers and may ensure a more even distribution of added nutrients in the field. They therefore require less technical knowledge in their use. On the other hand, the use of single fertilizers also has advantages which may be important. Single (or straight) fertilizers containing only one nutrient element allow the different nutrients to be applied at different times and by different methods, as when phosphates are applied in concentrated pockets or bands at planting time, and nitrogenous fertilizers are broadcast or sidedressed later in the season. Nitrogen- and potassium-containing fertilizers, because of their solubility, are more likely, in wet areas, to have their effects increased by being given as split applications than are the less soluble and less mobile fertilizers. In some cases applications of only one, or of two, of the major nutrients may be more profitable than applications of complete mixtures.

Whether single or mixed fertilizers are used, the farmer and research worker interested in interpreting fertilizer responses must be fully aware of the chemical composition of the added fertilizers, and not merely of the N, P_2O_5, and K_2O contents. The oversimplified habit of thinking in terms of these nutrients only can be misleading, for we do not and cannot add nitrogen, phosphorus, or potassium to a soil—we can only add these elements in combination with others. If the addition of a particular compound produces an increase in yields, this increase might, in theory at least, be due to any or to all of its constituent elements, and not just the N, P_2O_5, or K_2O written on the bag and calculated as a percentage of the total fertilizer. Failure to remember this simple fact has led to some wrong conclusions in the past. When groundnut yields in northern Ghana were increased by single superphosphate applications this was assumed to be a response to phosphorus, but single superphosphate contains calcium sulphate as well as calcium phosphate and in fact the response was due mainly to the sulphate added. This was discovered when triple superphosphate, which contains hardly any sulphur, was later substituted for the single superphosphate and failed to produce the response expected. In the same way, single superphosphate responses in Sierra Leone were found to be due, not to the phosphorus, but to the calcium in the added fertilizer.

FERTILIZER RESPONSES IN WEST AFRICA

Although fertilizers are still used to only a slight extent in West Africa, a number of agricultural stations and a few commercially run plantations have been conducting agronomic and fertilizer experiments for a number of years. The results obtained, though they vary locally with the soil and the crop, indicate in general that fertilizer responses in the savanna areas are more frequent than in the forest areas. In the forest areas the general level of soil productivity is naturally higher, and traditional land rotation fallows have been more effective in restoring soil fertility after a period of cropping than have the fallows of the savanna areas. Differences in responses in the two zones are related to differences in climate and vegetation, and to the lower organic matter levels of the savanna soils, but also appear to be connected with the differences in the crops involved in the two areas, for the tree crops of the forest zone make smaller demands on the soil than the annuals of the savanna, and afford the soil greater protection.

Nitrogen responses

The broad differences between the forest and savanna zones appear to be particularly marked in the case of nitrogen. Nitrogen responses are relatively frequent in savanna areas, and grass fallows are thought to have an inhibiting effect on nitrification in some cases, particularly where the dominant grasses are species of *Andropogon*. Nitrogen is often deficient in the first cropping season immediately after clearing, and this is related to the widespread practice of the African farmer of planting yams and sometimes cotton or tobacco as the first crop, rather than a cereal which has a higher nitrogen requirement. In long-term rotational trials in northern Ghana, nitrogen responses were initially large but later fell off somewhat, though they were still moderate.[1] In more exhausted West African savanna areas where fallows are generally fairly short, a considerable number of widespread trials indicate that cereals, yams, and cotton show moderate to large responses to nitrogen.

In the Zaria area of Northern Nigeria a standard recommendation for guinea corn is 112 lb of ammonium sulphate per acre, but for maize heavier dressings of $2\frac{1}{2}$ cwt of sulphate of ammonia are recommended, as well as 1 to 5 tons of farmyard manure per acre. In the same area farmers are advised not to apply sulphate of ammonia to groundnuts as it merely increases the vegetative growth of the plant without increasing nut yields, nor are nitrogen applications recommended for cotton. Nitrogen responses in West African savanna areas have often been shown to be increased by phosphorus applications, though they may be limited by water shortages.

In the forest areas, in contrast, nitrogen responses are not usually obtained from crops grown on ground which has been newly cleared or

[1] Responses are conveniently described as very small when of the order of 0 to 5 per cent increase over the control, small when 5 to 10 per cent, moderate when 10 to 20 per cent, large when 20 to 40 per cent, and very large when over 40 per cent.

cleared from an adequate period of fallow. On more exhausted, longer-cultivated soils with short fallows, the responses can become large. On acid, exhausted forest soils on Tertiary sands in south-eastern Nigeria, yams, maize, and cassava showed large responses to sulphate of ammonia. Along the southern borders of the Ghana forest zone, light, sandy granite-derived soils, exhausted by a long history of cultivation and short fallows, also gave large responses to sulphate of ammonia. On the other hand, six trials in the Ghana forest zone where the land was planted to a continuous rotation of maize and cassava for 8 years showed no shortage of nitrogen even after 8 years of cropping. Nitrogen responses in the forest zone appear to be closely related to organic matter levels in the soil and the history of previous cultivation. Where humus levels are still high, little or no response can be expected, but where humus levels have been reduced by intensive cultivation and too short fallows, then nitrogen responses are sometimes large.

Potassium responses

Responses to potassium also illustrate the broad differences between the savanna and forest zones. Responses to potassium in savanna soils are usually small or absent, and this lack of response, even on long-cultivated soils, is remarkable. Reasons for it have been suggested in Chapter 6 (see p. 175). Long-term trials involving continuous crop rotations on impoverished soils in northern Ghana and in Northern Nigeria failed to show any consistent responses to potassium. Similarly, savanna zone responses to the other basic cations, calcium and magnesium, can be expected to be small since savanna soils generally have reactions of 6·5 to 7·0 or above in the topsoil and are normally well supplied with these cations. However, it may be misleading to over-generalize, and there certainly are savanna soils capable of giving potassium responses.

Responses to potassium in the forest zones of West Africa have occurred much more frequently than in trials on savanna soils, and responses have generally been small to moderate in size: they occur mainly on fairly long-cultivated land already cropped for several years, and are more marked for cassava than for maize. Coconuts growing in the sandy littoral areas of West Africa have given widespread and often large or very large responses to potassium applications.

Phosphorus responses

Responses to phosphorus, in contrast to those to nitrogen and potassium, show a less consistent relationship to the broad savanna and forest soil and vegetation belts. Phosphorus responses have been obtained in both belts, but are erratic and appear to be related more to the intrinsic qualities of individual soils than to their history of cultivation, as might be expected from the discussion in Chapter 6 of the factors affecting phosphorus availability and its fixation in soils.

In trials on cocoa in Ghana, the use of fertilizers gave very erratic results but responses to phosphorus were more frequent than to other nutrients. Responses of food crops sometimes increase after the first year of cropping. On upland soils in Sierra Leone superphosphate applications gave large responses with cassava, cereals, and groundnuts, though the same soils usually failed to respond to nitrogen and potassium applications. On the exhausted Tertiary sand soils of south-eastern Nigeria, in contrast, no consistent responses to superphosphate were obtained, though large responses were given by nitrogen applications and small but consistent ones by potassium. In the exhausted sandy soils of the southern Ghana forest areas food crop responses to superphosphate were moderate but erratic. In the continuous maize and cassava trials carried out for 8 years in the Ghana forest zone, phosphorus gave large and increasing responses when applied to maize but had little effect on cassava.

In savanna areas responses to phosphorus are also generally rather erratic, though small to moderate responses are widespread. They may be small following a long fallow but increase if the cropping is prolonged. Responses have been obtained from cereals, yams, and cotton and also from groundnuts. In Northern Nigeria the standard recommendation of single superphosphate for guinea corn is 112 lb per acre, and for groundnuts 84 lb an acre. These are fairly low application rates. For cotton the recommendation is 184 lb per acre of single superphosphate, and the same quantity is recommended for maize. In northern Ghana the FAO recommendation for maize and guinea corn is 20 lb of P_2O_5 per acre, equivalent to 111 lb of single superphosphate, and 30 lb P_2O_5 (167 lb single superphosphate) for groundnuts. These figures are given as examples of the type of recommendation made in some areas; wherever possible farmers should attempt to obtain the latest local recommendations from local stations, extension service personnel and others competent to advise them, for responses to phosphorus in particular can be expected to vary considerably from soil to soil.

Sulphur and lime responses

Responses to sulphur applications also exhibit a broad zonal pattern, being frequent in the savanna areas of West Africa, particularly with leguminous crops such as groundnuts, and with cotton. They are much less likely in the forest areas. This is probably because organic sulphur levels are much higher in the forest areas and there is not usually the annual loss through grass burning experienced in the savanna. Sulphate applications have often caused responses in groundnuts when single superphosphate or sulphate of ammonia were applied, and some of these responses were originally wrongly attributed to the phosphorus or the nitrogen in the added fertilizer. Although sulphur deficiencies in groundnuts have been widespread in the West African savanna zone, no responses appear to have been obtained with cereal crops.

Responses to lime have been considerable only when applied, often in relatively small quantities, to very acid forest soils with pH values below 5·0, though small lime responses have been reported from slightly acid savanna soils planted to groundnuts, cereals, and yams.

Micronutrient deficiencies

Not much is yet known about micronutrient deficiencies and possible responses in West Africa. Although analyses of some export crops have shown low levels of certain micronutrients, responses have not often been obtained in the field. In extensive trials in Ghana, no response was obtained from manganese, boron, copper, zinc, iron, or magnesium supplied to cereals or groundnuts. A locally induced zinc deficiency has been demonstrated in cocoa farms where dumps of rotting cocoa pods upset the nutrient balance, and high pH values have been shown to reduce the availability to this crop of zinc, iron, and manganese. In 19 trials on groundnuts in Ghana molybdenum applications (as sodium molybdate) increased yields by 12 per cent. In Senegal groundnuts have shown small responses to this element and also to copper and magnesium. It is likely that further work will reveal other local trace element deficiencies, particularly on alkaline soils and soils over poor sandy parent materials.

The FAO fertilizer demonstrations

More recently, in 1962–5, the Food and Agriculture Organization of the United Nations (FAO) have conducted widespread fertilizer trials and demonstrations in Nigeria, Togo, Ghana, Gambia, and Senegal, as well as in countries outside West Africa, within their Freedom from Hunger Fertilizer Campaign. This campaign has the broad aim of demonstrating to farmers that economic responses can be obtained from fertilizer use. Results of the trials and demonstrations are published.

The results show the yield increases due to the treatments, the estimated profit/cost ratio, and the fertilizer mixtures, of those tried, which give the best and the most profitable responses. These demonstrations are not as carefully conducted, or as long-term, as the agronomic trials which are discussed in the preceding paragraphs and the results are averages, often for considerable numbers of demonstrations, which may hide wide and important differences in response. Moreover, the weather conditions of a single season may be abnormal, so that results for several seasons are desirable before making firm recommendations. Nevertheless the campaign and the numerous trials undertaken are of value because of the large number of individual trials and demonstrations involved, usually on typical African-owned farm patches, and the broad picture which evolves.

In Nigeria demonstrations in 1964–5 were confined to the southern regions of the country and were mostly on maize, yam, and rice. Results with maize were disappointing or only moderate, and the economic returns generally small or negative except in the case of complete 45–11–45 applications[1] in the eastern regions where responses were economic. With rice, on the other hand, the responses and the economic returns were generally good, both with swamp and hill rice, and were generally more profitable with NP than with NPK applications. Yam responses to NK treatments were generally small to moderate, but relatively profitable, with value/cost ratios of about 4 to 11, thus giving the farmer a profit of 4 to 11 times the cost of the fertilizer used.

In Ghana numerous demonstrations and trials were conducted in 1964–5 on maize, groundnuts, rice, yams, and guinea corn. In general, responses to N, NP, and NPK applications (at about 22 lb/acre each of N, P_2O_5, and K_2O) were good, and showed a satisfactory profit, with the biggest yield increases generally coming from the complete fertilizer treatment. Maize increases in the Ghana forest zone, generally to applications of complete fertilizer, gave yield increases which were claimed to average 30 to 50 per cent above the control and to give value/cost ratios of about 3, but in the savanna areas, where yield increases were similar or slightly higher, value/cost ratios were generally only a little above 1, so that the fertilizer applications showed very little profit. Groundnut responses in the savanna areas to complete NPK treatments averaged about 40 to 50 per cent, with value/cost ratios averaging about 4. Yam responses, both in the forest and savanna areas, gave value/cost ratios which averaged about 9 to 11, so that fertilizer applications appear relatively profitable in the case of this crop, as was also found in Nigeria. Forest zone rice increases averaged 40 to 60 per cent, but value/cost ratios were generally only 2 to 4. It should, of course, be stressed that these are average figures hiding considerable variations between individual demonstrations and trials, and that they are only for 1 cropping year.

[1] In lb/acre N, P_2O_5, K_2O

In the Gambia, demonstrations were confined to rice. Responses were moderate to good, depending on the district, but it appeared that nitrogen applications alone (at about 45 lb/acre) were probably the most economic.

In Senegal demonstrations were mainly on millet, and generally showed good responses, though the economic returns were rather variable.

The campaign so far has indicated fairly widespread responses to fertilizer applications on a range of crops and soils, but has shown that the increases obtained are not always profitable at local selling prices. Mass demonstrations of this type cannot be as carefully controlled and checked as agronomic experiments on stations, and the increases claimed must in some cases be regarded with some caution. The results have shown that it is sometimes necessary to distinguish, in the areas of West Africa which have two wet seasons, between responses in the main and minor growing seasons. The results also indicate that the variety of the crop used, particularly maize, sometimes considerably influences its ability to make use of added nutrients. If the campaign is continued, further refinements appear to be desirable in order to relate responses to particular soils, and to distinguish the effects of individual nutrients where they have usually been added only in combination.

NITROGEN-CONTAINING FERTILIZERS

Nitrogen and the nitrogen cycle have been discussed briefly in Chapter 6 (see pp. 152–9) where it was stated that nitrogenous fertilizers, both organic and inorganic, are used by farmers in greater quantity than any other. Animal manures and green manures (see pp. 255–9) are examples of ways in which organic nitrogen can be applied to the soil, but most of the nitrogen now given to crops by commercial farmers in the more developed countries is in the form of chemical compounds. The nitrogen fertilizer manufacturing industry is based mainly on the production of ammonia (NH_3) formed by reacting nitrogen and hydrogen gases.

Classes and specifications of nitrogeneous fertilizers

Unlike the accepted conventions which express potassium and phosphorus contents of a fertilizer, not as K or P, but as K_2O and P_2O_5, nitrogen in fertilizers is simply calculated as the percentage nitrogen by weight. Thus, sulphate of ammonia with the formula $(NH_4)_2SO_4$ has a molecular weight of 132 of which the two nitrogen atoms account for 28, so that the nitrogen in the compound is 28/132 or about 21 per cent. The sulphate anion is relatively heavy, but if it is replaced by a nitrate anion as in ammonium nitrate (NH_4NO_3) then higher nitrogen percentages are obtained giving more concentrated fertilizers. The percentage nitrogen in some of the commoner nitrogenous fertilizers is given in Table 9.3.

Nitrogen and nitrogenous fertilizers are of particular interest because the nitrogen can be given as a cation (ammonium, NH_4^+), or as an anion, (nitrate, NO_3^-), or as both. Although plants can absorb nitrogen in either of these combinations, it must be remembered that the ammonium cation in the soil is likely to be nitrified by soil bacteria to the nitrate form if not quickly taken up by plants, as explained in Chapter 6 (see pp. 153–4). Since the ammonium ion is a cation it is held in the soil by the cation exchange capacity of the soil colloids (see Chapter 2, p. 35) and is thus less readily leached from the soil than the more mobile nitrate anion.

In the following paragraphs the commoner nitrogenous chemical fertilizers are grouped into those containing (1) ammonia (or forming ammonia when in the soil); (2) nitrate nitrogen; and (3) other forms of nitrogen.

Ammonia-containing nitrogenous fertilizers

The ammonia-derived nitrogenous fertilizers include ammonium sulphate, the most widely used in West Africa, and other forms such as ammonium nitrate, ammonium chloride, and anhydrous ammonia. Urea is also included in this section: it does not contain ammonia when manufactured but produces ammonia when allowed to react with the soil.

Sulphate of ammonia or *ammonium sulphate* $(NH_4)_2SO_4$ is one of the oldest of the ammonia-containing fertilizers and has been popular in West Africa because of its good handling and storage qualities and its relatively low cost. It is a white, crystalline substance containing 21·2 per cent nitrogen and 24·2 per cent sulphur by weight. The sulphur content may have beneficial effects on soils deficient in this element, as are many of the West African savanna soils.

When ammonium sulphate is applied to the soil and dissolved in the soil solution, the ammonium ion, a cation, is held, with other cations, by the cation exchange positions on the clay and humus fractions of the soil. This makes them less likely to be leached from the soil than the very mobile nitrate anion, but if not absorbed by the plant the ammonium cation is likely to be converted first to nitrite then to nitrate by soil bacteria.

Ammonium sulphate, like all ammonia-containing fertilizers, can lead to acidification of the soil. This is due to the fact that the ammonium cation displaces other cations, such as calcium and magnesium, from the soil exchange complex, and these might then be lost in the drainage water. The sulphate anion may be washed out of the soil with the displaced cations: it is normally assumed that there is an approximate balance between the anions and cations contained in the drainage water. It has been calculated that for every 100 lb of ammonium sulphate added to the soil, between 75 and 150 lb of calcium carbonate will be needed to make good the calcium likely to be washed out of the soil.

On acid sandy soils, such as those of Samaru, Northern Nigeria, the continued use of ammonium sulphate has been shown to increase the acidity further and to be harmful for this reason. Increased acidity may be associated with harmfully high amounts of free aluminium or free manganese in the soil. The acidifying effects of sulphate of ammonia are, however, likely to be important only on poorly buffered soils (i.e. soils low in clay and humus which change their pH relatively easily) and if the fertilizer is applied over a long period. In these cases it may be better to apply a non-acidifying nitrogenous fertilizer (Table 9.3) or to use mixtures, such as nitrochalk, consisting of ammonium nitrate with calcium carbonate or dolomite. On clay soils with a good organic matter content which are not already acid it is unlikely that ammonium sulphate applications will have a marked effect on soil pH. Occasionally soils are acidified deliberately for crops such as pineapples or tea which are thought to prefer acid soils.

Ammonium nitrate (NH_4NO_3) contains nitrogen in both the ammonium and the nitrate forms and therefore as both cations and anions. The nitrate anion is probably the more immediately available but also the more likely to be lost by leaching during wet periods. The ammonium cations may be held by the cation exchange capacity of the soil until absorbed by the plant as such or nitrified. Ammonium nitrate contains 32 to 33·5 per cent nitrogen. It is a good source of nitrogen and is widely used in the United States but it is little used as yet in West Africa. It needs particular care in handling and storage because it is hygroscopic (i.e. it picks up moisture from the air) and also because it may form an explosive mixture if mixed with certain carbonaceous substances such as oil.

Ammonium nitrate is frequently supplied ready mixed with calcium carbonate or lime (as in nitrochalk). The lime is included to correct the acidifying tendency of the ammonium. The mixture is also easier to handle than ammonium nitrate by itself, but contains a lower percentage of nitrogen (20·5 per cent as compared with 32 to 33·5 per cent).

Ammonium nitrate sulphate is a double salt of ammonium sulphate and ammonium nitrate now being produced experimentally. It is designed to give a fertilizer with a high nitrogen content and some sulphur, and has very good handling qualities.

Ammonium phosphates are considered under phosphorus-containing fertilizers (see p. 280).

Ammonium chloride (NH_4Cl) contains about 26 per cent nitrogen and is used in particular in the Far East on rice paddies, in preference to ammonium

TABLE 9.3. Approximate composition of some of the commoner fertilizers, with their equivalent acidity or basicity.

The *equivalent acidity* is the number of lb of calcium carbonate ($CaCO_3$) required to neutralize 100 lb of the fertilizer; the *equivalent basicity* shows the acid neutralizing capacity, expressed as lb of $CaCO_3$, of 100 lb of the fertilizer; for example 100 lb of calcium cyanamide have the same neutralizing effect as 63 lb of $CaCO_3$. The symbol xx indicates that the compound is basic, but the strength varies with the composition, since both rock phosphate and basic slag have no fixed composition. The acidifying effects of fertilizers such as ammonium sulphate are likely to be important only on soils with a low buffer capacity (i.e. soils low in clay and humus whose pH is relatively easily changed) and only if applications are repeated for several years running.

FERTILIZER AND FORMULA	% N	% P_2O_5	% K_2O	EQUIVALENT ACIDITY	EQUIVALENT BASICITY
Nitrogen fertilizers					
Sodium nitrate $NaNO_3$	16				29
Ammonium sulphate $(NH_4)_2SO_4$	21			110	
Ammonium nitrate NH_4NO_3	33·5			60	
Calcium nitrate $Ca(NO_3)_2$	15·5				21
Ammonium nitrate— limestone (including nitrochalk and similar mixtures of NH_4NO_3 and $CaCO_3$)	15–26				
Urea $CO(NH_2)_2$	45			80	
Calcium cyanamide $CaCN_2$	21				63
Ammonium chloride NH_4Cl	24			128	
Ammonium sulphate nitrate $(NH_4)_2SO_4$ and NH_4NO_2	26			93	
Phosphate fertilizers					
Single superphosphate $Ca(H_2PO_4)_2$ and $CaSO_4$		16–20			
Triple superphosphate $Ca(H_2PO_4)_2$		43–52			
Di-calcium phosphate $Ca(HPO_4)$		35			25
Rock phosphate		20–40			xx
Basic slag		16–20			xx
Potassium fertilizers					
Muriate of potash, or potassium chloride KCl			50–60		
Potassium sulphate K_2SO_4			50		
Potassium magnesium sulphate $K_2SO_4 \cdot 2MgSO_4$			21		
Potassium nitrate KNO_3	13		44		23

sulphate, where conditions in the paddies would reduce the sulphate of the ammonium sulphate to hydrogen sulphide (H_2S), a substance thought by some investigators to be harmful to rice.

Anhydrous ammonia (NH_3) is, unlike the other fertilizers listed here, not a solid but is stored as a liquid and volatizes to ammonia gas when applied to the field, often by injecting it through tubes into the soil, though it can also be dissolved in irrigation water. Because of the very high nitrogen content and low price, this method of nitrogen application is practised in the U.S.A. but care is needed in its application and it has not yet been used in West Africa.

Urea is an important nitrogen-containing fertilizer with the formula $CO(NH_2)_2$. It contains a relatively high percentage of nitrogen—45 per cent. It is not an ammonia-containing fertilizer as such, but when applied to the soil it rapidly reacts with water to form ammonium carbonate which in turn decomposes to ammonia and carbon dioxide. It is therefore considered here with other ammonia-containing fertilizers.

In most cases the hydrolysis of urea added to the soil is rapid. If applied to the surface of the soil or mixed in lightly to only a shallow depth, some of the ammonia released will escape as gas. Too much urea placed very close to a seed can injure the seedling through excess ammonia, but placement at the correct distance from the seed avoids injurious effects.

Urea is a popular fertilizer in some parts of the world. It has the advantages of low cost per pound of fertilizer nitrogen, and a high nitrogen content which reduces transport costs. It normally has little effect on soil reaction. Urea can also be applied in leaf sprays.

Urea-sulphur is a relatively new fertilizer containing 40 per cent nitrogen and 10 per cent elemental sulphur. The sulphur is left behind when the urea hydrolyses and is ultimately converted to sulphates by bacteria. Another recent innovation is the production of urea phosphates (29 per cent nitrogen, and 29 per cent P_2O_5, equivalent to 12·7 per cent P).

Nitrate-containing nitrogenous fertilizers

Nitrate-containing fertilizers are very soluble and the nitrate ion is mobile in the soil, easily absorbed by the plant but also easily leached out of the soil. Ammonium nitrate, considered above, is the nitrate fertilizer used in the largest quantity, but sodium nitrate, calcium nitrate, and potassium nitrate are all used to lesser extents. These three metallic nitrates are not, as is ammonium nitrate, acid forming; in fact, since the nitrate anion is usually absorbed more rapidly than the accompanying sodium, potassium or calcium cation, these fertilizers may even have a slight tendency to the opposite, i.e. to increase soil pH to less acid or more alkaline levels.

Sodium nitrate $NaNO_3$ occurs in natural deposits in Chile and was once a relatively more important fertilizer than it is now, though it is still used. It contains 16 per cent N. The natural deposits contain some trace elements, particularly boron. There is also a purer synthetic sodium nitrate on the market.

Potassium nitrate KNO_3 contains 13·8 per cent N and 36·5 per cent K, while *calcium nitrate* $Ca(NO_3)_2$ contains 15·5 per cent N and 19·5 per cent Ca.

Other nitrogen-containing fertilizers

There are a variety of minor nitrogen-containing fertilizers which do not fall into the two broad classes considered above. These include calcium cyanamide and a number of slowly available nitrogen-containing compounds.

Calcium cyanamide ($CaCN_2$) contains 21 to 22 per cent nitrogen. When added to the soil it reacts with soil water to form (urea $CO(NH_2)_2$). It is necessary to mix the cyanamide well with the soil to allow the reaction to take place. It is also advisable to apply the fertilizer 2 to 3 weeks before planting. Failure to mix the cyanamide well with the soil can result in harmful side effects due to the formation of toxic by-products, particularly in dry weather. Calcium cyanamide is sometimes applied in fairly heavy doses, well before a crop is planted, as a weed killer. It is not a particularly cheap form of nitrogen, nor is it immediately available, and it is little used in West Africa as yet.

Slowly available nitrogenous fertilizers are of particular interest where, in areas of heavy rainfall, much of the nitrogen added in nitrogenous fertilizers is liable to be washed out of the soil in the nitrate form. If a slowly available fertilizer releases nitrogen over the whole growing period of the plant, it is likely that a greater proportion of the total released will be absorbed by the growing crop. Compounds which have been developed to meet this need include the urea-formaldehyde compounds, which vary from very soluble to quite insoluble depending on the proportion of formaldehyde they contain, and such metal ammonium phosphates as magnesium ammonium phosphate (about 9 per cent nitrogen) which releases ammonia slowly. These products might be used for perennial tree crops or grass but have not been used in West Africa as yet to any extent.

Applying nitrogenous fertilizers

As is the case with all fertilizer applications, the best way to use nitrogenous fertilizers depends on a range of factors which include soil, climate, the crop grown, and economic considerations of cost and expected return.

Nitrogenous fertilizers differ from phosphatic and, but to a lesser extent, potassium-containing fertilizers inasmuch as they are generally very soluble and once dissolved in the soil solution move rapidly within the soil. The nitrate ions in particular may, where rainfall is heavy, be leached right out of it. This high solubility means that chemical fertilizers such as ammonium nitrate can be applied simply as a surface dressing to the soil and will rapidly find their way into the soil and to the plant root. This is in strong contrast to the relatively immobile phosphatic fertilizers. This makes it easy to give a quick-acting shot of nitrogen to plants at that point in their growth cycle when it will do most good. With maize, for example, extra nitrogen is frequently applied at tasseling time.

Nitrogenous fertilizers, particularly in heavy rainfall areas, may be washed out of the soil. Such losses can be reduced by giving split applications (i.e. smaller applications, at more frequent intervals) but this increases the cost of handling and applying the fertilizer. Alternatively, less immediately available fertilizers can be applied, e.g. urea or calcium cyanamide or some of the slowly available nitrogenous fertilizers.

As indicated above, nitrogen can be applied as either a cation or an anion. If applied as the ammonium cation, it is held for a short time against leaching by the cation exchange capacity of the soil colloids, and this effect is more marked in soils high in clay and organic matter and least in sandy soils containing little organic matter. Nitrogen applied as the nitrate anion is not held in this way. Ammonium ions are normally fairly rapidly oxidized to nitrate. Top dressings of nitrate fertilizers are likely to move down in the soil more rapidly than ammonium-containing fertilizers.

Fertilizers which release ammonium must not, however, be placed too near the plant root, or injury may result from excess ammonium ions. Calcium cyanamide must be applied well before planting and well mixed in the soil.

In many cases the final choice of a nitrogenous fertilizer may depend on the other elements it contains besides nitrogen: sulphur, as in sulphate of ammonia, is beneficial on many West African sulphur-deficient soils, and the effects of trace elements must also be considered. In West Africa sulphate of ammonia is still much used, partly because of its good handling qualities, partly because many users continue to use a substance with which they are familiar.

The acidifying effects of sulphate of ammonia and of other ammonia-containing fertilizers are likely to be most noted when repeated applications are given to light-textured soils low in organic matter. On heavier soils and soils high in organic matter the pH is less easily changed. Table 9.3 gives information on the relative acidifying powers of some common fertilizers.

Applied nitrogen may be lost again in various ways; the plant recovery of added nitrogen varies very widely according to conditions but is usually less than 60 to 70 per cent. Some may be lost as nitrogen gas, some as ammonia gas, and some by fixation of the ammonium on the clays, but the main loss, particularly in wetter areas, is by the leaching out of the soil of nitrates.

PHOSPHATE-CONTAINING FERTILIZERS

When phosphate fertilizer manufacture was started in the nineteenth century, bones were used as the source of phosphate. Today the very large phosphate manufacturing industry is based on natural deposits of rock phosphate, of which two high quality deposits occur in West Africa, in Senegal and in Togo.

Classes and specifications of phosphate-containing fertilizers

It is necessary to be familiar with the technical or trade terms used to measure the amount of phosphate in a fertilizer and its availability to the plant. The amount of phosphorus or phosphate in a fertilizer has long been calculated and referred to commercially as the content of P_2O_5. P_2O_5 is phosphorus pentoxide, and the phosphorus in the fertilizer is expressed as though it were present in this form. Thus, if a fertilizer contained 7 per cent phosphorus by weight this would be considered the equivalent of 16 per cent P_2O_5 and this would be the percentage or grade marked on the bag. The phosphorus is not actually present in this form, so that the use of the P_2O_5 content is a rather artificial convention. More recently there has been a tendency to express the phosphate content in terms of the percentage by weight of elemental phosphorus. These percentages are easily converted one to the other by the use of the following conversion factors:

$$P \text{ (elemental phosphorus)} = P_2O_5 \times 0.436$$
$$P_2O_5 \text{ (phosphorus pentoxide)} = P \times 2.29.$$

Hence, in the example given above, 7 per cent phosphorus is equivalent to 7×2.29 per cent P_2O_5, or 16 per cent.

However, not all the phosphorus in a fertilizer is available to the plant, and when buying a fertilizer, the buyer is entitled to know what percentage is or is not available. The phosphate in the fertilizer may or may not be soluble in water. Of that which is not water-soluble, some may be soluble in dilute acids, such as citric. Both the water-soluble and the citric acid-soluble phosphate is conventionally considered to be *available* to plants. It is therefore necessary to distinguish between the following:

Water-soluble phosphorus is that phosphorus which can be dissolved in water. It is expressed as a percentage by weight of the total fertilizer. This is the phosphorus most easily and quickly available to the plant.

Citrate-soluble phosphorus is that phosphorus which is not soluble in water but which is soluble in a solution of neutral normal ammonium citrate. This citrate-soluble phosphorus is also expressed as a percentage by weight of the total fertilizer. It is assumed that the citrate-soluble phosphorus is also available to plants, though it may not be so quickly and easily available as the water-soluble forms.

The available phosphorus is all that phosphorus which is either water- or citric acid-soluble. The available phosphorus in a fertilizer is therefore the sum of the water-soluble and the citric acid-soluble percentages.

The total phosphorus is the total phosphorus percentage in the fertilizer, whether available or not.

Water-soluble phosphatic fertilizers

The more important phosphatic fertilizers which are water-soluble are the single and triple superphosphates and the ammonium phosphates. Others are listed in Table 9.4.

Single superphosphate is formed by mixing rock phosphate with an equal weight of sulphuric acid. Considerable heat is given off by the reaction, which helps in the drying, and the final product sets hard and has to be ground up. The resulting fertilizer material is a mixture of calcium sulphate (gypsum) and calcium phosphate. Most of the calcium phosphate is monocalcium phosphate and is water-soluble. Single superphosphate contains about 16 to 20 per cent P_2O_5, equivalent to 7 to 9·5 per cent phosphorus, of which almost all is water-soluble. Its average composition is approximately the following:

	%
Calcium sulphate	48
Monocalcium phosphate	30
Dicalcium phosphate	9
Iron and aluminium oxides and silica	9
Tricalcium phosphate	2
Moisture	2
	100

Single superphosphate has been successfully used in West Africa in many areas. Where soils are sulphur-deficient, as they often are in the West African savanna areas, the sulphur content of single superphosphate may also be beneficial. Single superphosphate is often mixed with other ingredients to make mixed fertilizers. Where the sulphur is not needed and transport distances and costs are high, then savings may be effected by using more concentrated phosphatic fertilizer such as triple super-phosphate.

Triple superphosphate is formed when rock phosphate is treated with phosphoric acid instead of with sulphuric acid. The resulting product has 2 to 3 times the phosphate content of single superphosphate, for it contains 43 to 52 per cent of P_2O_5, equivalent to 19 to 23 per cent elemental phosphorus. Nearly all of this is water-soluble. Triple superphosphate consists mainly of monocalcium phosphate. It lacks the high sulphur content of single superphosphate (though it does contain a little—up to 1 per cent) and therefore may be less suitable for sulphur-deficient areas. The higher phosphate content gives it an advantage where it has to be transported long distances and at considerable cost.

Enriched superphosphates are superphosphates intermediate in composition between single and triple superphosphates, containing more monocalcium phosphate than single superphosphate but less than triple superphosphate.

Ammoniated superphosphates are superphosphates (either single or triple) which have been reacted with ammonia. This makes them a source of relatively cheap nitrogen but unfortunately ammoniating the superphosphate decreases the solubility of the phosphate in the fertilizer. Ammoniated superphosphates should not be confused with ammonium phosphates.

Ammonium phosphates are made by allowing ammonia to react either with phosphoric acid or with phosphoric and sulphuric acids. A range of different compounds is obtained containing 11 to 21 per cent nitrogen and 20 to 61 per cent P_2O_5 (see Table 9.4). These fertilizers have several advantages. First, the phosphate is 100 per cent water-soluble. Secondly, they contain a high total percentage of nitrogen and phosphorus and therefore reduce transport, storage, and handling costs. Thirdly, like the super-phosphates, they have good handling qualities. For these reasons they are becoming increasingly popular in some parts of the world.

Nitric phosphates vary in composition and phosphate content. They also vary very much in the percentage of the contained phosphate which is water-soluble, this percentage varying from 0 to 70 per cent. Those with the lower percentages of water-soluble phosphate are relatively slow-acting and are best considered under the next section on water-insoluble phosphatic fertilizers.

An important recent development in phosphate fertilizer manufacture has been the invention of a method to produce large quantities of super-phosphoric acid (Table 9.4), which in turn is used to produce phosphates with a higher phosphorus content. Superphosphoric acid contains 34 per cent phosphorus (79 per cent P_2O_5) as against the 24 per cent phosphorus (55 per cent P_2O_5) of ordinary phosphoric acid: it is a more concentrated acid containing polyphosphates (condensed phosphate radicals). It is used

TABLE 9.4. Composition of some of the more common phosphatic fertilizers.

The percentage of the phosphorus available refers to that which is removed by neutral normal ammonium citrate. The extent to which the phosphorus is water-soluble is indicated by (1), (2), and (3), where (1) means all or almost all is water-soluble, (2) means that some or most is water-soluble, and (3) means that very little or none is water-soluble. (Adapted mainly from a table in *Soil Fertility and Fertilizers* by S. L. Tisdale and W. L. Nelson, 2nd ed., New York, The Macmillan Co.)

FERTILIZER	% P	% P₂O₅ (a)	% AVAILABLE (b)	OTHER CONSTITUENTS				
				% N	% K	% S	% Ca	% Mg
Single superphosphate	7–9·5	16–21·8	97–100 (1)	..	..	11–12	18–21	..
Triple superphosphate	19–23	43–52	96–99 (1)	..	..	0–1	12–14	..
Enriched superphosphate	11–13	25–30	96–99 (1)	..	..	7–9	16–18	..
Ammoniated single superphosphate	6·1–8·7	14–20	96–98 (2)	2–5	..	10–12	17–21	..
Ammoniated triple superphosphate	19–21	43·5–8	96–99 (2)	4–6	..	0–1	12–14	..
Dicalcium phosphate	23	52·7	98	(3) ..	..	..	29	..
Phosphoric acid	23	52·7	100	(1) ..	..	0–2	..	..
Superphosphoric acid	34	78	100	(1) ..	..	..	..	..
Potassium phosphate	18–22	41–50	100	(1) ..	29–45	..	..	..
Ammonium phosphate nitrate (c)	4	9	100	(1) 30	..	..	..	..
Ammonium polyphosphate	25	57	..	(1) 15	..	..	..	..
Magnesium ammonium phosphate	17	40	..	(3) 8	..	..	..	14
Raw rock phosphate	11–17	25–39	14–65	(3) ..	..	..	33–36	..
Heated (defluorinated) rock phosphate	9	20·6	85	(3) ..	..	..	20	..
Rhenania phosphate	12	27·5	97	(3) ..	..	..	30	0·3
Basic slag	3·5–8	8–18	62–94	(3) ..	..	0·2	32	3
Ammonium phosphates % N; % P₂O₅; % K₂O								
21–53–0	23	52·7	100	(1) 21	..	..	..	..
21–61–0	27	61·8	100	(1) 21	..	..	..	..
11–48–0	21	48	100	(1) 11	..	0–2	..	..
16–48–0	21	48	100	(1) 16	..	0–2	..	..
18–46–0	20	45·8	100	(1) 18	..	0–2	..	..
16–20–0	8·7	20	100	(1) 16	..	15	..	..

(a) % P × 2·29   (b) Ammonium citrate method.   (c) Essentially a mixture of ammonium phosphate and ammonium nitrate.

to make ammonium and calcium polyphosphates. These compounds are more concentrated and have a higher P content than fertilizers made with ordinary phosphoric acid, and because they form complexes with such metallic ions as iron, zinc, and manganese may also be used in the future as carriers of trace elements.

Water-insoluble phosphatic fertilizers

Phosphatic fertilizers in which the phosphate is all or mainly water-insoluble include raw rock phosphate, basic slag and some other fertilizers of minor importance.

Raw rock phosphate consists mainly of apatite (see p. 165). The phosphate is insoluble in water, but some of it is citric acid-soluble. Since raw rock phosphate is relatively cheap as compared with the more concentrated and more soluble treated fertilizers such as the superphosphates it is often applied in relatively large quantities. To some extent and under some conditions the higher quantities of total phosphate applied can have beneficial effects comparable with smaller quantities of more soluble fertilizers. This is most likely to be the case where (*a*) the rock phosphate is finely ground, so that the surface exposed to reaction with the soil is increased; and (*b*) the rock phosphate is applied to acid soils. It is relatively ineffective in neutral and alkaline soils.

Apart from its cheapness, raw rock phosphate has the advantage that since it dissolves in the soil only slowly, it has a long-lasting effect and a single heavy application may therefore give crop increases for many years after application. In West Africa it seems to be most useful in high rainfall areas of acid to very acid soils where it becomes slowly available over a period. It thus appears to be worth further investigation for tree crops in these areas. Where a quicker-acting effect is needed, some water-soluble phosphate can also be given as a starting dose. In French West Africa some agronomists put in large quantities of rock phosphate in order to reduce the phosphate fixing capacity of the soil and to become available over a long period, and small quantities of water-soluble phosphate for an immediate effect. Further investigation remains to be done on these lines.

Heat-treated rock phosphates are rock phosphates which have been heated to high temperatures with or without added ingredients. These do not contain any water-soluble phosphate but the content of citrate-soluble phosphate is increased. Heating drives off the fluorine in the apatite and the result is known as defluorinated phosphate rock, containing 8 per cent citrate-soluble phosphorus, equivalent to 18 per cent citrate soluble P_2O_5. Rhenania phosphate (27·5 per cent citrate soluble P_2O_5) is another heat-treated rock phosphate. These products are also more likely to be effective on acid soils than on neutral or alkaline ones.

Basic slag (or Thomas slag) is another source of phosphate which is popular in Europe and which has proved successful in some parts of the tropics, particularly on acid soils. Basic slag is a by-product of the steel-making industry by the open-hearth process. Its P_2O_5 content is very variable, usually anywhere from 8 to 18 per cent (equivalent to 3·3 to 8 per cent elemental P) of which over half is citric acid-soluble. Because of the basic nature of this product, it has a high acid-neutralizing capacity and therefore acts like lime when applied to acid soils (see Table 9.4). It has been found to be effective for rubber grown on acid soils in Malaya.

What happens when phosphate is applied to the soil

What happens to phosphate fertilizer applied to the soil depends on both the nature of the fertilizer, particularly whether it is water-soluble or not, and also the nature of the soil. In addition climate, particularly rainfall, has an influence. The following paragraphs give a simplified account of what happens when a commonly used water-soluble phosphate such as single or triple superphosphate is applied to the soil.

A granule of single superphosphate (a mixture of calcium phosphate and calcium sulphate) or a granule of triple superphosphate (mainly calcium phosphate) when applied to the soil first attracts moisture to itself (see Fig. 9.1). This moisture dissolves some of the calcium phosphate and forms a concentrated and very acid solution. The acid solution moves away from the fertilizer granule into the soil immediately surrounding the granule and may there react with other substances in the soil. The nature of the reactions depends on the pH of the soil and the substances it contains.

In an acid soil the acid solution containing phosphate ions may dissolve iron, aluminium, or manganese in the soil. The phosphate ions then react with the dissolved iron or aluminium or with free iron or aluminium ions already present. Insoluble compounds of iron and/or aluminium may then be formed: these are either precipitated as small particles or crystals, or attach themselves to the clay fraction of the soil. If the granule is near to plant roots, a proportion of the phosphate ions will be taken up by the plant roots before they can react with other soil constituents to form insoluble compounds. The extent to which this type of fixation takes place varies very much with the nature of the soil, being influenced by the extent of the surface contact between the phosphate-containing solution and the soil, and by the amount of iron and aluminium present in the soil.

In an alkaline soil the phosphate-containing solution may react with calcium ions in the soil to precipitate relatively insoluble dicalcium phosphate (see Chapter 6, p. 164). In soils containing free calcium carbonate the dicalcium phosphate will be precipitated on the surface of the calcium carbonate. The more calcium carbonate in the soil and the more finely divided it is, the greater the surface area exposed, and the greater the likelihood of added phosphate being precipitated as dicalcium phosphate or as apatite on this surface.

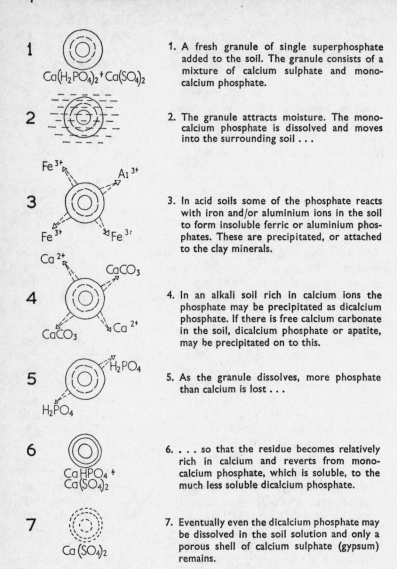

1. A fresh granule of single superphosphate added to the soil. The granule consists of a mixture of calcium sulphate and mono-calcium phosphate.

2. The granule attracts moisture. The mono-calcium phosphate is dissolved and moves into the surrounding soil . . .

3. In acid soils some of the phosphate reacts with iron and/or aluminium ions in the soil to form insoluble ferric or aluminium phosphates. These are precipitated, or attached to the clay minerals.

4. In an alkali soil rich in calcium ions the phosphate may be precipitated as dicalcium phosphate. If there is free calcium carbonate in the soil, dicalcium phosphate or apatite, may be precipitated on to this.

5. As the granule dissolves, more phosphate than calcium is lost . . .

6. . . . so that the residue becomes relatively rich in calcium and reverts from mono-calcium phosphate, which is soluble, to the much less soluble dicalcium phosphate.

7. Eventually even the dicalcium phosphate may be dissolved in the soil solution and only a porous shell of calcium sulphate (gypsum) remains.

Fig. 9.1. What happens to a granule of single superphosphate in the soil.

The water attracted to the fertilizer granule dissolves the monocalcium phosphate it contains but in fact it removes more of the phosphate ions than it does calcium ions. As a result, the ratio of calcium to phosphate in the residue of the granule increases and its composition changes from monocalcium phosphate, which is soluble, to dicalcium phosphate, which is relatively insoluble. If the original granule were a single superphosphate granule containing both monocalcium phosphate and calcium sulphate, it might later consist of a mixture of dicalcium phosphate and calcium sulphate. Eventually the dicalcium phosphate may also be slowly dissolved and a porous gypsum (calcium sulphate) shell of the granule remains.

If water-insoluble phosphate fertilizers are added to the soil, the reaction between fertilizer and soil solution may be much slower. Some cases are known where rock phosphate added to soil gave no immediate effect but increased yields some years afterwards. Calcium phosphates which are insoluble in pure water are to a slight extent soluble in the soil solution, or the phosphate is liable to be released by reacting with other soil constituents, including plant root secretions and organic matter decomposition products. This interaction between soil and added rock phosphate is speeded up when the rock phosphate is finely ground, thus increasing its surface area. Thus, though contact between the soil and water-soluble fertilizers should be reduced to a minimum, this contact is beneficial in the case of the insoluble fertilizers because it increases their slow availability.

The soil solution is, as was seen in Chapter 3, a weak but complex solution. It is able to react with added phosphatic materials in a variety of ways. Not enough is known about the ability and the ways in which plant roots can obtain phosphate from sparingly soluble compounds, but it is known that some plants are more efficient extractors of soil phosphate than others. Citric acid soluble phosphate appears to be generally available to plants, though some investigators consider that the phosphate extracted by alkaline ammonium citrate is a better indication of relative availability than that measured by extraction with neutral ammonium citrate.

Applying phosphatic fertilizers

The best method of applying phosphatic fertilizers to the soil depends on the type of fertilizer used, the soil, the climate and, in some cases, on the crop. Sometimes the choice of fertilizer is influenced by whether the plant also needs other nutrients, such as sulphur, which are contained in some phosphatic fertilizers.

Generally speaking, the placing of phosphorus in the soil is far better than merely applying dressings to the soil surface. The placement is best done at or before planting time. With tree crops, phosphate can be applied in the planting hole below the roots. With annuals, placement is often done a little below and a little to one side of the seed, often 2 in below and 2 in to one side in the case of maize and beans. With mature trees, the phosphate can be placed in holes or in shallow trenches dug round the tree, or between rows, approximately below the outer edge of the crown. Placement is necessary because phosphate does not move far in the soil and must therefore be near the growing root. At the distances mentioned there is, in the case of most phosphatic fertilizers, no danger that the fertilizer will harm the root. Closer proximity to the roots must be avoided in the case of ammonium-containing phosphates, such as the ammonium phosphates because, particularly in alkaline soils, they may release too much free ammonium near the roots and thus injure the plant.

Where water-soluble fertilizers are used, applying the fertilizer in large granules or even coated pellets slows down the release of the phosphate and lessens the percentage loss through fixation. The water-insoluble fertilizers, in contrast, are best ground up finely and mixed more thoroughly with the soil to give a more intimate contact between added fertilizer and the soil and the roots. In low rainfall areas the more soluble fertilizers should normally be used.

POTASSIUM-CONTAINING FERTILIZERS

In contrast to phosphatic fertilizers, all the widely used potassium-containing fertilizers contain potassium in the water-soluble form. For this and other reasons potassium fertilizers and their use form a less complicated subject than phosphorus-containing fertilizers. Very large deposits of soluble potassium salts occur in various parts of the world, some of them of a high degree of purity, and these are mined for the production of fertilizers and of industrial potassium salts.

Specifications of potassium-containing fertilizers

The potassium content of fertilizers is at present calculated as the percentage of K_2O, potassium oxide. This is measured by determining the amount of the salt that dissolves in a solution of ammonium oxalate. There is a more recent trend to express both phosphorus and potassium not in terms of their oxides but in terms of the percentage of the element itself. In the case of potassium, this can be achieved by the following conversion factors:

$$\% \text{ K (elemental potassium)} = \% \text{ } K_2O \times 0.83$$
$$\% \text{ } K_2O \text{ (potassium oxide)} = \% \text{ K} \times 1.2.$$

The principal potassium-containing fertilizers

Potassium fertilizers are mainly simple compounds of potassium with chloride, sulphate, or nitrate.

Potassium chloride (KCl) is by far the most widely used potassium-containing fertilizer, both by itself and in mixed fertilizers, and this is the potassium salt mined in the largest quantities. The natural salt frequently contains about 40 to 50 per cent KCl and other potassium salts but is usually purified to contain 83·5 or 96 per cent KCl which is equivalent to 50 and 60 per cent K_2O, or 41·5 and 49·8 per cent K. This salt is often referred to commercially as *muriate of potash*.

Potassium sulphate (K_2SO_4) contains about 48 to 53 per cent K_2O, depending on its purity, equivalent to about 40 to 44 per cent K. It is used mainly on crops such as potatoes and tobacco which are sensitive to large quantities of chlorides. It has the advantage of supplying sulphur to the plant, which is more frequently needed than is chlorine, and is particularly recommended for drier areas.

Potassium magnesium sulphate (K_2SO_4, $MgSO_4$) is a naturally occurring double salt, a combination of potassium sulphate and magnesium sulphate. It contains 22 per cent K_2O (18 per cent K), 18 per cent MgO (11 per cent Mg), and 18 per cent S and is of value where soils are deficient in sulphur and magnesium as well as potassium.

Potassium nitrate (KNO_3), also known as saltpetre, contains 44 per cent K_2O (37 per cent K) and 13 per cent N, and is a good source of both these nutrients, though up to now its relatively high cost has restricted its use to particularly high-value crops.

Potassium metaphosphate (KPO_3) is a highly concentrated fertilizer, not soluble as such but becoming available by hydrolysis, which is little used as yet because of its high price.

Applying potassium fertilizers

Agronomic experiments have suggested that of the above fertilizers, one form is as good as the other as a source of potassium, and usually the cheapest form per pound of potassium is preferable. In the case of potassium nitrate and potassium metaphosphate the value of the nitrogen and phosphorus, if needed, should be included in the calculation, as must the value of sulphur, magnesium, or other elements included. In the case of chloride-sensitive crops such as tobacco, sweet potato, and citrus, care must be taken in the use of high quantities of potassium chloride.

Factors affecting the uptake of potassium from the soil were discussed in Chapter 6 (see pp. 173–178), where it was pointed out that plants differ considerably both in their potassium needs and in their ability to extract potassium from low potassium soils.

Since all the important potassium-containing fertilizers are soluble, they are all quickly available to the plant. Potassium is not as mobile in the soil or as easily leached as are the nitrates, but is considerably more mobile than phosphorus. Because of this, potassium fertilizers can be applied either by placing in the soil, often as bands to the side and below the seed or plant, or by being broadcast. Placement is advisable on particularly heavy soils, or where rainfall is light. When large quantities are applied, then broadcasting is more usual, with or without subsequent working into the soil. In most West African soils where potassium fixation is thought to be unimportant, broadcasting is not likely to result in significant potassium loss through fixation, though in soils high in micas and illite, banding might be preferable since it reduces fixation.

The potassium cation is held by the exchange complex so that leaching losses of added potassium fertilizer are not as likely as is the case with nitrates, particularly where the soil has a good cation exchange capacity. Leaching losses would be expected to be greatest on sandy soils low in humus, but slight on loam and clay soils with a good humus content except in areas of particularly heavy rainfall. In some cases potassium may be washed down from the upper horizons of the soil to be held by subsoil clays.

SUPPLYING CALCIUM, MAGNESIUM, AND SULPHUR TO THE SOIL

Liming has been discussed earlier (see Chapter 6, pp. 180-181) where it was stressed that this is practised very little as yet in West Africa and there is therefore not much experience of liming and its likely effects. The commonest compounds used in order of effectiveness or calcium carbonate equivalent neutralizing value (where the effectiveness of calcium carbonate is taken as 100), are the following:

Amendment	Calcium carbonate equivalent
Calcium oxide CaO	179
Calcium hydroxide Ca(OH)$_2$	136
Dolomite CaMg(CO$_3$)$_2$	109
Calcium carbonate (limestone or chalk or calcite—CaCO$_3$)	100
Calcium silicate slag CaSiO$_3$	86

The calcium carbonate equivalent makes it possible to compare easily the neutralizing value of different compounds used in liming. Of the above, calcium oxide (true lime) and calcium hydroxide (slaked lime) are quick-acting but unpleasant to handle, and the most commonly used commercial liming materials are ground limestone, chalk, or calcite (a crystalline form of limestone), all of which are impure calcium carbonate. Where magnesium is needed as well as calcium, then dolomite (half calcium carbonate, half magnesium carbonate) or dolomite limestone (other combinations of calcium and magnesium carbonate) is preferable to ordinary limestone.

The effectiveness of liming materials depends very much on the degree of fineness of the limestone. Limestone is ground mechanically, and the finer the end product the greater the surface area and the quicker and more complete the reaction with the soil, though the cost of the limestone increases with the fineness of the grinding. To be effective, limestone is best mixed rather thoroughly with as much of the soil as possible.

The principle behind liming is that the soil acidity is neutralized by the calcium-containing compounds added to it. However, the amount of lime needed does not depend only on the pH of the soil but on the buffer capacity of the soil. The buffer capacity of a soil is its resistance to change in reaction: a soil with a low buffer capacity changes its pH relatively easily, but a soil with a high buffer capacity requires greater quantities of lime to change the pH a similar amount.

The buffer capacity of soils is related to their content of colloids, and cation exchange capacity. A soil with a high content of clay and humus has a high buffer capacity and it requires a relatively strong influence to change the pH, whereas a sandy soil low in humus has a low buffer capacity and the reaction is relatively easily modified.

When calcium or magnesium carbonate is added to acid or very acid soils, then the calcium or magnesium replaces some of the hydrogen and aluminium ions on the cation exchange positions with the formation of carbon dioxide and aluminium hydroxide $Al(OH)_3$.

The amounts required to affect a pH change of one unit vary according to the buffer capacity of the soil and this is best calculated by adding a small and carefully measured amount of base (such as calcium hydroxide) to a known weight of soil and measuring the change in pH produced. The amount of lime needed to be applied to a field to raise the pH a specified amount can then be calculated. In practice, much larger quantities of lime are needed on heavy soils than on light and sandy ones, and even higher quantities are needed for very acid organic soils than for clay ones.

When liming is carried out the usual aim is primarily to decrease the acidity of the soil rather than to supply calcium or magnesium to the plant directly. Calcium and magnesium may be added when other commercial fertilizers are used: calcium occurs in the calcium sulphate of single superphosphate, and magnesium in magnesium sulphate, and the addition of these compounds has little or no effect on soil pH. Magnesium applications may become necessary when potassium applications have given too high a potassium/magnesium ratio in the soil. Potassium magnesium sulphate (see p. 287) is a fertilizer supplying both these elements.

Sulphur is an important nutrient which has received increasing attention recently: it is needed by the plant in about the same quantities as phosphorus but, as explained on p. 181, shortages have only recently become widely recognized. In West African savanna areas sulphur deficiencies are probably the result of long periods of annual burning. Sulphur is conveniently supplied to the soil as the sulphate anion, the form usually taken up by the plant. The sulphate anion is contained in the calcium sulphate of single superphosphate, in ammonium sulphate, in potassium sulphate, in potassium magnesium sulphate, in magnesium sulphate, and in a range of other fertilizers, of which only the first two are much used in West Africa and even these are used only to a very small extent so far. Thus it appears that sulphur shortages in the savanna areas at least might be a widespread limiting factor not yet corrected on any scale. The sulphate anion can be leached from soils moderately easily, and this is more likely in the wetter areas.

Sulphur can be applied to the soil as elemental sulphur, but as such it has a marked effect in increasing soil acidity, and is often used for the purpose of deliberately acidifying (or acidulating) soils and reclaiming alkaline soils. Elemental sulphur is oxidized to sulphate in the soil by the sulphur-oxidizing bacteria which are species of the genus *Thiobacillus*, and the end product of the process is sulphuric acid. Conversion is quickest when the sulphur is added as very fine particles. Some modern fertilizers are now being developed which mix elemental sulphur with urea, triple superphosphate, ammonium phosphate, and granular mixed N-P-K fertilizers. Polysulphides are marketed as ammonium polysulphide and calcium polysulphide, and the sulphur in these forms is converted to sulphates fairly rapidly.

CORRECTING TRACE ELEMENT DEFICIENCIES

Trace element deficiencies and their correction are a relatively new aspect of soil science and practical agriculture, but one which has, under certain circumstances, achieved considerable production increases. In general, however, trace element deficiencies in West Africa have received little attention as yet.

The trace element content of soils appears to depend mainly on the parent rock, but in practice an important source of trace elements is the mineralizing organic matter in soils. The availability to the plant of the trace elements present in the soil is influenced by reaction. Molybdenum is most available in alkaline soils but the metallic trace elements are more available in acid soils, and liming may seriously decrease their availability. In very acid soils aluminium and manganese may be present in quantities which are harmful to plants.

Trace element deficiencies can often be cured either by changing the soil reaction, or more commonly, by supplying the element itself, usually in very small quantities indeed, either to the soil or direct to the plant, as in the case of leaf sprays.

Chelates. The chelates (also known as sequestering agents) are complex organic compounds capable of attaching themselves to a metallic atom with various degrees of tenacity. Their advantage is that they are soluble in water, but that when dissolved the metallic atom and the remaining organic part of the molecule dissociate only to a small degree, so that the metal can be absorbed by the plant but is not very likely to be fixed by forming combinations with inorganic anions in the soil (combinations such as iron phosphate, for example, which would render added iron insoluble). Exactly how the plant absorbs the metal chelate is not fully known: whether as the whole molecule or whether as the metallic cation and the organic anion separately.

The metals commonly chelated are iron, copper, manganese, and zinc. In other forms the chelates can exist as acids or sodium salts and, if these are added to the soil, they have the power of dissolving and extracting the trace element metals from their insoluble forms in the soil, and iron deficiencies have been corrected in this way simply by adding sodium chelate to the soil. Chelates of iron, manganese, copper, and zinc are efficient correctors of deficiencies of these trace elements and can be applied to the soil or as leaf sprays.

Iron deficiencies are most likely on calcareous soils and those high in phosphate: they are not likely in acid soils. Most West African soils have high total iron contents, though the total iron is not necessarily any indication of available iron to the plant. Iron deficiencies are associated with an imbalance between ions such as copper, iron, and manganese and can be induced by particularly high manganese or copper levels in some soils. High concentrations of phosphorus have been shown to interfere with iron uptake by the plant. Iron shortages can be corrected by using ferrous sulphate ($FeSO_4.7H_2O$), either by applying it to the soil or as a leaf spray. When applied to the soil the ferrous iron is rapidly oxidized to the ferric form, so that this is not an efficient method. Ferrous iron used as a leaf spray is both quicker-acting and more efficient: a solution of 4 to 6 per cent iron sulphate is commonly used. Iron chelates are being used for the same purpose in increasing amounts: these contain 6 to 12 per cent iron, are water-soluble, and can be applied either to the soil or to the foliage. Although more expensive than ferrous sulphate, much smaller quantities are necessary to correct deficiencies.

Manganese is probably least available in soils with neutral or near-neutral pH values and most available in acid soils. Manganese deficiencies have sometimes been induced by liming. Deficiencies can be prevented in some cases by keeping the soil pH moderately acid (with sulphur, for example) or by adding salts such as manganese sulphate to the soil. Manganese chelates are also used. For quick results plants can be sprayed with manganese sulphate solution (5 to 10 lb manganese sulphate to 100 gal of water) or with manganese chelates in solution.

Zinc is less available in neutral and alkaline soils than in acid ones, but some acid soils can be deficient through having very low zinc contents. Deficiencies have also sometimes been correlated with high phosphorus levels in soils, or with high organic matter levels due to farmyard manure additions. Zinc deficiencies have been induced by liming, and zinc is adsorbed by calcium and magnesium carbonates. Zinc deficiencies are often corrected by applying zinc sulphate to soils at rates of 40 to 80 lb per acre, or as a leaf spray. Zinc chelates, zinc ammonium sulphate and zinc ammonium phosphate are also used.

Copper is often low in organic soils, probably due to the formation of copper-humus complexes, and in some cases copper availability has been shown to be reduced in alkaline soils. Uptake by the plant appears to be influenced by the amounts of other metals such as aluminium and iron in the soil, so that the ratios of these elements to each other are more important than the absolute amounts. Excess copper causes iron deficiencies. Copper sulphate is frequently used to correct copper deficiencies, both by applying to the soil and as a leaf spray. More recent materials used include copper ammonium phosphate and copper chelates.

Boron is widely applied as a trace element but plants differ considerably in their needs. Boron is usually applied in the form of borax ($Na_2B_4O_7$. $10H_2O$), but is very soluble and easily leached from soils: a mineral, colemanite, which is a naturally occurring calcium borate ($Ca_2B_6O_{11}.5H_2O$) is less soluble and often preferable for this reason, especially on light soils. To reduce the borax solubility, borax is sometimes fused with glass, shattered, and applied as glass frits which slowly dissolve to release the boron. Boric acid (H_3BO_3) can be applied in leaf sprays.

Molybdenum is present in particularly small quantities in soils—the average is probably only 2 parts molybdenum per million parts soil. The availability of the molybdate anion is greater in alkaline soils than acid soils, and phosphate applications have been shown to increase molybdenum uptake. The correction of molybdenum deficiencies is usually achieved by adding relatively small quantities of molybdenum compounds, such as ammonium and sodium molybdate or molybdenum trioxide, with normal N-P-K or phosphatic fertilizers so as to give 2 oz to 2 lb of the compound per acre, but leaf sprays can also be used. In Australia, clover seeds have been successfully soaked in sodium molybdate solution as an alternative to applying the compound to the field.

APPENDIX: FOR FURTHER READING

In this appendix a few suggestions are given for further reading which can supplement the introductory information contained in the text. No attempt has been made to prepare a full bibliography relevant to West African soils; rather it has been the aim to introduce the reader to a cross section of the literature in the hope of indicating the breadth of the subject and stimulating him to dig further for himself. The number of books and journal articles which are relevant to the environment, agriculture, and soils of West Africa is very great indeed, and it is not possible to do more here than list a very small percentage of them, but most of the references given here themselves contain numerous additional references which will assist the reader in following up further those aspects of the subject which are of interest to him.

For convenience the references are numbered, and grouped under the chapters to which they are especially pertinent.

Chapters 1 and 2: *Introduction*

The following references deal primarily with the study of the soil in the field and the description of soil profiles:

1. CLARKE, G. R. (1957) *The Study of the Soil in the Field*, 4th ed., London, O.U.P.
2. U.S. DEPT. OF AGRICULTURE. *Soil Survey Manual*, U.S. Dept. of Agriculture Handbook, No. 18.

There are a large number of general soil textbooks which contain sections on soil structure, texture, consistency and the description of profiles, in addition to chapters dealing with soil physics and chemistry relevant to later chapters in this book. For convenience, a short selection of general textbooks is given here:

3. BERGER, K. C. (1965) *Introductory Soils*, New York, Macmillan.
4. BUCKMAN, H. O., and BRADY, N. C. (1968) *The Nature and Properties of Soils*, 6th ed. (Revised N. C. Brady), New York, Macmillan.
5. COMBER, N. M. (1960) *An Introduction to the Scientific Study of the Soil*, London, E. Arnold.
6. DEMOLON, A. (1952) *La dynamique du sol*, Paris, Dunod.
7. DONAHUE, R. L. (1958) *Soils: An Introduction to Soils and Plant Growth*, Englewood Cliffs, New Jersey, Prentice Hall.
8. DUCHAUFOUR, P. H. (1960) *Précis de pédologie*, Paris, Masson.
9. GRIM, R. E. (1968) *Clay Mineralogy*, 2nd ed., New York, McGraw-Hill.
10. LEEPER, G. W. (1957) *Introduction to Soil Science*, 3rd ed., Victoria, Australia, Melbourne University Press.

11. RUSSELL, E. W. (1961) *Soil Conditions and Plant Growth*, 9th ed., London, Longmans Green.
12. TAMHANE, R. V., MOTIRAMANI, D. P., BALI, Y. P., and DONAHUE, R. L. (1964) *Soils: Their Chemistry and Fertility in Tropical Asia*, Englewood Cliffs, New Jersey, Prentice Hall.
13. THOMPSON, L. M. (1957) *Soils and Soil Fertility*, New York, McGraw-Hill.
14. U.S. DEPT. OF AGRICULTURE (1957) *Soil: The Yearbook of Agriculture, 1957*, Washington.
15. —— (1958) *Land: The Yearbook of Agriculture, 1958*, Washington.

Of the above, References 4 and 13 are widely used college texts written particularly for users in the U.S.A.; References 3 and 7 are more introductory texts also written primarily for American users. Reference 11 is relatively advanced and the ninth edition has benefited from the author's experience in East Africa, so that this book is more relevant to tropical soils than most general texts. Reference 12 is an introductory book primarily for readers in tropical Asia.

The following references are to general books on the West African environment, some regional geographies, and general books on soils, agriculture and land-use:

16. BOATENG, E. A. (1966) *A Geography of Ghana*, 2nd ed., London, Cambridge University Press.
17. BUCHANAN, K. M., and PUGH, J. C. (1955) *Land and People in Nigeria: The Human Geography and Its Environmental Background*, London, University of London Press.
17a. COBLEY, L. S. (1956) *An Introduction to the Botany of Tropical Crops*, London, Longmans Green.
18. GOUROU, P. (1966) (translated Laborde, E. D.) *The Tropical World*, 4th ed., London, Longmans Green.
19. GROVE, A. T. (1967) *Africa South of the Sahara*, London, O.U.P.
20. HARRISON CHURCH, R. J. (1966) *West Africa: A Study of the Environment and Man's Use of It*, 5th ed., London, Longmans Green.
21. JARRETT, H. R. (1961) *A Geography of Sierra Leone and Gambia*, London, Longmans Green.
22. NIGERIA GOVERNMENT (1954) *The Nigeria Handbook*, 2nd ed., London, Crown Agents.
23. PERKINS, W. A., and STEMBRIDGE, J. H. (1957) *Nigeria: A Descriptive Geography*, London, O.U.P.
24. RICHARD-MOLARD, J. (1956) *Afrique-Occidentale française*, 2nd ed., Paris, Berger-Levrault.
25. SMYTH, A. J., and MONTGOMERY, R. F. (1962) *Soils and Land-use in Central Western Nigeria*, Ibadan, Govt. of Western Nigeria, Ministry of Agriculture and Natural Resources.
26. THOMPSON, V., and ADLOFF, R. (1958) *French West Africa*, London, Allen and Unwin.
27. WILLS, J. B. (Editor) (1962) *Agriculture and Land Use in Ghana*, London, O.U.P., and Accra, Min. of Food and Agriculture.

Of the above, References 25 and 27 are particularly valuable to students of West African soils. The textural classification shown in Fig. 2.4 is taken from Reference 25, and individual chapters in Reference 27 are referred to subsequently.

This book also contains an extensive classified bibliography, and lists other West African bibliographies. Other recent bibliographies include the following:

28. BAUDIN DE THÉ, B. M. S. (1960) *Essais de bibliographie du Sahara français et des régions avoisinantes*, Paris, Arts et Métiers graphiques.

29. BRASSEUR, P. (1964) *Bibliographie générale du Mali*, Dakar, IFAN.

30. HARRIS, J. (1962) *Books about Nigeria: A Select Reading List*, 3rd ed., Ibadan.

31. JOHNSON, A. F. (1964) *A Bibliography of Ghana, 1930–61*, London, Longmans Green.

32. PORGES, L. (1964) *Éléments de bibliographie sénégalaise, 1959–63*, Dakar, Archives nationales — Centre de documentation.

33. RYDINGS, H. A. (1961) *The Bibliographies of West Africa*, Ibadan, Ibadan University Press.

34. SAIX, E. (1963) *Bibliographie sur la cuvette du lac Tchad: ouvrages publiés et études réalisées dans les cadres de la république du Tchad*, Paris.

There are a number of organizations producing bibliographies and abstracts dealing with soils and agriculture. Particularly useful is *Soils and Fertilizers* (*Abstracts of World Literature*) published bimonthly by the Commonwealth Agricultural Bureaux, Farnham Royal, Bucks, England, and compiled by the Commonwealth Bureau of Soils, Harpenden, Herts. This organization also issues the following bibliography at intervals:

35. COMMONWEALTH BUREAU OF SOILS (1957, 1960, 1963) *Bibliography of Soil Science, Fertilizers and General Agronomy, 1953–6, 1956–9, 1959–62*, Harpenden, Herts.

In addition, the Commonwealth Bureau of Soils issues very useful *annotated bibliographies* on a wide range of subjects. Several hundred of these are usually in print, and subjects, number of references and price are listed at intervals in *Soils and Fertilizers*. Examples include:

36. COMMONWEALTH BUREAU OF SOILS (1965) *Soils of West Africa*, Annotated bibliography 282, 1964–53, 282 references, Harpenden, Herts.

37. —— (1966) *Texture Classification*, Annotated bibliography 1001, 1965–53, 25 references, Harpenden, Herts.

38. —— (1966) *Iron Concretions in Soils*, Annotated bibliography 1057, 1965–36, 51 references, Harpenden, Herts.

The reader will also find much that is relevant in the numerous journals devoted to soils and related subjects. Examples, in addition to *Soils and Fertilizers*, mentioned above, include:

The Journal of Soil Science,
Soil Science,
Soil Science Society of America Proceedings,
Canadian Journal of Soil Science,
Pédologie (Ghent),
African Soils (*Sols africains*),
Experimental Agriculture (formerly: *The Empire Journal of Experimental Agriculture*),
Agronomy Journal,
Australian Journal of Agricultural Research,
Nature.

In addition, there are local West African journals such as the *Journal of the West African Science Association*, the *Ghana Journal of Science*, the *Journal of the Nigerian Science Association* and others. Information is contained in the annual reports of organizations such as the Cocoa Research Institute, Tafo, Ghana (formerly the West African Cocoa Research Institute), the West African Institute for Oil Palm Research (WAIFOR), the West African Rice Research Station (Rokupr, Sierra Leone), IRHO (Institut de Recherches pour les Huiles et Oléagineux, Paris), IFAC (Institut des Fruits et Agromes Coloniaux) (Paris, Abidjan) and similar organizations, some of which also publish scientific papers and reports. The work of these organizations includes soil investigations. Systematic soil surveys in West Africa are carried out by a number of organizations, in particular, by the Soil Research Institute of the Ghana Academy of Sciences (formerly the Ghana Department of Soil & Land-Use Survey), Kumasi, Ghana, the Institute for Agricultural Research, Ahmadu Bello University, Samaru, Zaria, Northern Nigeria, and by the French research organization, ORSTOM (Office de la Recherche Scientifique et Technique d'Outre-Mer) with centres at Hann, Dakar, Senegal and at Adiopodoumé, Abidjan, Ivory Coast. Soil and related investigations are also carried out by the Ministries of Agriculture of several West African territories and by the Faculties and Departments of Agriculture at West African universities.

Chapter 3: *Soil formation—parent material, relief and site*

The following references deal with soil formation in general, general geology, and rock weathering and its products, including clays:

39. BATES, D. A. (1962) Geology in *Agriculture and Land Use in Ghana*. (Reference 27)
40. BERRY, L., and RUXTON, B. P. (1959) Notes on weathering zones and soils on granite rocks in two tropical regions, *Journal of Soil Science*, **10**, 54–63.
41. BIDWELL, O. W., and HOLE, F. D. (1965) Man as a factor of soil formation, *Soil Science*, **99**, 1, 65–72.
42. COMMONWEALTH BUREAU OF SOILS (1967) *Weathering of Micas*, Annotated bibliography 1043, 39 references, Harpenden, Herts.
43. CROMPTON, E. (1962) Soil formation, *Outlook on Agriculture*, Vol. III, No. 5, 209–18.
44. DE VILLIERS, J. M. (1965) Present soil-forming factors and processes in tropical and subtropical regions, *Soil Science*, **99**, 1, 50–7.
45. FURON, R. (1963) *Geology of Africa* (translated Hallam, H. and Stevens, L. A.), London.
46. HALLSWORTH, E. G., and CRAWFORD, D. V. (Editors) (1965) *Experimental Pedology*, London, Butterworth.
47. HAUGHTON, S. M. (1963) *The Stratigraphic History of Africa South of the Sahara*, Edinburgh.
48. JACKSON, M. L. (1965) Clay transformations in soil genesis during the Quaternary, *Soil Science*, **99**, 1, 15–22.
49. ——, and SHERMAN, D. G. (1953) Chemical weathering of minerals in soils, *Advances in Agronomy*, 1953, 219–318.
50. JENNY, H. (1941) *Factors of Soil Formation*, New York, McGraw-Hill.
51. JUNGERIUS, P. D., and LEVELT, T. W. M. (1964) Clay mineralogy of soils over sedimentary rocks in Eastern Nigeria, *Soil Science*, **97**, 2, 89–95.

52. LENEUF, N. (1959) *L'Altération des granites calco-alcalins et des granodiorites en Côte-d'Ivoire forestière et les sols qui en sont dérivés*, Paris, ORSTOM.

53. MARSHALL, C. E. (1964) *The Physical Chemistry and Mineralogy of Soils*, vol. i—*Soil Materials*. New York, John Wiley.

54. MUIR, A., ANDERSON B., and STEPHEN, I. (1957) Characteristics of Some Tanganyika soils, *J. Soil. Sci.*, **8**, 1, 1–18.

55. NYE, P. H. (1954–5) Some soil-forming processes in the humid tropics, ibid., **5**, 7–21; **6**, 51–62, 63–72, 73–83.

56. OLLIER, C. D. (1959) A two-cycle theory of tropical pedology, ibid., **10**, 2, 137–48.

57. READ, H. H. and WATSON, J. (1962) *Introduction to Geology*, vol. i; *Principles*, London, Macmillan.

58. REICHE, P. (1950) *A Survey of Weathering Processes and Products*, Mexico, University of New Mexico Press.

59. RUXTON, B. P., and BERRY, L. (1957) Weathering of granite and associated erosional features in Hong Kong, *Bull. Geol. Soc. America*, **68**, 10, 1263–91.

60. SMITHSON, F. (1961) The microscopy of the silt fraction, *J. Soil Sci.*, **12**, 1, 145–57.

61. VINE, H. (1949) Nigerian soils in relation to parent material. Commonwealth Bureau of Soil Science, Harpenden, Herts, *Technical communication*, **46**, 22–9.

62. WEMBLEY, D. M., HENDERSON, M. E. K., and TAYLOR, I. F. (1963) The microbiology of rocks and weathered stones, *J. Soil Sci.* **14**, 1, 102–12.

63. WEBSTER, R. (1960) Soil genesis and classification in Central Africa, *Soils and Fertilizers*, **3**, 77–9.

There are numerous textbooks on general geology in addition to the single volume (Reference 57) referred to above: this can be recommended as a fairly full introduction to the subject. Similarly, there are a very large number of books on geomorphology. The following list includes only two general textbooks and a selection of other references on soils in relation to geomorphology, stone lines and related topics. The book on relief formation in the forest zone of the Ivory Coast (Reference 70) deals particularly with the importance of the weathering mantle.

64. BRASH, H. T. (1962) Geomorphology in *Agriculture and Land Use in Ghana*. (Reference 27)

65. DE CRAENE, A. (1954) Les sols de pédimentation ou les sols à 'stone line' du N.-E. du Congo belge, *Fifth International Congress of Soil Science*, **IV**, 451–60.

66. HUNTER, J. M. (1961) Morphology of a bauxite summit in Ghana, *Geog. J.* **CXXVII**, 4, 469–75.

67. MOSS, R. P. (1965) Slope development and soil morphology in a part of south-west Nigeria, *J. Soil Sci.*, **16**, 2, 192–209.

68. PEEL, R. F. (1952) *Physical Geography*, London, English University Press.

69. PUGH, J., and KING, L. C. (1952) Outline of the geomorphology of Nigeria, *South African Geographical Journal*, **43**, 30–7.

70. ROUGERIE, G. (1960) *Le façonnement actuel des modelés en Côte-d'Ivoire forestière*. Mémoires de l'Institut Français de l'Afrique Noire, 58, Dakar, IFAN.

71. RUHE, R. V. (1956) Geomorphic surfaces and the nature of soils, *Soil Science*, **82**, 441–55.

72. —— (1956) *Landscape Evolution in the High Ituri, Belgian Congo*, Brussels INEAC (Institut national pour l'étude agronomique du Congo belge), Série scientifique, 66.

73. RUHE, R. V. (1959) Stone lines in soils, *Soil Science*, 87, 4, 223–31.
74. SPARKS, B. W. (1960) *Geomorphology*, London, Longmans Green.
75. STEPHENS, C. G. (1961) *Soil Landscapes of Australia*, Soil Publication No. 18, CSIRO, Australia.
76. WAEGEMANS, G. (1953) Signification pédologique de la 'stone line', *Bulletin agricole du Congo belge*, XLIV, 3, 521–32.

Information on West African soil catenas is available in many of the soil survey reports (often mimeographed) issued by the West African soil survey organizations such as those listed under Chapters 1 and 2. The following is a short selection of references relevant to this subject:

77. ADU, S. V. (1961) The soils of Zuarungu agricultural station, Upper Region (Ghana) Ghana Ministry of Agriculture, Scientific Services Division, Tech. Report No. 54, Kumasi, Ghana.
78. —— (1962) The soils of Manga agricultural station, ibid. Tech. Report No. 56.
78a. AHN, P. M. (1960) The soils of Aiyinasi agricultural station (Ghana). Ghana, Department of Soil and Land-Use Survey, Tech. Report. No. 26, Kumasi, Ghana.
79. —— (1961) *Soils of the Lower Tano basin, south-western Ghana*, Ghana Ministry of Agriculture, Soil and Land-Use Survey Branch, Memoir No. 2, Kumasi, Ghana, Government Printer, Accra.
80. —— (1961) The soils of Wamfie cocoa station, Brong-Ahafo area, (Ghana), Ghana Scientific Services Division, Tech. Report No. 43, Kumasi, Ghana.
81. —— (1962) The soils of Goaso cocoa station, Brong-Ahafo area, (Ghana), ibid. Tech. Report No. 47, Kumasi, Ghana.
82. —— (1962) Soil studies in the Asenanyo forest reserve, Ashanti, Ghana, ibid. Tech. Report No. 46, Kumasi, Ghana.
83. BOCQUIER, M., and GAVAUD, M. (1964) Étude pédologique du Niger oriental, ORSTOM, Hann, Dakar, Senegal.
84. BRAMMER, H. (1962) Soils in *Agriculture and Land Use in Ghana* (Reference 27).
85. HILDEBRAND, F. H. (1966) Report on the soil survey of the United Hills area, Sardauna Province, Nigeria, Institute for Agricultural Research, Ahmadu Bello University, Soil Survey Bull. 31, Samaru, Zaria, N. Nigeria.
86. KALOGA, B. (1966) Étude pédologique des bassins versants de Volta blanche et rouge en Haute-Volta, Cahier ORSTOM, Hann, Dakar, Senegal, Série pédologique, IV, 1, 1966.
87. MONNIER, G. (1955) Études pédologiques à la station de l'IFAC à Azaguié, IFAC, Annales 10, Abidjan, Ivory Coast.
88. MOULD, A. W. S. (1960) Report on a rapid reconnaissance survey of the Mambilla plateau, Regional Research Station, Ministry of Agriculture, Bull. 15, Samaru, N. Nigeria.
89. OBENG, H. B. (1963) Soils of the Seilo-Tuni land planning area, Wala District, near Wa, Upper Region (Ghana), Ghana Academy of Sciences, Agricultural Research Institute, Tech. Report No. 62, Kumasi, Ghana.
90. PULLAN, R. A., and DE LEEUW, P. N. (1964) The land capability survey prepared for the Niger Dams Resettlement Authority, Institute for Agricultural Research, Ahmadu Bello University, Soil Survey Bull. 26, Samaru, Zaria, N. Nigeria.
91. PURNELL, M. F. (1960) Report on the detailed soil survey of proposed oil palm plantations at Pretsia, Avrebo and Sukusuku estates, (Ghana) Ghana Ministry of Food and Agriculture, Soil and Land-Use Survey Branch, Tech. Report No. 39, Kumasi, Ghana.

92. RADWANSKI, S. A., and OLLIER, C. D. (1959) A Study of an East African catena, *J. Soil Sci.*, **10**, 2, 149–68.

93. SMITH, G. K. (1962) Report on soil and agricultural survey of Sene-Obosum river basins, Ghana, U.S. AID—Ghana, Accra, Dept. of State, AID, Washington 25, D.C.

94. VALETTE, J., and HIGGINS, G. M. (1967) The reconnaissance soil survey of an area near Auna, Niger Province, N. Nigeria, Institute for Agricultural Research, Ahmadu Bello University, Soil Survey Bull. 34, Samaru, Zaria, N. Nigeria.

95. WATSON, J. P. (1964) A soil catena on granite in Southern Rhodesia, *J. Soil Sci.*, **15**, 238–257.

Chapter 4: *Soil formation—climate, vegetation and soil fauna; 'laterite'*

The following publications deal with vegetation in general and with West African vegetation in particular, with soil-vegetation relationships, with West African climate and with soil fauna (including soil microbiology).

96. AHN, P. M. (1958) Regrowth and swamp vegetation in the western forest areas of Ghana, *J. West Afri. Sci. Assoc.*, **4**, 163–73.

97. —— (1959) The savanna patches of Nzima, ibid. **5**, 10–25.

98. —— (1961) Soil-vegetation relationships in the western forest areas of Ghana, in *Tropical Soils and Vegetation*, Paris, UNESCO (Reference 142).

99. ALEXANDER, M. (1961) *Introduction to Soil Microbiology*, New York, John Wiley.

100. AUBREVILLE, A. (1936) *La Flore forestière de la Côte-d'Ivoire*, Paris, Larose.

101. —— (1938) *La Forêt coloniale: les forêts de l'A.O.F.*, Annales de l'Académie des Sciences coloniales, 9, Paris, Société d'Éditions géographiques, maritimes et coloniales.

102. —— (1949) *Climats, forêts et désertifications de l'Afrique tropicale*, Paris, Société d'Éditions géographiques, maritimes et coloniales.

103. BAKER, H. G. (1962) The ecological study of vegetation in Ghana, in *Agriculture and Land Use in Ghana* (Reference 27).

104. BATES, J. A. R. (1960) Studies on a Nigerian forest soil, i. The distribution of organic matter in the profile and in various soil fractions, *J. Soil Sci.*, **11**, 2, 246–56.

104a. BURGES, A. (1958) *Micro-organisms in the Soil*, London, Hutchinson.

105. CHARTER, J. R., and KEAY, R. W. J. (1960) *Assessment of the Olokomeji Fire Control Experiment (investigation 254) 28 years after institution*, Nigerian Forestry Information Bull. (New Series) 3, Lagos, Federal Government Printer.

106. CHIPP, T. F. (1927) *The Gold Coast Forest: A Study in Synecology*, Oxford, Clarendon Press, Ox. For. Mem., 7.

107. COMMONWEALTH BUREAU OF SOILS (1956) *Termites and soil formation*, Annotated bibliography 49, 1964–33, Harpenden, Herts.

108. EYRE, S. R. (1963) *Vegetation and Soils*, London, E. Arnold.

109. HESSE, P. R. (1955) A chemical and physical study of the soils of termite mounds in East Africa, *J. Ecol.*, **43**, 449–61.

110. —— (1961) The decomposition of organic matter in a mangrove swamp soil, *Plant and Soil*, **14**, 249–63.

111. —— (1961) Some differences between the soils of *Rhizophora* and *Avicennia* mangrove swamps in Sierra Leone, ibid. **14**, 335–46.

112. HOPKINS, B. (1965) *Forest and Savanna*, Heinemann, London.

113. KEAY, R. W. J. (1953) *An Outline of Nigerian Vegetation*, 2nd ed., Lagos, Government Printer.

114. KEAY, R. W. J. (1959) *Vegetation Map of Africa south of the Tropic of Cancer*, London, O.U.P.

115. —— (1959) Derived savanna—derived from what? *IFAN Bulletin*, Series A, **21**, 427–38.

116. LANE, D. A. The forest vegetation, in *Agriculture and Land Use in Ghana* (Reference 27).

117. LAWSON, G. W. (1966) *Plant Life in West Africa*, London, O.U.P.

118. LEMÉE, G. (1961) Effets des caractères du sol sur la localisation de la végétation en zones équatoriales et tropicales humides, in *Tropical Soils and Vegetation* (Reference 142).

119. LENEUF, N., and AUBERT, G. (1956) Sur l'origine des savanes de la basse Côte-d'Ivoire, Paris, *Comptes rendus de l'Académie des sciences*, **243**, 859–60.

120. LONGMAN, K. A. and JENIK, J. (In preparation) *Tropical Forest and its Environment*, Edinburgh, Oliver and Boyd.

121. MANGENOT, G. (1955) Études sur les forêts des plaines et plateaux de la Côte-d'Ivoire, *Études éburnéennes*, **IV**, 5–61, Abidjan, Institut français d'Afrique Noire, Centre de Côte-d'Ivoire.

122. MIÈGE, J. (1955) Les savanes et forêts claires de la Côte d'Ivoire, ibid. 62–81.

123. MOONEY, J. W. C. (1961) Site indices in natural and selection forest, Vienna, 13th Congress, International Union of Forest Research Organizations.

124. —— (1961) Classification of the vegetation of the high forest zone of Ghana, in *Tropical Soils and Vegetation* (Reference 142).

125. NYE, P. H. (1961) Some effects of natural vegetation on the soils of West Africa and on their development under cultivation, ibid.

126. —— (1961) Organic matter and nutrient cycles under moist tropical forest, *Plant and Soil*, **13**, 333–46.

127. PRESCOTT, J. A. (1949) A climatic index for the leaching factor in soil formation, *J. Soil Sci.*, **1**, 9–19.

128. RAMSAY, J. M., and ROSE INNES, R. (1963) Some observations on the effects of fire on the Guinea Savanna vegetation of northern Ghana over a period of eleven years, *African Soils*, **8**, (1), 41–85.

129. RATTRAY, J. M. (1960) *The Grass Cover of Africa*, Rome, FAO, Agricultural Studies, 49.

130. RICHARDS, P. W. (1952) *The Tropical Rain Forest*, London, Cambridge University Press.

131. —— (1961) The types of vegetation of the humid tropics in relation to the soil, in *Tropical Soils and Vegetation* (Reference 142).

132. RILEY, D., and YOUNG, A. (1966) *World Vegetation*, London, Cambridge University Press.

133. RODALE, R. (Editor) (1961) *The Challenge of Earthworm Research*, The soil and health foundation, Pennsylvania, Emmaus.

134. ROSEVEAR, R. D. (1953) Vegetation, in *The Nigerian Handbook*, London, Crown Agents.

135. RUSSELL, E. J. (1957) *The World of the Soil*, London, Collins.

136. SCHNELL, R. (1950) *La Forêt dense. Introduction à l'étude botanique de la région forestière d'Afrique occidentale*, Paris, Le Chevalier.

137. SCOTT, R. M. (1962) Exchangeable bases of mature, well drained soils in relation to rainfall in East Africa, *J. Soil Sci.*, **13**, 1, 1–9.

138. STEPHENS, C. G. (1965) Climate as a factor of soil formation through the Quarternary, *Soil Science*, **99**, 1, 9–14.

139. TAYLOR, C. J. (1952) *Vegetation Zones of the Gold Coast*, Gold Coast Forestry Department, Bull. 4, Accra, Government Printer.
140. THOMPSON, B. W. (1965) *The Climate of Africa*, Nairobi, O.U.P.
141. TOMLINSON, T. E. (1957) Relationship between mangrove vegetation, soil texture and reaction of surface soil after empoldering saline swamps in Sierra Leone, Trinidad, *Tropical Agriculture*, 34, 41–50.
142. UNESCO (1961) *Humid Tropics Research. Tropical Soils and Vegetation*, Paris, Proc. of the Abidjan symposium of 1959.
143. WAKSMAN, S. A. (1952) *Soil Microbiology*, New York, John Wiley.
144. WALKER, H. O. (1962) Weather and climate, in *Agriculture and Land Use in Ghana* (Reference 27).
145. WATSON, J. P. (1961) Some observations on soil horizons and insect activity in granite soils, Salisbury, S. Rhodesia, *Proc. 1st Federation Science Congress, 1960*.
146. —— (1962) The soil below a termite mound, *J. Soil Sci.*, 13, 1, 46–51.
147. WEST, O. (1965) Fire in vegetation and its use in pasture management, Hurley, Berkshire, Commonwealth Bureau of Pastures and Field Crops, mimeographed publication 1/1965.

The literature on 'laterite' is particularly extensive. The following references are but a small selection dealing with laterite formation, iron movements in soils, gleying and allied phenomena. Many of these, particularly References 148, 157, 158, and 163, contain extensive further bibliographies.

148. ALEXANDER, L. T., and CADY, J. G. (1962) *Genesis and Hardening of Laterite in Soils*, U.S. Dept. of Agriculture, Washington, Tech. Bull. 1282.
149. AUBERT, G. (1963) Soil with ferruginous or ferrallitic crusts of tropical regions, *Soil Science*, 95, 235–42.
150. BLOOMFIELD, C. (1950) Some observations on gleying, *J. Soil Sci.*, 1, 205–11.
151. —— (1951). Experiments on the mechanism of gley formation, ibid. 2, 196–211.
152. —— (1952) The distribution of iron and aluminium oxides in gley soils, ibid. 3, 167–71.
153. D'HOORE, J. (1954) *L'accumulation des sesquioxydes libres dans les sols tropicaux*, Brussels, INEAC, Série scientifique, 62.
154. DU PREEZ, J. W. (1949) Laterite: A general discussion with a description of the Nigerian occurrences, *Bull. agricole du Congo belge*, 40, 53–66.
155. FOLLET, E. A. C. (1965) The retention of amorphous, colloidal 'ferric hydroxide' by kaolinites, *J. Soil Sci.*, 16, 2, 334–41.
156. FRIPIAT, J. J., and GASTUCHE, M. C. (1952) *Étude physico-chimique des surfaces des argiles. Les combinaisons de la kaolinite avec les oxydes de fer trivalent*, Brussels, INEAC, Série scientifique, 54.
157. MAIGNIEN, R. (1958) *Le Cuirassement des sols en Guinée*, ORSTOM, Strasbourg, Université de Strasbourg, Institut des Sciences Géologiques, extrait des Mémoires du Service de la Carte Géologique d'Alsace et de Lorraine, 1958, No. 16.
158. —— (1966) *Review of Research on Laterites*, Paris, Natural Resources Research, IV, UNESCO.
159. PRESCOTT, J. A., and PENDLETON, R. L. (1952) *Laterite and Lateritic Soils*, Slough, Commonwealth Agricultural Bureaux.
160. SEGALEN, P. (1965) *Le Fer dans les Sols*, Paris, Gauthier-Villars/ORSTOM.
161. STEPHENS, C. G. (1961) Laterite at the type locality, Angadipuram, Kerala, India, *J. Soil Sci.*, 12, 1, 214–17.

162. SCHOFFIELD, A. N. (1957) Nyasaland latterites and their indications on aerial photographs, Harmondsworth, Middlesex, Road Research Laboratory, Overseas Bull. No. 5.

163. SIVARAJASINGHAM, S., ALEXANDER, L. T., CADY, J. G., and CLINE, M. G. (1962) Laterite, *Advances in Agronomy*, 14, 1–60.

The following publications refer to tropical black earths:

164. BRAMMER, H. (1955) *Detailed Soil Survey of the Kpong Pilot Irrigation Area, Kumasi*, Memoir 1, Ghana Dept. of Soil and Land Use Survey.

165. DUDAL, R. (1963) Dark clay soils of tropical and subtropical regions, *Soil Science*, 95, 264–70.

166. FAO (1965) *Dark Clay Soils of Tropical and Subtropical Regions* (R. Dudal, Editor), Rome, FAO, Agricultural Development Papers 83.

Chapter 5: *Soil water and soil air*

The literature on soil water and irrigation is now very extensive indeed: the following brief selection is concerned mainly with practical aspects of soil moisture utilization in Africa, but numerous additional references are contained in References 167, 168, 174, and 175.

167. BAVER, L. D. (1956) *Soil Physics*, New York, John Wiley.

168. COMMONWEALTH BUREAU OF SOILS (1967) *Reduction of Evaporation from Soil*, Annotated bibliography 1106, 1966–56, 58 references, Harpenden, Herts.

169. FOSTER, L. J., and WOOD, R. A. (1962) Observations on the effects of shade and irrigation on soil moisture utilization under coffee in Nyasaland, *Empire Journal of Experimental Agriculture*, 31, 122, 108–114.

170. GILCHRIST, J. L. (1964) *Evaporation in Nigeria*, Lagos, Nigerian Meteorological Service, Tech. Note 6.

171. HAGAN, R. M., HAISE, H. R., and EDMINSTER, T. W. (Editors) (1967) *Irrigation of Agricultural Lands*, Agronomy monograph 11, Madison, Wisconsin, American Society of Agronomy.

172. HILL, P. R. (1961) A simple system of management for soil and water conservation and drainage in mechanised crop production in the tropics, *Emp. J. Exper. Agric.* 29, 116, 337–49.

173. LAWES, D. A. (1961) Rainfall conservation and the yield of cotton in Northern Nigeria, ibid. 29, 116, 307–18.

174. MARSHALL, T. J. (1959) *Relations between Water and Soil*, Commonwealth Bureau of Soils, Technical Communication 50, Harpenden, Herts.

175. PENMAN, H. L. *Vegetation and Hydrology*, Commonwealth Bureau of Soils, Technical Communication 53, Harpenden, Herts.

176. PEREIRA, H. C. (1956) A rainfall test for structure of tropical soils, *J. Soil Sci.*, 7, 68.

177. —— (1957) Field measurements of water use for irrigation control in Kenya coffee, *J. Agric. Sci.*, 49, 450–66.

178. —— WOOD, R. A., BRZOSTOWSKI, H. W., and HOSEGOOD, P. H. (1958) Water conservation by fallowing in semi-arid tropical East Africa, *Emp. J. Exper. Agric.* 26, 103, 213–28.

179. —— and HOSEGOOD, P. H. (1962) Comparative water-use of softwood plantations and bamboo forest, *J. Soil Sci.*, 13, 2, 300–31.

180. —— *et al.* (1962) Special issue on land-use hydrology experiments, *East African Agriculture and Forestry J.*, 27, 1–131.

181. ROSE, C. W. (1961) Rainfall and soil structure, *Soil Science*, 291, 49–54.

182. ROSE, C. W (1962) Some effects of rainfall, radiant drying, and soil factors on infiltration under rainfall into soils, *J. Soil Sci.*, **13**, 2, 286–98.

182a. —— (1966) *Agricultural Physics*, London, Pergamon Press.

183. SALTER, P. J., and WILLIAMS, J. B. (1963) The effect of farmyard manure on the moisture characteristic of a sandy loam soil, *J. Soil Sci.*, **14**, 1, 73–81.

184. —— —— (1967) The influence of texture on the moisture characteristics of soils, IV. A method of estimating the available water capacities of profiles in the field, ibid. **18**, 1, 174–81.

185. SHAW, B. T. (Editor) (1952) *Soil Physical Conditions and Plant Growth*, Agronomy Monograph 11, New York, Academic Press Inc.

186. THORNTHWAITE, C. W. (1951) The water balance in tropical climates, *Bull. Amer. Met. Soc.* **32**, 5, 166–73.

187. —— and MATHER, J. R. (1955) *The Water Balance*, New Jersey, Centerton.

188. TROUSE, A. C., and HUMBERT, R. P. (1961) Some effects of soil compaction on the development of sugar cane roots, *J. Soil Sci.*, **91**, 208–17.

189. VERSHININ, P. V. *et al.* (1967) *Fundamentals of Agrophysics*, London, Oldbourne Press, Publishing House for Physics and Mathematics, Moscow.

190. WALTON, P. D. (1962) The effect of ridging on the cotton crop in the Eastern Province of Uganda, *Emp. J. Exper. Agric.*, **30**, 117, 63–76.

191. WOOD, R. A. (1960) The relationship between soil moisture utilization and rooting depth in the tropics, *Trans. 7th International Congress of Soil Science*, i, 364–8.

Chapter 6: *Soil chemistry and the supply of plant nutrients*

Chapters on soil chemistry and on plant nutrient needs and how these are supplied by the soil are contained in most of the general soil science textbooks listed under Chapters 1 and 2 (References 3 to 15). Other books dealing with these topics include the following.

192. BEAR, F. E. (Editor) (1964) *Chemistry of the Soil*, 2nd ed., New York, Rheinhold.

193. —— (1965) *Soils in Relation to Crop Growth*, New York, Rheinhold.

194. BLACK, C. A. (1968) *Soil-Plant Relationships*, 2nd ed., New York, John Wiley.

195. COMMONWEALTH AGRICULTURAL BUREAU (1962) *A Review of Nitrogen in the Tropics with particular reference to Pastures, A Symposium*, Ed. Committee of the Division of Tropical Pastures, CSIRO, Australia, Commonwealth Bureau of Pastures and Field Crops, Berks., England, Bull. 46.

196. FOGG, G. E. (1963) *The Growth of Plants*, Harmondsworth, Middlesex, Penguin.

197. MILLAR, C. E. (1955) *Soil Fertility*, New York, John Wiley.

198. MINISTRY OF AGRICULTURE, FISHERIES AND FOOD (United Kingdom) (1965) *Soil Phosphorus*, London, H.M.S.O., Tech. Bull. No. 13.

199. STEWART, W. D. P. (1966) *Nitrogen Fixation in Plants*, London, The Athlone Press.

200. SWAINE, D. J. (1955) *The Trace Element Contents of Soils*, Harpenden, Commonwealth Bureau of Soil Science, Tech. Communication 48.

To some extent the subject matter of Chapter 6 and that of the books listed above overlaps with that of Chapter 9 on manures, fertilizers, and their use. The following are a small selection of the many journal articles relevant to the chemistry of West African soils: a wide selection of further general references will be found in the books listed on the subject, such as References 192–200 above.

201. ACQUAYE, D. K., MACLEAN, A. J., and RICE, H. M. (1967) Potential and capacity of potassium in some representative soils of Ghana, *Soil Science*, **103**, 2, 79–89.

202. ARNOLD, P. W. (1962) Soil potassium and its availablity to plants, *Outlook on Agriculture*, III, 6, 263–7.

203. BATES, J. A. R., and BAKER, T. C. N. (1960) Studies on a Nigerian forest soil, II, The distribution of phosphorus in the profile and in the various soil fractions, *J. Soil Sci.*, **11**, 257–65.

204. BURRIDGE, J. C., and AHN, P. M. (1965) A spectrographic survey of representative Ghana forest soils, ibid. **16**, 2, 296–309.

205. —— and CUNNINGHAM, R. K. (1960) Cacao yield maps and soil fertility in Ghana, *Emp. J. Exper. Agric.*, **28**, 112, 327–34.

206. CHENERY, E. M. (1950). Some aspects of the aluminium cycle, *J. Soil Sci.*, **2**, 97–109.

207. ENDREDY, A. S. DE, and QUAGRAINE, K. A. (1960) A comprehensive study of cation exchange in tropical soils, *Trans. 7th International Congress of Soil Science*, Madison, vol. ii, 312–20.

208. FULLER, W. H., CAMERON, R. E., and RAICA, N. (1960) Fixation of nitrogen in desert soils by algae, ibid. 617–24.

209. GASSER, J. K. R., and BLOOMFIELD, C. (1955) The mobilization of phosphate in waterlogged soils, *J. Soil Sci.*, **6**, 219–32.

210. GREENLAND, D. J. (1958) Nitrate fluctuations in tropical soils, *J. Agric. Sci.*, **50**, 82–92.

211. HENZELL, E. F., and NORRIS, D. O. (1962) Processes by which nitrogen is added to the soil/plant system, in *A Review of Nitrogen in the Tropics* (Reference 195).

212. HESSE, P. R. (1962) Phosphorus fixation in mangrove swamp muds, *Nature*, **193**, 295–6.

213. JEFFERY, J. W. O. (1961) Defining the state of reduction of a paddy soil, *J. Soil Sci.*, **12**, 172–9.

214. MEIKLEJOHN, J. (1962) Microbiology of the nitrogen cycle in some Ghana soils, *Emp. J. Exper. Agric.* **30**, 118, 115–62.

215. MOORE, A. W. (1962) The influence of a legume on soil fertility under a grazed tropical pasture, ibid., **30**, 119, 239–48.

216. —— and AYEKE, C. A. (1965) HF-extractable ammonium nitrogen in four Nigerian soils, *Soil Science*, **99**, 5, 335–8.

217. —— and JAIYEBO, E. O. (1963) The influence of cover on nitrate and nitrifiable nitrogen content of the soil in a tropical rain forest environment, *Emp. J. Exper. Agric.*, **31**, 123, 189–98.

218. MORTLAND, M. M. (1961) The dynamic character of potassium release and fixation, *Soil Science*, **91**, 11–13.

219. NORRIS, D. O. (1962) The biology of nitrogen fixation in *A Review of Nitrogen in the Tropics* (Reference 195).

220. NYE, P. H., and STEPHENS, D. Soil fertility, in *Agriculture and Land Use in Ghana* (Reference 27).

221. SIMPSON, J. R. (1960) The mechanism of surface nitrate accumulation on a bare fallow soil in Uganda, *J. Soil Sci.*, **11**, 1, 45–59.

222. STEPHENS, D. (1962) Upward movement of nitrate in a bare soil in Uganda, ibid., **13**, 1, 52–9.

223. STEWART, W. D. P. (1967) How do plants fix nitrogen? *Span*, **10**, 2, 110–13.

224. TEWARI, G. P. (1962) Note on a preliminary investigation of the efficiency of two introduced strains of cowpea rhizobium in the nodulation of a local cowpea variety at Ibadan, W. Nigeria, *Emp. J. Exper. Agric.*, **30**, 118, 155–8.

225. TINKER, P. R. H., and ZIBOH, C. O. (1959) A study of some typical soils supporting oil palms in Southern Nigeria, *J. W. Afr. Institute for Oil Palm Research*, III, 9, 18–51.

226. TOMLINSON, T. E. (1957) Changes in a sulphide-containing mangrove soil on drying and their effect upon the suitability of the soil for the growth of rice, *Emp. J. Exper. Agric.*, 25, 98, 108–18.

Chapter 7: *Surveying, classifying and analysing soils*

Publications dealing with soil survey and classification are also very numerous: information on soil survey methods is contained in Reference 2 and in some of the soil survey reports (References 77–95) listed above. The following are a short selection of further soil maps and reports dealing mostly with West African soil surveys:

227. DABIN, B., LENEUF, N., and RIOU, G. (1960) *Notice explicative sur la carte pédologique de la Côte-d'Ivoire au 1/2 000 000*, Secrétariat d'État à l'agriculture, Direction des sols (ORSTOM-IDERT), Abidjan.

227a DEVELOPMENT AND RESOURCES CORPORATION (1967) *A report to the Government of the Republic of Ivory Coast. Soil survey of the south west region.* New York, Development and Resources Corporation.

228. D'HOORE, J. L. (1964) *Soil Map of Africa, scale 1 to 5 000 000, Explanatory Monograph*, CCTA: Lagos.

229. FAUCK, R., TURENNE, J. F., and VIZIER, J. F. (1963) *Étude pédologique de la Haute-Casamance*, I. Rapport général, II. Carte pédologique de la Haute-Casamance au 1/200 000, ORSTOM, Dakar-Hann, Sénégal.

230. KALOGA, B. (1966) *Carte pédologique du Sénégal oriental à l'échelle du 1/200 000: notice explicative de la feuille de Dalafi*, ibid. Dakar-Hann, Sénégal.

231. KELLOGG, C. E., and DAVOL, F. D. (1949) *An Exploratory Study of Soil Groups in the Belgian Congo*, Brussels, INEAC, Série scientifique, 46.

232. MAIGNIEN, R. (1965) *Carte pédologique du Sénégal au 1/1 000 000. Notice explicative*, ORSTOM, Dakar-Hann, Sénégal.

233. PEREIRA BARRETO, S. (1966) *Cartes pédologiques du Sénégal au 1/200 000: Notice explicative des feuilles Tambacounda–Bakel-Sud*, Dakar-Hann, Sénégal, idem.

234. REED, W. E. (1951) *Reconnaissance Soil Survey of Liberia*, Washington, U.S. Department of Agriculture, Information Bull. 66.

235. SEGALEN, P. (1957) Les sols du Cameroun, Legend for *Atlas du Cameroun, planche VI, carte pédologique, 1/2 000 000*.

236. SYS, C. (1960) *Notice explicative de la carte des sols du Congo belge et du Ruanda-Urundi* (with 1/5 000 000 soil map), Brussels, INEAC.

The following books and journal articles deal with soil classification, mapping and interpretation:

237. AHN, P. M. (1959) The principal areas of remaining original forest in western Ghana and their agricultural potential, *J. West Afr. Sci. Assoc.*, 5, 2, 91–100.

238. —— (1963) The mapping, classification and interpretation of Ghana forest soils for forestry purposes, *Proc. Fifth World Forestry Congress, Seattle*.

239. AMERICAN SOCIETY OF AGRONOMY (1967) *Soil Surveys and Land Use Planning*, Wisconsin, Amer. Soc. of Agronomy, Madison.

240. AUBERT, G. (1962) La classification pédologique utilisée en France, Paper in Soil Classification, *Pédologie*, Special number 3, Ghent, Belgium, (Reference 252).

241. CHARTER, C. F. (1957) Suggestions for a classification of tropical soils, Kumasi, Ghana Ministry of Food and Agriculture, Soil and Land Use Survey Branch, Miscellaneous paper 4.

242. DUCHAUFOUR, P. H. (1963) Soil classification, A comparison of the American and French systems, *J. Soil Sci.*, **14**, 1, 149–55.

243. FINK, A., and OCHTMAN, L. H. J. (1961) Problems of soil evaluation in the Sudan, *J. Soil Sci.*, **12**, 1, 87–95.

244. GIBBONS, F. R. (1961) Some misconceptions about what soil surveys can do, ibid. **12**, 1, 96–100.

245. GREENE, H. (1963) Prospects in soil science, ibid. **14**, 1, 1–11.

246. JACKS, G. V. (1946) *Land Classification for Land Use Planning*, Harpenden, Herts., Imperial Bureau of Soil Science.

247. KELLOGG, C. E. (1961) *Soil Interpretation in the Soil Survey*, Washington, U.S. Dept. of Agriculture, Soil Conservation Service.

248. —— (1963) Why a new system of soil classification? *Soil Science*, **96**, 1, 1–5.

249. MUIR, J. W. (1962) The general principles of classification with reference to soils, *J. Soil Sci.*, **13**, 1, 22–30.

250. SIMONSON, R. W. (1963) Soil correlation and the new classification system, *Soil Science*, **96**, 1, 23–30.

251. SMITH, G. D. (1963) Objectives and basic assumptions of the new soil classification system, ibid. **96**, 1, 6–16.

252. THIRD INTERNATIONAL SYMPOSIUM ON SOIL CLASSIFICATION, Ghent (1962) Soil Classification, special issue of *Pédologie* (Special Number 3), Ghent, Belgium.

253. U.S. DEPARTMENT OF AGRICULTURE (1960) *Soil Classification. A Comprehensive System*, 7th Approximation, Washington, U.S. Department of Agriculture, Soil Conservation Service, Soil Survey staff.

254. U.S. DEPARTMENT OF AGRICULTURE (1967) *Supplement to Soil Classification System*, (7th Approximation), ibid. Washington.

255. VAN WAMBEKE, A. R. (1962) Criteria for classifying tropical soils by age, *J. Soil Sci.*, **13**, 1, 124–32.

256. VINK, A. P. A. (1963) Soil survey as related to agricultural productivity, ibid. **14**, 1, 88–101.

It is not possible in a short selection of references such as this to enumerate even a small percentage of the many publications referring to the wide subject of soil analysis, but copious lists of references are contained in some of the following books and articles on the subject, particularly in the very comprehensive two-volume publication by the American Society of Agronomy (Reference 257):

257. BLACK, C. A. *et al.* (Editors) (1965) *Methods of Soil Analysis.* (2 vols.), Madison, Wisconsin, American Society of Agronomy Inc., No. 9 in the series 'Agronomy',

258. BRITISH STANDARDS INSTITUTION (1961) *Methods of Testing Soils for Civil Engineering Purposes*, British Standards Institution, London, B.S. 1377.

259. CHAPMAN, H. D., and PRATT, P. F. (1961) *Methods of Analysis for Soils, Plants and Waters*, Berkeley, University of California.

260. DABIN, B. (1956) Considérations sur l'interprétation agronomique des analyses de sol en pays tropicaux, *Proc. VI International Congress of Soil Science, Paris*, D, 403–9.

261. GREWELING, T., and PEECH, M. (1960) *Chemical Soil Tests*, Ithaca, New York, Cornell University Agricultural Experiment Station, Bull. 960.

262. JACKSON, M. L. (1958) *Soil Chemical Analysis*, London, Constable.

263. KELLOGG, C. E. (1962) *The Place of the Laboratory in Soil Classification and Inter-pretation*, Washington, U.S. Dept. of Agriculture, Soil Conservation Service.
264. MUKHERJEE, H. N. (1963) Determination of nutrient needs of tropical soils, *Soil Science*, 95, 276–80.
265. OEEC (1956) *The Organization and Rationalization of Soil Analysis*, European Productivity Agency of the OEEC, Paris. (Organization for European Economic Co-operation).
266. SALMON, S. C., and HANSON, A. A. (1964) *The Principles and Practice of Agricultural Research*, London, Leonard Hill.
267. SAUNDER, D. H., ELLIS, B. S., and HALL, A. (1957) Estimation of available nitrogen for advisory purposes in Southern Nigeria, *J. Soil Sci.*, 8, 2, 301–12.
268. SPENCER, R. (1961) Analytical methods at present used to determine plant nutrient status and readily available nutrients in the soil by the Federal Department of Agricultural Research, Ibadan, *Fed. Dept. Agric. Research, Memorandum* 30, Moor Plantation, Ibadan.
269. STEWART, A. B. Soil in the field and in the laboratory, *J. Soil Sci.*, 16, 2, 171–82.

The following references deal with soil micromorphology and the microscope study of thin sections: the first two in particular contain numerous further references:

270. BREWER, R. (1964) *Fabric and Mineral Analysis of Soils*, New York, John Wiley.
271. JONGERIUS, A. (Ed.) (1964) *Soil Micromorphology*, (*Proc. of the Second International working meeting on Soil Micromorphology, Arnhem, Holland, 1964*). Amsterdam, Elsevier Publishing Co.
272. KUBIENA, W. L. (1938) *Micropedology*, Ames, Iowa, Collegiate Press.
273. LARUELLE, J. (1956) Some aspects of the micro-structure of soils in the north-east of the Belgain Congo, *Pédologie*, 6, 38–54.

Chapter 8: *Shifting cultivation, soil erosion and mechanical agriculture.*

The literature on shifting cultivation, both in Africa and in other parts of the tropics, has grown very considerably in recent years. An extremely useful summary and analysis of the information available up to about 1960 is contained in the book by Nye and Greenland (Reference 293) which pays particular attention to soil changes and contains about 400 references. The following short list of references also includes some referring to soil erosion and to farming practices and mechanization:

274. ALLAN, W. (1965) *The African Husbandman*, Edinburgh and London, Oliver and Boyd.
275. AUBREVILLE, A. (1947) Érosion et bovalisation en Afrique Noire française, *L'Agronomie tropicale*, 2, 7–8, 339–57.
276. BATES, W. N. (1957) *Mechanization of Tropical Crops*, London, Temple Press Books.
277. BENNET, H. H. (1955) *Elements of Soil Conservation*, 2nd ed., New York, McGraw-Hill.
278. BRAMMER, H. (1962) Soil erosion and conservation, in *Agriculture and Land Use in Ghana* (Reference 27).
279. CHARTER, C. F. (1958) Report on Environmental Conditions Prevailing in Block 'A', Southern Province, Tanganyika Territory, Kumasi, Ghana Department of Agriculture, Division of Soil and Land Use Survey, Occasional Paper 1.
280. CLARKE, R. T. (1962) The effect of some resting treatments on a tropical soil, *Emp. J. Exper. Agric.* 30, 117, 57–62.

281. COMMONWEALTH BUREAU OF SOILS (1962) *Ley Farming in Tropics and Sub-tropics*, Annotated bibliography 678, 1961–44, 59 references, Harpenden, Herts.

282. CUNNINGHAM, R. K. (1963) The effect of clearing a tropical forest soil, *J. Soil Sci.*, **14**, 2, 334–45.

283. D'HOORE, J. (1961) Influence de la mise en culture sur l'évolution des sols dans la zone de forêt dense de basse et moyenne altitude, chapter in *Tropical Soils and Vegetation* (Reference 142).

284. FAO (1960) *Soil Erosion by Wind and Measures for its Control on Agricultural Lands*, Rome, FAO, Agricultural Development Paper 71.

285. GREENLAND, D. J., and KOWAL, J. M. L. (1960) Nutrient content of the moist tropical forest in Ghana, *Plant and Soil*, **12**, 154–74.

286. —— and NYE, P. H. (1959) Increases in the carbon and nitrogen contents of tropical soils under natural fallows, *J. Soil Sci.*, **10**, 284–99.

287. HILL, P. (1963) *The Migrant Cocoa Farmers of Southern Ghana*, London, Cambridge University Press.

288. IGNATIEFF, V., and LEMOS, P. (1963) Some management aspects of more important tropical soils, *Soil Science*, **95**, 243–9.

289. LEBRUN, J., and LEFÈVRE, P.-C. (1965) Fertilité des sols et éléments de la sociologie rurale en Afrique au sud du Sahara, Brussels, Collection CEDESA, Fasc. X.

290. MCEWEN, J. (1962) Raising cereal yields in northern Ghana, *Emp. J. Exper. Agric.*, **30**, 120, 330–4.

291. NYE, P. H. (1958) The relative importance of fallows and soils in storing plant nutrients in Ghana, *J. W. Afr. Sci. Assoc.*, **4**, 31–41.

292. —— (1958) The mineral composition of some shrubs and trees in Ghana, ibid. **4**, 91–8.

293. —— and GREENLAND, D. J. (1960) *The Soil under Shifting Cultivation*, Commonwealth Bureau of Soils, Technical Communication 51, Farnham Royal, Berks., Commonwealth Agric. Bureau.

294. PEAT, J. E., and BROWN, K. J. (1962) The yield responses of rain-grown cotton, at Ukiriguru, in the Lake Province of Tanganyika. II. Land resting and other rotational treatments contrasted with the use of organic manure and inorganic fertilizers, *Emp. J. Exper. Agric.*, **30**, 120, 305–14.

295. STALLINGS, J. H. (1957) *Soil Conservation*, Englewood Cliffs, New Jersey, Prentice-Hall.

296. TEMPANY, H. A. (1949) *The Practice of Soil Conservation in the British Colonial Empire*, Harpenden, Herts., Commonwealth Bureau of Soil Science, Technical Communication 45.

297. TRAPNELL, C. G., and CLOTHIER, J. N. (1938) *The Soils, Vegetation and Agricultural Systems of North Western Rhodesia*, Lusaka, Government Printer.

298. —— (1943) *The Soils, Vegetation and Agriculture of North Eastern Rhodesia* Lusaka, Government Printer.

299. WALDOCK, E. A. *et al.* (1951) *Soil Conservation and Land Use in Sierra Leone*, Freetown, Government Printer.

Chapter 9: *Manures, fertilizers, and their use.*

The use of fertilizers and manures are discussed in many of the general texts listed under Chapters 1 and 2 (References 3–15) and under Chapter 6 (References 192–200). The following references are to books dealing with soil fertility and fertilizer use and to a publication dealing with fertilizer trial results in West Africa:

300. COOKE, G. W. (1967) *The Control of Soil Fertility*, London, Crosby, Lockwood.

301. FAO (1967) *FFHC Fertilizer Program: Review of Trial and Demonstration Results, 1964/5*, Rome, FAO (Reference LA; FFHC).

302. JACOB, A., and UEXKUELL, H. (Translated by Whittles, C. L.) (1960) *Fertilizer Use, Nutrition and Manuring of Tropical Crops*, 2nd ed., Hanover, Germany, Verlagsgesellschaft für Ackerbau.

303. IGNATIEFF, V., and PAGE, H. J. (1958) *Efficient use of Fertilizers*, Rome, FAO, Agricultural studies No. 43, FAO.

304. SAUCHELLI, P. (1965) *Phosphates in Agriculture*, New York, Rheinhold.

305. TISDALE, S. L., and NELSON, W. L. (1966) *Soil Fertility and Fertilizers*, 2nd ed., New York, Macmillan.

Most of the above books contain a great many further references to journal articles and other publications dealing with the use of fertilizers and manures. The following are a short selection of journal articles on these subjects of particular interest to West African soils and agriculture:

306. BOLLE-JONES, E. W. (1964) Incidence of sulphur deficiency in Africa. A review, *Emp. J. Exper. Agric.*, **32**, 127, 241–8.

307. BOSWINKLE, E. (1961) Residual effects of phosphorus fertilizers in Kenya, ibid. **29**, 114, 136–42.

308. BROCKINGTON, N. R. (1962) Fertilizer trials on some cultivated grasses in Northern Rhodesia, ibid. **30**, 120, 345–54.

309. COOKE, G. W. (1956) The value of rock phosphates for direct application, ibid. **24**, 294–36.

310. CUNNINGHAM, R. K. (1964) Micronutrient deficiency in cocoa in Ghana, ibid. **32**, 125, 42–50.

311. DENNISON, E. B. (1961) The value of farmyard manure in maintaining fertility in Northern Nigeria, ibid. **29**, 116, 330–6.

312. DJOKOTO, R. K., and STEPHENS, D. (1961) Thirty long-term fertilizer experiments under continuous cropping in Ghana. I, Crop yields and responses to fertilizers and manures. II, Soil studies in relation to the effects of fertilizers and manures on crop yields, ibid. **29**, 114, 181–95; **29**, 115, 245–58.

313. ELLIS, J. R., QUADER, M. A., and TRUOG, E. (1955) Rock phosphate availability as influenced by soil pH. *Soil Sci. Soc. America Proc.*, **17**, 357–9.

314. EVELYN, S. H., and THORNTON, I. (1964) Soil fertility and the response of groundnuts to fertilizers in the Gambia, *Emp. J. Exper. Agric.*, **32**, 126, 153–60.

315. GOLDSWORTHY, P. R., and HEATHCOTE, R. (1963) Fertilizer trials with groundnuts in Northern Nigeria, ibid. **31**, 124, 351–66.

316. —— —— (1964) Fertilizer trials with soya beans in Northern Nigeria, ibid. **32**, 127, 257–62.

317. —— (1964) Methods of applying superphosphate to groundnuts in Northern Nigeria, ibid. **32**, 127, 231–4.

318. GREENWOOD, M. (1954) Sulphur deficiency in groundnuts in Northern Nigeria, *Trans. 5th International Congress of Soil Sci.*, **3**, 245–51.

319. HEMINGWAY, R. G. (1961) The mineral composition of farmyard manure, *Emp. J. Exper. Agric.*, **29**, 113, 14–18.

320. HENZELL, E. F. (1962) The use of nitrogen fertilizers on pastures in the sub-tropics and tropics, in *A Review of Nitrogen in the Tropics* (Reference 195).

321. JAMESON, J. D., and KERKHAM, R. K. (1960) The maintenance of soil fertility in Uganda, *Emp. J. Exper. Agric.*, 28, 111, 179–92.

322. JONES, P. A., ROBINSON, J. B. D., and WALLIS, J. A. N. (1960) Fertilizers, manure and mulch in Kenya coffee growing, ibid. 28, 112, 335–52.

323. NYE, P. H. (1951–2) Studies on the fertility of Gold Coast soils. I, General account of the experiments. II, The nitrogen status of the soils. III, The phosphate status of the soils, ibid. 19, 217–23; 19, 275–82; 20, 47–55.

324. —— (1953–4) A survey of the value of fertilizers to the food farming areas of the Gold Coast, ibid. 21, 176–83; 21, 262–74; 22, 42–54.

325. —— (1954) Fertilizer responses in the Gold Coast in relation to time and method of application, ibid. 22, 86, 101–11.

326. MAINSTONE, B. J. (1962) Manuring of *Hevea*: effects of 'triple' superphosphate on transplanted stumps in Nigeria, ibid. 31, 121, 53–9.

327. —— (1963) Manuring of *Hevea*, VI. Some long-term manuring effects with special reference to phosphorus, in one of the Dunlop (Malaya) experiments, ibid. 31, 122, 175–85.

328. PEAT, J. E., and BROWN, K. J. (1962) The yield responses of rain-grown cotton, at Ukirigu in the Lake Province of Tanganyika, I, The use of organic manure, inorganic fertilizers and cotton-seed ash, ibid. 30, 119 215–31.

329. PIGOTT, C. J. (1960) The effect of fertilizers on the yield and quality of groundnuts in Sierra Leone, ibid. 28, 109, 59–64.

330. ROBINSON, J. B. D., and HOSEGOOD, P. H. (1965) Effects of organic mulch on fertility of a latosolic coffee soil in Kenya, *Exper. Agric.*, 1, 67–80.

331. SCHUTTE, K. H. (1955) A survey of plant minor element deficiencies in Africa, *Sols africains*, 3, 285–97.

332. SMITH, R. W., and ACQUAYE, D. K. (1962) Fertilizer responses on peasant cocoa farms in Ghana: a factorial experiment. *Emp. J. Exper. Agric.*, 31, 122, 115–23.

333. STEPHENS, D. (1959) Field experiments with trace elements on annual food crops in Ghana, ibid. 27, 108, 324–32.

334. —— (1960) Fertilizer trials on peasant farms in Ghana, ibid. 28, 109, 1–15.

335. —— (1960) Fertilizer experiments with phosphorus, nitrogen and sulphur in Ghana, ibid. 28, 110, 151–64.

336. —— (1960) Three rotation experiments with grass fallows and fertilizers, ibid. 28, 110, 165–78.

337. THORNTON, I. (1964) The effect of fertilizers on the uptake of nitrogen, phosphorus and potassium by the groundnut, ibid. 32, 127, 235–40.

338. WATSON, K. A., and GOLDSWORTHY, P. R. (1964) Soil fertility investigations in the middle belt of Nigeria, ibid. 32, 128, 290–302.

ALPHABETICAL LIST OF AUTHORS

cited in the Appendix: for Further Reading

The numbers in this list refer to references listed on pages 294–311)

GENERAL INDEX

For list of authors mentioned in the section 'For Further Reading' see pages 312–15. In this index references in the text are given first, followed by references to the tables, figures, and plates.

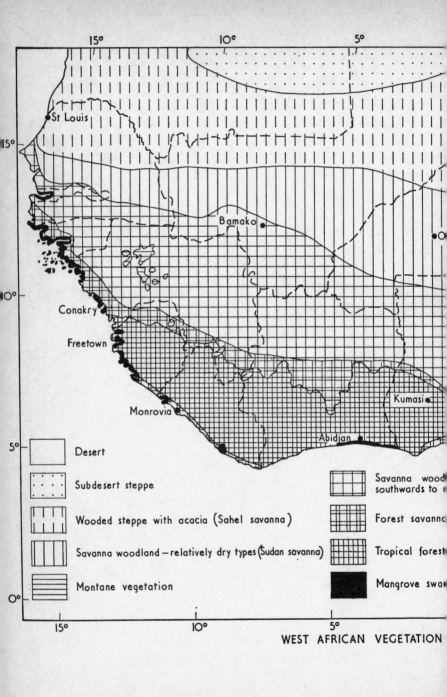

WEST AFRICAN VEGETATION

Desert

Subdesert steppe

Wooded steppe with acacia (Sahel savanna)

Savanna woodland – relatively dry types (Sudan savanna)

Montane vegetation

Savanna wood
southwards to

Forest savanna

Tropical forest

Mangrove swa

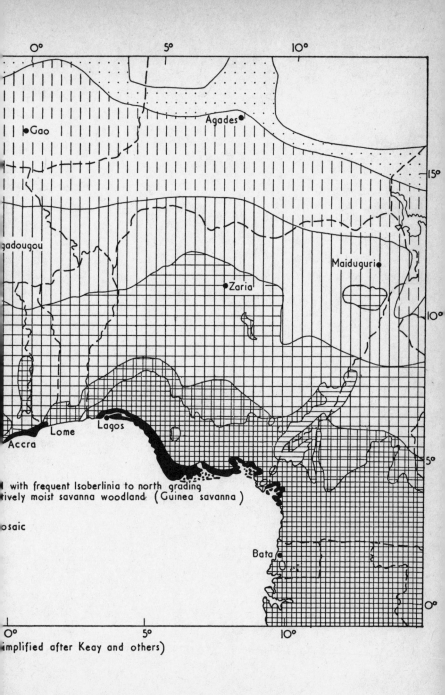

with frequent Isoberlinia to north grading
tively moist savanna woodland (Guinea savanna)

osaic

(implified after Keay and others)